THE GOLDEN PASSPORT

THE GOLDEN PASSPORT

Global Mobility for Millionaires

KRISTIN SURAK

HARVARD UNIVERSITY PRESS

Cambridge, Massachusetts & London, England

2023

Library of Congress Cataloging-in-Publication Data

Names: Surak, Kristin, author.
Title: The golden passport : global mobility for millionaires / Kristin Surak.
Description: Cambridge, Massachusetts ; London, England : Harvard University Press,
    2023. | Includes bibliographical references and index.
Identifiers: LCCN 2022061131 | ISBN 9780674248649 (cloth)
Subjects: LCSH: Citizenship—Economic aspects. | Investments, Foreign. |
    Investments—Developing countries. | Rich people. | Geopolitics.
Classification: LCC JF801 .S87 2023 | DDC 332.67/3091724—dc23/eng/20230113
    LC record available at https://lccn.loc.gov/2022061131

Contents

THE GOLDEN PASSPORT

Chapter 1

Selling Citizenship

I N OCTOBER 2017, the tiny country of Montenegro was abuzz. Nestled in the mountains along the Adriatic coast and with a population of a mere 620,000, it's a place that has been overlooked by many. Formerly a part of Yugoslavia, it remained an appendage of Serbia until it gained full independence in 2006. If the country is known at all, it's perhaps through the film *Casino Royale*, in which it served as the stage for James Bond's high-stakes poker game. Yet even then the microstate was too small to play itself: the scene was actually shot in the Czech Republic.

Given the country's size, it didn't take much to create a lot of hype for the Global Citizen Forum. In the capital city of Podgorica, billboards projected mammoth images of the GCF's headline speakers, a glitterati lineup including actor Robert De Niro, rapper Wyclef Jean, and General Wesley Clark. Along the Adriatic coast, black and gold forum banners lined the highway, challenging drivers to "inspire change" and "provoke innovation." At the airport, posters greeted new arrivals by proclaiming, "The future starts now: keep the conversation going." Over two days, nearly four hundred participants would gather in the small Balkan country to discuss the most pressing issues facing the world today.

The main events took place along a private beach in a glamorous Italianate villa worthy of James Bond and a trio of geodesic domes worthy of Disney World. Floating above, an enormous hot air balloon announced the encampment with a huge "Global Citizen" sign emblazoned across a multicolored patchwork of passports. Under it wandered the delegates, dressed in elegant casuals better suited for a cocktail hour than morning coffee. Millionaires milled around the samovars and chatted with deejays and supermodels. Prime ministers and politicians dropped in by helicopter. Filling the spaces in between was a hodgepodge of philanthropists, NGO workers, bankers, creatives, and a few royals.

The event did not hold back in trotting out the world's major and minor elites to trumpet the glory of the global citizen. Opening the event, former UN president Kofi Annan gave his blessings by video. On a spotlighted stage, Cherie Blair, wife of the former UK prime minister, drove home the importance of women's empowerment. Beside her First Lady Jeannette Kagame of Rwanda, whose husband had been—again—returned to power with 99 percent of the vote, sang the praises of entrepreneurial mothers. In between, José Manuel Barroso, the former European Commission president turned Goldman Sachs executive, offered his thoughts on the best way to manage refugees. The prime minister of Antigua, an island hit a few weeks before by a massive hurricane, spoke passionately about climate change, while the director general of UNESCO told the audience about the importance of giving back to create a sustainable world. A session on philanthropy provided inspiration for saving the planet. In another on "universal creativity," artists and entertainers debated the impact of smart phones on the imagination. With three heads of state and two princes to boot, the event was clearly one for the powerful, elite, and glamorous. All spoke fluently on how to solve global problems without bringing up uncomfortable questions of responsibility, not to mention redistribution. Certainly, nothing was to shake up the status quo. No Global Citizen at this Forum was to be inconvenienced.

As the hours rolled on, the delegates shifted their attention from the stage to their phones, glancing up occasionally between taps and swipes. After a full day of it, expressing concern about global problems and patting oneself on the back for leadership can grow tiresome. Some wandered back to the garden to network with other attendees, but those with serious business met in the well-guarded villa. It would take real star power to draw the highfliers back into the geodesic dome, and Robert De Niro rose to the occasion. All eyes were on the Hollywood actor as he casually strolled onto the stage. "We are one world, global citizens, stronger united than divided," he pronounced.

The finale was an evening not to be missed. The geodesic dome transformed into a dining club with projections of the day's inspirational phrases traveling across the ceiling's arc. If the conference had addressed problems concerning the shared fate of humanity, the dinner put the spotlight back on the megarich, cordoned off in the center of the room. Throughout the meal, an array of entertainers kept up the eclectic spirit. An artist with an oversized Etch-a-Sketch drew pictures of refugees with sand. A charity auction brought a mix of goodies under the gavel, from a golden map of the world portrayed in passports to dinner with the prime minister of a Caribbean country. The highlight was the conferral of the Global Citizen Award to a music-star-turned-philanthropist who funded solar power projects in Africa. Wrapping it up, another hip-hop celebrity took the stage and reflected on what it means to be a refugee before launching into a private performance that kept the global citizens dancing until dawn.

Little suggested the source of money behind the proceedings: golden passports. Several guests I spoke with had never heard of them. When the topic came up, it was almost in passing. Still, it lurked in the background. A representative from the Montenegrin government in one session described the new citizenship by investment (CBI) program they were planning: "It's a way to attract people who have knowledge and experience to come and teach others, and to move the country forward. If executed and monitored properly, it's a big opportunity for countries like Montenegro. . . . We don't want to sell passports, we want to buy excellence." I spoke with him and a few officials from other places who were looking to develop CBI programs. Georgia, Macedonia, and Moldova were all showing interest. A civil servant from Armenia explained to me over coffee that his country, lacking oil or gas, was exploring ways to build a business environment that would attract foreign capital, and saw citizenship by investment as a means to develop competitiveness. "We're looking for a tool to place the country within the right networks," he clarified. If inserting oneself in elite networks was the goal, the Global Citizen Forum was the place.

The event's host, Armand Arton, a successful businessman who made his money helping people move across borders, described his own history of immigration to launch the occasion. Uprooted by genocide, his family traveled from country to country in search of a better future. Cross-border mobility had taught him much: "The place I was born, I decided, will not dictate who I am, where I can go, and who I can become." His words drew attention to one of the strongest pillars of inequality in the world today. No one chooses their country of birth, yet no other status has a greater impact on one's life chances.[1] People born in Burundi live, on average, to the age of fifty-seven on an income of around $300 per year; their counterparts in Finland will likely survive over eighty years on a far more generous income of $42,000.[2] It comes as no surprise that the most impoverished people in low-income countries fare worse than their counterparts with citizenship in wealthier states, but the disparity holds across all income levels. Wealth does not insulate the rich from the consequences of what the economist Branko Milanovic terms "citizenship penalties." The Burundians in the top one percent also occupy a lower position on the global income distribution than their Finnish counterparts. The difference, Milanovic notes, represents a "citizenship premium" for those born in countries higher up the global income ladder.[3] Of course, moving to a more prosperous state may offer a solution, but border controls work to block this route for many. Countries are reluctant to give easy entrance to the citizens of poorer places. The result, as the philosopher Kwame Anthony Appiah observes, is that "All individuals in the world are obliged, whether they like it or not, to accept the political arrangements of their birthplace, however repugnant those arrangements are to their principles or ambitions—unless they can persuade somebody else to take them in."[4] Political borders transform citizenship into what the legal scholar Ayelet Shachar has termed a "birthright lottery."[5]

However, many still search out possibilities for improving their lot. Some may migrate and naturalize, others might find an ancestral connection that can get them in, and for those who can afford it, citizenship by investment supplies an inroad. Individual motives vary. A Bangladeshi businessperson might seek faster visa approvals for travel. An Iranian ex-pat professional in the United Arab Emirates may have problems opening a bank account in Dubai due to sanctions against her home government. A wealthy Chinese national may be unsure of what Beijing will do next and seek out an insurance policy against political change—and an American tech entrepreneur might do the same. Often, though, it's people from the Global South with the resources to spare, for whom borders are barriers and politics perilous, who seek to improve their options by investing money in a country and getting citizenship in return.

The Global Citizen Forum's host was well aware of the conundrums they face, which have gained salience with the rise of anti-immigrant movements across the globe. "We must shift away from seeing migration as a potential political tool to a tool of potential. Too many politicians are using human lives and tragedy to gain votes and retain power," Arton explained in his keynote speech. "We must change our view of seeing migration as a cost to bear to an investment that bears fruit." What was the key issue? "Migration needs a new brand."

Why this, in Montenegro of all places? At the time, it was a hot spot for those interested in the sale of citizenship. The government had long been willing to use its discretionary powers to extend membership to the wealthy and powerful. This, for example, was the basis for naturalizing Thailand's former prime minister Thaksin Shinawatra who was living in self-imposed exile after being convicted in absentia for corruption and the abuse of power. In 2009, he deposited €15 million in the erstwhile First Bank of Montenegro, an institution co-owned by the prime minister's brother. The bank was short of liquidity in the face of bad real estate loans and needed the injection. Shortly thereafter, Shinawatra was made a citizen and acquired a passport. This likely came in handy since his Thai documents had been cancelled.[6]

Such discretionary awards, well known in Montenegro, differ from the formal CBI programs behind the Global Citizen Forum. In these, government policy sets out the minimum investment amount and type, background checks, timeframe, and application procedures. The result is an official program for which anyone who qualifies can apply. At the time of the conference, the leading firms in the investment migration industry had been lobbying the government to establish such a formal scheme. This would diversify the options they could offer clients, and if a company could swing it, it might even secure for itself the role of "concessionaire," managing or advertising the program in exchange for a cut of each investment. Industry professionals flew in to meet with officials, present policy options, and proffer the services they might offer the Montenegrin government to attract the best applicants and ensure the program would be a success.

In June 2010 (a year after Shinawatra showed up in Libya on Montenegrin papers), Montenegro made its first attempt at a formal program. It amended the Citizenship Act to allow for the naturalization of individuals with special achievements in science, business, culture, or sports. The implementation manual specified that individuals who invested €500,000 could naturalize based on their contribution to business and economic interests. This opened a channel for citizenship by investment, but it didn't last long. Internal and external criticism induced the government to suspend the program within three months.[7] Still, the cat was out of the bag. Montenegro continued to grant citizenship to people making exceptional contributions, a parliamentarian attending the Global Citizen Forum told me, but on a case-by-case basis for those with good connections to the government.

This would change. In 2016, the government began again to move toward a formal program, but slowly. Service providers had been lobbying for over a year for a clear channel that they could sell to clients while collecting handsome fees in return, and eventually the government came around. It launched a public tender for the scheme's design and implementation, and secured a number of proposals from the private sector. With a set of blueprints in hand, the government withdrew the tender and established an internal commission to set up the program.[8] The companies stood rebuffed. It's not always easy for the private sector to move into the terrain controlled by the state.

By 2018, a new law was finally on the books, if not yet translated into an operational program. The government announced the scheme was to contribute to trade and economic development, and accordingly channeled the money into two areas: four- and five-star hotels or agriculture and the processing industry. The choices were not surprising for a country where farming and light manufacturing, traditionally important sectors, had been on the decline, and tourism was seen as a replacement. For projects in more prosperous regions, applicants would have to invest €450,000, but this fell to €250,000 for ventures in poorer areas. In addition, all were required to donate €100,000 to a government fund that supported economic growth in underdeveloped regions. The new citizens were to drive the country's redevelopment.

Limits were built in, too: no more than 2,000 applications would be approved, and the program would run for no more than three years. Why curtail a moneymaker? The move was possibly made with a glance over the shoulder at the European Parliament, which had expressed concern about such schemes in countries hoping to join the European Union. If Montenegro had legal control over how it chose to admit full members, it still had to balance the interests of more powerful countries and alliances.

Even with a timer set, the program was predicted to bring in at least €700 million—a significant sum for a country whose foreign direct investment inflows amount to a mere €450 million per year.[9] Indeed, the application fees alone would be a boost to the government coffers, with each main applicant paying €15,000 to file the forms, and a family of four laying out €45,000 in fees. Additional family members—new children or spouses—could be added, but at a whopping €50,000 per head. Service providers would also pay the government generous fees for the privilege of submitting applications: licenses were set at €50,000, to be renewed annually. The flow of money seemed unstoppable as the country opened a new domain to market forces.

The state would not manage the operation alone; it planned to team up with the private sector. A new government agency would oversee the scheme, but companies would be responsible for much of the on-the-ground implementation, including initial application checks, background screening, and marketing. After that, the government took over again, running the applications past three ministries for further assessments before they reached the prime minister for final approval. Gone were the days when a simple negotiation with a high-ranking official sufficed. This would be a clear-cut, bureaucratic, and marketable option.

Yet the government stalled on the launch, again and again.[10] If the "public" doesn't move in a public-private partnership, the "private" has to wait, and in this case, that meant until 2020 for a promised 2018 launch. The capitalists groaned about an incompetent state that was dragging its feet through neoliberal reforms, but the government had more to worry about. Part of the delay came from the management of a decades-long balancing act between East and West. When Yugoslavia dissolved in 1992, Montenegro was the only state that opted to remain in the federation, leaving it appended to Serbia as the rump Federal Republic of Yugoslavia. Over time, however, it would distance itself from Slobodan Milošević's machine until the tiny republic of just over 600,000 people gained independence in 2006. The microstate didn't even establish its own currency—it just adopted the euro, even without Eurozone membership. Since independence, its history has been one of navigating between Russia, the EU, and the interests of the country's small ruling class. Cigarette smuggling worth billions of euros kept cash moving through the country in the 1990s. By the 2000s, Russian wealth arrived, with major oligarchs, including the aluminum king Oleg Deripaska and the oil baron Viktor Ivanenko, putting money into major projects. Soon Russia was the top source of inward investment by a sizeable margin, pumping in more money than the next two countries, Serbia and Italy, combined. Around 80,000 Russians bought property in the Adriatic country—one for every eight Montenegrins.[11]

At the same time, the country looked west. It applied to become a member of the EU in 2008 and began formal negotiations a few years later. Keeping in good stead, it also followed the EU in imposing sanctions against Russia in 2015, at some cost to itself. The economic punishment of Vladimir Putin resulted in a 15 percent drop in property prices in Montenegro.[12] In a further snub to its former benefactor, Montenegro joined NATO in 2017.

For those in the citizenship industry, the pivot to Brussels was welcome.[13] Acquire citizenship in Montenegro now and get in on the ground floor for a burgundy passport embossed with "European Union" in a couple of years. A service provider I spoke with described the run-up to EU entry as a "golden opportunity" for a golden passport. He knew it was a "touchy subject" with the European Union, but with a path to EU membership at hand, the country was offering new investors a potential future return on their membership asset. For just €250,000—half the price of a "golden visa" in Spain and a quarter of the price of a "golden passport" in Malta—an investor could become a citizen of Montenegro today. If it joined the Union a few years down the road, this would convert into the much-coveted EU citizenship. Of course, there was the risk that the accession process could be delayed, but risk is just a part of doing business.

Finally, in early 2020, the program opened. The timing could not have been worse. Approvals were rolling out within the first few months, but by early summer, no one was yet an investor citizen. New members were required to pick up their papers in person, and the Covid-19 pandemic had blocked most international travel. Even if the passports remained in Podgorica, the program was at least off the ground.

———

SO WHY, BACK in 2017, was Robert De Niro in Montenegro trumpeting the benefits of investor citizenship? On stage at the Global Citizen Forum, he spent most of his time dispensing a pull-no-punches tirade against Donald Trump worthy of the "Raging Bull," but he wound down with the more instrumental reason for his trip to the Adriatic: a $250 million resort, Paradise Found, that he was planning on the tiny island of Barbuda.

The sidekick in a federation with Antigua, Barbuda is perhaps the most pristine spot in the Caribbean, home to one of its largest nature preserves and a rare bird sanctuary. Or it was until Hurricane Irma—a Category 5 storm with winds topping 150 miles per hour—decimated the island in 2017. With 95 percent of its buildings and infrastructure destroyed, the island's 1,700 residents were relocated to Antigua. Barbudans have a strong independent identity within the federation. When slavery formally ended in the British Empire in 1833, the island's sole plantation owner sought to gain compensation by forcibly relocating his formerly enslaved workers to Antigua. However, the freed Barbudans refused to budge and instead ran out their erstwhile tyrants. In their wake, they established perhaps the purest expression of communitarian democracy in existence, with all land communally held. Owning a house means applying for a lease from the community. Business development is possible, but on a fifty-year tenancy and only if a majority of islanders vote in favor. As one member of the island's governing council describes it, the place is run "like a co-op."[14] If there was ever a utopian socialist dream, this was it. Plus beaches.

And that was the problem—both the beaches and the communitarian democracy. Developers have long wanted to build in Barbuda, but for them, accustomed to full control, democratic participation and negotiation with local interests is irksome, to say the least. Hurricane Irma, however, proved a useful tool for those outside the island looking to grab a piece of paradise. Within a week of the storm, Prime Minister Gaston Browne announced plans to privatize the land. Borrowing a page from the economist Hernando De Soto, who argues that all economic development depends on ownership rights, he proposed giving the islanders deeds to the land they occupy. They could use these as collateral for loans to rebuild their dwellings and businesses—and then possibly sell them to bigger developers. The locals were against it.

By 2018 the government in Antigua repealed the law that had enshrined Barbuda's communal land ownership. Suddenly it was legal to sell property without local approval.[15] The communitarian utopia was against the wall and facing cocked guns. Yet the Barbudans put up a fight, turning to the courts to challenge the constitutionality of what critics termed a land grab.

In the face of community resistance, De Niro and his investment partner at the time, billionaire media mogul James Packer, pursued their own deal with the prime minister.[16] For them, Hurricane Irma was a godsend. It forced the evacuation of the inconvenient residents, who were now without power, running water, or permanent shelter. From the government's point of view, teaming up with the actor could stoke interest in its CBI program. If it approved the resort, a person making a sizeable investment into Paradise Found would be able to qualify for Antiguan citizenship.

Initially, the government in Antigua blocked Barbudans from returning as it reconfigured its strategy with the Hollywood actor, now crowned a "special economic envoy."[17] When locals were finally allowed back, they found that they had to rebuild much of the basic infrastructure themselves while the government focused its efforts on expanding the airport. Even two years after the hurricane, there were still periodic water shortages, the hospital was not yet repaired, and many residents lived in tents.

Not everyone on the island was against De Niro's Paradise Found—a communitarian democracy isn't necessarily antibusiness. Yet even its local supporters embraced the importance of the democratic processes that had defined their community for nearly two hundred years. Some invited De Niro to stand with them to ensure that their system of self-government and communal land ownership would continue. As one resident put it, "We as Barbudans don't want automatic development—we want control. It has to be developed according to our own population's needs."[18] Others had less hope that a cooperative relationship that respected democratic processes would be possible. A school principal on the island put it plainly when describing the stakes around Paradise Found's maneuverings: "You are coming into someone's territory and there are laws and regulations, which govern how you should operate. You do not like these laws, so you ignore them. You go even further and change those laws to suit yourself. Your actions therefore demonstrate that you have elevated yourself above the people you are dealing with."[19] Who gets to rule the day?

One might think that the democratic participation, shared ownership and responsibility, and community spirit that define the Barbudans might also be characteristic of a global citizenry. Such debates, though, didn't make their way into the Global Citizen Forum's geodesic dome, where highfliers were encouraged to not let anything get in the way of their dreams. Nonetheless, in the lush playgrounds of the Adriatic coast, two extreme ends of global mobility met, at least in concept, under the aegis of promoting one of the most compelling, yet understudied, transformations in state membership today: the sale of citizenship.

What Is Citizenship?

Citizenship, in the contemporary world, is a sovereign prerogative over which governments retain exclusive control. Only a state can make a citizen, and little in international law impinges on this power. International norms stipulate that citizenship should not be revoked if it results in statelessness. They also proscribe forced naturalization. Yet beyond such cautions—toothless in any event—states have wide berth in deciding who is theirs.[20] At the same time, citizenship is a remarkable sorting mechanism. Virtually everyone in the world has one, which connects each person to a country where they are usually found. The exceptions are few. About twelve million stateless people have no country. Dual citizens—also a tiny population—lay claim to more than one state. International migrants, only about 3 percent of humanity, are exceptions to the rule of staying where one belongs. For the vast majority of people, where they live is where they hold citizenship, which is assigned to them at birth and serves to attach them to and keep them within a state.

Viewing citizenship as fundamentally a legal status binding sovereign and subject means rethinking some common assumptions.[21] First, democratic participation and civic engagement, though they loom large in debates about what citizenship ought to entail, do not define the status. An Australian may be fined for not voting in national elections, but she won't be denaturalized for it. Nor will she be forced to look for a new country if she fails to volunteer in her local area. Some may believe that citizens are bound in a "community of fate" that characterizes a nation, but in truth this view attaches only derivatively to citizenship. Plus, democracies are not the norm. According to the Economist Intelligence Unit, in 2021 less than half of the world's population benefited from a democratic government. Of those who did, 39 percent were in "flawed" variants and only 6 percent enjoyed "full" democracy.[22]

Identity also does not determine citizenship. A person may think of herself as, say, an American, but as over two million "Dreamers," whose parents brought them to the United States at a young age, know too well, identity alone does not change one's legal status. Citizenship may in some cases have a strong emotional side. To be a citizen of a country is often to be a member of the imagined community of the nation as well. Typically, it is presumed that citizenship represents a "genuine link" to the nation, binding its members together.[23] However, this is rarely a determining factor in practice. Some people may feel such bonds while others do not, yet they may still share the same legal status. Plus the identity side of citizenship doesn't stop many people from being purely instrumental about acquiring it, especially if they are from more impoverished parts of the world. People from middle- to low-income countries typically naturalize on instrumental or pragmatic grounds, while those from wealthy states more frequently do so for emotional or identity reasons.[24]

In democracies, citizenship is often cast as a social contract defining a set of duties and rights granted and guaranteed by the state. A contract, however, is an agreement that its parties enter willfully, and on this score, citizenship does not pass muster. Most people have no choice in the matter: citizenship is ascribed at birth. Only in the cases of naturalization—quite rare across the globe—do adults make a clear choice in picking a state. Usually the options are limited by strict qualification regimes. An Argentinian dissatisfied with her country cannot simply throw her lot in with, say, New Zealand. She would need to find a spouse, a work permit, or some other means to qualify. Citizenship is often more about keeping people out rather than inviting them in.[25]

We usually think of citizenship as granting rights in exchange for duties, but this too frays under inspection. Obligations, such as paying taxes, voting, and serving in the military, are thin in most cases and thinning yet further.[26] Plus they usually fall on all individuals living in a territory, not merely the citizens. Income taxes are levied on resident foreigners and nationals alike, and even short-term visitors pay sales tax. With the decline of conscripted armies, military service is no longer expected of most national populations, and in many places, foreigners can find employment in the armed forces—and sometimes receive postmortem citizenship if killed in the line of duty. In the United States and the United Kingdom, only jury duty remains fully in the hands of citizens—and even then with the qualification that the person must be resident in the country.[27] The shift away from mutual obligations has been long in the making. Over sixty-five years ago, T. H. Marshall, doyen of citizenship studies, observed that the rights of citizenship were superseding its duties, a trend that appears resilient.[28]

Even when it comes to rights, citizenship adds very little in many cases. Western countries, in the main, now grant extensive rights to long-term resident foreigners rather than reserve them only for citizens. A permanent resident can claim a large number of benefits and protections, including access to schooling, health care, unemployment payments, and pensions.[29] However, most people in the world hold citizenships that do not come close to supplying such a prized basket of benefits, even in exchange for duties. A citizen of Tajikistan can expect to live on an average income of $5000 per year under a tight-fisted authoritarian regime without access to quality public schools or unemployment benefits, let alone freedom of speech. Plus the Tajik national is unlikely to be able to move abroad to better her chances. Citizenship documents are the first point of screening when people cross borders, and those from poorer countries face far greater hurdles than those from wealthier ones. The upshot is that the Tajik citizen will encounter roadblocks should she try to move, for example, to the United Kingdom to improve her lot, while the Australian will find open doors instead. For many, the citizenship that they were assigned at birth is more of a liability than an asset.[30]

At its root, citizenship is a legal status: it connects an individual to a state.[31] Of course, rights, identities, duties, and the like may accrete around citizenship, but they are not minimum conditions for it.[32] As we will see, it is the *differences* in citizenship's rights and benefits that create demand among people willing to pay for it. This legal status is nearly ubiquitous in the contemporary world, where it acts as a filing system for placing people within states. Except for a tiny number of stateless people, everyone on the planet is attached to a country whether they like it or not. The connection is a sticky one, for it follows its holder wherever she goes: a citizen of India is a citizen of India anywhere in the world. Citizenship is hard to shake off.

Furthermore, citizenship is universally assigned at birth, which ensures that almost everybody has one.[33] Thereafter, states have a range of tools at their disposal to naturalize new citizens. Immigration is perhaps the most familiar: a person who moves to a country and lives there for an extended period may eventually gain full membership as a citizen. Yet it is not the only grounds for naturalization or necessarily even the predominant one.[34] Marriage, military service, ancestry, scientific achievement, and service in the public interest are common as well. Some countries, like Hungary, naturalize more people based on ancestral ties than they do immigrants. Others, like China or the United Arab Emirates, naturalize virtually no one at all, even people resident in the country for generations. There is almost nothing in international law that limits the grounds states use to naturalize a person. Governments have largely free rein in this domain.

Citizenship by Investment

States can also—to get to the heart of this book—extend citizenship in recognition of economic contributions to a country. This might be done on an exceptional basis, as when New Zealand naturalized PayPal billionaire Peter Thiel after he spent twelve days in the country, purchased a few luxury properties, and donated to an earthquake relief fund. In exchange for the anytime-access to his escape villa on the South Island, he promised to promote the country internationally.[35] France has done the same for Snapchat billionaire Evan Spiegel, mobilizing a law that extends citizenship to those who contribute to the "standing of France and the prosperity of international economic relations." He also bypassed all the standard residence requirements and naturalized at the consulate in Los Angeles.[36] France and New Zealand are wealthy states with strong bureaucratic infrastructures where one might think that it's not so simple to "pay to play." Smaller countries, where top officials are easier to access, can readily give in to—or eagerly jump on—such overtures. Such examples are not isolated cases. As long as one has enough money and the right connections, it is possible to negotiate citizenship in many places.[37]

Citizenship by investment programs, however, are different. Unlike the discretionary grants of the sort enjoyed by Peter Thiel, they provide a clearly delineated, relatively swift route for applying for citizenship outright in exchange for a defined financial contribution for which anyone—with the cash—can apply. The timeframe, cost schedule, investment options, and due diligence expectations are plainly specified by a publicly available policy, transparent and formal, that can be replicated. To qualify, an applicant makes a donation to a government fund or invests in an approved channel, typically real estate, businesses, or bonds. Countries that offer "top tier" citizenships, as Cyprus did, whose citizens also become citizens of the European Union, may ask for more than $2.5 million for the privilege. Others, like small island countries in the Caribbean, may expect as little as $100,000 to grant membership.

Yet citizenship is not gained immediately upon investment; these are not just cash-for-passport exchanges. Bureaucrats review the applications, which typically include financial statements, police reports, and medical certificates, while due diligence companies carry out background checks. Those with riskier profiles may be flagged and further investigated before final approval or rejection is reached, usually by a panel or the government Cabinet. Notably, permanent residence is often not needed, or else reduced to bureaucratic box-ticking. Indeed, some countries do not even require naturalizers to ever visit. The entire process usually takes six weeks to one year and may be capped with a swearing-in ceremony. In Malta, these rites of passage take place in an ancient fortress that once housed its famous knights. In Vanuatu, the ceremony transpires in a traditional hut and includes drinking a potent semi-hallucinogenic brew. Some countries, however, will take care of matters at an embassy abroad—or even allow their bureaucrats to be flown out to administer the oath at the naturalizer's convenience and expense.

Such CBI or "golden passport" programs stand apart from "golden visa" options, which secure residence rather than citizenship. Portugal, Canada, Spain, Australia, and the United States are among the fifty or so countries that supply an easy route to a visa in exchange for an investment.[38] But these residence by investment (RBI) programs are fundamentally different from their citizenship counterparts, a point that cannot be stressed firmly enough.[39] Many commentators and analysts slip from one golden option to the other without recognizing the vital distinctions between visas and passports. First, far more is at stake with citizenship. Golden visas secure only residence rights, which are more easily lost than full membership. If an applicant fails to maintain the investment, she can expect to lose her visa. Citizenship, by contrast, is far harder to revoke: denaturalization is rare and subject to court challenges. Citizenship, too, is inheritable, whereas residence is not, raising the stakes of its acquisition for future generations. Citizenship is a new state membership that comes with access to a passport rather than a mere visa in a passport, which affects border crossing options and the utility of the document for identification purposes. A person with a residence permit for Nigeria will not have the same reception as one with a Nigerian passport. Some business opportunities are also limited to citizens. Of course, RBI programs may supply a pathway to citizenship, but not all do. Several countries with popular golden visa schemes, like Thailand and the United Arab Emirates, do not allow their investor residents to naturalize.[40] Even when the option is there, most investor residents do not seek out an additional citizenship in the first place. If a country does not recognize dual citizenship, the case with China and India, a new citizenship may be more a risk than a benefit. Although some golden visa schemes provide a foot in the door for citizenship—and some people do use the schemes to eventually naturalize—this status is acquired through a second and separate step that not everyone takes. When it comes to rights, stakes, trajectories, and demand, citizenship by investment and residence by investment are very different.

Furthermore, CBI programs are more than mere "cash-for-passport" exchanges. As Chapter 2 will show, such an equivalence ignores what makes citizenship by investment a formal citizenship *program* in the first place.[41] The extended application procedure means that it takes time—typically a few months—to become an investor citizen as the application is assessed and vetted through an official process, and that an application can be rejected as well. Those who make it through can, after naturalization, apply for a passport, which for many is the goal. These travel documents, however, are a privilege rather than an entitlement and remain the property of the granting state (take a look at the fine print on any passport). They hardly equal citizenship. Indeed, the vast majority of citizens in the world, most Americans included, don't even have one.[42] Nevertheless, for many investor citizens, state membership itself is far less of a goal than the "golden passport," to use a pithy moniker that has proliferated.[43]

Just how common is citizenship by investment? More than one might expect. Over a dozen countries host operational programs. The Caribbean is home to five: Antigua, Dominica, Grenada, Saint Kitts, and Saint Lucia. In the Mediterranean, Malta sits alongside Cyprus, which froze its long-standing scheme in the autumn of 2020, and is accompanied by Egypt, Jordan, Montenegro (until 2023), North Macedonia, and Turkey. In Asia, Cambodia offers an option, and in the South Pacific, Vanuatu has a smorgasbord of channels in operation. Around them are countries that have laws on the books allowing investors to naturalize, but in much smaller numbers, if at all. These countries have yet to develop reliable, marketable programs, as we will see in Chapter 4. Including them into a maximalist definition yields at least twenty-two countries

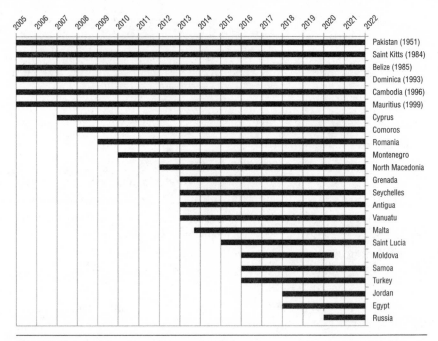

FIGURE 1.1. Timeline of recent legal provisions enabling citizenship by investment

Note: The legal provisions in Pakistan, Saint Kitts, Dominica, Cambodia, and Mauritius date from before 2005, as the parentheses indicate. Malta and Vanuatu have hosted more than one program. Several countries have stopped accepting CBI applications, though the legal provisions remain on the books. These include Belize (2001), Cyprus (2020), Comoros (2018), and Vanuatu (VCP, 2015; VERP, 2017).

that in 2022 had a legal basis for naturalizing individuals who invest or donate a specified amount into the country (Figure 1.1). Some countries, like Austria, have legal provisions that allow people who make a significant economic contribution to the country to naturalize, but do not specify the investment amount and type. Instead these are negotiated on a case-by-case basis, resulting in a route to citizenship that is individualized rather than formalized into the sort of clearly defined program that is the focus of this book.

Until recently, CBI schemes have been the preserve of small island countries with populations of less than one million. For such microstates, a sizeable injection of foreign funds brought through citizenship by investment can have a considerable economic impact. However, the scene has recently begun to change as more substantial nations, like Russia and Egypt, enter the game (Figure 1.2). With these newest programs still embryonic, it is difficult to judge their poten-

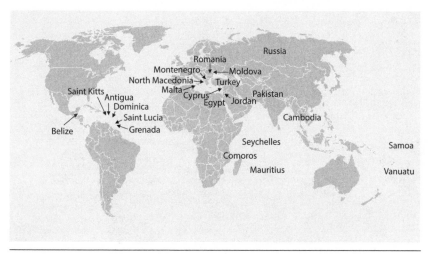

FIGURE 1.2. Countries with recent provisions for citizenship by investment

tial, but future growth appears to be moving away from tropical islands. As countries like Armenia, Croatia, Georgia, and Panama discuss options, citizenship by investment doesn't seem to be going away anytime soon.

How big are the programs? On the face of it, they're miniscule. Only around 50,000 individuals naturalize though them each year—a negligible number in comparison to a global population of eight billion people.[44] Yet, as we will explore in Chapter 9, the significance of the figure is much clearer when placed in context. The population of likely consumers is relatively small. They're largely members of the nouveaux riches from countries outside the Global North. Figures available from Malta, Antigua, Cyprus, Saint Lucia, and Dominica suggest that buyers come mainly from three regions: China and Southeast Asia, Russia and the post-Soviet countries, and the Middle East. Some people from wealthy democracies may apply, including a growing number of US citizens. However, driving demand is a smaller population of wealthy people from countries with "bad passports" and authoritarian regimes. It's the non-Western winners of globalization—those doing well on Branko Milanovic's famous elephant curve—who want it.[45] For governments aiming high, these global elites are the target audience of citizenship for sale.

Yet not all countries have been equally successful in attracting investor citizens, despite the continuous growth of demand (Figure 1.3). In the early 2010s, investors went for Caribbean programs, which accounted for about 90 percent of naturalizations globally. By the middle of the decade, however,

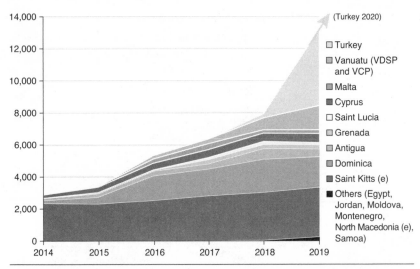

FIGURE 1.3. Total approved applications for citizenship by investment

Note: (e) indicates estimates based on statements by government representatives.

Data source: InvestMig database

they began turning to new offerings in the Pacific and Mediterranean, and since 2018 have sent Turkey to the top of the charts. It's now the country of choice for most investor citizens and accounts for around half of all such naturalizations globally. Even at the height of the Covid pandemic in 2020, Ankara was approving around a thousand applications per month. Demand concentrates around a few places. Egypt, Samoa, North Macedonia, and Jordan may have programs, but so few investors select them that they hardly register on the wider scene. Though over twenty countries offer CBI options, only nine have approved significant numbers of investor citizens: Antigua, Cyprus, Dominica, Grenada, Malta, Saint Kitts, Saint Lucia, Turkey, and Vanuatu. They sit alongside the Comoros, which is excluded from the count of formal programs due to the uncertainties and legal questions around the channel. Because of the numerical predominance of these nine cases—they account for over 95 percent of all CBI naturalizations—this book focuses on these countries to reveal how this unusual market operates.[46]

In assessing the figures, it is important to note that the number of naturalizations is not equivalent to the total applications approved. Investor citizens, like many privileged migrants, are typically able to bring along spouses and children, and sometimes even parents or siblings. Some may choose to naturalize alone if they need a passport to facilitate business travel, but often it is a family affair. Each approved application includes, on average, not only the "main applicant" but an additional 1.81 relatives.[47] The multiplier is important to bear in mind when assessing the overall magnitude of the programs: usually several people gain citizenship from one investment.

As we will see, demand for citizenship by investment stems from citizenship's inequities. That is, global disparities produce its selling points. The inequalities of citizenship within states are well known, including "second-class citizenship," racialized or gendered differences in rights, or other forms of semi-citizenship. But there are also marked differences *between* states in what citizenship secures, whether in social welfare provisions, stable political rule, legal protections, or mobility to other countries. Typically low- and middle-income countries offer packages of rights and benefits inferior to those of their wealthier counterparts.[48] Thus it should come as no surprise that many people in the world would be interested in acquiring a second citizenship if the option were available.[49]

Given that the programs are small, why should we care about them? For one, the market in golden passports highlights dynamics that are restructuring our world but go easily unobserved. As this book will show, dissecting this trade can tell us much about the multifaceted and multilayered nature of global inequality: the wealthy may buy their way in, but not always, and states may have sovereign control, but not always. A closer look at citizenship by investment also reveals the machinations of extraterritorial privileges and power. These supply the globally mobile with additional backing even when they are foreigners, and they give strong countries great leverage over weaker ones even when it comes to the most sacrosanct state powers. Observing the power plays and competitive dynamics between governments and the businesses of the citizenship industry can encourage us to rethink the so-called neoliberal transformations that occur when markets expand into new realms. Finally, understanding the world of citizenship by investment can challenge us to reconsider our basic assumptions about citizenship, including what it means for rights, duties, and identity.

For T. H. Marshall, citizenship was the great equalizer, providing a level starting ground on which capitalist growth could be built. By granting legal, political, and welfare rights, it helped dislodge persistent inequities to produce more egalitarian and redistributive societies.[50] However, the rise of citizenship by investment suggests a movement in the opposite direction as the wealthy leverage economic resources to circumnavigate the limits of the citizenship ascribed to them at birth. The resulting world of peripatetic, self-interested "global citizens" undermines the notion, however mythic, of citizenship as the bedrock of an interdependent political community. For this reason, many people see it as a threat.

The Marketization of Citizenship

This perceived threat raises a crucial question: Should countries offer citizenship by investment at all? Most people do not think of citizenship as an economic good. Indeed, the prospect that the wealthy might purchase citizenship rights to facilitate "residence planning" often raises concerns about inequality and other moral questions. Many people, especially if they are from wealthy and well-functioning democracies, see the sale of citizenship as irredeemably illegitimate.

The first common objection revolves around inequality: citizenship by investment lets the rich "pay to play" at the exclusion of the poor and refugees. However, the country with the largest number of refugees, Turkey, is also home to the largest CBI program. Ankara was providing refuge to nearly four million displaced people in 2022—far more than any Western country—and approved about 12,000 investor citizenship applications in the same year, also far more than any other state.[51] The two are not mutually exclusive.

More fundamental is the selectiveness of all naturalization policies. All countries allow some people in while keeping others out, and it's usually those most in need who are left in the cold. Take, for example, the possibility of naturalizing after immigrating to a country and living there for many years. To many, this may seem like a valid path to citizenship, open to all who have thrown in their lot with a community. But all countries screen migrants at the door, allowing some to enter while excluding others. In OECD member states, skills and family ties are currently the favored points for selection: those with the right CV or kinship ties—essentially human or social capital—have an easier time of it than others. Yet these valuable currencies rarely lie far from their more powerful sibling: economic capital.[52] In consequence, it is not the poorest of the poor who can improve their chances through migration, but those in the lower-middle classes and often above, with investments in education and skills, as well as the means to travel. People with fortunate family trees may discover that they can expand their options by using ancestry-based naturalization. Several EU countries, for example, readily hand out membership to anyone who can find the right ancestor. However, this privilege often maps onto class and race in exclusionary ways. It is a whiter, wealthier population in

Argentina, for example, who is able to pick up an Italian passport because they can prove an ancestor left Italy centuries before and can afford the fees.[53] Naturalization channels rarely operate in the service of those in greatest need.

A second objection turns on the impact of commodification. Citizenship by investment raises questions about what happens when political membership carries a price tag. Seen from this angle, the programs allow people to exchange economic capital for a public good, namely membership in the body politic, that ought not to be commodified.[54] The result, some scholars warn, is a transactional or contractual version of citizenship that threatens to degrade the institution globally and erode the moral bonds sustaining it.[55] Assigning a price to belonging devalues the principles of equality, solidarity, and participation by rendering them commensurable.[56] These economic equivalencies, some argue, can make CBI options little different from fake marriages, forged ancestries, and birth tourism as means to circumvent the barriers of membership in a country.[57] On this score, quantification and exchange are thorns: economic valuation debases the normative underpinnings of this quasi-sacred status.

Yet, as economic sociologists have observed, not all price tags leave residues.[58] Since ancient times, money has been offered in compensation for murder, but this has not subverted the sacrosanctity of life or the vilification of killing. The same might be said of the trivial effect of payments for egg and sperm donations on the love later accorded to the child.[59] Researchers have shown that when people create markets for normatively loaded items like blood, organs, or endangered species, they will try to overcome our lingering doubts by promoting the trade's moral legitimacy—and sometimes with great success.[60] Few people these days see life insurance as morally repugnant for assigning a price to life, though many did in the nineteenth century.[61] The same efforts, as we will see, occur in the market for citizenship.

No matter if one is for or against citizenship by investment, debates about whether citizenship should be commodified concern outcomes. They rest on the prior, still unexplored issue of how citizenship operates as a commodity in the first place, and how its value is established and maintained in the market. The point is crucial for dissecting market dynamics because, as anthropologists have shown, items reveal new properties when they are commodified.[62]

Market Properties

Citizenship is not only an unusual commodity—it is also unusual *as* a commodity, which presents distinct challenges when building a market around it.

The first challenge comes from the role of the state, which is typically the great market-enabler. States set the rules that structure markets and facilitate play within them.[63] Their regulations may affect the type of producers in the market, the forms of competition among them, their possibilities of failure, as well as the kinds of goods available and how they are exchanged, whether legally or illegally.[64] Though a state may provide the backing that sustains trust between market actors, it is itself never disinterested and may be persuaded by players to alter the rules in their favor.[65] States can also shield populaces from the worst effects of the market by compensating them when markets fail.[66]

Yet in the case of citizenship, the state is both the key market regulator and the sole producer of the good, for in the contemporary world, only states make citizens. If a government does not recognize a grant of citizenship as its own, the status is null and void. Even Stefan Černetić, prince of Montenegro and Macedonia, had to face this reality. His high-society life, which included knighting Hollywood actress Pamela Anderson, came to an abrupt end when the police discovered this Italian citizen, with a closet full of fake uniforms and royal robes, was merely posing as the head of state. He could not even turn to his claimed kingdom for help. Stateless people, like the Rohingya of Myanmar or ethnic Russians of Latvia, know the dire consequences that can result when a government disavows them as outsiders. Even if they once had claims to belonging, their citizenship no longer counts if the state doesn't stand behind it.

The result is that the state is the only legitimate seller of citizenship. Even if bureaucratic hurdles extend the naturalization process, and even if chains of intermediaries connect the buyer and seller, the state must sign off on every citizenship transaction. As such, there can be no legal secondary market.[67] In this, citizenship resembles flags of convenience, another sovereign prerogative that has become a market good.[68] It is possible to imagine a world with a secondary citizenship market, in which those looking to expatriate could sell or swap their membership to others hoping to join a polity.[69] Yet as prized as US citizenship is by some, no disaffected American can sell her state membership to a willing buyer.

Because citizenship is a state monopoly, even its smallest incumbents, microstates of less than a million inhabitants and lacking the economic and military heft that we typically associate with statehood, can employ this tool to raise revenue. What matters is not size but sovereignty. For this reason, territories and protectorates and other places of semi-independence, like Greenland, or the Cayman Islands, cannot start their own CBI programs, whereas an enclave like Monaco, the size of New York's Central Park, or a newly minted country like South Sudan can.

Effectively, the state wears two hats when it sells citizenship, serving as both the sole product producer and the ultimate market rule maker. The double role has at times yielded ethically questionable but entirely legal cases of countries selling citizenship to the criminally suspect. Tadamasa Goto, a Japanese mafia boss who became Cambodian for a sizeable donation, is one example. Still, when the state both structures the field of play and serves as an indispensable player in the game, it presents challenges to conventional assumptions about what is needed for a market to work: namely, that a separation of these roles mitigates conflicts of interest and stabilizes market transactions.

The multiple-hat issue is not merely acute, it is unavoidable when states build a market around a sovereign prerogative. In the case of sovereign debt, for example, the possibility of default without compensation remains a looming risk because sovereign immunity limits the available tools for enforcing payments or seizing assets. Governments can also influence macroeconomic indicators, making it difficult for creditors to verify their economic health.[70] To protect against such threats and secure liquidity, intermediaries with separate reputational risks enter the transaction. Historically, banks and corporations have played this role, as happened in London when joint-stock companies got involved in the early issuance of English debt.[71] By the nineteenth century, investors relied on the reputation of these third-party actors that sold, certified, and even guaranteed sovereign debt for assurance that the deal was solid and they would be repaid. Indeed, buyers even paid premiums for "big name" underwriters because these firms would have more to lose if their brand were sullied by sovereign default.[72] Today credit rating agencies play a similar role in evaluating a state's ability to make good on a loan.[73]

Citizenship has its own version of sovereign default: nonrecognition. As described above, if a state does not acknowledge a citizenship, the status is void. When, for example, Grenada closed down its economic citizenship channel in 2001 following pressure from the United States, it dealt with its investor citizens by simply refusing to recognize them as such, effectively erasing their citizenship. Similar incidents occurred in the Pacific across the 1990s. However, this strategy becomes more difficult once these channels are formalized into full-fledged CBI programs. When citizenship is granted through an extended bureaucratic procedure involving a division of labor and external oversight, such willful disregard is more readily challenged, and instead membership can be severed only through formal, legal denaturalization.

When Cyprus sought to disavow over two dozen investor citizens in 2019, it did so by officially denaturalizing them. In a further nod to the power of formalization, this has since been challenged in the courts.

One consequence is that states hoping to increase the scale of their citizenship business create a division of labor that separates the executive from the operation and oversight of the program. It's easier for a state to gain legitimacy—and sales—if citizenship is granted through a clear application process managed by several separate units within and outside the government, and with externally handled background checks to make sure the process is on track. These add more credence and standing than, say, just buying a passport off the king of Tonga. For buyers and intermediaries, a formal process signals that the state can be held accountable and that the citizenship granted is not a fly-by-night offering.

Commodity Properties

In addition to particular market properties, citizenship carries with it distinctive properties as a commodity. These, too, test common assumptions about the nature of citizenship. As with many economic goods, product differentiation marks citizenship: not all versions are equal. Setting its value are the rights and privileges it secures. Usually we think of these in terms of the benefits that citizenship brings within the granting state—rights to political representation, welfare assistance, free access to the labor market, and the like. Yet the utility of citizenship does not end at the national border: it affords advantages outside a state as well. In this, reputation plays no small part. People with more prestigious citizenships benefit when abroad from the stature accorded to their associated state, and vice versa. States may also safeguard their citizens when away from home through protection offered at embassies. For global movers, however, of more immediate concern is visa-free access. On this measure, the most powerful passports, like Japan's, allow their holders to enter over 190 countries without requiring a visa in advance; the worst, Iraq and Afghanistan, will grant access to about thirty. Of course, not all countries are equally desirable. For most people, easy entry into the United States is worth far more than free entry to Tuvalu. Yet the differences matter. Even if Turkish citizens have visa-free access to only 110 countries, it's still far better than trying to travel on Syrian documents.

More than access to other states, citizenship can secure rights within them, as members of regional groups know well. If the EU is the most prominent case, it is hardly the only one. The Economic Community of West African States (ECOWAS), Caribbean Community and Common Market (CARICOM), Southern Common Market (MERCOSUR), Association of Southeast Asian Nations (ASEAN), the Gulf Cooperation Council (GCC), and the Nordic Council, among others, grant extensive rights to the citizens of member countries, which can include rights to vote, own businesses, invest, and claim social welfare benefits. Beyond regional clubs, states can negotiate extended rights on a bilateral or multilateral basis as well. Notable pairings include Switzerland and the European Union, Monaco and France, Lesotho and South Africa, and New Zealand and Australia.[74] Citizens of any Commonwealth country who are resident in the United Kingdom can vote in British elections. As such, Canadian, Maltese, and Indian nationals living in London had a say in the Brexit referendum, whereas French, German, and Spanish residents did not.

Multiplying citizenships multiplies a person's benefits both within and outside a state. It gives its holder an à la carte range of options to select from, increasing possibilities that can be used to hedge against risks.[75] Of course, there are some intriguing caveats to this general pattern, like individuals who become "foreign" in their own country to access more benefits, as we will see. In either case, an additional citizenship is effectively the right to more rights.[76]

The outcome is important for the geopolitics of the market. Because the value of citizenship is set both internally and externally, the granting government does not hold exclusive control over it. Foreign states can curtail a citizenship's worth by forbidding access to or restricting rights within them. Thus, legitimacy in the eyes of more powerful actors is crucial when microstates look to expand their CBI programs. Countries that supply the CBI market are often concerned with securing and maintaining good relationships with regional powers to protect the value of their product. The issue of legitimacy is important because even if we typically think of citizenship as a bond between sovereign and subject, these two defining properties of citizenship as a commodity mean that third-party actors—foreign states securing value and private businesses implementing divisions of labor—play important roles in forming the market for it.

———

TO UNPACK HOW THIS WORKS, the following chapters travel the world of golden passports, revealing in turn its political, economic, and social dynamics. Excavating the political origins and expansion of the schemes, Chapter 2 uncovers how they grew out of an unruly scene of discretionary grants and took root in the Caribbean as more formal programs, driven forward by both public and private interests. Chapter 3 lays bare the dynamics of their highly politicized spread into the European Union, as well as the unintended consequences big powers can provoke when regulating schemes from the outside. Chapter 4 turns to the countries around the historical core of the market. By assessing smaller, newer, and more borderline programs that are rarely documented, it reveals what defines the market proper and how it functions. Chapter 5 examines the geopolitical hustling that shapes the market: how powerful third countries and supranational organizations gain leverage over the way a country decides to make someone a citizen. It looks at how the programs themselves reconfigure states as they try to get buy-in within a world defined by power hierarchies.

The next pair of chapters address the economics of citizenship by investment. Chapter 6 dissects the transnational citizenship industry, much of which is invisible to even the investors themselves. It is these intermediaries, knit together by the flow of commissions, who create the market by profiting from borders and inequality. Chapter 7 analyzes the economic upshot for the states hosting programs. If the schemes are implemented to drive development forward, do countries really benefit?

The final chapters turn to the social side of citizenship by investment. Chapter 8 asks the locals in the countries offering CBI programs what they think of the schemes, revealing a wider array of viewpoints than one might expect. In Chapter 9, we turn to the investor citizens themselves to understand why they seek out these programs and what they hope to gain from them. Their stories reveal several unexpected patterns driving choice. They also provide the opportunity to assess the impact of the Covid-19 pandemic on the market and consider the implications of citizenship by investment for identity and global citizenship.

Drawing these strands together, Chapter 10 distills the dynamics of supply, demand, and the intermediaries that keep the market moving. The book closes by laying out what all this means for citizenship and globalization today, focusing on inequality, extraterritoriality, neoliberalization, and strategic action. A Methodological Appendix follows for those curious about how I carried out this research, who I interviewed, how I assembled my database of statistics, and how one gets to Vanuatu in the first place.

Chapter 2

A Product Is Born

To our global citizen,

Delivering tailor-made solutions to your unique immigration needs has been the focus of our CBI program for over three decades. The St. Kitts & Nevis Citizen takes stock of our Platinum Standard milestones inspired by you, as we endeavor to safeguard your deserved piece of paradise.

S O OPENS THE 2018 edition of a thick coffee table book that the government of Saint Kitts presents to its new investor citizens. Dominating the cover is a gold image of the country's coat of arms bearing the nation's motto, "Country Above Self." Yet the tone of the introductory welcome makes clear that investor citizens need not worry about undue sacrifices: We are here to serve—you deserve it.

The book provides an overview of the country to its newest members who may not know much about the national club they have joined. For some, this can come in handy. Citizenship clients are occasionally stopped at airports when using their new passports, and it doesn't help for them to stand dumbfounded when a border guard asks them to point to Saint Kitts on a map. Yet for the government of Saint Kitts, the book does more than that. Full-page images of the country's beauty spots accompany articles on its recent economic performance, new financial service provisions, and latest technological advancements. Toward the end come the exotic tourist spots, local life, and cultural highlights. In between are advertisements parading as articles about various hotels, malls, and marinas offering investment opportunities that can turn into a passport. The resulting citizenship book reads like a cross between a business guide and an in-flight magazine.

On the opening pages, the prime minister greets those looking to "re-home" with the guarantee that they will receive only the best when joining the nation that invented citizenship by investment. "St. Kitts and Nevis has long been a pioneer in creating innovative solutions to add value to the lives and experiences of individuals of high net worth," he announces. New members are assured that the status they are gaining is secure. "Our platinum standard is maintained through effective global partnerships, careful due diligence, robust regulatory compliance, and an insistence that all our investors and economic citizens demonstrate integrity in their business relations, and legal and private actions." As a nation with a long history of immigration, "We believe strongly that prospective citizens can add great value to the economic and social well-being of our beautiful islands . . . Our country will become yours when you bring your talents, resources, and vision onto our shores."

For Saint Kitts, the promise of new sales is critical. Citizenship by investment accounts for over 40 percent of GDP by most estimates. The government receives more from the application fees than it does from all tax revenue. This is big business.

Yet the absolute numbers are small. In fact, the population of the entire country, at 55,000, could fit inside a single football stadium. In terms of geography, Saint Kitts resembles something like a cricket bat and ball: an oblong island proper reaches out via a narrow, handle-like peninsula toward the round sister island of Nevis. Dominating the skyline is the extinct volcano Mount Liamuiga, home to thick rainforests, monkeys, and ancient stone forts. Encircling it are the villages, businesses, university branches, and tourist resorts that define the economy. It's not a place of sprawling white sand beaches, though a few can be found. Instead it offers stunning unbuilt coastline, particularly on the peninsula. Nevis is yet smaller, with a population of just 10,000 to Saint Kitts's 45,000. With its own extinct volcano and numerous colonial-era buildings, it carries an off-the-beaten-path appeal and is easily circumnavigated in about forty-five minutes by car.

Walking around the capital, Basseterre, makes one think that an additional revenue source might be welcome. The port area is home to some shops, the national history museum, and the headquarters of the philatelic society—an important site for any small country with sovereignty to sell. On the promenade, a mundane array of chain stores and trinket stands, cracking from sun and sea exposure, extend out to the water. Basseterre has the feeling of an aging small town, carrying on in its own way. Its seasoned clapboard buildings have charm, but development is uneven across the island. Driving around the country takes about an hour and reveals villages of small wooden houses in need of repair at the ends of dirt roads. Tiny shops keep credit tabs for their regular customers who don't have cash on hand for their daily purchases. Interspersed are a few university satellite campuses and some small manufacturing, alongside the Caribbean staple of holiday resorts, where foreigners come to let go.

But this island confederation wasn't always so out of the way. In the seventeenth and eighteenth centuries, the "white gold" of sugar ensured that Saint Kitts and Nevis were two of the wealthiest British colonies. Despite its tiny size, Nevis produced as much as 20 percent of the British Empire's entire output. So important was the sweetener that by the time of the American Revolutionary War, Saint Kitts was the richest colony in the region on a per capita basis. It was sugar from Saint Kitts and its neighbors that built the fortunes of English merchants and pushed forward Britain's Industrial Revolution.[1] In the seventeenth and eighteenth centuries, the islands were indispensable—and rich.

Prying open this history of economic success, however, makes the sale of mere citizenship look tame in comparison. The beneficiaries were a small set of white and wealthy elites whose affluence depended on the torturous work of enslaved Africans, who comprised 90 percent of the population.[2] The labor conditions in sugar production were so punishing that 40 percent of the workers in Saint Kitts died within a year of arrival. Nevis had the ignominious role of serving as administrative center for the entire region's slave trade, overseeing the passage of hundreds of thousands of Africans through its ports who were subsequently sold as chattel. The trade fueled fortunes, and the island became a hub for successful merchants who built Georgian houses—now a major tourist highlight—from Scottish stone intended to weigh down ships once empty of their human cargo. As the French and British expanded their footprint, the local populations of Carib peoples stood little chance against their diseases and superior weaponry.

With the native population decimated, the country as we know it today is the inheritor of an economy built on the export of a good that enriched the few and sacrificed the many, with little thought toward development of domestic subsistence or shared prosperity. Even after the abolition of slavery in the British Empire enacted in 1833, Saint Kitts remained dependent on sugar, which would continue to be its economic mainstay until the 1970s. Alternatives have been slow to develop, but over the past forty years, tourism has emerged as the new monetary motor, bringing in much of the country's foreign exchange. Yet the industry has grown at a snail's pace on this tiny island confederation off the luxury track. In the 1990s, cruise ships took over across the Caribbean, cutting into the demand for longer stays at local hotels and the secondary benefits to restaurants and shops. Now most visitors simply disembark for a few hours at the port, leaving some dollars—and their rubbish—behind.

By the 2000s, sugar was a loss-making industry, with production costs exceeding sales. The St. Kitts Sugar Manufacturing Corporation had accumulated over $100 million in debt.[3] It still employed about 10 percent of the labor force but contributed less than 5 percent to the GDP. The World Bank diagnosed the industry's future as bleak, and from 2001, the government considered exit strategies from the sweetener that had defined its modern history.[4] It was perhaps a blessing in disguise when the EU began discussions in 2005 to cut the price paid for Caribbean sugar even further, which led to the liquidation of the island's last production center. Yet it was still an economic blow, and Saint Kitts needed to secure a stable revenue stream. A series of hurricanes and the global economic downturn in 2001 had hit the tourist industry hard, while cruise ships continued to transform visitors into day-trippers. In 2000, a study funded by the Caribbean Development Bank found that 30 percent of the population was poor.[5]

Microstates

Nearly all small states face economic challenges. Those that do not have typically carved out a profitable niche for themselves. Monaco went from rags to riches in the early twentieth century by developing casinos, tax breaks, and a luxury-driven economy. Vatican City has the wealth of the Catholic Church to keep it in good stead. Yet for most geographically small countries with populations under 1 million—often known as *microstates*—the situation is far more challenging. Limited resources and little access to economies of scale mean that almost everything must be imported and that foreign exchange is in great demand. For these tiny places, the institutions that make a country—everything from militaries and transportation infrastructure to school systems—are costly. Supplying even basic services is challenging with a national population that could fit into a football stadium or two. Historically, it might have been possible to get by, but the rise of capitalism has meant that states need to be of medium to large size in order to develop a competitive economy. By the late nineteenth century, microstates, in the words of historian Eric Hobsbawm, "were at best tolerated freaks."[6]

For this reason, it's often easier for small places to eke out an economic existence as dependencies of more powerful states, usually former colonizers, than it is for them to become fully sovereign countries. Dependent territories have the benefit of receiving regular fiscal transfers, which given their size, need not be very large to matter. The metropole can also buffer them against economic disasters, easily magnified by their small scale.[7] Indeed, places that achieve full independence quickly find that it usually comes at a financial loss. Small sovereign states have on average a lower per capita income than small dependencies that remain attached to a larger power.[8] Since the 1960s, referenda on independence have been almost always heartily rejected in microstates—and sometimes by margins of over 95 percent. Their populaces clearly prefer to maintain a continued connection to a more powerful metropole.[9] In fact, many islands fight for *dependence* rather than independence, as seen in the cases of Mayotte, Turks and Caicos, and Anguilla.[10] Even some states that would eventually turn to citizenship sales took the offering of full sovereignty—a prerequisite for issuing citizenship—gingerly. In Grenada, opposition to going it alone led to riots and looting on the cusp of independence in 1974. In Antigua, the Labor Party turned the rejection of independence into an election issue in 1976 and won. Malta chose independence in 1964 only after attempts to remain integrated with the United Kingdom failed.[11] Had history been different and these countries remained attached to a rump British Empire, they would have no independent citizenship to sell.

If microstates have anything in outsized amounts, it is sovereignty. The combined member states of CARICOM, the Caribbean's regional alliance, have a population of just 18.5 million people, comparable to a large Chinese city. Yet as a group, they muster fifteen votes in the United Nations. With sovereignty, these and other tiny places can name diplomats, open embassies, assert sovereign immunity, serve on the UN Security Council, and send athletes to the Olympic Games. They can claim large swaths of ocean around them, miles of atmosphere above them, and anything found underground. And they can grant citizenship and issue passports.

Sovereignty is thus a resource that microstates can capitalize on when other options are lacking. Like Saint Lucia, they can strategically switch between giving diplomatic recognition to China or Taiwan at the UN, depending on the foreign aid that their allegiance musters. Like Tuvalu, they can sell access to the thermosphere for hosting satellites. Like Nauru, they can lease themselves out as refugee processing facilities to countries thousands of miles away. Like Monaco, they can enjoy rents by transforming themselves into tax havens.[12]

For small places that are economically unviable on their own, sovereignty offers possibilities for creative solutions to financial problems. These are no trifling matter, for if microstates don't produce creative solutions, they produce emigrants.

Behind all this—why microstates can use sovereignty as a resource—lies the legal fiction that all states are equal. The line of reasoning is usually traced back to Emer de Vattel, who posited in *Le droit de gens* in 1758 that if men are equal in the state of nature, despite their many differences, then so too are states. As such, Vattel reasoned, small kingdoms are as much states as large republics.[13] The approach serves as the foundation of international positive law, which is premised on the equality of its incumbent countries. The reality, of course, is hardly so equitable, and historically asymmetrical relationships of domination and subordination have defined the international sphere.[14] What we find most often, when it comes to sovereignty, is "organized hypocrisy," in the words of Stephen Krasner.[15] If it's in their interest to break the rules, states will do so—and they do it regularly, though this rarely changes what we think about states and our assumptions about how they act, let alone the fundamental presuppositions of international law. What's crucial is that the legal fiction of equality between states allows small places that qualify as states to grant citizenship in whatever way they please—and have it recognized in the international sphere. Indeed, there is virtually nothing in international law that impinges on how states choose to naturalize people. The result is that if a state wants to sell citizenship, it can—even if it's a tiny speck of an island.

Notably, the microstate pioneers of citizenship by investment are all former British colonies. Two reasons stand behind this link. First, Britain fostered independence among its overseas possessions where possible, and did so more often and more successfully than other Western empires.[16] Of the twenty-two separate territories in the Eastern Caribbean that have a population of less than 1 million, for example, all eight that are fully independent states are former British colonies. Meanwhile all the French, Dutch, and American possessions remain semi-sovereign, along with a few British holdings. Some of them, like the Cayman Islands and Anguilla, do have residence programs, yet they cannot offer citizenship. In the contemporary world, this is the domain of only sovereign states.

Second, and more significantly, British common law offers useful resources for developing offshore structures.[17] In comparison to civil law, common law typically specifies what is prohibited, rather than what is permitted, and it places great importance on judicial precedent. This combination has done much to facilitate protections for businesses and the accumulation of capital through the development of offshore structures.[18] Furthermore, the history of imperialist projects has endowed British common law with a range of precedents that allow companies and individuals deemed nonresident to avoid regulation. This amalgam has proved propitious for producing "business solutions" that enable global financial flows to circumvent state regulation.[19] Indeed, these structures in former colonies have helped London retain its importance as a banking center, particularly as it was teetering in the 1960s. The City's financial institutions found that legal provisions in the country's dependencies were useful for circumventing disadvantageous regulations. The government in Westminster even encouraged the development of such offshore structures in its colonies and post-colonies to lessen its own costs for maintaining dependencies.[20]

The link between offshore financial centers and the sale of citizenship, however, isn't direct. The biggest, most important offshore locations are in substantial and powerful countries like the United States, the United Kingdom, and Switzerland.[21] Furthermore, highly specialized and high-volume offshore hubs like the Cayman Islands, British Virgin Islands, Jersey, and the Bahamas are dependent territories, which cannot sell citizenship. The Financial Secrecy Index by the Tax Justice Network ranks countries based on the scale of their offshore financial activities and secrecy. Here, too, CBI countries fail to stand out. The highest-ranked country that has offered investor citizenship in recent years is Cyprus, which comes in only at number 15—just above South Korea. Malta follows at a distant number 38.[22]

All CBI pioneers have some offshore facilities. These can take on sizeable proportions in their small economies, but they are not the key global hubs. Furthermore, as will be discussed in Chapter 9, almost anything people do to "structure" their wealth and keep it hidden from the tax collector can be done without an additional citizenship. Trusts, foundations, special purpose vehicles (SPVs), captive insurance, and other tools in the standard tax avoidance kit simply don't require it. To the extent that there is a connection between the sale of citizenship and offshore finance, it is largely through network advantages. Service providers who work in wealth structuring are connected to the wealthy individuals (if often via other service providers) who may want a second citizenship.

Origins

So where do these programs come from in the first place? Saint Kitts is usually given credit for inventing CBI schemes, and it remains one of the most prominent—and most popular—examples today. However, what "economic citizenship" meant in 1984 when the island rolled out the law on which it's based is quite different from the sleekly packaged programs that define the market now. A look into its history reveals much about the transformation of the field, once dominated by passport sales, into a formal transnational market in citizenship.

In Saint Kitts, discussions about granting citizenship to investors started on the eve of the island's independence, which it gained from the United Kingdom in 1984. Behind the law was Dr. William (Billy) Herbert, a local man who trained in law in Britain and was a central figure in the independence movement. Though he never held a cabinet position, he was always closely involved with the government and served as the country's first ambassador to the UN. It is in New York that he likely got the idea for citizenship by investment, a retired government official who knew him well told me. Already in November 1983, cabinet minutes note that the prime minister recommended setting the minimum investment at US$50,000 and adding a substantial registration fee, payable to the government. Eventually they settled on a higher price: applicants could qualify by either purchasing a ten-year government bond for $100,000, paid back with an enviable 10 percent interest, or investing $75,000 in property. The revenue would have come in handy, as the government amassed a deficit of $2.5 million, or 15 percent of its revenue, while bringing in only $900,000 in taxes in its first year after independence. In these conditions, even the fees from a few extra citizenships would make a difference. However, not everyone stood behind the proposal, and the opposition party sought to make hay out of the controversial scheme, branding it a magnet for criminals, murderers, and drug-pushers. In their flagship newspapers, the two main parties hurled at each other the same accusations of corruption through the sale of (real or fake) passports to criminals.[23] Yet by February 23, 1984, the new parliament approved the motion to allow investor citizenship, and soon after the legal provision was up and running.

The first approvals on record went to Mr. and Mrs. Cheung and Wong, followed by the Britt family. In some cases, the new citizens invested in tourism infrastructure and made charitable donations to the country that went beyond the minimum qualification requirements.[24] Robert Dreyer (a pseudonym) was one of these first investor citizens. In the early 1980s, he moved as a child to the island with his father, a Canadian hotelier, who was advised by doctors to seek early retirement. Not able to fully disengage, the businessman purchased a hotel and turned it around. Buying the property qualified the family for citizenship, so they all naturalized as well. Though Robert has spent most of his life outside the Caribbean, the Kittitian-Canadian returned to the island as an adult to take on a new project: following in his father's footsteps, he is revamping an aging hotel.

However, not everyone who received a passport in these early years is recorded in the government files. A sizeable portion of the processing seems to have been carried out by Dr. Herbert on his own, who supplemented his ambassadorial labor with work as an offshore lawyer. Equipped with diplomatic immunity, he based his practice in Anguilla, a tiny Overseas Territory of Britain. Initially slotted into a federation with Saint Kitts and Nevis, Anguilla broke away from what it saw as the domination of its microstate neighbors and remained under British protection. Usefully, it had few laws regulating capital controls but strong laws protecting secrecy. Deals considered money laundering elsewhere were simply legal—and confidential—transactions in Anguilla. Kenneth Rijock, a lawyer who laundered money for drug smugglers before going straight and becoming a financial crime consultant, remembers working often with Herbert, and even securing bundles of blank passports for drug cartels.[25]

More benignly, the citizenship program catered to American, Canadian, and British citizens with a libertarian bent who looked to expatriate to a place with low to no taxes. "Asset protection," it was often called. One service provider estimated that the government processed a few dozen applications per year for such people; another suggested that they handled fewer than four hundred applications before the 2000s. Even so, the process wasn't onerous. It involved filling out a three-page form that asked for the name, address, and nationality of the applicant and family members. More space was given over to listing the languages they spoke than to specifying their source of wealth and reason for applying. The applicant also had to supply passport photos, a certified copy of a birth certificate, a standard police report, and a credit report or bank reference. That was it. An old hand in the field described how he would fill out the forms for his clients: "Profession? Investor. Source of funds? Investment. And that was enough. No background checks, no nothing." Foreign service providers sent the pack to a local lawyer who then sent it to the government, where it would go to the minister in charge of immigration, who was often the prime minister, for approval.

For those looking for passports, Saint Kitts wasn't the only country on the international scene, or even a major player. At the time, demand was surging, and many potential buyers had greater worries than the Western retirees trying to escape taxes.[26] In the 1980s and 1990s, Hong Kong was the center of the action. The British had a ninety-nine-year lease on the New Territories that abutted the mainland, but the heart of Hong Kong—the island and the peninsula—was theirs in perpetuity. Two years of negotiations ended in 1984 with the Joint Sino-British Declaration, under which the British committed to returning the colony in its entirety to a then far more communist China—a move that left many residents of the capitalist entrepôt hunting for alternatives. The territory posted nearly 6 percent annual growth across the 1980s, and Hong Kong's per capita GDP was greater than that of Ireland or Spain. Its successful middle and upper classes looked to secure mobility, schooling, and financial protection before Beijing took over. The brutal crackdown on democracy protesters in Tiananmen Square in 1989 only stoked fear for the future, pushing emigration numbers above 60,000 annually.[27]

In response to demand, Kowloon became a hotbed of investment migration services. As many as five hundred businesses, some carrying pithy names like "Emergency Exit Company," opened up shop once it became clear that the United Kingdom would not extend British citizenship to most Hong Kongers. For consumers, a glossy magazine called *The Emigrant* offered guidance on moving families and investments abroad, its circulation soaring to 25,000. Indeed, so many people were looking for alternatives that the *South China Morning Post* wondered in 1990 if the country would soon be "full of people of every nationality except Chinese."[28]

Canada, the United States, and Australia were the preferred exit options, if one could figure out how to get in. Student visas supplied a common route, and some employers sponsored workers, but many businesspeople took advantage of the entrepreneurial and investment programs those countries offered. Investing in a project or opening a company was enough to secure a residence permit. After a few years, naturalization was the next obvious step.

Yet getting a residence visa for Australia or Canada didn't always mean moving house permanently. Many businesspeople were making money hand over fist in the region as it opened to capitalist development, and they were reluctant to abandon their ventures entirely. They simply wanted an alternative base for the family with a high quality of life and good schools for the children, as well as an insurance policy against an uncertain future.[29] The result was a boom in circular migration for these "flexible citizens" with various footholds along the Pacific Rim.[30] By the early 2000s, an estimated 250,000 individuals living in Hong Kong held Canadian passports.[31] Ottawa's consulate was one of the small island's busiest, identifiable by the long lines of citizens queuing to renew their papers from abroad.

Hong Kong was the regional if not global leader in visa and passport sales at the time, but it was not alone. Taiwan and to a lesser extent Singapore and South Korea were also bubbling as countries with remarkable GDP growth under still comparably authoritarian regimes in the process of relaxing control. The promise of business opportunities, mobility, security, and improved quality of life encouraged individuals to invest in citizenship or residence options abroad. Geopolitics also buoyed the trend, with events like the 1996 Taiwan Strait Crisis sounding alarms that some found too loud to ignore.

If the traditional Anglophone countries of immigration were in greatest demand, they were also the most expensive, with investor visa options setting an individual or family back between $150,000 and $500,000. Plus, they offered up front only residence, which might turn into citizenship, but didn't always. Citizenship in a lesser-ranked country, however, could be had for as little as $15,000. Such places didn't offer the prestige and quality of life of their larger counterparts, but they did secure a travel document and some business opportunities. A newly minted Belizean citizen might make use of the market access to Canada and Europe that the Third Lomé Convention secured. Samoan citizenship came with a generous quota from New Zealand to support Samoan business migration. Some wealthy Chinese nationals even sought an additional passport to facilitate easier border crossing into Hong Kong. For that, documents from Lesotho, a fellow commonwealth country, would do the trick. Taiwanese looking for easy access to Hong Kong would often select Tongan documents. By one estimate, around a thousand citizenships or passports—the difference was rarely significant—were sold annually in Hong Kong during these years.[32]

Among the sellers, Belize was a powerhouse. In 1985 it revised its Nationality Act to include a clause that allowed citizenship to be conferred on those contributing to the economy or the well-being of the country. By the late 1980s, this meant that citizenship could be had for an investment of just $35,000. In Hong Kong alone, an estimated 1,000 people gained citizenship through this route in two years. A change in government in 1989, however, closed the program and canceled the passports that had been issued. Yet the caesura didn't last long. By 1991, the country had opened a consulate in Hong Kong and was offering a special package: anyone who purchased $100,000 worth of land would get a passport.[33] The following year saw another channel launched, this time at just $44,000, plus a registration fee of $25,000. Three years later, the government added a new option allowing investors to pool contributions in a national investment fund. With so much on offer, demand soared, and service providers working in the field at the time describe Belize as the go-to option for most.

Other Central American and Caribbean countries got into the game as well. Honduras provided citizenship in exchange for a $25,000 investment, attracting almost three thousand buyers, though not without controversy. In 1993 the new president accused his predecessor of selling passports at inflated rates for personal gain. Still the sales continued, if dubiously. By 1996, officers busted a passport ring involving top immigration officers and diplomats in the United States, Hong Kong, and Tegucigalpa.[34] As early as 1983, Dominica's prime minister visited Hong Kong, where she touted her discretionary authority to grant citizenship in exchange for financial investments, a practice the country had regularized by 1993.[35] Its honorary council for Hong Kong and Taiwan proffered membership in exchange for a $35,000 investment in a hotel under (very, very slow) construction, rumored to be owned partly by the prime minister. As expensive as this was, it remained a better bargain than Jamaica, which required a deposit of $1,000,000 held in the national bank for ten years. Applicants didn't need to move to the country to become citizens, but they did need to wait five years after putting their money down to get full membership and passports.[36]

Closer to home, a number of Pacific islands opened shop, selling an estimated 14,000 passports and raising over $150 million between 1982 and 2002. The Marshall Islands, Nauru, Samoa, and Vanuatu all had offerings of various sorts, but Tonga was the most popular, moving over 8,000 passports and attracting buyers from former Philippines president and first lady Ferdinand and Imelda Marcos to the vice president of General Motors and head of the Hong Kong Stock Exchange.[37] An early adopter, the archipelago entered the scene when the king approved the sale of "Tonga Protected Person" (TPP) passports in 1981, targeting the Hong Kong market. The passports did not provide the right to enter and reside in the country, let alone signify citizenship. However, they did offer a means for travel, and a number of countries accepted the document. Obtaining the papers required only an oath of allegiance to the Tongan king and a lease of some land on an uninhabited island for twenty years for about $23,000. Expanding options, the government added a citizenship channel three years later, when a new Nationality Act gave the king the discretion to naturalize foreigners. In practice, this simply required leasing a larger tract of land on the same uninhabited island for a mere $35,000, a pittance for wealthy participants whose net worth could be greater than the country's GDP.[38] By 1988, the courts declared the controversial sales unconstitutional. The more than four hundred people who purchased citizenship through this route saw their membership erased with the repeal of the Nationality Act. Yet some within government claimed that the program was still operational, and the consul in Hong Kong continued to issue both TPP passports and citizenship to willing investors for another two years.[39] In 1990, the king announced that a new program for millionaires was in the works, and the following year the consulate in Hong Kong (which the local newspapers were now comparing to a business front) restarted passport sales. On the eve of Hong Kong's return to China, Tonga's minister of immigration announced yet another scheme, this one aimed at selling 7,000 passports for $20,000 each in just twelve months. If the legal status of the documents and sales during these years was blurry, so was the amount of revenue coming in, with reports of proceeds varying wildly. The media variously claimed that the schemes attracted $6.5 million over two years to over $150 million in six years. The finance minister announced that the first ten years for the program generated a mere $2.2 million, held in a bank account in San Francisco, while the king, by contrast, claimed that receipts were already $20 million by 1990.[40]

The scene in other Pacific islands was similarly murky, featuring multiple short-lived schemes, one part of the government selling passports unbeknownst to other parts, and travel documents in bulk going unaccounted for. All Nauru required was a ten-minute interview and medical test before giving out a travel document. It even allowed applicants to choose a new name on the spot—an easy way to reinvent oneself. Representatives for the Marshall Islands duped buyers into thinking that they could use the membership to get permanent residency in the United States. The chief of immigration was convicted for illegal sales in 1999.[41]

The wider field presented a wealth of choice, including options in Sri Lanka, Bolivia, Peru, São Tomé, Sierra Leone, Grenada, and Cabo Verde. The end of the Cold War even saw Eastern European countries, including East Germany, Czechoslovakia, and Hungary, investigate possibilities for extending citizenship to wealthy citizens of Hong Kong. They didn't develop CBI programs per se, but organized bespoke citizenship packages in recognition of substantial investments.[42] Closer in, Bangladesh charged a hefty $1 million but still received one or two inquiries per month.[43] A passport from Sierra Leone could be had for an investment of $28,000 in land and a quick visit to the country. If one were looking for diplomatic documents, Liberia would supply. Sometimes the distinction between consulate and company blurred completely.[44]

For those reluctant to apply through a program, there was always the time-tested means of the obliging government employee willing to supply a few passports through a greased palm. To obtain a travel document from Para-guay, for example, all that was needed was a simple application for residence and a payment to an official who would backdate the permit three years so that one could immediately apply for citizenship—a "favor" that reportedly cost about $16,000.[45] By 1993, Hong Kong's commission for dealing with corruption complaints registered a wave of cases against consular staff who reportedly took bribes for issuing passports. The Lesotho consulate alone fired three employees who had sold over 250 passports for about $35,000 apiece.[46] When Benin travel documents began to spread in Hong Kong, its govern-ment officials hastily denied that the country offered citizenship by invest-ment.[47] Kenya forced a company that was selling its passports to close.[48] In some cases, the number of missing documents is staggering. Between 1991 and 1997, the Samoan consulate couldn't account for 4,500 passports issued, likely sold. Yet at least the documents were for an actual country. In the final months of UK rule, two hundred people who were still looking for exit op-tions bought passports for the Dominion of Melchizedek—a nonexis-tent paradise supposedly somewhere in the Pacific—for $33,000 per useless document.[49]

Throughout the 1980s and 1990s, the economic citizenship scene in Hong Kong and elsewhere was murky. Programs came and went in rapid succes-sion. One hand of a government wouldn't know what the other hand was doing—or in whose pocket it was reaching—and accountings of the revenue generated could vary wildly. There may have been a legal basis for the sales in some of the cases, but even then, the application process wasn't always trans-parent, external oversight was nonexistent, due diligence on the applicant or source of funds largely absent, and there was rarely a division of labor among the vested interests to ensure trustworthiness.[50] A lawyer I met in Hong Kong described looking into Lesotho's citizenship option in the 1990s to see if he could offer it to clients. They had the law on the books, he said, but the Min-istry of Foreign Affairs was selling it for more than the Ministry of Justice, and the whole scheme broke down in inter-ministerial fighting. Such was the world of passport sales in the 1980s and 1990s.

Even the number of issuances often remained unclear. In 1990, Saint Kitts sought to gain more of the Hong Kong market by offering three thousand passports at the bargain-basement price of $25,000—substantially below the going rate at the time of $100,000. Local newspapers confirmed that it had nearly reached its quota in 1992, but once the opposition party began hounding the government over irregularities and missing money, the prime minister publicly announced that the number of applicants was "embarrassingly few."[51] Honduras, too, was hard to pin down. The *New York Times* claimed that the country sold around twenty thousand citizenships in the 1990s; media outlets with a closer view on the scene put the figure in the low thousands. In several cases, numbers remained small. Ireland, for example, naturalized only 156 individuals over ten years.[52] In the Pacific, volume was larger, but the channels were more unstable. The Marshall Islands sold two thousand passports, but its program lasted only one year; Vanuatu issued three hundred through a similarly short-lived scheme. Nauru's option was open for four years and naturalized one thousand people.[53]

Clearly, too, it was the passport rather than citizenship that was most often on sale. If a program went under or was axed after a change of party in power, the new government would either declare the citizenships null and void or wouldn't renew the passports, effectively invalidating the membership. According to service providers operating at the time, there was little guarantee that the countries would continue to recognize the citizenship status of clients. As one based in London told me, "officials might sell them and then the next regime would come along and cancel all of them, saying that they didn't follow the statutory procedures." The state could not be trusted. There was no question of citizenship being passed down to future generations either. Intermediaries who remember the scene describe it as "quasi-official" and "under the radar." A lawyer at a global accountancy described the situation to me: "They weren't seen as programs back in the day. They were seen as shady," and added that even minimal due diligence was lacking.

Today one might be surprised to learn that Ireland was a paradigmatic merchant of passports. In 1989 it opened a pathway to economic citizenship by broadly interpreting Article 16(a) of its Nationality and Citizenship Act to include financial investments as sufficient to fulfill the requirement of "Irish descent or Irish association." The government didn't publicly announce the expanded channel or its specifics, nor did it make clear how the applications were processed and decisions made. One former government bureaucrat I spoke with said that no one had any idea how many people came through the program. "It was all money under the table and into the pockets of politicians." By 1998, reports of fraud brought down the scheme, with rumors floating that politicians were engaged in horse-trading—quite literally—by accepting the finest Arabian thoroughbreds in exchange for country membership. Feargal Quinn, a parliamentarian and one of the most prominent businessmen in the country, captured the dubious operation of the channel during senate debates:

> The scheme was apparently perfectly legal in that it broke no law, but the basis for it was not set down either in the form of legislation or a ministerial order. It worked entirely within the scope of the discretion available to the Minister of the day under the nationality and citizenship legislation. It came into being with an informality that is quite staggering, particularly in view of the importance of the issues involved. There seemed to have been no rules governing the scheme at all. A number of unofficial rules were applied later, but these made no difference. It is a matter of record that little or no effort was made to keep to those rules or to discover whether they were being observed.[54]

The citizenship trade in the 1980s and 1990s was quite a different scene than the one that would emerge in the new millennium. Certainly, passports could be had for a buck, if one knew where to go, but scaling up required a number of transformations to make citizenship into a trustworthy product—a story of gradual transformation beginning in the 2000s.

Birthing a Product

Saint Kitts was the trailblazer. In 2006, the government contracted the "residency planning firm" Henley and Partners to expand its economic citizenship stream into a marketable citizenship by investment program. The company, headed by Christian Kälin, had previously focused on how people could lower their taxes through residence options in places like Switzerland and Belgium. The man who would eventually take the title of "Passport King" saw an opportunity in Saint Kitts to shift from mere wealth structuring to include mobility too. Yet for it to work, it needed to be transparent. Under the firm's guidance, the Saint Kitts government expanded its channel into a widely marketable CBI program.

Scaling up required formalization, and that meant developing a more clearly defined application process with oversight and a separation of interests. Under

Henley's advice, the government undertook a series of reforms over several years. Initially, it moved from a minimal three-page application to a more lengthy and detailed form in line with international standards, and it began to check more closely for health, criminal activities, and the source of funds. It also established a dedicated Economic Citizenship Processing Unit under the Ministry of Finance to handle applicant screenings and approvals. To keep it all moving, it set up communication guidelines and an official time frame for assessing applications. To manage the flow of money, the government created the Sugar Industry Diversification Fund (SIDF) under the Ministry of Security to monitor and distribute government donations. The move was well placed. Saint Kitts had lost EU subsidies for this historically key sector in the prior year, leaving about 10 percent of the workforce unemployed, and the government needed to expand into new sectors to keep things afloat.

Vetting was also to be taken more seriously than before. As a due diligence professional who worked in the scene at the time described to me, the countries claimed they were checking the applicants, "but they weren't doing much." This would begin to shift under the revamped program as the government called for tighter screening procedures to "enhanc[e] its reputation and minimiz[e] any possible risk."[55] The Citizenship Processing Unit was charged with commissioning independent professional due diligence firms to carry out background checks for the government, which had been under pressure from more powerful countries over vetting. Saint Kitts was also facing criticism from the United States over possible money laundering through the channel. In response, it suspended the bond option and established two qualifying investment possibilities: a contribution of $250,000 to the SIDF or the purchase of $400,000 in approved real estate projects. On top of this came processing fees that ran around $60,000, depending on the number of family members naturalizing.[56]

The government contracted Henley and Partners to handle both escrow services and applications before sending them on to the government's Citizenship Processing Unit, a role that would become known as that of the "concessionaire." Effectively, it outsourced both the financial and the assessment side of program management. The government doubted it had the infrastructural capacity to reach a substantial client base without the firm's networks and economic resources, and so it contracted Henley to promote the program internationally.[57] In exchange for this work, the company received a commission of 10 percent of every contribution to the SIDF, or an enviable $25,000 for every application coming through that route. The concessionaire could file applications too. The result was a terrific incentive to go out and market the program.

Large multinational banks with private client divisions, as well as private wealth managers, were already assisting an affluent clientele with residence by investment options—golden visas, not golden passports—in places like Canada. Henley connected to these firms, pitching the new mobility tool in Saint Kitts and offering its services. Citizenship in Saint Kitts could be not only lined up beside investment residence in Canada but also paired with it to facilitate mobility while would-be Canadians waited the years it took to move from residence to citizenship. Henley also pioneered the large-scale professional conferences in global hubs like Dubai and Hong Kong, which would become an industry standard for advertising programs and connecting buyers to sellers.

In 2011, the government further formalized the program, bookending a five-year transformation begun in 2006.[58] The Citizenship Processing Unit became the Citizenship Investment Unit (CIU) and gained more control over the program and its supply chain of service providers. The government would now grant licenses to authorized agents in Saint Kitts, and only they could bring applications forward to the CIU. The result not only increased rents through licensing fees, but also added the potential for quality control. Agents were the first bastion of background checks, and those submitting problematic files could be barred. Furthermore, the Citizenship Investment Unit took final say on all marketing materials—no agent could publicize the program without the CIU approving the advertisement first. The move was intended to protect the image and reputation of the country, at least inside it, for the state's jurisdiction ended at its borders. In the key places of demand outside Saint Kitts, only indirect pressure could ensure adherence to the rules. By 2012, the SIDF became an independent body, run by a CEO but answering to the Ministry of Finance.

The new law also required background checks on all adult applicants, and after some foot-dragging, the government eventually contracted an international due diligence firm in 2012 for the job, elaborating the levels of vetting and cross-checking applications. New rules rendered ineligible anyone who had been denied a visa to a country that grants Kittitian citizens visa-free access, as well as anyone who posed a security risk not only to Saint Kitts but also to any other country. People working in due diligence at the time remember pressure from Western governments concerned about who might be coming through the programs. With a nod to those interests, the microstate took itself out of play as a possible workaround for people who had been denied visas to places like the United States, Canada, or the United Kingdom.

In addition, the revamp established basic procedures for assessing the value of real estate investments and ensuring that projects reached completion.

Properties, too, had to be held for at least five years before they could be re-sold. However, in a rider crucial for any developer, those purchased after 2012 and sold after five years could be used again as a qualifying investment: effectively, the same building could now be recycled through the program. The option was a boon to buyers, or at least service providers trying to make a convincing case about possible returns on investment. But it also meant that not every application through the real estate route would bring new infrastructure with it.[59]

Formalization over these years resulted in a scalable product. What had been a murky channel was now a clearer process, and a far more transparent one, structured by a division of labor, involving third-party oversight through external due diligence firms, and appeasing regional powers.[60] In 2009, the country gained visa-free access to the Schengen Area, which proved an additional boon. Thereafter a Kittitian passport would allow its bearer to enter the EU for ninety days without the hassle of acquiring a visa first—much more than could be asked of Russian or Chinese documents at the time. With visa-free access to the United Kingdom and Canada to boot, the result was a true mobility tool.

It was also a revenue-generating success. In 2006, program receipts constituted about 1 percent of the country's GDP; by 2015 the figure rose to over 35 percent.[61] On the cusp of the Covid-19 pandemic, income from CBI accounted for nearly half of the government's recurrent revenue.[62] The steady growth seen over the past decade dropped slightly in 2015 after Saint Kitts lost visa-free access to Canada following a scandal involving diplomatic passports, yet with naturalization rates for investor citizens several times higher than those of its neighbors, the country still leads the Caribbean programs.

En voyage, Christian Kälin became the "Passport King." In the ten years after the Saint Kitts government began the revamp, his firm reportedly earned $250 million from the program.[63] From the four thousand applications processed during the time Henley and Partners held the concessionaire's contract for Saint Kitts (2008–2013), it would have gathered tens of millions in fees alone.[64] To that can be added the professional fees it charged to its own clients applying for citizenship, which could exceed $100,000 per file.

What were the exact dynamics of the relationship between Henley and Partners and the Kittitian government? Who was really in control? The questions, intriguing and important, are unfortunately difficult to answer. There are virtually no accessible records of the negotiations, and those involved in the development of the program offer few details when asked. Government proposals gave the concessionaire a wide range of powers and discretion. The journalist Atossa Abrahamian recounted the scene in 2015 when a new coalition government took power: no one had a clue of how the program worked, and questions from the new government about what to do had the Passport King's phone ringing off the hook.[65] It may have been a welcome shift, as some wondered whether his firm was backing the dog that lost the race—the long-standing prime minister Denzil Douglas. "Dougie," as he is affectionately known, was already on the edge of losing his office in 2010 when a video went viral casting his opponent as on the take. He remained in his seat, but close enough to the edge to be dislodged in 2015. Meanwhile, speculation swirled that the video had been staged by the SCL Group, the parent of Cambridge Analytica, which had been active in a number of elections across the region.[66] Indeed, the head of Cambridge Analytica, Alexander Nix, even testified in 2018 that his company was involved in Saint Kitts as well, and that he had discussed campaign financing with Kälin.[67] Speculation swirled again: where did the government stop and the business begin?

If definitive answers are challenging to find, the close connection between the two during the birth of the formal program is undoubtable. As one migration agent working in the field at the time described it to me, Kälin "was in the delivery room for [the CBI scheme in] Saint Kitts." The metaphor is remarkably apt. It took two to create the formalized scheme and launch it globally. Of the duo, only the state of Saint Kitts could give birth to an investor citizenship program, but Henley and Partners put the sparkle in its eye and helped it on its way.

Exporting Citizenship by Investment

The reformatted program's financial success, for the country and for Henley, was reason enough to export it. Saint Kitts wasn't happy about the absent father, but there was little that it could do about it. As one Kittitian lawyer complained to me, "We gave Henley exclusivity, but they didn't give it to us. It should have been a two-way street like a marriage, but now there are so many other countries trying to compete." The firm courted a number of governments, in the region and outside it, to assess interest in its services, and in 2013 both Antigua and Grenada passed CBI laws with Henley's input. Antigua was new to the field and simply mirrored Saint Kitts's program. Grenada, by contrast, had some experience. In 1996 it opened a channel that focused on the Hong Kong market but shut it down and negated the passports under US pressure following September 11.[68] Rather than build on this institutional legacy, it adopted a design based on the Saint Kitts model. Dominica, too, followed suit. Its channel for investor citizenship had approved a few dozen to a few hundred applications per year since 1993.[69] In 2013, it followed regional trends and passed a new law implementing the same set of changes enacted by its neighbors, creating—as in Saint Kitts—a more formal and transparent program.[70] Two years later, in 2015, Saint Lucia joined the club with a new law in the now well-established format.[71]

Why did they go for it? Each island had its own story of economic challenges precipitating a turn to the program, or—as with Dominica—its formalization and expansion. Antigua was dealt a sharp blow in 2009 when the US Securities and Exchange Commission brought fraud charges against billionaire Allen Stanford, who was later convicted of running one of the biggest international Ponzi schemes in history.[72] Until then, much of the island's economy was intertwined with the fortunes of a man whose own fortune was valued at nearly twice the country's GDP—and who was extraordinarily popular too. He owned the main newspaper, the major bank, and the cricket grounds, among other assets, and was the country's largest private-sector employer. When the American who the Antiguan prime minister described as having "a lien on our whole country" landed in US federal prison, it was a serious financial challenge for the island.

Further south, the scene was also economically grim. Dominica, the least developed of the group, lost out against Chiquita. Before the 2000s, it was primarily dependent on banana exports, which brought in half of its foreign exchange. The country of just seventy thousand people had twenty thousand workers in its over six thousand banana farms, which exported mainly to Europe through a special arrangement. In 1996, the American firm Chiquita applied new rules from the World Trade Organization to challenge the preferential access that Dominica and its neighbors had to European markets. Two years later, the "Banana Wars" wrapped up with Chiquita winning and the small Caribbean islands bearing heavy losses. On Dominica, half of the farmland was abandoned. By 2008, bananas were just 1.2 percent of GDP, and the unofficial unemployment rate ran as high as 30 percent.[73] In Saint Lucia, also dependent on the fruit, 85 percent of its banana growers went out of business.[74] Grenada, momentarily safe with nutmeg production, was instead hit by powerful hurricanes. This bane of the region dealt Grenada a double blow in 2004 and 2005, when two fierce storms damaged 90 percent of its homes.[75] Against these backdrops, the promise of conjuring funds from nothing but the magical legal principle of sovereignty must have seemed a no-brainer.

For the other fully independent microstates in the region, citizenship by investment had less appeal. Saint Vincent and the Grenadines had a long-standing Socialist—with a capital S—prime minister in Ralph Gonsalves, in power since 2001. It's hardly surprising that a scholar-politician who authored books like *The Non Capitalist Path to Development* and *The Spectre of Imperialism: The Case of the Caribbean* would have no truck with the citizenship trade. Opposition candidates may flirt with the possibility, but they have yet to unseat the popular Comrade Ralph, who is keenly against the option. In other microstates, there was simply no need: Trinidad and Tobago had oil wealth to stay afloat, and Barbados has long had a diversified economy that has kept it on the World Bank's list of high-income countries. Why open the door to more citizens when tourists suffice?

The islands that went for it, however, went in lockstep. As suggested above, the new programs differed little in organization and operation. Henley and Partners courted all the governments while its business competitors tried to woo them away, but the general format for program design was the same everywhere. All adopted the divisions of labor, external checks, and clear procedures pioneered in Saint Kitts. All established CIUs to handle and assess the applications, set up similar regulations around the addition of family members, developed a system for licensing service providers and accepted applications only through them, set out basic due diligence requirements and fees, and established procedures for approving real estate projects. As in Saint Kitts's renewed design, Antigua, Grenada, Saint Lucia, and eventually Dominica specified that those who have been denied a visa to a country granting visa-free travel to its citizens would be rejected, ensuring that the security concerns of more powerful countries were not ignored.

When asked about program origins or reform, government representatives usually say that financial need drove them to it. As an official in Saint Lucia explained to me, the schemes offered a way to re-attract the foreign direct investment inflows that had dropped off significantly after 2008. They needed to find "creative mechanisms" to draw in money. Governments described setting up task forces, issuing white papers, and meeting with different law firms and service providers to understand what it takes to establish a program. Officials typically say that they looked at all the models and adopted the best practices, but there was really only one dominant model out there. And of course the governments did not do it all on their own. As in Saint Kitts, the main design typically came from Henley, with some additional input from other service providers.[76] Those working in the industry describe the laws behind the programs as simply cookie cutter in form, rather than an expression of individual sovereign choice. Indeed, comparing the legislation across cases reveals astounding similarities—but with some tweaks. Grenada took the opportunity to open an RBI option by tagging "permanent residence or" to all relevant occurrences of "citizenship" in its legislation. For its part, Antigua added a business investment option. Dominica copied its neighbors on a number of provisions but kept its price of $100,000, lower than Saint Kitts. Saint Lucia imposed a ceiling of five hundred applications annually and initially required all applicants to prove a net worth of at least $3 million.[77]

Grenada and Antigua also made efforts to bring their new citizens into the fold, hoping to build connections and—more importantly—to capture secondary spending. Grenada obliged those who chose to donate to the National Transformation Fund to obtain permanent residence first and spend at least fourteen days in the country before becoming a citizen—a provision that it soon dropped. Antigua wanted to see its new investor citizens every year: all were required to spend at least five days in the country annually for the first five years of their membership. Those who didn't visit would, according to the law, find their citizenship revoked. Over time, however, officials have taken a more lenient stance, stating that absent investor citizens would merely see their first passport—issued for five years—not renewed. Yet it soon became clear that investor citizens didn't want to be told where to spend their time, particularly when places like Saint Kitts placed no demands on them. Within a year, Antigua amended the clause to require only five days within a five-year period, and eventually it would scuttle the duty entirely. The countries saw a need to remain competitive.

They also stepped up program oversight. Ordinarily, prime ministers in the region decide who can take the role of "Minister Responsible for Citizenship" and then allocate to themselves this prized portfolio that allows them to make the final call on naturalization. Yet with the formalization of the programs, countries shifted decision-making power out of the hands of the prime minister alone and into those of the cabinet or a multimember citizenship by investment board.[78] The division created more checks on final decisions and further distanced the executive from the issuance of citizenship.[79] Improving transparency, Grenada and Antigua instituted a legal requirement to provide biannual reports that give figures for applications and funds, providing clarity to the flows unheard of among the schemes in the 1980s and 1990s.[80]

Vetting also increased across cases and over time. Laws included clauses requiring background checks, established fees to cover their costs, and provided for the appointment of external due diligence companies. More was expected of the applicants too. By 2017, Grenada's application had gone from nine pages at its launch to over twenty-five, with ever more details asked about potential risks such as whether applicants had outstanding criminal lawsuits against them or whether they had ever had a visa cancelled. The forms for Saint Lucia ran to about fifty pages—a far cry from the three-page application Saint Kitts collected in the early 2000s.

Of course, what looks good on paper is not always what happens in practice. An application might be long, but it might also be easily skimmed and approved pro forma. An external due diligence report might consist of a thin search and no more, supplying only a sheen of legitimacy. A bipartisan committee might make final approvals, but this may be only to bring down a rubber stamp. And, of course, prime ministers or other top officials might go it on their own—the salary is often not the main allure of a job in politics. The point of formalization is not necessarily to completely clean up a program. Much can still happen on the side. Rather, it is to supply credibility so that others in the market know that the sovereign will not default, as discussed in Chapter 1, and that the new citizens are getting a product they can trust.

Party politics in the Eastern Caribbean can be fierce, with general elections as passionately contested as cricket matches. Remarkably, however, there has been broad support of the programs across the political spectrum. This might be expected for the long-standing options in Saint Kitts and Dominica: an initially skeptical populace can become habituated over time. Indeed in Saint Kitts, I met outright nationalist pride among everyday folks over its offering, as we will see in Chapter 8. Governments, too, if initially skittish, can easily warm to a lucrative income source with few costs involved. Newer programs, with less economic dependence on their yet nascent income streams, may be more easily scuttled. Nonetheless, all the Caribbean offerings have weathered changes in government. In election years, investor citizenship programs are often a hot-button issue. Opposition parties liken the programs to cash cows for the party in power, and the local media may attack governments for carelessly prostituting the nation or siphoning funds from the programs. Yet even if they complain about poor management or bad ideas, no newly elected party has implemented pre-election promises to end the programs, though opportunities have abounded. Antigua's government changed shortly after its program opened in 2014; Saint Lucia elected new rulers in 2016 and 2021, and in Grenada the government flipped just before passing the CBI law in 2013, when the country was already in discussions about the program. Saint Kitts saw turnovers in 2015 and 2022. Yet the schemes continued even when new parties came to power. For small economies, the money is simply too hard to pass up.

The flow of funds also stimulates competition. Individual countries try to separate themselves from the pack in marketing their programs: Antigua is home to 365 beaches; Saint Kitts is the legacy product; Saint Lucia is the honeymoon capital. Prime ministers pitch their offering at investment migration conferences to draw in top dollar. "We are working hard to ensure that our product and your experience of Saint Kitts is of the highest quality," the prime minister of Saint Kitts told a captive audience in London in 2016. Appealing to the purse strings, a representative from Dominica touted their low investment amounts: "We're the best value option out there." In Dubai, the prime minister of Antigua flaunted his country as the "economic tiger of the Caribbean" and "the best way to diversify your portfolio of holdings overseas." He went on, "there are no bulls or bears in Antigua, just lovely people and investment opportunities." Meanwhile, a representative from Grenada painted a glowing picture of economic growth and positioned Grenada as "the choice for a discerning clientele," adding, "We are happy to move our country forward and happy to share our sovereignty." Although market-speak around a quasi-sacred status like citizenship may rankle some, such sales pitches are a dime a dozen. They are also not terribly surprising when a key function of the prime minister is to attract foreign direct investment, and the country generates upwards of 50 percent of its GDP through citizenship by investment. In such cases, country branding is the name of the game.

The key selling points, though, are not in the countries themselves, but outside them. The principal asset, shared by all in the Caribbean market, is visa-free access to Europe's Schengen Area of twenty-six countries, which Saint Kitts and Antigua acquired in 2009 and Dominica, Grenada, and Saint Lucia in 2015.[81] For many people from the Global South, the option of smoothly entering Europe at will is highly desirable—a privilege taken for granted by most in the Global North. Gaining such access is not sudden. Rounds of negotiations and diplomatic work precede it and the outcome is usually known about two years in advance. Yet positive signals are enough to send the industry scrambling. Dominica, for example, was seeing some applications in the early 2010s, but "Schengen [visa-free access to the Schengen Area] really changed the landscape," as one developer explained. In anticipation of access to Schengen and the boost to product value, investment migration firms moved into Dominica in 2014 and saw their sales soar: between 2013 and 2015 applications doubled annually. To deal with the huge influx of applications, the CIU quadrupled its personnel. By 2017, they were processing between 1,500 and 2,000 files per year, the head of the CIU told me, and sometimes receiving as many as thirty applications per day.

There were also some third-country benefits that set individual countries apart. Citizens of Saint Kitts and Antigua had the right to enter Canada without a visa, at least in the early years of their programs. Grenada and Dominica have visa-free access to China. Most crucially, though, Grenada boasts a trade treaty with the United States that enables its citizens to apply for an E2 visa. A Grenadian citizen who makes a substantial investment in a US business—about $200,000 will usually suffice—can qualify for an E2 residence visa that allows businesspeople and their families to reside in the US. Around eighty countries have signed E2 treaties with the US, allowing their citizens to apply. A Vietnamese national cannot make use of the provision because Vietnam does not have such a treaty, but a Vietnamese national who has become a Grenadian citizen can readily apply for an E2 residence permit. This work-around to the US immigration regime is intriguing. The residence permit can be renewed indefinitely, but it does not lead to a green card or automatically into citizenship. For some investors, nothing could be better. Permanent residence or citizenship would transform its holder into a "US person" in legal terms, placing them under the American tax net for life. Plus the United States levies tax on the global income of its "persons" even if they spend no time on its soil. The result is that a Chinese citizen looking to gain the right to reside in the US but avoid some of the tax implications might become an investor citizen of Grenada and then lodge an E2 visa application at an American consulate in China. The process would take less than a year and cost about $500,000—far less than the $900,000 now needed to qualify for the US RBI program, the EB-5 investor visa, which now has a waiting list of over ten years for Chinese nationals.

Third-country benefits, such as visa-free access and other privileges secured outside the granting state, add value to a citizenship in a country—or, rather *outside* a country—that is otherwise easily overlooked. Yet it also adds vulnerabilities as the value of the citizenship, in such cases, ends up controlled by more powerful actors outside the state granting it. The result is a geopolitically charged scene.

The Loss of Canada and Vetting

In some cases, the lesson about the extraterritorial clout of superpowers has been learned the hard way. In May 2014, FinCEN—the financial investigation unit of the US Treasury—issued a warning to Saint Kitts that individuals may be buying citizenship to evade sanctions or engage in financial crimes. The report did not mince words, noting that although the Kittitian government had announced that citizens of Iran would no longer be able to participate in the program, it continued to offer them passports through it.[82] Service providers on the island complained about being strong-armed into serving as a confederate in American imperialist adventures in the Middle East. "Why should I have any misgivings about helping people around illegal, immoral sanctions?," one told me indignantly. Sanctions are a controversial tool: they are intended to make it difficult for an enemy regime to rule, but often they place restrictions on the whole populace. Many in the citizenship industry are more than happy to assist individuals—particularly businesspeople with the money to hand—to circumvent geopolitics in order to carry on with their lives and economic ventures.

In June, the Canadian High Commission in the region dispatched an immigration official to the island to inform them about Canada's concerns with the program.[83] Shortly thereafter Saint Kitts announced that citizens of Iran and Afghanistan could no longer apply. Still, Canada revoked visa-free access for Kittitian citizens by the close of 2014. Two Iranian businessmen had arrived in Toronto on diplomatic passports from Saint Kitts but without official diplomatic business in the country. They were allowed across the border, but upon questioning they revealed that their documents were had for a government donation of $1 million.[84] The CBI program doesn't supply diplomatic passports, which would have come through a different channel within the government, but nonetheless the incident had negative reverberations for the program—and for all Kittitian citizens. About eight thousand visitors enter Canada each year on Kittitian documents. Since this incident, they all have had to send their passports first to the Canadian High Commission in Trinidad to apply for a ten-year multientry visa, a process that takes about a week.

The "loss of Canada" was a deep blow to a country that at the time collected more than a quarter of its GDP from citizenship sales. The fiasco contributed to the electoral defeat of reigning prime minister Douglas, who had been in office for twenty years. I met him a year later at an investment migration conference in Dubai, where he didn't say much but still passed me a business card with his new affiliation: Global Lifestyle Foundation.

Yet the new government, led by Prime Minister Timothy Harris, didn't cancel citizenship sales, for the country was too economically dependent on it. Instead, it "reset the program," as the new head of state described to an audience in London. The result was a third round of improvements. Concerned about security risks and looking to tighten its procedures in general, the government brought in a Big Four accountancy and international due diligence firm to audit the scheme and subsequently implemented their recommendations.[85] During the review, the country revoked the passports of those who had questionable elements in their files. Notably, however, their citizenship was left intact. This flipped the script of the 1980s and 1990s, when new governments would claim that past CBI memberships were illegally issued, rendering them null and void. Program formalization meant that even a new party in power would have challenges if it were to take the route of "sovereign default" and erase the naturalized citizens. The product had staying power.

In 2018, the head of the CIU walked me through the reformed assessment process, which consisted largely of background checks if the application was complete. An international due diligence company screens the file, which then goes to the Joint Regional Communication Center (JRCC)—CARICOM's subagency for border protection—for checks through the International Criminal Police Organization (INTERPOL) and other databases. Finally it heads off to the "international partners," or powerful countries. This layer includes checks to see if an applicant has ever been denied a visa to the United Kingdom, EU, Canada, or crucially the United States, which runs its own screening. If Washington gives the nod, the file will usually be approved. However, it can also withhold support without explanation. Red flags are rare, affecting only about one percent of applications. Yet "if the international partners deny, then the application is denied," the CIU head explained. Finally, a committee above the CIU decides whether to accept or reject the application before it moves to the desk of the prime minister for a final signature. Legally the prime minister has the discretion to override a rejection, but this doesn't occur in practice, I was told. Given the stakes—and the price paid for past missteps—they seemed to be keeping a tight ship.

Most of the application assessment process concerns vetting, which itself is aimed at ensuring that third-party countries—those powerful states to the north—do not disapprove of the applicant. As such, the final selection in Saint Kitts is contingent upon the decision of stronger players. And for good reason. It is these more powerful countries that control the value of investor citizenship by offering passport holders smooth entry at the border—or not. They have shown that they are willing to use this influence as well by revoking visa-free access and pressuring countries to shut down programs. Countries with schemes might choose to ignore the recommendations of their "international partners," but they do so at their own risk.[86] Antigua, for example, followed Saint Kitts down the path of losing visa-free access to Canada in 2017. No clear catalyst was in public view, but Ottawa declared that an interest in "protecting the integrity of our immigration system and ensuring the safety of Canadians" lay behind the move.[87] Antigua was the last country in the Caribbean with a CBI program to have visa-free access to Canada.

In the wake of these jolts, due diligence companies began bringing countries together to share best practices and strengthen background checks. A key concern was to prevent "venue shopping"—individuals rejected by one program trying their luck with another. Initially the governments were reluctant to sit around the table with their competitors to discuss what they believed was a right of a sovereign state, but after regional powers began to flex their muscles, the microstates became more willing to talk. The Caribbean Investment Program Association (CIPA) was formed in 2015 to strengthen the transparency, rigor, legitimacy, and stability of the programs. It brought together the CIUs from the region in quarterly meetings and—crucially—invited along representatives from the US Department of State, UK High Commission, Canadian High Commission, the International Monetary Fund (IMF), and FinCEN. The point was to encourage two-way communication over best practices and—perhaps more importantly—foster the big players' toleration of their programs. Due diligence was the central focus, and discussion centered on issues like biometric data and synching information with the EU, Canada, and the United States. As such the meetings also helped ensure the backroom support of the major countries that do much to control the value of the product. Yet it remained a challenge to keep the islands together, and since 2019, CIPA has existed in name only. More than the Covid-19 pandemic, I was told, intercountry squabbling and the difficulty of coordinating change made it a dead letter.

Of course, some individuals get past formal vetting procedures. Arguably, if a person commits a crime *after* becoming a citizen, there is little way for a country to predict it in advance, and there are some instances of people on the brink of exposure for criminal activities who have received citizenship through the programs. But there are also some who have gotten through even when red flags are raised. A solid vet, due diligence experts advise, means not simply running background checks, but doing so systematically and with periodic auditing. A secure system will have multiple moving parts. It will use a dedicated office to assess applications and set up a regulator to oversee it. It will employ multiple independent due diligence companies for external checks and carry out regular financial auditing. And it will monitor everything with an independent board distanced from the government and issue annual parliamentary and public updates that involve also the political opposition. However, not all governments are interested in going all the way with such reforms, due diligence experts told me. Some are genuinely committed, others have reluctantly started after facing external pressure, and some countries remain blasé. There may be a vetting procedure and even a separation of power, but if not used consistently, these are of little use.

Perhaps a greater threat than undesirables who get *through* the due diligence checks are those who get *around* them. There is always the risk that officials will succumb to the temptation to relax their rules for big spenders. A service provider I met in Dubai offered a sardonic comparison: If you put a million dollars into a Swiss bank, they'll check out everything about you; if you put 50 million in, they'll lighten up. The media have increasingly exposed high-profile cases that should not have gotten past vetting, as we shall see. Unless checked by a systematically enforced division of labor, executive authority can override, and undermine, a carefully constructed system. A person whose application is rejected by due diligence firms or the CIU can otherwise go straight to the prime minister, promise great investments—and perhaps a cut on the deal—to try to get the decision reversed. The systems will never be watertight; no migration screening system ever is. Indeed, it is probably easier for a potential terrorist to obtain a student visa than investor citizenship. However, some CBI countries are letting in more water than others.

The end effect of the background checks—whether solid or not—is to bolster legitimacy, which is essential for the market to function. Countries even tout their screening when marketing their programs. "We are all about due diligence, due diligence, due diligence," the head of the Saint Kitts CIU told a professional audience in 2016. "You will not be approved if it puts the reputation of the country at risk." His counterpart from Grenada on the same panel went on, "We have a much wider responsibility when we grant approvals. We look at the potential impact on our country's reputation and that of the wider Caribbean." Meanwhile, the prime minister of Malta was boasting at a conference, "We are very careful about our reputation. Sometimes that doesn't make us popular with agents because we end up refusing the very wealthiest around. We may be a bit snobbish in our approach, but our program has the best due diligence around." He went on explain that much was due to the division of labor and formalization. "I cannot change a decision made by [the government unit assessing the applications], and they spend a hell of a lot of money on due diligence. There is no political interference. Our system is top-heavy with a lot of paperwork." Such statements not only reassure their audiences that the wrong people don't get approved, but also convey the right image of the programs. "Our biggest challenge is the 'perception challenge,'" one of the CIU heads commented to an audience in Europe, referring to the negative associations the programs carry. "We cannot overemphasize the importance of due diligence for [addressing] that." And indeed, rather than repelling interest, strict due diligence can attract it. As a London-based lawyer told me, CBI clients are used to "robust" regulatory environments. "If there isn't a framework around it, they're suspicious." The wealthy are risk averse: they want the protection of the law behind them—as long as it's working in their favor.

Formalization and the Global Market

The formalization process introduced degrees of transparency, divisions of labor, and third-party oversight to the programs. They may not be watertight, but for market players, the occasional leak doesn't matter as much as the credibility of the programs overall. How do you know that the citizenship will be good ten years from now? That the sovereign won't default? That other countries will accept the passport as valid? Formalization was secured against the backdrop of a cowboy world of discretionary grants. A partner at a major international accounting firm encapsulated the shift. About fifteen years before, a longtime client asked about purchasing an additional passport in the Caribbean. Unfamiliar with shadowy business, she conducted a risk analysis, which threw up red flags. A fact-finding mission left her just as mystified: no public information was available, the steps were unclear, and it was impossible to determine how much was paid to whom. "There was no transparency," she said, describing odd figures in dark sunglasses who met her at the airport and took her into government meetings. Soon after she returned, the country closed the program under international pressure. Yet much has changed since, she stated. "All the things that were so wrong then are so good now." When the same client recently approached her again about the programs, she set out an array of options, some with solid investment opportunities, and none of which raised the risk flags of the firm's legal division.

Her company was not the only one to change its stance. Indeed, by the 2010s, the London branches of three of the Big Four accountancies deemed the programs credible enough to regularly assist clients with investment-based naturalization. A service provider captured the transition from the 1990s to the present: "They didn't have a dedicated team like the CIU . . . they didn't have a system of licensed agents. That's all a lot more transparent now." A due diligence professional working in the field noted that in early days, "the same people were doing everything, which wasn't good": too many conflicts of interest arose. As another migration agent explained, in the 1990s, there wasn't even minimal due diligence. The required real estate investment was a way of legitimizing what was, effectively, just crudely paying an officer. "Back in those days, it was seen as quasi-official . . . it was almost a guilty secret." But, he went on, much has changed since the formalization of programs. It's become "more transparent," he told me. As a former Swiss banker put it: Ten or fifteen years ago, if a client came in with a Saint Kitts passport to open a bank account, no one knew where the country was and they wouldn't do it. "Now all the compliance departments know all about it, and know where the islands are." A due diligence company employee I spoke with who runs background checks for international financial firms said that they used to regularly advise banks to increase the risk rating on clients who used identity documents from countries with CBI programs. Now, however, it is a different story, he explained.

Yet not everyone has hopped on the train. A lawyer in Asia told me that he was "not a fan" of the citizenship schemes, though he assists clients with residence by investment programs. The governments don't do much of a background check, and the application file is just a few inches thick, he said, unimpressed. Service providers may also avoid programs not because they question their credibility but because others might. A partner at an international accountancy said that she doesn't recommend the Caribbean programs to her clients. "They're expensive for what you get. There are a lot of uncertainties around them." She went on to describe a client with a Caribbean passport who was always pulled over at airports and asked why he had it and if he had something to hide. "It can be a huge inconvenience." She did, however, help clients apply for the European CBI programs because they raised fewer problems at borders. Sufficient legitimacy and credibility have been secured for many actors to engage with the programs, but not all. In some corners it remains an ongoing project.

How effective is formalization in ensuring that things don't go wrong? The head of one of the CIUs explained to me, "Once you have ministers and political parties directly engaged [with the applications], then you can have problems with politics"—effectively, a polite way to say "corruption," which has been evident. "The politicians are the problem," I would often hear, gesturing to the kickbacks they might receive when cutting deals for service providers. A few CIU employees, past and present, told me of cases in which they pushed back on politicians who were tempted by offers difficult to refuse. A cabinet minister might own a construction company that could do well if hired by a real estate developer to build a resort with CBI funding, for example. In one case, a prime minister made the fiat decision that Iraqis, still on the country's banned list, could apply for the program. The timing came just as an Iraqi developer secured a lucrative contract for a real estate project that could be used to qualify for citizenship. However, the CIU's head rejected the application and remained firm against subsequent arm-twisting. When another prime minister backed a pie-in-the-sky proposal for an overpriced private jet hangar, possibly with a part reserved for himself, a CIU official formed a subcommittee to assess the project's viability and persuaded the cabinet to vote it down. If corruption is not fully stemmed—perhaps a delusory goal when it comes to high-ranking politicians in many places—formalization and divisions of labor may provide mechanisms for pushing back.[88]

Of course, there are alternatives to formalized programs too. In many countries, fixers can arrange citizenship—or, rather, a passport—via officials with "flexible ethics." Yet in these cases, there is no guarantee that the government will recognize the grant, whether in the present or the future, and if it decides to annul the membership, the buyer has no legal recourse. As a fixer I met in China told me, one might get a passport for five years, but after that it's unlikely to be renewed, and there's nothing one can do about it. He had a whole list of countries where it's possible to get membership documents by cutting a deal with a government official for a passport. Yet "without the backing of the law, you never know what could happen," a lawyer in Hong Kong told me. "Fake programs can easily explode." This includes falsifications. A popular route among Russians, for example, is to simply purchase documents attesting to Romanian heritage and then apply for citizenship through Romania's ancestry options. One can acquire a Romanian grandfather for a mere €25,000, according to estimates I received. Yet anyone who naturalizes based on fake documents remains at risk. Without the law behind you, "they can come and take it [the citizenship] away from you—or away from your children" an agent in Russia explained. Does the Romanian government try to stamp this out? A service provider in Eastern Europe told me he went to the Romanian embassy to let them know what was going on. The Russians buying fake papers for ancestry-based naturalization were eating into his own business, which dealt only with the formal programs. However, he lamented, the officials didn't seem to care.

Surveying the Scene

Citizenship by investment programs did not appear *ex nihilo*, but on ground prepared by more murky discretionary options. These supplied a base that service providers and governments retooled into more formalized and transparent offerings that could be pitched to a wider wealthy market. For the industry to go big, it needed credibility, and that meant standardization and transparency. The prices and investment options had to be explicit, the application form had to be serious, the attribution of citizenship needed to have clear expectations and separate steps involving different actors, and there needed to be checks on the process. In addition, powerful third countries needed to be appeased.

Formalizing wasn't like flipping a switch: the transformations were gradual and sometimes incomplete. In Saint Kitts, the main changes took place from 2006 to 2011 and resulted in a relatively clear-cut and replicable program that was far from swapping briefcases of money for envelopes of passports, or from just negotiating with a top official. A simple cash-for-passports exchange wouldn't work for a mass-market product. Formalization also meant that sovereign default—a new government coming into power and erasing the citizenships—was not likely. The process was too legalized now. These reforms also contributed to the credibility and future calculability of the program.

Of course, one can still seek out a "boutique option," like negotiating citizenship in recognition of a large investment in a country. Panama reportedly does this regularly for wealthy individuals from Latin America, but the practice is not limited to such places, as we saw with France and New Zealand. However, these "non-formatted solutions," as one lawyer in London put it tactfully, cannot become the basis of an expandable business model. That requires credibility, which rides on divisions of labor to make sure that dubious characters don't slip around the system, and on strong background checks to make sure they don't slip through them. It can also mean allowing a powerful third country to play a role in selection to keep it appeased. Additional rules haven't curbed demand either. Rather than repelling interest, strong due diligence can attract it, with governments now even using regulatory rigor as a marketing pitch to assure potential investors that what they offer is rock solid. Of course, countries talking the talk may not always walk the walk, and the extent to which the two diverge is an important concern. But notably the talk itself has become important—a situation different to the one that existed before the formal programs, when pitches focused on how easily a passport could be had. It sends the right signals by reassuring potential investors that their choice is legitimate and safe. For a market to be created, the product couldn't be one that might easily go under.

Scaling up also meant that it was no longer simply passports that were on sale—even if many still think and speak in those terms. It was citizenship, which is a relatively sticky legal status. When Grenada closed its first program in 2001, it simply did not renew the passports. Problem solved. The move was similar to the sovereign default adopted by most countries in the 1990s that sought to disavow their channels, often after a change in government. However, the formalization of programs in the 2000s meant that this was no longer a fly-by-night transaction. States could not cancel the status en masse: they could be held to account. Countries would need to adhere to formal legal procedures of denaturalization if they were to get rid of their new members, which Cyprus learned the hard way when it tried to denaturalize nearly thirty investors, a case that has been hung up in the courts since 2019. How did it get there?

Chapter 3

EU Citizenship

A CROSS THE ATLANTIC, other microstates were getting into the game, but with a more valuable proposition on offer: citizenship in an EU member state. At stake was not merely membership in a tiny country with visa-free access to the EU, but citizenship *in* the EU, with the right to reside in any EU country and be treated as, effectively, its own citizen. Caribbean countries have something similar on offer within CARICOM, but few people seeking citizenship by investment in the region were doing so to island-hop. The European Union was a very different wager. On top of it, EU citizens lay claim to extensive business rights and rights of establishment across the Union. The result is a powerful combination.

Malta

In 2013, as several countries in the Eastern Caribbean passed CBI laws, a surprise newcomer entered the field: Malta. In March, Malta's Labour Party unseated the ruling Nationalist Party, which had been in power for fifteen years. Initially elected on a pro-EU platform, the Nationalists lost their luster over time and eventually lost their power as well to a revamped opposition trumpeting a Tony Blair–style "New Labour" platform of pro-business reform and liberal social policies. Within months of taking the helm of state, the dynamic and young prime minister, Joseph Muscat, announced a new legislative initiative: the sale of citizenship.

The proposal caught many off guard. It hadn't been part of the campaign or general policy discussions. Malta had long employed its migration policies to harness revenue, but until this point, only residence had been on offer. Indeed, the strategy stretched back to its independence in 1964 when the country rolled out the "Six-Penny Settler Scheme." The idea was to get British retirees to spend time—and money—in the country. All they needed to do for a residence visa was purchase a property and prove a minimum annual income. This was set at a rate similar to the annual pay of the UK military services, which happened to be decamping from the island.[1] Taking a page from British law, the program worked on the distinction between "residence," or where one lives, and "domicile," or having a permanent home outside the country where one resides. Under the program, non-domiciled residents paid the equivalent of only six pennies on the British pound in tax, or the exact inversion of the highest tax rate in the United Kingdom at the time.[2] When combined with a double tax treaty, people who purchased a residence in Malta would pay only 2.5 percent in income taxes and be free of similar obligations back home.

In 1988, the pro-business Nationalist Party, then newly back in power, began developing an offshore financial sector. It rallied the country's migration policies for the endeavor by shifting residence options from merely attracting penny-saving retirees to more sharply focus on tools useful for tax structuring. The Permanent Resident Scheme, introduced that year, offered a tax rate of 15 percent to foreigners who rented or owned property and paid a minimum amount in taxes to Malta. This would become the first of a series of residence by investment (RBI) programs, now more colloquially known as "golden visa" schemes, that provided a way to draw in foreign revenue through taxes and property investment or rental.[3] These options seem to have been widely accepted across the years, with both political parties rolling out new programs. The *Malta Independent*, one of the country's main newspapers, even ranked the Labour Party's Global Residence Programme, introduced in June 2013, as number one among the top ten best moves of the new government. Golden visas appeared to be a golden opportunity.

Golden passports, however, proved to be a very different wager. Naturalizing foreigners was not traditionally a part of Malta's migration regime. As a former civil servant who spent a career working on migration policy explained to me, Malta was simply "not an immigration country." Until recently, the government offered mostly permanent residence or multiple extensions to stay. Even the "six-penny settlers" were handled in this manner rather than put on a path to citizenship. Furthermore, dual citizenship was not a possibility until 2000 when the government gave into pressure from the large Maltese diaspora, which wanted to have multiple memberships. Once the law was passed, the few naturalizations the country saw were largely of Maltese people who had become Australian or British.[4]

As such, most people were blindsided when the prime minister in October 2013 proposed legislation for a new Maltese Individual Investor Programme (MIIP) that would confer citizenship on people who "contribute to the economic development of Malta." The design was straightforward: applicants would donate €650,000 to the government to qualify, family members could be added for an additional €25,000 or €50,000 per person, and due diligence and processing fees would be assessed at around €8,200 for an individual and €20,700 for a family of four. The law barred individuals with criminal convictions or cases against them, as well as money launderers and terrorists, and multiple background checks were required of all applicants.

The timing seemed propitious. The new RBI program was getting rave reviews in the newspapers. Even the Nationalist Party supported a golden visa scheme in principle, though it bickered about the adjustments made to the format it had launched years before.[5] If golden visas were well accepted, why not golden passports? How different would citizenship be?

Controversy

As it turned out, the answer was "very." The uproar in the media was immediate. Leading newspapers came out strongly against the move, and many in the public were skeptical or opposed.[6] An opinion poll carried out by the newspaper *Malta Today* revealed that 53 percent of the population was against the scheme, while just over 35 percent supported it as proposed or if an investment was included, with the remainder undecided.[7] The results were divided strongly along party lines with 60 percent of Labour voters supporting the scheme, compared to just 10 percent of Nationalist voters.[8] On top of it, local lawyers were up in arms that they could not simply file a client's application with the government but would have to go through a foreign service provider.

Yet the opposition Nationalists were slow off the block to come out against the program.[9] Initially they were more critical of the design than of citizenship by investment in principle. They wanted to see a serious residence and clear investment component built in to ensure that membership went to committed investors, rather than merely "sold" to the distant rich.[10] The Nationalist Party had worked with Henley and Partners when overhauling its High Net Worth Individuals RBI program a few years before,[11] but as one of its politicians told me, they rejected the firm's overtures to start a citizenship program at the time. Some local law firms saw the advantages that Cyprus was securing through its CBI program and even assisted clients with their applications on the neighboring island. They also had lobbied the Maltese government to start a scheme. However, the Nationalists didn't budge. Even if the party was ready for golden visas, its buy-in for golden passports was hardly guaranteed, especially when it became clear that the subject touched a nerve with many Maltese.

As in the Caribbean, the law established a new agency to handle the program and license service providers, though in this case it was given the sleeker name of "Identity Malta" rather than the clunky "Citizenship Investment Unit." The government also guaranteed that applicants would go through a multilevel background check, ensuring that no one who had been charged or convicted with a range of criminal offenses would be approved.[12]

The policy built in a role for a "concessionaire," namely a firm contracted to "design, implement, administer, operate, and promote the program." Such outsourcing is not unusual. Private-public partnerships have become not only common, but sometimes de rigueur across a range of functions that lie at the heart of the modern state. Military defense, border control, education, postal services, transportation and communication infrastructure, and visa screenings are now regularly turned over to companies even by powerful states with the capacity to carry out the tasks themselves. Yet the prospect of private-sector involvement in the naturalization process grated on many and would become a bone of contention in the EU. At the end of September 2013 and following a public tender, which some saw as barely competitive, the firm Henley and Partners was awarded a ten-year concessionaire's contract to design, administer, and promote the program.

In the letter of the law tabled in parliament, the remit of the concessionaire was hard to disaggregate from the duties of Identity Malta. Both could run due diligence checks, both were to be informed of the outcomes of all applications, both could recommend that an applicant be called for an interview. The concessionaire would also disburse the government contribution to Identity Malta and thus, ostensibly, serve as an escrow agent in the process, holding the money for a stint. Notably, too, the concessionaire could examine applications in place of Identity Malta. And—even more notably—it could submit them as well, leading to queries about potential conflicts of interest.[13] As such, the position of concessionaire was an enviably sweet one: it could get paid by clients for assembling their application and then get paid by the government for vetting the application. The cherry on top was an additional payment from the government for the successful application.

The contract the government signed with Henley and Partners, just over two weeks before rolling out the legislation, tasked the firm with processing applications and implementing the program. For this work, as well as for designing and promoting the scheme, it would receive 4 percent of each donation, or a tidy €26,000 per application. Others watching the island state were surprised. "Malta is a serious country, an EU member. It's a proper democracy," a long-time service provider based in London told me. He didn't expect it would partner with a private firm to run its program. In the Caribbean, the paucity of government resources for managing such a scheme—whether in know-how, infrastructure, or finances—was clear; in Malta, it was less so. However, as controversy expanded, the government increasingly distanced itself from the private sector. Despite the contract, Identity Malta took control of the operation of the program and the assessment of the applications.[14] Initially the Henley offices were co-located with Identity Malta, but when I visited in 2018, they had moved to a different part of town, and the migration officials I spoke to said that all the vetting was handled within the government. The new arrangement bypassed potential conflicts of interest, which were glaring and glared at. Plus, Henley still got paid.

There was also a pressing need to get the program through. The contract with Henley specified that the scheme should be operational by November 1, and the prime minister was scheduled to travel to Miami and London that month to tout the newborn program at investment migration events.[15] The opposition, shifting between outright rejection and mere disagreement on implementation, demanded a string of amendments: the names of the naturalizers should be made public, and participants should be required to spend at least one month in the country annually for the first five years. The key bone of contention, however, was that under the initial proposal, no investment was required: the applicant just gifted money to the government. This meant, the Nationalist Party argued, that citizenship was merely being sold.[16] They instead wanted proper investment requirements, which they saw as doing more for the economy, and proposed that a minimum of €5 million would be appropriate.[17] In a throwback to the practices of the 1990s, they also threatened, if elected, to revoke the citizenships should their demanded changes not go through. At this point, the attorney general stepped in to confirm that such a move would be unconstitutional.[18] Citizenship, and not mere passports, was at stake. And precisely because of these heightened stakes, debates raged in the media and on the streets, questioning whether the country was selling its soul.[19]

By mid-November, the parliament—divided along party lines—approved an amended version of the law that incorporated the thrust of the opposition's key demands, if in modified form: the names would be published in the national gazette, an investment dimension would be included, and applicants would have to obtain a residence. In practice, however, it simply meant that applicants would need to invest an additional €150,000 and purchase or lease a property at a minimum amount.[20] The revisions also stated that the final decision would be made not by the executive of the country but by a committee within Identity Malta, removing the prime minister's power of discretion. In a new development, adding a level of transparency still unknown in the Caribbean, an ombudsman would audit the program annually and publish a public report on its findings. The changes also clarified what would happen to the money: 70 percent of the contributions would go into a newly established National Development and Social Fund, which aimed for the "advancement of education, research, innovation, social purposes, justice and the rule of law, employment initiatives, the environment, and public health." Who could be against that? The result was a program that cost around €890,000 for a single applicant and €975,000 for a family of four, netting between €620,000 to €700,000 for the government, €150,000 for finance and businesses, €80,000 for landlords, and €32,000 for Henley and Partners.[21]

The European Union

But the battle wasn't over. The leader of the opposition, Simon Busuttil, had been a member of the European Parliament (MEP) in the years preceding the 2013 election, and he still possessed strong connections there.[22] The EU was a natural environment for the Nationalist Party, which had championed membership in the Union and saw through the referendum that brought Malta into the fold in 2004. As such, it could be a savvy strategic move for the Nationalist Party to shift their domestic political struggles to a venue in the supra-national sphere where they would land on their front foot rather than their back one.

MEPs from the Nationalist Party lobbied intensely at the European Parliament against the citizenship program, and with great success.[23] It was blatantly clear that the main advantage of citizenship in Malta was not membership in the tiny island, but in the EU. Any Maltese citizen can move to and enjoy extensive rights in any member state, without question, and as EU citizens, they possess rights of establishment for doing business as well.

MEPs from other member states immediately recognized the backdoor into their own backyard and reacted. Service providers did as well and launched advertising campaigns around it.

Moving a debate about citizenship over to Brussels wasn't an obvious option at first. Since the EU's founding, citizenship attribution has remained firmly ensconced within the sovereign domain of each member state. The result is that EU citizenship is fundamentally derivative: it is only if a person is a citizen of a member state that she can become an EU citizen. With citizenship attribution a sovereign function, it is the individual countries, rather than the EU, that decide who can obtain the prized burgundy passport. The European Court of Justice (ECJ) has even ruled against countries that raise questions about the legitimacy of another member state's naturalization policies.[24]

Nonetheless, in January 2014 the European Parliament debated "EU citizenship for sale." Viviane Reding, then vice-president of the European Commission and the EU justice commissioner, opened the discussion with a strident condemnation of such programs. Drawing on "the spirit of sincere cooperation with other Member States" enshrined in the Treaty on European Union, she argued that only people with a "genuine link" or "genuine connection" to a country should be awarded its citizenship.[25] Declaring plainly that "citizenship must not be up for sale," she proclaimed to a round of applause that "one cannot put a price tag on it." Voices from across the political spectrum echoed the vice-president's concerns in the debate that followed. Representatives from the Maltese Labour Party's own political group within the parliament abandoned their colleague and came out against the scheme. Even warring parties were united in the condemnation. In other matters, far-right Euroskeptics denounced the EU's encroachment on sovereign rights, and the communist group condemned the EU's hypocrisy, as it violated the putatively universal values on which it is built.[26] Yet even the extreme ends of the political spectrum—along with all the parties in the middle—came out forcefully against the prospect of citizenship sales. Only the Maltese Labour Party MEPs stood behind it.

Thus it came as little surprise when the European Parliament on the following day adopted a nonbinding resolution, supported by nearly 90 percent of MEPs, that condemned the sale of EU citizenship.[27] The declaration read like a hymn to the European project, announcing that the "values of and achievements of [the Union] are invaluable and cannot have a price tag attached to them," and further that "the rights conferred by EU citizenship are based on human dignity and should not be bought or sold at any price." (No doubt, a large swath of the world's population, including many asylum-seekers, wish that the rights EU citizenship confers were based on human dignity, rather than citizenship in an EU member state.) Malta's CBI program, it proclaimed, amounts to "the outright sale of EU citizenship as a whole without any residency requirement" and "undermines the mutual trust upon which the Union is built."

Some of the specific contentions rested on dubious grounds, such as the claim that investor citizens would use the status to shirk taxes even though, across the EU, income taxes are a matter of residence and physical presence, rather than citizenship.[28] A Maltese citizen living in Paris pays income taxes in France, just as a French citizen living in Frankfurt pays taxes in Germany.[29] Even the assertion that "EU citizenship ... depends on a person's ties with Europe and the Member States or on personal ties with EU citizens" was questionable: spouses of EU citizens, for example, are not automatically entitled to EU citizenship. Odd, too, was the focus on the absence of a residence requirement in Malta's program. Arguably, other routes to EU citizenship—and far more common ones as well—fall afoul of the same concerns but have rarely raised eyebrows. The number of naturalizations through ancestry channels approaches, if not exceeds, those seen through immigration routes in some member states, even though they often do not require any physical presence or demonstration of ties beyond a lucky family tree. Italy, for example, approved around 85,000 ancestry-based naturalizations each year between 1998 and 2010, while it naturalized a mere 25,700 immigrants annually in the same period. Furthermore, 75 percent of the ancestry passports were handed out not in Italy, but in South America, where most of the new Italians continued to reside.[30] Yet the large-scale naturalization of far-off foreigners with the right great-great-great-grandparent has never been taken up by the European Parliament.[31]

Notably, too, only Malta stood in the crosshairs. Cyprus had long hosted a CBI program, as we shall see, and had even recently adjusted it in reaction to economic penalties imposed by the EU. Yet the European Parliament had remained mute on Cyprus's CBI scheme. When a MEP raised questions about Cyprus's program in 2011, Vice-President Reding dismissed the query on grounds that it addressed an issue outside the purview of the EU.[32] However, with Malta on the stand, this would change entirely, and the debates that followed turned largely on it. Investment migration programs elsewhere in the EU came up occasionally, but only Malta would be mentioned by name in the resolution eventually adopted.

The European Parliament's resolution, however, was a testament of the general weakness of the institution in the matter of controlling member states. Nonbinding, it had the legal force of mere suggestion and could be ignored. If the EU had no legal grounds for direct interference with naturalization principles of a member state, the Parliament's pressure—in addition to negative press coverage—was enough to bring the small island to the table. At the end of January, Maltese authorities met with Union powers to discuss the situation. The result was a joint press statement in which the European Commission and Malta declared that they had reached a common understanding on the program and affirmed that the commission welcomed good-faith changes to the residence requirement.

The "Citizenship Journey"

The upshot was that Malta didn't scuttle the scheme but passed a reformed law in February 2014 with some changes to the "citizenship journey" that participants would undertake. To appease the EU, applicants now had to prove that they had been "a resident of Malta for a period of at least twelve months" prior to naturalization. The obligation, however, sounds far more stringent on paper than what it means in practice, for residence, in the eyes of the law, is different from physical presence. Legal residence concerns a connection to a place, but it doesn't result just from being there: it isn't physical, but metaphysical. Even if a California resident moves to New York for a few months, the law will still treat her as though she is in California when it comes to voting, acquiring a driver's license, or attending public universities. And it gets more extreme. A US citizen who has not been in the country for decades will still be able to cast a ballot in elections as though she were living in her last state of residence. As legal scholar Richard Ford puts it, "residence operates by analogy to physical presence. We assume that people are usually at home, that they care most about home, that they identify with home, and therefore we will 'find' them at home for legal purposes, even if they are physically somewhere else."[33] It is this disjuncture that would prove useful when implementing residence requirements for Malta's CBI program.

In practice, satisfying the residence requirement meant not moving home but showing the *intent* to make Malta home. This could be enacted by joining neighborhood clubs, establishing some business ties, or giving charitably to local causes, on top of the required purchase or rental of a residential property. Yet it couldn't be merely a box-ticking exercise: each person was expected to build an individual "citizenship profile," submitted as a plan to the government with the emphasis on intention rather than actual execution. As the head of Identity Malta explained to an audience in Switzerland, "When we look at residence, we look at it in a practical manner. It's about creating synergies and links to the local community." Showing a "genuine connection" was crucial but "workable," he clarified.

"Light touch" is how one lawyer described the government's approach to residence in his experience. The service providers I met gave a range of answers to what residence entailed in practice. Most advised their clients to spend anywhere from one week to one month or more in the country. (Those who upped the ante to two months could also qualify for tax residence.) Still, no one could get away with not visiting at all, as is possible in some Caribbean countries. Applicants needed to travel to the island at least twice: once to give biometric data, and a second time to swear their citizenship oath if successful.[34] The head of Identity Malta later explained to me that this was the only way the program could work. Wealthy business elites are simply too internationally engaged to be able to commit an entire year to a small island. "We don't want people who will sit around and do nothing for twelve months. We want people who are active and successful in their fields, which means living a transnational life. They can't run their businesses if they are just sitting around in Malta." Yet without clear boxes to tick, some applicants remained concerned about the uncertainty around fulfilling program requirements. For others, the residence stipulation made the program appear more serious and desirable.[35] In the end, this concession to EU demands was hardly a hindrance for the program to grow.

And to grow economically as well. The residence requirement supplied applicants with the opportunity—and incentive—to invest yet further in a country they might not have known existed before they naturalized. The idea behind the genuine connection, the head of Identity Malta explained to an audience in Switzerland, is that becoming a citizen is "not a one-time transaction" but rather something "mutually beneficial." He went on, "People start off wanting to tick as few boxes as possible and then fall in in love with the place." Whether or not this is indeed the case, there is an incentive for moving businesses to the island to create a "genuine connection profile." One of the country's financial experts explained to me that the CBI program helped the wealthy to learn about the country in the first place. The multiplier effects have been substantial, he averred. "People start off interested in citizenship and then discover the financial services they have to offer." Like Luxembourg, he continued, Malta's low tax regime means that it can serve as an "advantageous staging ground" for moving capital and goods into the EU. My interviews turned up investors who had set up family offices on the island or moved their financial structures to it, boosting the country's insurance, banking, and financial services industries.

Indeed, an unlikely outcome of the EU's insistence on a residence requirement was a synergy with changes moving through the offshore financial sector. The OECD and the United States, along with the EU, had been cracking down on the legal sleights of hand that individuals and companies use to structure wealth as they game or ghost residence. Where a mere post office box or name plate would have sufficed in the past, now greater connections—"substance" behind the claim—are needed to prevent legal challenges. A mere "flag of convenience" of the classical offshore world is no longer enough. This "mid-shore" variant demands a thicker web of relationships to anchor a person in a place for legal purposes, with consequent benefits for the local financial industry. Thus the residence requirements for the CBI program also made it easier to claim legal protections and tax benefits.

The new "citizenship journey" in Malta was time-consuming and selective. From start to finish, it took about fourteen to eighteen months and offered no guarantee that those who headed down the path would make it to the end.[36] Indeed, around one in five applications was rejected—an astounding number in comparison to the Caribbean programs, where rejection rates rarely broached 5 percent.[37]

Strict due diligence may partly explain the rejection numbers, but the cap of 1,800 might have also played a role, since demand for EU citizenship was strong. Service providers and officials involved with the program had long expected it to be renewed once the cap was hit, but it was clear that this would have to be delicately timed. After steering through a bumpy launch, the government hardly wanted to see the contentious program made into an issue at the ballot box. In this context, the pace of approvals could be managed to avoid the general elections scheduled every five years. The high rejection rate—which, for any failed applicant, meant a loss of several thousand euros in fees—might also be a boon for well-placed service providers. It could incentivize any would-be naturalizer to select a lawyer or agent with close links to the government in Valetta and a record of past approvals. The situation was one in which the concessionaire, which was also filing applications, could hardly complain.[38] Already in 2017, the government was making public statements about the next iteration of the program in anticipation of reaching the cap. However, the path ahead would prove rocky enough to move the targets down the road, slowing the pace of approvals until the maximum was hit in 2020.

One might think that the long and tumultuous process of launching the program could have done irreparable damage to it, but its proponents transformed every hurdle into a selling point. The cap of 1,800 became a hallmark of elite privilege. "Ours is a small and exclusive program," the prime minister would boast to audiences on the investment migration conference circuit. Explaining the high refusal rate, stringent due diligence, and cap on numbers, he went on, "Our program is not the cheapest or the fastest. What we give is value." The residence requirement was converted into a feeder for the financial services industry. He even renovated the tussle with the EU into an endorsement from Brussels.[39]

All of this was to great success. In the first two years of the program, the government saw 564 applications go through, resulting in just over 2,000 investor citizens, including the naturalized family members. It generated €70 million in residential property sales, brought €50 million to the rental market, and garnered €85 million for the stock market. The government donations themselves amounted to nearly €370 million, though Henley netted €14 million of that. The program's average annual revenue amounted to about 5 percent of what the country collected in tax. By 2019, the scheme was keeping the government in the black and adding 2.1 percent to the GDP.[40] It was also proving to be an important source of foreign investment, generating the equivalent of 7.6 percent of foreign direct investment inflows.[41] Economically, it was making a mark.

Yet the program had many critics, including the country's leading blogger, Daphne Caruana Galizia. A longtime opponent of the Labour Party and no friend of Joseph Muscat's government, she had been relentlessly reporting on corruption and particularly on cases of alleged wrongdoing that involved high-level Labour politicians.[42] She was also a fierce opponent of the CBI program. She railed against the over-friendly relationship between the prime minister and Henley and Partners, churned out stories on foreign politicians who obtained citizenship through the scheme, and exposed an alleged kickback to the prime minister's chief of staff for seeing through the citizenship application of a Russian family. Then in October 2017, she was tragically killed by a car bomb. No evidence has been found to prove that her reporting on Malta's CBI program led to her murder—she was prolific and addressed a wide range of dubious, suspicious, and illegal practices among the Maltese elite—but the two issues became intertwined in the media coverage and subsequent debates around corruption and press freedom.[43] As the government dragged its feet in investigating her death, the EU and the international media pressured it from the outside and public vigils and demonstrations did the same from within.[44] If the CBI program was controversial to begin with, now it was bringing people out to the streets with placards and candles. The EU even sent an ad hoc delegation to assess the rule of law, producing a non-binding resolution bitingly critical of the course of events in the country.[45] By the end of November 2019, the prime minister's chief of staff and the minister of tourism, once minster of energy, had resigned. Both were allegedly involved in payments moving through Panamanian shell companies, and questions were being raised about related irregularities in the process of privatizing energy in Malta.[46] Within a week, the prime minister too announced that he would step down after unrelenting pressure over how the murder investigation was handled and repeated accusations of corruption at the highest levels of his government. For a small, arid island, the swamp seemed deep.

Yet the CBI program remained. Once the planned 1,800 applications were approved, the Maltese Individual Investor Programme was wrapped up and replaced in 2021 with a new channel. However, the government was still facing heat. The new option, the Maltese Exceptional Investor Naturalization (MEIN), was to be quite deliberately not a "program"—a term that evoked an image of cash-for-passports—but a "policy" for rewarding citizenship to those who had made exceptional economic contributions to the country. With an overall cap of 1,500 and an annual cap of four hundred approved applications, it was meant to be small and temporary. It raised the minimum costs and stretched out the naturalization process to three full years, but with a one-year shortcut available to those willing to up the ante, and it threw in a few more requirements around charitable contributions and background checks. It also shelved the role of concessionaire: program management was to be clearly in-house. The revisions were to make the option more palatable, but by this point, the EU was unwilling to compromise. In October 2020, the European Commission sent a formal notice to Malta requesting that it end its CBI program and later that year initiated infringement procedures against the country. The European Parliament carried the ball further in September 2022 by passing a motion that called for the abolition of all such schemes. Six months later came the final weapon in the arsenal: the European Commission referred Malta to the ECJ for not addressing its concerns. The case will likely take several years to move through the court, but the outcome may not be surprising. It's rare for the ECJ to rule against the desire of the commission, let alone the expansion of EU power, and this is a stellar opportunity to bring citizenship under the EU's regulatory auspices on an issue that makes for great PR as well.[47] "European values are not for sale" has become the battle cry, if an incoherent one. The political game promises to keep going.

Cyprus

Malta may have dominated much of the early press coverage of CBI programs in the EU, but it wasn't the first member state to offer citizenship by investment. That title Cyprus had claimed long before. Its history, however, stands in contrast with the pattern seen among its island colleagues in the Caribbean and Mediterranean, for it undertook formalization without close cooperation with service providers and never had a company play the role of concessionaire. Why?

To some extent, size matters. With a population of 850,000, the republic is substantially larger than its Caribbean counterparts and even Malta, lending its government in Nicosia more weight against private firms. Just as important has been its long-standing role as a conduit between regional blocks. As part of the nonaligned movement in the postwar years and with one of the most vibrant communist parties in the West, the island became a link between the Soviet Union and Europe during the Cold War. Leftist university students read Marx, learned Russian, and took part in party activities (of the communist sort, though perhaps not only). These gave them skills and connections that would come in handy once the USSR collapsed. Student exchanges in Moscow and Leningrad were particularly important, for they produced a generation of university-educated lawyers and accountants who had links to what was becoming the Wild East of privatization and capitalism. In addition, Cyprus's enviable list of double-taxation treaties with both the West and the Rest made it a convenient offshore base for moving money out of the country and into more stable legal systems. The result was that Cyprus began banking Russian oligarchs long before financial centers in London or New York would touch them. As one service provider summed it up, the country was "a bit like the Russian Hong Kong."[48] The client base boosted the financial services industry and offshore sector in the country, which developed tools and systems that places like Malta would later emulate. When foreign service providers came in to try and set up a CBI program around 2012, they were slow off the blocks: the government was already running one.

Origins

The program itself grew organically. Back in 2003, the Council of Ministers—the cabinet chosen by the country's president—began naturalizing wealthy foreigners if they had contributed to economic growth. Rather than formulating a new legal provision, as Malta and the Caribbean countries did, they based the move on the Civil Registry Law, which allows for naturalization "by exception." Why it began to use this clause with regularity is still cloudy. Some suggest that it was a Chinese magnate doing business on the island who first proposed that he and his co-investors receive citizenship in recognition for their economic efforts. No matter its source, it seemed to the Council of Ministers to be a practice worth continuing. As a civil servant described it to me, the point in these early years was to offer something to people who had already contributed to the economy. If someone had, for example, started a shipping firm, citizenship would be given "as a reward," she said. And as an anchor. Making an investor a full member in the state would ensure that "investors already in Cyprus would stay in Cyprus," she clarified.

Though the policy wasn't specifically built for wealthy Russians, they immediately became the main participants and would continue to dominate the CBI numbers. Cyprus, for many of them, was not solely a financial center. Long-standing connections to Moscow made the Mediterranean island an easy choice when newly wealthy Russians began looking for vacation homes. Their first port of call was the resort town of Limassol, which soon found itself brimming with Russian schools, Russian shops, Russian media, Russian clubs, and Russian restaurants. For locals, the influx transformed the town into "Limassolgrad," and for Russians into "Sunny Moscow." As such, the country already had connections to a population of potential naturalizers—it didn't need foreign service providers to supply it with the concept, or with "clients."

In its operation, the channel initially worked on an individualized basis rather than as a depersonalized program. There was no set investment amount, just a rule of thumb that an "exceptional benefit" to the country's economy was required. In practice, this ranged around €20 to €30 million or more per person. Furthermore, investors couldn't apply for the status per se. Rather, it was something the government conferred post hoc in recognition of their achievements—or economic injections. The decision was made by the Council of Ministers, which convenes every Wednesday, and a minister could put forward a potential new citizen at any of these meetings for approval. Yet this occurred only rarely, and old hands in the field confirm that only about a dozen or so people were naturalized in this way in the 2000s. It was a discretionary channel rather than a formal program, similar to the way New Zealand naturalized PayPal billionaire Peter Thiel.

This would change in 2007 when the Council of Ministers, then controlled by the centrist Democratic Party (DIKO), decided to expand the practice. It set a minimum investment amount of €17 million and came up with a more clear-cut set of expectations. Would-be naturalizers needed to present an investment proposal to the minister with the relevant portfolio—energy, shipping, tourism, and so forth. If the minister supported the proposal, it then went to the Council of Ministers for a final decision. No longer was citizenship merely a post hoc reward for unspecified services but a status gained through a more formalized route. The number of naturalizations increased from a few dozen in total to around thirty or forty annually.

The following year saw the election of the leader of the communist Progressive Party of Working People (AKEL) to the presidency. One might assume that a Marxist-Leninist movement would scuttle a VIP naturalization route for the wealthy, but instead it took a more pragmatic view and not only kept it but eventually expanded the channel into a full-fledged CBI program aimed at attracting foreign investment. The global economic crunch that began in 2008 hit Cyprus hard. From 2009, the country fell into recession, and its GDP was shrinking by nearly 1.7 percent annually. With the economy flagging, the government saw the citizenship option as one tool of several it could use to address the ailing bank and real estate sectors. These twinned segments of the economy were dragging each other under. The banks held books of bad loans secured by real estate that had lost value, and so they stopped lending to developers, who were themselves overleveraged. The economic downturn had a deleterious impact across the property and construction industry, a sizeable 18 percent of the economy, which saw the production of new buildings halve between 2010 and 2014.[49] Even when I visited in

2018, banks were still reluctant to lend to developers, who had to source their funds through other means, including citizenship by investment.

In 2011, the government finished transforming the channel into a full program aimed at attracting investment. First, the state dropped the minimum investment from €17 million to a "more affordable" €10 million. It also set out specific investment options. Applicants could make a direct investment in real estate, businesses, stocks, or financial assets; establish a company; introduce innovative technology or a research center; or deposit €15 million in a bank. A final possibility—never taken up, an official told me—granted citizenship to those who had paid an average of €500,000 in taxes per year on income generated through Cyprus-based businesses or spent the same on legal or financial services. The program's orientation to business and investment was made clear in the minimum age of applicants: only those at least thirty years old (enough time to get some experience under one's belt) could qualify. Due diligence wasn't as stringent as it would later become. The policy specified simply that applicants could not have property in the EU that had been frozen by authorities, and they needed a clean criminal record from their country of origin "and/or" the Cyprus police. The flexibility of "and/or" granted the government fairly wide berth when deciding who merited admission into the national fold. Finally, in what would become a hallmark of the Cyprus scheme, the applicants had to purchase and continue to hold a private residence worth at least €500,000. Though the other investments could be sold or cashed in after three to five years, the new citizen had to continue to possess a residential property on the island. This, a civil servant explained, helped ensure that they maintained a genuine connection to the country. Where else is home but where (one of) your home(s) is?

With these reforms, the number of applications soared from a few dozen to over a hundred annually, even though the minimum cost still stretched into eight figures.[50] Who would go for such an option? "They were all Forbes List people," someone working with the scheme at the time told me. "Ultra-, ultra-, ultra-high net worth individuals." The vast majority continued to hail from Russia, though interest from the Middle East began to pick up.

Yet the government's measures were far from a financial panacea, and two years later the economy was still flagging. Commercial property, frequently used as collateral for loans, fell 30 percent between 2012 and 2013, and bad debt rose precipitously. In March 2013, the Troika—the European Commission, European Central Bank, and International Monetary Fund—and Cyprus agreed to a €10 billion package that would address expiring debt and budget deficits, and recapitalize the banks through a controversial bail-in. The agreement dissolved the failing Laiki Bank (Cyprus Popular Bank), the second largest in the country, rolled it into the Bank of Cyprus, and imposed dramatic levies at both institutions on bank deposits over €100,000.[51] This infamous "haircut" in which depositors paid for the recapitalization took a heavy toll on retirees, savers, and small businesses.[52] It also impacted a substantial number of Russians who had been using the island as their financial center of choice, a role that Cyprus had built up since the fall of the Soviet Union. A local lawyer described the scene as desperate. "You have to imagine what it's like to have everything you have in the bank over €100,000 suddenly disappear. You have a great house, a great car, but no money. One of my friends went crazy and started popping pills."

In April, the new president of Cyprus, elected just two months before, announced that any foreigner who lost more than €3 million in the haircut would be eligible to apply for citizenship under the CBI program—a proposition seen by many as a consolation prize. Those who had already acquired Cypriot papers wondered what they were supposed to do with a *second* second citizenship. A month later, the government adjusted the array of investment options, dropped the price yet further, and did away with the age requirement. In a new move, applicants could invest €2 million in a state investment company plus donate €500,000 to a research and technology fund to qualify. The other main routes were simply rolled over from 2011. Most important was the change in their price: the minimum investment was halved from €10 million to €5 million.

When foreign service providers approached Cyprus about managing its program in 2012, the government knew that Malta was receiving a similar call about starting a scheme, though likely at a lower cost. The first concern was how to reduce their minimum investment to keep it competitive. Government consultations with the private sector, one participant in them explained to me, led to the conclusion that a quick drop might raise questions about the integrity of the program or the true value of what was on offer. If citizenship is €5 million today and €500,000 tomorrow, why not make it €50,000? What establishes its value? The solution was to curate the price decline. In 2013, Nicosia lowered the minimum investment to €2.5 million in state companies and to €5 million in other qualifying sectors. The next year, the lowest investment threshold dropped further to €2 million while other options stayed at €5 million. By 2015, €2 million had become the standard minimum across the range of investment options—plus, of course, the €500,000 house. The total might not seem competitive against Malta's offering, which approached just €1 million in price, but a savvy investor would see otherwise. In Malta, the bulk of the money—around €750,000 or so—was spent on donations, fees, and rent, and the investor would never see it again. In Cyprus, by contrast, the new citizen invested the money and had to retain the asset for three years—increased to five in 2019—after which it could be sold, with the exception of the house. As such, the end cost could be calculated as just the price of the residence, plus fees. It was a very different proposition to donating to the government and "kissing your money good-bye," as one service provider put it.

Notable in this mix is the process of elaboration and reform. The program came into being by executive fiat rather than legislative act, and evolved through regular modification. To make changes, the Council of Ministers simply expanded, formalized, and bureaucratized the powers it had to grant citizenship by exception, guaranteed under Article 111 of the Civil Registry Law—even while noting that it continued to maintain the discretion to naturalize whomever it wanted anyway, with or without the new program. At any of the council's weekly assemblies, it could change the program, or even end it, should the cabinet agree. Yet the scheme remained different to naturalization through mere sovereign discretion. With specified investment options, the government could easily direct the inflow of funds toward areas of the economy that it wanted to boost—tinkering that would happen nearly annually. In practice, the Ministry of Finance assessed where need lay and recommended amendments to the financial criteria to the Council of Ministers. The result was a more flexible tool for economic improvement.

Indeed, fiddling with the scheme was continuous: 2014, 2015, 2016, 2018, and 2019 all saw changes to the investment options, and sometimes amounts, with even more minor adjustments to application requirements. By 2015, the guidelines had grown from just three pages in 2011 to seven pages, with nearly every year in between bringing more specificity to the process. When the banking sector flagged, real estate tanked, sovereign debt continued to be downgraded, and unemployment rose, the program was shifted to address those sectors. In 2013, a category for investing in innovative technology and research was added, but by the next year it was gone. Options for alternative investment funds and for investors who lost money in the 2013 haircut were also introduced and removed when no longer deemed useful. When it became difficult for the government to borrow on the open market, it added a government bond option, which it then dropped once it left the EU's assistance program. In 2019 the government added a required donation of €75,000 to the government's Research and Innovation Foundation and an equal amount to the government's social housing fund to channel more money into social welfare—provisions again tinkered with in summer 2020.

Since the government produced the policy on its own, without involvement of service providers interested in marketability and profits, the design itself—like most naturalization channels—was not very fussy. There was no elaborate table of fees because there was no need to create a pot of funds to pay commissions to agents. The policy also didn't include intricate differences in cost based on the number and age of family members on the application. Simply €10 million—later €5 million, then €2.5 million—was the fare, whether the application was for a single individual or a large family. The government didn't worry about promoting the program or controlling advertising around it, two important components found in the Caribbean, and later in Malta, where service providers pitched their marketing proficiency as a "must-have" for any government looking to attract applicants. Instead, it relied on interest generated through the financial services industry.

Indeed, the government took a strong stance against its own involvement in promoting the program. If agents wanted to advertise the naturalization option, they could, but this was not seen as the role of the state. "We're a government, not a marketer," I was told flatly when I visited the Ministry of Interior, where an official added with a note of sarcasm, "How desperate are we?" Service providers offered to fly out officials, all expenses paid, to become the face of the program and pitch it at conferences, yet the government refused each time. "Why would a government official go to a private event to promote it?" I was told that the Cyprus International Businesses Association (CIBA), a semi-governmental body that encourages investment in the country, handles such things. The result was dramatically different to the situation in the Caribbean and Malta, where the state actively engages in product promotion, working with the private sector to ensure its economic success. In Cyprus, the division between state and market was more starkly drawn in program design and operation—at least, as we shall see, in the *formal* program.

The result is not for want of trying by the citizenship industry. In 2012, foreign service providers approached the government about revamping its program, angling to create a concessionaire role and manage the scheme. Where Malta went for the lure, Cyprus casually turned its head: it was perfectly capable of implementing a naturalization policy on its own. Its decisions, of course, were not made in total isolation from industry actors. As with other policy domains, it would hold consultations to gather input from stakeholders such as financial services, lawyers, or real estate professionals, to inform its choices. Yet it wasn't dependent on—or under contractual obligations with—any of them.

Notably, too, the program in Cyprus was not politicized. A centrist party opened the channel, the communists transformed it into a formal program, and the conservatives expanded it further still. Of the eight major parties, only the xenophobic extreme right was consistently against it. In 2018, I visited a week before national elections and was surprised to find that citizenship by investment wasn't an issue at all. With such a broad base of support among parties, transformations in program operation would come from the outside.

There was also strong agreement that the program was meant to reward economic endeavors. Everyone I spoke with, from public officials through the service providers, was adamant that, in contrast to Malta, a government donation was not—and would never become—the main way to qualify. The scheme was to build the economy by addressing areas of need and potential through investment. And because it is fundamentally about investment, many explained to me, it is far from a mere passport trade. The typical response was offered by an accountant: "We don't sell citizenship. It's not for sale; it's based on investment. Our goal is not to stop with the passport, but to build on it, so that people continue to invest and do other business in Cyprus ... Once they get the passport and start feeling connected to the country, then you start promoting other structures or businesses that they can do through Cyprus." Another service provider explained, "If you look at the structure, we're far away from selling citizenship. It's an actual solid investment that makes sense ... We're not selling citizenship or giving it away. We are rewarding individuals who have provided benefits to Cyprus."

The Program on the Ground

How did this all work? Initially, the application process took around three months, sometimes less. First the file went to the Ministry of Interior, where a civil servant evaluated the application, sometimes requesting clarification if anything was amiss, and inquired with the police for background checks. Next the Ministry of Finance assessed the investment, and the Central Bank carried out due diligence on the source of funds. Finally, the Minister of Interior took the files that passed vetting to the Council of Ministers for approval. A passport could be applied for immediately following naturalization, and it usually arrived within a week. Even if there was a required residence, there was no residence requirement—nor even the need to visit the island at all, at least in the early years. The oath of allegiance could be taken at an embassy overseas.

Though the overall process was straightforward, assembling the proper documentation was not. As a result, lawyers rather than individuals submitted virtually all applications. Any clarifications to the file had to be accompanied by a lawyer's letter. Lawyers also carried out the first round of due diligence on the investor and the investment, not an easy task. Because there was no list of approved investment options and most real estate developers were bankrupt, the lawyer was left negotiating between the investor, the real estate developer, and the bank, which stood in the middle. Service providers would complain about the paperwork required to get the title and tax clearance—work that could be eliminated if the government would simply issue a list of approved investments. Plus, Nicosia required yearly updates. If a client bought five plots of land to construct five houses, they would have to show evidence of annual progress on each building. "You can't do this as a fly-by-night operation," a lawyer explained. "Each file is about two box files for us." She pulled out some applications to illustrate, each over six inches thick. "There are so many things you have to do from the beginning to approval" in the paperwork jungle—contracts of sale, agreements, bank accounts, source of funds checks, on top of the application itself. "There's a lot of legal work, and financial work as well."

On top of it, Cyprus's economic travails left some skittish about losing money, and when Malta opened its program, the smaller neighbor was seen as a safer option. "With Cyprus, they're afraid they won't get their money back," a London-based service provider told me. Yet Cyprus was seen as "easier" than Malta when it came to getting in. Malta had an overall cap, which set a time limit on the program and led to a rejection rate as high as 30 percent in some years. Cyprus's cap, introduced in 2018, was annual rather than total. Plus it was generous, allowing 700 families per year to get through. Of those, less than 3 percent were rejected or withdrawn during the application process, a huge contrast to Malta.[53]

Compared to other EU countries, Cyprus has been relatively generous with granting citizenship. On a per capita basis, it comes in third in the EU, behind Luxembourg and Sweden. Between 2009 and 2018, it naturalized 21,400 individuals.[54] Of these, an estimated 4,550 were through the CBI program, or about one in five.[55] Still there are complaints, and for those not going through the CBI route, naturalization can be a hassle. Several people I encountered said the government drags its feet and finds excuses for not processing files when it comes to regular folks. Rebecca, for example, a British woman running a B&B, had married a Cypriot and moved to the island twelve years before. She recalled to me the endless run-arounds from different bureaucratic offices in the struggle to naturalize. After she gathered the required documents and took them to the Ministry of Interior, they told her told to turn over the copies and keep the originals until her interview. But the interview never came. When she followed up, she was told that her application hadn't been considered because she hadn't given over the originals. Back to square one. The route was smoother for the investors.

Cyprus, too, has an unusually public element of vetting: all prospective citizens, whether investors or not, need to publish a notice in a daily newspaper on two consecutive days stating their intent to naturalize. The major dailies even have a dedicated section for these formulaic declarations: "It is brought to the attention of all interested that [name] who resides at [address] has submitted to the Minister of the Interior a M127 application [if for CBI] for naturalization as a Cypriot citizen. If anyone knows any reason for which the person should not be granted the requested citizenship, they are requested to send to the Minister of Interior in Nicosia a written and signed report of the facts." The practice has been around for decades and is intended to serve as a check on new adults entering the national family. (However, just as at weddings, peace is always held and objections unknown.) The publication requirement is serious and copies of the original newspapers must be submitted with each citizenship application. Whenever I visited law offices, there were newspapers lying about, but none could be taken home: they had to be saved for the files.

The government wanted to hang on to its new members. More than a single injection of funds, Nicosia hoped investors would build on the citizenship connection and move other business to or—in the case of financial services—*through* the island. For all of this, the requirement to buy and keep a residential property was key. "We believe that if a person has a house here, they will visit and retain a bond with the country," a civil servant told me. The foothold, she explained, was intended to facilitate further ties, even trickle-down benefits for the country. The scene was similar to the one found in Malta: a symbiotic, "mid-shoring" relationship with the island's financial services that would see investor citizens moving their financial structures over to it. The result for the investors would be a stake in the future of the country, if a pecuniary one. Yet the connection was crucial for the government. As a civil servant who vetted applications told me, "a relationship to Cyprus is the main thing we look for." In principle, this did not mean cultural or familial ties, but an investment in the island's economic future.

Did this work for the benefit of all? The more cynical might note that the direct economic injection was concentrated in the hands of three groups—lawyers, accountants, and property developers—and that all generously fund political campaigns. A drive along the coast in Limassol runs past the enormous footprints of massive luxury residential towers, many of which are still construction sites. These are surrounded by glamorous advertisements of what is to come: a sleek metropolitan landscape of opulent condos that would stretch high against modest, low-slung buildings of the town. With construction funded mainly through presales, completion depends on continued interest, which if it dried up would leave unsightly skeletons on the beachfront. What would happen if the program were to end?

EU Pressure

When the "sale of EU citizenship" hit newspaper headlines and the European Parliament's docket in 2013 and 2014, it was Malta that stood at the center of attention. Though Cyprus's program was older, it gained mention as an addendum at best. Indeed, the vice-president of the European Commission even turned down a request to investigate the Cypriot program, raised in 2011, on grounds that the naturalization policies lay beyond the EU's remit. The EU also made no noise when Cyprus extended its CBI options to those who lost €3 million or more in the haircut in early 2013. Some people working with the scheme hypothesized that Brussels had stung the country hard enough with the so-called haircut that it held its tongue when it came to the CBI program. "We had a bail-in of billions from depositors. Do you imagine that they [the EU] want to crush an alternative source of money? How else can a country reboot?" one lawyer asked me incredulously. Cyprus wouldn't remain insulated for long. The Maltese domestic political fight, catapulted into a new political arena in Brussels, may have been the catalyst for debate, but the origin hardly mattered once the issue was on the radar of the EU and the media.

After the European Commission concluded discussions with Malta in 2014, it began exchanging letters with Cyprus about its program. Initially, the pace was slow and the pressure light. Brussels had no legal jurisdiction over how Cyprus grants citizenship, but it could make unpleasant noises about it. These increased in volume from the summer of 2017 when a delegation from the parliament's committee dealing with money laundering and tax evasion undertook a mission to Cyprus. In its final report, it raised concerns that the CBI program naturalized a large number of Russians and might serve as a means for money laundering. Other back-channel pressure was being placed on the island, and the government began to discuss reforms in alignment with it. In January 2019, the squeeze tightened as the European Commission issued a report to the parliament that supplied a critical appraisal of the programs and warned member states that it would continue to monitor compliance with EU law.

The Cypriot government, like the Maltese, fell in line by overhauling the program. According to a person involved in government consultations, "a fear of Brussels coming and stopping it [the program]" drove the continuous changes. Others described the EU as incessantly "dropping hints" or offering "constructive criticism" over changes it wanted to see. Following pressure over the lack of a residence requirement—first raised in the European Parliament debates on Malta—Cyprus added a stipulation in 2016 that all investor citizens must hold a residence permit before naturalizing.[56] It also required investors to supply evidence annually that they were retaining their investment and property. The biggest revisions came in 2018, however, as the reprove from Brussels grew louder. In response, Cyprus set out plans for a Committee of Supervision and Control, something akin to the CIUs in the Caribbean or Identity Malta next door to manage the program separately from other naturalization streams. It began licensing service providers, which had to adhere to a newly established Code of Practice and carry out separate background checks on applicants before submitting files to the government. The government, too, made moves to control marketing. Any advertisement needed approval from the Committee of Supervision and Control, and any suggestion that passports were on offer was banned. By summer, the country added an annual cap of 700 applications, extended the processing time from three months to six, and began running additional due diligence checks through international databases. The program's rebirth brought a new name too: the Cypriot Investment Scheme.

The one thing that Cyprus didn't do, as it bent to Brussels, was phase out the program as requested. At the same time, none of the other seventeen member states with CBI or RBI schemes in the EU's crosshairs was doing so either.[57] Instead Cyprus reformed. However, the parliament and commission wouldn't let up. By 2019, they were pressing harder on due diligence procedures and raising concerns about security, money laundering, corruption, and tax evasion.[58] When the vice-president of the European Commission visited Cyprus in February of that year, she reiterated these apprehensions instead of praising the restructuring. Bending again, the Cypriot government reformed vetting: would-be naturalizers would need to secure a "Schengen visa"—a precious permit that enables its holders to visit most of the EU visa-free—before they applied for investor citizenship. No longer would Cyprus be a back door to the EU. It also created more categories of people ineligible for the program, including those under sanctions by third countries, those who had held public office in the past five years, and those with criminal cases against them.

Crucially, it also began a retrospective audit of all files submitted in previous years to ensure that they complied with the new standards. Though the legal grounds for doing so were questionable, the auditors found nine cases of applications that raised red flags. These had secured citizenship for twenty-six individuals. The number was miniscule in comparison to the more than 5,000 citizenships granted by that time, but it included some eyebrow-raising applicants. Among them were members of Cambodia's authoritarian ruling class, but the most glaring was Jho Low. He became a Cypriot citizen in 2015, adding a new passport alongside the one from Saint Kitts that he gained in 2011. In 2018, the United States indicted Low as the mastermind behind the 1MDB scheme that sought to divert over $4 billion from Malaysia's state investment fund. At the time of his approval, the news stories of 1MDB were beginning to break and should have raised red flags, but Low's record in Cyprus was unimpeachable. His passport application even included a letter supporting expedited service from the archbishop of the country's orthodox church, written as His Beatitude accepted a €300,000 donation to the archdiocese from the financier—a gift he later returned.[59]

Despite EU pressure, numbers continued to grow. In 2014, Cyprus approved around 200 applications, rising to nearly 340 the following year, and then almost 450 in 2015. Russia remained a key driver of demand, and geopolitical tensions did nothing to abate it. When the United States imposed sanctions in 2017, many Russian businesspeople found themselves facing an in-or-out choice since doing business across borders became more challenging. Those whose main business interests were within Russia remained in the country and cut ties externally, while those who were more invested outside concentrated their resources there—which would have made an additional citizenship more appealing. In addition to the Russian applications, interest in citizenship by investment was picking up globally as knowledge of and familiarity with the programs spread. Cyprus began to see more Chinese applicants coming through, alongside longer-standing yet still-growing demand from the Middle East. The program looked to be here to stay.

Al Jazeera

And then it didn't. The CBI program was just one route that the wealthy took to citizenship. The Council of Ministers still maintained the discretion to naturalize individuals and could decide to do so at any of its Wednesday meetings. At these, any minister could present a special file directly to the council, circumventing the system of formal vetting. How special did such a file have to be? About €20 or €30 million special. This route Al Jazeera dramatically exposed in summer 2020.

In August, the news agency released "The Cyprus Papers," a tranche of 1,400 leaked documents that included the names of over 2,500 people who had naturalized through the CBI program. Initially, local institutions closed ranks. The government condemned the leak while the *Cyprus Mail* newspaper observed that the Qatari broadcaster is owned by a close political ally of Turkey. It suggested that it was far from happenstance that the leak came just as a dispute was heating up between Nicosia and Ankara over oil fields in the Mediterranean. Al Jazeera declared that ninety-seven out of 2,500 naturalized individuals were high risk. However, local investigations found the claim overstated: fifty-four were merely "politically exposed persons," otherwise known as PEPs, or individuals in high-ranking government offices who might not have a court case brought against them should they commit a crime. In banking, such people require "enhanced due diligence," or extra-strong background checks. The remaining forty-three people—1.7 percent of the naturalizers—fell afoul of the rules. This could mean that they held an executive position at a company under the 2014 US sanctions against Russians and Ukrainians, or that they were convicted of a crime after acquiring citizenship, something that authorities may not have foreseen. According to a local reporter, the real mistakes could be counted on a single hand.[60] Of course, "Cyprus Sold Passports to Criminals and Fugitives" is more eye-catching than "Cyprus Naturalized Investors, 96% of Whom Passed Due Diligence Checks," but still several cases were very concerning.[61]

If anything, the list of naturalizers that Al Jazeera exposed reads like an indictment of global capitalism. There was the Ukrainian tycoon Mykola Zlochevsky, owner of the Burisma energy company that named Hunter Biden to its board, arousing controversy in the US presidential election. And Mir Rahman Rahmani, a general-turned-businessman who made his fortune by handling contracts between the Afghan government and US military before becoming speaker of Afghanistan's Lower House. On the list too was the richest woman in China (and sixth wealthiest in the world), Yang Huiyan, the daughter of a real estate scion who also holds a high-ranking advisory position within government. And it included Pham Phu Quoc, a businessman serving in Vietnam's national assembly, who is the CEO of a major state-owned finance and investment company, and who founded the country's first industrial zone. Great wealth may be acquired in a legal and political context in which people amass fortunes by "playing in the gray"—the ambiguous space between legality and illegality typically navigated via government connections—a hallmark, often with brutal consequences, of capitalist regimes everywhere.[62]

If August and September 2020 saw the Cypriot media stand together in defense of the country, few offered justifications in October when Al Jazeera released a damning undercover film. In an impressive piece of reportage, two journalists captured the president of the legislature (who ironically had introduced a code of ethics for the governing body just a few months before) and a real estate mogul-turned-parliamentarian for the communist party offering a smoothed path to citizenship to a bogus Chinese businessman with a criminal record. Service providers told undercover reporters with hidden cameras that the wealthy communist MP was the go-to person for "solutions" whenever there are "headaches." The businessman parliamentarian could solve problems for the price.[63] He was close to the managing director of the Ministry of Interior, as well as the president of the legislature, who previously sat on his firm's board of directors. "When you know the angels, you don't need God," a lawyer with flexible ethics explained to the hidden camera. The workaround he organized involved more than a simple payoff for passports. Banks would be carrying out due diligence, and a convincing story would be needed for them to get the money into the country. But once it was in, everything would be smooth sailing; the team would help the bogus investor "to dance to the rhythms of the music of regulation."

The report exposed the operation of what insiders called a "two-track" route. Alongside the formal program, corrupt politicians would facilitate naturalization on a case-by-case basis for a price, circumventing the official procedures and bureaucratic vetting. As a lawyer explained to the undercover reporters, "You can still get a passport for €2 million and nobody will say no. But a different and preferential treatment is given to [some] people. . . . Those over the limit [that is, investing more in the country] are treated differently." The fictitious Chinese businessman was offered the opportunity to cruise through the VIP lane, leaving his criminal conviction behind, for a €20 million investment in a massive real estate project under development by the MP.

Though the officials involved denied any wrongdoing, the exposé was hard to refute. Within a few weeks, the two politicians caught on video had resigned, and the government terminated the CBI program. It also appointed a committee headed by a former Supreme Court judge to probe all the naturalization cases while the police investigated possible criminal activity. Yet the scandal—and the likelihood of exposure—did little to quell interest in the scheme. Instead, it skyrocketed. After the government announced it would shut things down, over four hundred new applications arrived, nearly a dozen a day, as aspirants rushed to submit their files before the door closed.[64]

What had once been a program with relatively wide buy-in among the populace became a contentious debacle that brought people to the streets in protest of political corruption. Yet the government sailed through it. Parliamentary elections in 2021 saw the ruling party returned to power, and the president—a former lawyer whose law firm processed many applications—remained in seat. Service providers expected that once the smoke cleared, the program, which was merely on ice, would be revived. However, EU pressure continued, and it was plain that the government couldn't simply call its own shots when it came to its naturalization processes. Bigger players could not be ignored.

Enter(ing) the European Union

The traditional countries of citizenship by investment—those in the Caribbean and the Mediterranean introduced in the past two chapters—know that they are not where an investor wants to be. The key benefits of investor citizenship are found outside rather than inside the granting country. For Cyprus and Malta, the reward is big and reflected in the hefty price tag. Citizenship brings not merely membership in the islands, but citizenship rights across the EU. The upshot is that external powers gain considerable leverage over what is, at heart, a sovereign prerogative. Yet their influence doesn't always work as intended.

When the opposition party in Malta catapulted its domestic conflicts over citizenship into the EU arena, it seemed that it had made a master move against the program. The controversy around the scheme, bubbling at the outset, rose to a rapid boil as the European Parliament and European Commission took up the cause of shutting it down. The murder in 2017 of Daphne Caruana Galizia, an investigative reporter who focused on corruption in Malta, only added fuel to the fire. The EU didn't have legal jurisdiction over the CBI programs, but it could pressure countries, and the cause was an appealing one. As neoliberal reforms expanded the market into new domains and turned functions once carried out by the state over to the private sector, the sale of citizenship was an easy target.

Yet EU pressure has had unintended consequences too. In Malta, the key concern initially was that the investors did not have a "genuine link" to the country. In response, the island instituted a perfectly legal residence requirement that had little to do with investors' physical presence in the country. Wealthy individuals needed merely to make some overtures that could be had for a few extra donations and some trickle-down spending. The government transformed the residence requirement and the EU's "approval" into a selling point for the program's seriousness and resilience. The changes even worked in tandem with the country's expanding financial sector and new regulations impacting the offshore world. When the European Parliament raised concerns that the programs could be used for tax avoidance, the residence requirement helped add "substance" to a person's business links running through the island's mid-shore financial structures. Navigating the rocky waters in Malta, citizenship by investment came out on the other side.

In Cyprus, EU pressure transformed what began as a government-developed naturalization policy into a scheme that increasingly resembled the cookie-cutter CBI "products" of its neighbors. Left to its own devices, Cyprus had evolved a CBI program that worked like other naturalization channels in design and operation. Yet by 2018, things had changed. Applicants had to undergo stricter due diligence checks than those imposed on other migrant streams. Lawyers assisting clients and submitting applications had to be specially licensed and uphold an additional code of ethics beyond the bar. No longer were bureaucrats within the Ministry of Interior in charge of managing the application procedure; a special monitoring unit, outside the standard migration bureaucracy, oversaw the program. Where the government once viewed advertising as the territory of the private sector and outside its concerns, it now asserted control. Despite Brussels's complaints about the involvement of private firms in the program, its pressure brought Cyprus's offering into closer alignment with the schemes that the private sector helped design and implement in Malta and the Caribbean. All the virtuous declarations against neoliberalization, against private-sector involvement in state activities, and against selling what some saw as a sacred status came to little. Rather, it was undercover reporters and the public square of the internet that brought it down. But that didn't slow the expansion of citizenship by investment.

Chapter 4

Beyond the Core Market

N OW THAT THE cow is out of the barn," a due diligence expert in New York told me in 2016, "any country can figure out how to do this on its own." His observation was prescient. A rash of new programs have appeared on the scene since 2018, but in none of them did the government turn over a complete monopoly role to a single service provider as was common earlier. Once the citizenship industry created a product and facilitated the growth of a global market around it, governments could get into the game on their own.

The resulting scene is different to what came before. Service providers may still knock on doors to proffer their wares and try to secure a prized concessionaire badge, but states are now more active too. Furthermore, the countries rolling out programs are larger, lending them heft against private interests. Some states have passed laws enabling citizenship by investment but have failed to see much uptake. Others have started down the path only to reverse the decision. A few have even developed programs, often small, aimed at an internal market. Expanding our view beyond the Caribbean and EU programs that have dominated public debate, we see a far more variegated field. Examining the miniscule, murky, or failed programs clarifies how the market is transforming and what is needed for schemes to flourish.

Wealthy Refugees: Egypt and Jordan

One new growth area is the Middle East, where countries like Jordan and Egypt have capitalized on regional instability to craft a new style of program: one aimed at wealthy, displaced foreigners already resident in the country. In this region "bad passport" and "political turmoil" are relative terms, and both Jordan and Egypt have ready-made clienteles among the Iraqis, Syrians, Palestinians, Yemenis, and Lebanese living there, often for many years, if not decades or their entire lives. Even if naturalization procedures exist on the books, the host governments are tight-fisted in extending full membership. Jordan, for example, requires naturalizers to be Arab and to have lived in the country at least fifteen years. Facing such walls, investors now have other options through CBI programs. The countries convert well-off foreigners and their business projects into Egyptian or Jordanian ones, nationalizing not just foreign wealth but the foreign wealthy—Nasser meets high capitalism.

In the case of Jordan, it wasn't foreign service providers knocking on the door who pushed the innovation but the country's own investment commission. Within a week of approving citizenship by investment in 2018, the country received sixteen applications, and over two hundred more requests by the end of the year.[1] However, processing was slow. A year after the program launched, the government was still fumbling its way forward: only twenty-one people had naturalized, and service providers complained that the steps were not clear. Jordan tried to boost numbers by cutting the investment amounts, bringing the minimum price down from $1.5 million to $1 million. Still the rate was high for what it brought: the program cost about as much as Malta or Cyprus, but without the bonus of EU citizenship. Yet this mattered little, for Jordan was trying not to compete for a global clientele but to embrace wealthy resident foreigners. By the end of 2020, the scheme had finally gotten off the ground. Just over two hundred investors received citizenship.

Egypt rolled out a legal provision in the same year as Jordan for similar reasons but at a significantly lower price. Foreigners who deposited nearly $400,000 with the government received a residence permit and after five years could become citizens if they turned the sum over to the state treasury.[2] In 2019, the government reformed the provision into a clear CBI scheme by setting out five investment options that directly led to citizenship. Most of these were variations on what was already in place—gifting money to the government—but now this could range from a $250,000 contribution to the state budget to a $1 million deposit in the central bank, interest-free, for three years. As in Jordan, the provocation and targets were internal—the program was about nationalizing foreign wealth (and its wealthy holders). The new move came at a strategic juncture too. Nearly one-third of Syrian businesspeople had evacuated to Egypt, bringing with them investments worth an estimated $800 million.[3] For them, citizenship by investment could supply a secure foothold in an insecure political situation. Yet those who work with the program state that uptake has been minimal and far below the tiny Jordanian rates. It's mostly longtime resident Palestinians who go for the option. As one service provider described, "They just put their money in an Egyptian bank and get the passport—but at least it's better than Palestinian papers." Both channels have work to do before becoming a humming naturalization stream, but for the governments, that doesn't appear to be the point: their orientation is internal.

Foreign Inward Investment: North Macedonia, Cambodia, Russia

Other countries use programs to support foreign inward investment rather than to nationalize foreign assets and their human owners. North Macedonia, for example, has gone this route, developing a program on its own that sits at some remove from the global market. Its citizenship law allows for naturalization based on "special interests for the country"—a clause that enables athletes and stars to become Macedonian. In 2012, the cabinet added specific criteria, setting down the types of qualifying investments and a minimum investment amount. No longer was citizenship through this route an individualized grant; it was now a more anonymous product. Anyone investing €400,000 into a new company and employing ten or more people would qualify. The government, though, was serious about using the program to attract foreign investment to build the economy. There was no talk of a real estate or donation option, and key sectors like restaurants were also off limits to protect local industries. More importantly, it required the applicant to demonstrate that the business was in place and ten people employed for at least one year before the government would extend the membership offer. The result, as a lawyer in the country described to me, "is a way of giving—let's say 'gifting'—citizenship." In 2019, the government added an option of placing €200,000 in an investment fund to qualify, broadening the focus away from the real economy. It also began licensing agents to submit applications, shifting gears to offer a more mass-market product. Yet without active promotion—the government has been reluctant—it attracts just a few dozen applications each year, even with visa-free access to the EU's Schengen Area on offer. International service providers have not swarmed around the channel, which is less cookie cutter than many. Instead, they treat it as a "boutique" option for those looking for a small program without a lot of exposure. Minus the involvement of these key market makers, the program remains on the margins of the global scene.

Cambodia has also been working the internal angle of its CBI provision. It took the country forty years from independence to roll out its first citizenship law, but when it did so in 1996, it included a proviso for naturalizing those who invest in the country or donate a minimum sum to the government. The clause seemed like a good thing at the time, given the bubbling demand in Hong Kong for exit options. But as a place with an unreliable government and few privileges on offer, Phnom Penh saw limited uptake. This began to change in the 2010s when the country turned to capitalism and began to open its economy. Although Cambodian membership doesn't bring many rights abroad, it does facilitate land ownership and access to government contracts. This proved a draw for Chinese and Korean businesspeople moving into the latest frontier market. By this time, the minimum investment amount hovered around $300,000 and government donations around $250,000—a threshold easily met by foreign developers with much larger projects in the country and a desire for stronger legal protections.[4] Hoping a golden goose would grow fatter, the government raised the minimum to nearly $1 million in 2018.

Yet demand was shifting by this time as well: it was no longer Chinese and Koreans but the Vietnamese next door who were driving the program. Their main interest, however, was not to be Cambodian in Cambodia but to become Cambodian in Vietnam. Why? In a country with a weak rule of law, sometimes being foreign can be a boon. Foreigners can avail themselves of legal protections and economic preferences meant to attract inward investment. Most importantly, they can turn to international arbitration rather than national courts should anything go wrong. For Hanoi, this was an imposition on its power. In a move rare for governments with citizens seeking CBI options, it tried to stem the tide in 2020 by banning the purchase of foreign real estate in order to acquire citizenship. The Cambodian government has thrown spanners in the wheels, sometimes accepting applications and at other times inexplicably not doing so for months, making the program notoriously difficult to market. Those familiar with the offering confirm that contacts and connections still matter, and that naturalization often rides on personalized ties acquired via the two law firms that handle ministerial negotiations.

Russia, too, has offered citizenship by investment since 2019 in a three-year process aimed at a business community. Interested investors must hold at least 100 million rubles worth of shares in a company, amounting to at least 10 percent of its value, or pay 6 million rubles in taxes and insurance on the company for three years. No physical presence is needed, but a certificate of knowledge of the Russian language is required to naturalize. On the whole, these cases are akin to business investor schemes. Some result in a few naturalizations, but in my research I rarely came across any. With the exception of Cambodia, none has become a magnet for investors nor is marketed as a program.

Not Quite There Yet: Mauritius, Samoa, Seychelles, Romania, Pakistan, Bulgaria

Other countries have legal provisions that enable investors to naturalize but have not yet fully commodified citizenship and entered the market. Mauritius is a case in point. It has a thriving financial services industry and offshore sector, as well as legal provision for citizenship by investment, but citizenship is not yet among the "products" in high demand. The country's Citizenship Act was amended in 1999 to allow those who invest at least $500,000 or "some other sum as may be prescribed" into the country to naturalize, but only after they have been in continuous residence for at least two years.[5] The extended residence requirement—even if physical presence is not specified—makes for what many interested buyers would find an unreasonable delay. As such, those looking for an easy investment-based Plan B or other "citizenship solution" would need to negotiate an individual exception with the government. In 2018, it looked as though the country might develop the offering when the prime minister slipped a line into his budget address about a planned CBI program. Citizenship was to be had for a contribution of $1 million, and a mere passport—without the membership—would cost $500,000. Family members could be added for $100,000 per person, and passport fees were an eye-watering $50,000. It was supposed to be a moneymaker. The uproar was immediate, however, both within the parliament and outside it. A local lawyer explained to me that strong community bonds drove the pushback: "We're a family-type of place—we would become strangers in our own country." With so much public outcry, the government had to listen, and a lingering silence followed. Despite the initial hype, five years later the government had still done nothing. Now the proposal is a forgotten blip.

Samoa also has an option but has done little to get it off the ground. In 2016, the government set up a legal basis by approving the Citizenship Investment Act. It then sat on it for more than a year before setting out an implementation plan and guidelines. And it continues to sit. A committee within the Ministry of Commerce is supposed to assess applications submitted by licensed service providers, but so far it has had little to do, with few lured in by the offering. Investors must put down at least $1.5 million on top of another $80,000 in government fees, sending the sticker price above even Malta's, with much less given in return.[6] Additionally, the naturalization process is slow. After making the investment, the applicant receives permanent residence, which morphs into citizenship three years later if the investor has spent at least fifteen days in the country. Between 2016 and 2018, Samoa received just one application, and even it was withdrawn before the investment was made and citizenship offered. The only money the program has brought in so far has been $35,000 to the government in registration fees from service providers.[7]

Some countries attempt to capture the wealthy with lengthy residence regulations that stunt growth. Since 2009, Romania has allowed investors to become citizens, but at a steep price in time and money. It requires eight years of permanent residency after putting up an investment of €1 million—not a competitive offering. Seychelles supplies something similar for $1 million but demands one to eleven years of continuous residence and doesn't bring EU citizenship with it. Others make the process easy but offer little in return. Since independence, Pakistan has allowed citizens of Commonwealth countries to naturalize in exchange for a specified sum. The hurdles are easy: those who transfer about $25,000 to the state bank will be granted citizenship upon arrival in the country. However, few find the membership desirable, and the government does nothing to promote this long-forgotten provision.

Some schemes skirt around a formal CBI option without fully fitting the bill. Bulgaria, for example, began a two-step solution in 2009: a golden visa program that can lead to citizenship. All that was required to gain residence was a €511,000 investment into company shares, government bonds, or real estate. Those looking to naturalize needed only to double the investment after holding residence status for at least one year. In total, the process took about three years to complete and was less certain than a clear-cut citizenship by investment offering. The circuitous route dented interest too. "It's not as straightforward," a service provider in Russia complained to me. Another in Hong Kong lamented the lack of clarity around the two steps. Yet it did have one draw: financing. Applicants needed to pay just half the money, which became effectively a fee to the service provider, who put up the invested funds and retained the asset. Even with this incentive, the vast majority of those who joined the golden visa (RBI) program—around 50 to 150 main applicants per year—did not naturalize but remained simply permanent residents, a more desirable option for those whose home countries do not allow dual citizenship. Though tiny, the program still fell under the European Parliament's relentless pressure, and in 2023 Bulgaria ended the scheme.

On the Border: Comoros and Vanuatu

There are also fuzzier offerings that skirt the boundary between a looser discretionary economic citizenship channel and a formalized CBI scheme. The most notorious is the case of the Comoros, which set up a legal provision in 2008 for granting citizenship in exchange for a cash transfer of $45,000. The program, engineered by a Syrian-turned-Frenchman born in Kuwait and based out of Dubai, was built around the provision of citizenship to stateless groups in Kuwait and the United Arab Emirates. Both countries offer substantial social welfare provisions to their citizens and thus are reluctant to extend membership to others. This includes long-standing populations within their borders who might be considered nationals elsewhere, but who never accumulated the paperwork to establish citizenship. By some estimates, Kuwait is home to at least 100,000 of such *Bidoon* ("without papers") people, and the Emirates to roughly the same.[8] For these rentier states, the Comoros offered a solution to demands from Bidoons for citizenship. The governments would supply them with papers—just not Emirati or Kuwaiti ones.

A similar offering had been set up by Eritrea in 2001 when its embassy in Kuwait began dispensing passports to Bidoon individuals for $13,000, which later dropped to $7,000. But these were just documents, and when Eritrea announced in 2014 that it would not be renewing the passports, the Bidoons were left with nothing. The deal with the Comoros was slightly different, for in this case there was a clearer legal basis: the Comorian parliament had passed the Economic Citizenship Act, enabling the investor naturalization route. Some willing investor citizens used the route, but they were not the only ones purchasing citizenship; the UAE government was doing so too. In an astounding deal, citizenship was sold in bulk between governments.[9] Comorian economic citizenship also did not come with the right to enter the Comoros—a unique legal provision that contravened international law. But for the small islands, this made sense since the citizenship was supposed to be operational not there but in the Middle East.

Working with the Comoros, Abu Dhabi reportedly paid $200 million for 50,000 passports to distribute to its Bidoon population.[10] Some may have been happy to get travel documents, but not all were. To bring them on board, the UAE government made it hard to refuse the offer. Simple bureaucratic procedures, like obtaining a driver's license, renewing health insurance, or marrying or registering a child's birth, suddenly became impossible for Bidoons to carry out without collecting Comorian papers first. The procedure, unsurprisingly, was informal and quick. Initially, the application was only half a page, and citizenship arrived in a matter of weeks. No significant background checks were required. One person I met told of her grandparents, who had arrived in the country as stateless refugees. Because they had no documents, they eventually received passports from the United Arab Emirates, but without naturalizing as Emirati citizens. When they attempted to renew those passports in 2012, they were told to go to the Comoros embassy to collect new documents. And that was that. Between 2009 and 2016, 52,000 passports were distributed through the Comoros's program, with an estimated 40,000 going to Bidoons in the United Arab Emirates.[11]

However, the Bidoons-cum-Comorians aren't completely foreign in the eyes of Abu Dhabi and are sometimes treated as nationals.[12] The United Arab Emirates is well known for granting citizens generous social provisions—free schooling, free health care, free land, and the like—that are inaccessible to foreigners, who constitute about 90 percent of the population. Surprisingly, individuals with Comorian citizenship are handled as though they are Emirati in some domains. People with either Emirati *or* Comorian passports are allowed to access state-run schools for free and—notably—even government jobs, which remain out of reach to foreigners like Filipinos, Indians, or the British. In schools, children with Comorian passports are treated as native Arabic speakers. Yet they are not full citizens in other domains. The government stance is to treat them as both in and out—like domestic servants who are also part of the household.

If Bidoons were served most often by the program, they were not the only takers. The fast-and-easy process and relatively low cost made it popular among Americans looking to bank outside the view of US authorities or travel around Africa on a friendlier passport than one with Uncle Sam's eagle. More significant were the long-standing foreign residents in the Emirates from places like Iran and Lebanon. Though many lived in the country for decades, sometimes generations, they faced challenges in naturalizing, which was never a well-defined process. If citizenship was gained at all, it was usually through connections. The Bidoons were getting some citizenship benefits based on Comorian papers, so other long-term foreign residents thought they might attempt it as well. Since so many bureaucratic processes remain ill-defined under the authoritarian regime, why not give the Comoros a try?

Things were not so clear-cut in the Comoros either. The deal was supposed to bring in hundreds of millions of dollars, but the islands saw little benefit and people wondered where the money was. In 2017, a new government established a parliamentary commission to figure out what was going on. It found that an estimated six thousand passports were sold by "mafia" networks and that most of the citizenships were issued without the Ministry of the Interior's awareness. Furthermore, the payments didn't go directly to the Comorian government but to a holding company in Dubai, and as much as $100 million of revenue from the citizenship sales never arrived in the state coffers. The lack of documentation around the program made it impossible to trace how such an enormous amount—nearly 20 percent of GDP—had gone missing.[13] On top of it, the Comoros started dragging its feet when the passports began to expire. It didn't want to renew them, which threw a wrench in the lives of those with the documents. Some with connections could get fresh passports, but for a hefty renewal fee of $10,000. Others, however, have been left in the lurch, stranded between expired Emirati documents and Comorian ones.

Though I met some service providers who worked with the program, many were wary of it. They didn't want to offer clients a service that was unreliable and could pose a reputational risk. Typical was a Hong Kong–based lawyer I spoke with who examined the offering and said that his firm "respectfully declined" when invited to explore the option: it did not follow the law. It was no longer the 1990s when such possibilities were a dime a dozen in Kowloon. Now, for many, the offering was simply too murky.

A similar murkiness marks the options in Vanuatu. Sometimes just which actors *are* the state is unclear when it comes to the manifold CBI options on the Pacific archipelago. The most recent wave of programs started in 2013 when a foreign jack-of-all-trades joined with a local lawyer and set up the Capital Investment Immigration Plan (CIIP, later "Program"), with little government involvement. Indeed, it's unclear how much the government knew about it at all. During the scheme's heyday from 2014 to 2015, the invested money—anywhere from $300,000 to $400,000 per application—ostensibly went into five-year government bonds.[14] However, the company that controlled it, the official-sounding Vanuatu Registry Service, directed the cash into a Hong Kong bank account. Even though it never saw a penny, the government was on the hook for paying back the funds when the bonds matured. The head of the Financial Services Commission described the program as a "scam" when we met, and local journalists said that even the prime minister was asking where the funds went.[15]

Next came the Vanuatu Economic Rehabilitation Program (VERP) in 2015, a recast version of the CIIP instituted after the archipelago was decimated by Cyclone Pam. Initially it offered only honorary citizenship—travel documents without complete membership—to avoid the ire of the Chinese government, but Vanuatu was willing to extend full citizenship to any interested takers. A simple government donation of $130,000 for a family of four sufficed. The Vanuatu Registry Service again held the contract and partnered with a firm based in Hong Kong to run the bulk of the program, while on the edges, a few other agents gained monopolies over other regions.

Yet there was again much that was not clear about the offering. When I queried the politician who was the minister of internal affairs when the program was rolled out, he didn't know what I was talking about, even though he had been in charge of the relevant ministry. I described citizenship by investment, giving examples from different countries, and he asked for a pen and began taking notes—CBI was new to him. Afterward, I observed to a local service provider that it seemed as though foreigners go to the country and set up what they want with little involvement by lawmakers. She grimaced and shook her head in despair, "That happens too often." One of the more jaded agents offered his own take on the scene. "A foreigner will come in, pitch an idea, and say there is a lot of potential, there is a great future. The government response is always 'Great idea!' But they don't care about seeing the project through. In fact, if you fail, it's better for them, because then the next guy comes, bringing them more things, maybe presents, free dinners, donations . . ." The end effect is akin to that of a cargo cult, he contended: politicians wait for the next tranche of aid and offerings, but do little otherwise.

And they kept on coming. The first scheme to follow was the Vanuatu Contribution Program (VCP) in 2016. Again a business in Hong Kong took over, but this time it was the Pacific Resource Consulting Group (PRG), a rival to the firm that had held the previous contracts. Other agents could submit files, extracting a donation of $180,000 from clients, but the PRG—as a "master agent"—was allowed to charge $130,000 and was given a monopoly on the Chinese market for ten years. In return, mixing country and company, the Hong Kong firm generously established a Vanuatu consulate at no cost to the state purse, just down the hall from its suite of offices looking across Kowloon Bay.

The monopoly system of a master agent controlling the flow of applications had local service providers in Vanuatu up in arms: why should a Hong Kong company control the game? In response to the outcry, the government launched the Vanuatu Development Support Program (VDSP) in 2017. It was similar to the VCP, but without a master agent monopoly: this one was for up grabs among service providers. One of them set up shop in Bangkok as the "Vanuatu Information Center" (VIC) and started working the investment migration conference circuit to tout the program. Given the name and the agent's self-presentation, even many seasoned professionals presumed that he was the face of the government. Yet he wasn't. One old hand approached VIC with great curiosity about the new offering, but after a few interactions with the service provider, he confessed to me that he had been taken in. "He looks like an official agent, but there is really no connection." He described how the firm led him on, pretending to represent the government until he realized he was being hoodwinked. When I visited Vanuatu and asked a few ministers and civil servants about the VIC, I got little in response beyond shrugs and indifference. They hadn't heard of it, but they weren't bothered either: Why should the government be concerned about what foreign firms are doing abroad? At one point, the VIC announced that the country was accepting Bitcoin, attracting global media attention. It was enough to rouse the government to respond that Bitcoin was indeed not accepted. Yet by then the deed was done—and to great marketing success for the VIC in free advertising.

For a long time, Vanuatu seemed marginal to the global market, serving mainly Chinese clientele through Hong Kong. Yet by 2018, numbers were climbing, with the country issuing an estimated 1,800 naturalizations that year alone.[16] Approvals were swift, taking only six weeks, and due diligence checks were minimal. Service providers in a range of global hubs started to supply the option. The growth of interest, however, raised concerns in Brussels, for Vanuatu had visa-free access to the EU. In April 2022, as a part of its crackdown on golden passport programs, the European Commission suspended visa-free access to anyone carrying a Vanuatu passport issued after 2015, when the programs started in force. The announcement left the government scrambling to figure out how to get it back, but to no avail: by November 2022, the EU had suspended visa-free access for all Vanuatu citizens.

The channel, however, remained open and serves as an ongoing experiment in how visa-free access—or its loss—alters demand.

Political Pressure: Moldova, Albania, Armenia

Yet not all programs, planned or actual, take off, and several countries in recent years have shelved efforts or mothballed fledgling attempts in reaction to EU pressure. Moldova, for example, passed a law in 2016 enabling citizenship by investment and began exploring options for structuring a program thereafter. An official from the Ministry of Justice whom I met in 2017 was enthusiastic and confident about the prospects. The pro-business regime is supportive, he confirmed, and with other countries in the region opening schemes, support has been easy to find. "It's just a part of retaining a competitive business environment." He wasn't worried about how the populace might respond and didn't expect the program to attract large numbers anyway. He was more concerned with developing a strong system and rulebook. In practical terms, this meant talking to—or being courted by—investment migration firms which hoped to gain a contract for designing and running the scheme. Yet the government shrugged them all off in the end, deciding that it had the capacity to manage it on its own and that demand was already there. The pro-Russia party in power at the time may have seen it as a way to draw in the Russian business community: by bringing their funds to the country, they could get a passport that would facilitate travel in the EU. By the autumn, new regulations were in place enabling no more than five thousand investors to naturalize if they donated at least €100,000 to a public fund or invested €250,000 for five years into real estate or government bonds.[17] The pattern followed the established norms: provisions for family members; a special commission to decide on the applications; rejections for terrorists, criminals, and those refused visas to countries Moldova shares visa-free access with; and so forth. All that was needed were the applicants. But they weren't forthcoming. The government just couldn't connect. In summer 2018, it started afresh, enlisting a consortium of service providers led by Henley and Partners to bring in the applicants. Within a month, they had a system put together, the cabinet approved the channel, and Moldova opened its first embassy in the United Arab Emirates.

As one might imagine, the design bore the markings of other Henley projects. It included an "implementation unit," similar to a Caribbean-style CIU, and a "four-tier" due diligence system of the sort boasted by Malta.

The program kept the same prices and investments from before but set the turnaround time at ninety days. Moldovan citizenship may not appear to be a prize at first glance, but it includes visa-free access to the Schengen Area, Russia, and Turkey—a useful proposition for businesspeople working in the region. Plus its free-trade agreements with both the EU and Russia provide business opportunities in these sizeable markets. By autumn 2018, the government proudly announced at one of Henley's Global Citizenship conferences that the program was open for business. Soon after, it had its first successful applicant: an IT entrepreneur interested in business possibilities in the country. The foreign minister even proclaimed that citizenship by investment would set Moldova on a clearer path to EU membership by strengthening its infrastructure and improving economic development.[18]

Yet the exuberance did not last. Elections in February 2019 resulted in a hung parliament, which evolved into an eleventh-hour, tottering coalition cobbled together between the pro-Russia Socialists and the pro-Europe ACUM alliance. The soon-to-be-former ruling party contested the coalition's constitutionality while its leader, a wealthy oligarch, fled to Moscow on a private jet, trailing behind him charges of massive bank fraud.[19]

The new government issued a moratorium on the program even though it had already attracted eighty applications, thirty-four of which had passed vetting and were awaiting approval. But it went on ice for four months— extended to six months, then to fourteen months, then yet further to sixteen months, and to twenty-four months—leaving service providers in the lurch while it evaluated the program and assessed risks of corruption and money laundering.[20] Possibly, the government was doing some math. The thirty-four applications represented about €4.6 million in investment. Cutting ties with the consortium contracted to run the program would cost another €3.5 million in fines.[21] This, however, paled in comparison to the risk of losing millions in EU financial aid. According to parliamentarians, the EU was leaning on the legislature, demanding the repeal of the CBI law as part of a package of changes it required to release an upcoming €30 million tranche of aid—and the next one as well of €40 million.[22] Plus there were concerns that the country might jeopardize the ninety-day visa-free travel it had recently gained to the Schengen Area.[23] Though the Socialists, the junior partner in the coalition, looked more often east than west, center-right ACUM was eager to comply with the EU's demands, and the math worked in its favor.[24] Processing proceeded slowly. By February 2020, five people had been approved, and a total of eight made it through by March of that year.[25] Then in June 2020, the government finally made a decision that it had telegraphed since 2019: it repealed the law.

A similar process unfolded in Albania. The tiny country had long held open a side door to citizenship for those making substantial economic contributions. Service providers would work with the country's trade commission to secure foreign investment, and in exchange the investors would get citizenship straight from the prime minister. An outlay of $200,000 in a business or a donation to the government of $250,000 were the required amounts, according to a China-based intermediary I met. She had been operating this way for a number of years and had helped several dozen people become citizens.

By 2019, though, things were changing in Albania. Its neighbor, Montenegro, had been in talks with service providers to start a program, and the investment prospects were too alluring to pass up. The government in Tirana began talking with service providers about how to revamp its offering. The citizenship industry was eager to supply a new product—especially for a country in the accession process to full EU membership. Even before the program was in place, agents were advertising the option. A savvy investor could get in on the ground floor for a passport "asset" destined to mature into EU citizenship in a few years—and at only a fraction of the cost of Malta or Cyprus.

By summer 2019, the minister of the interior announced that a program was in the works to great fanfare by the citizenship industry. Shortly thereafter, European Commissioner for Justice Věra Jourová signaled the EU's position on the matter. In an interview, she noted that CBI schemes are monitored by the European Commission as part of the EU accession process and warned ominously that "EU candidate countries should refrain from any measure that could jeopardize the attainment of the EU's objectives when using their prerogatives to award nationality."[26] If the diplomatic language was guarded, Brussels's stance was clear: no program. Albania came to heel. When it passed a new citizenship law in 2020, a clear-cut investment option for naturalization was noticeably absent. However, the government still reserved for itself the possibility of granting citizenship when in the "interest of education, science, art, culture, economy, and sport"—effectively what it had been doing for years already, if in a less formalized way.[27] The grounds for exceptional naturalization (here, if merely "in the interest of . . .") are not remarkable—a number of countries have such provisions. Yet the clause left Albania able to continue granting citizenship on a discretionary basis for economic contributions and, should things change, to create a full-fledged program in the future.

Armenia, too, shut down a nascent program, but there a change in government rather than international pressure precipitated the closure. The situation looked very different at the outset, however. I spoke with one official from the Ministry of Interior in 2017 who reckoned that starting a program would be relatively easy, and that they would be ready to go in only six months. "We are already giving citizenship for free to the diaspora," he told me. "Why not others?" If Armenia doesn't boast visa-free access to the EU, it does have visa-free access to Russia and most post-Soviet states, along with Iran. For business in that part of the world, it could be more convenient than a US passport.

The Ministry of the Interior was looking at a number of programs, the official told me, to select the best fit for the country. The CBI program would be "one more instrument for attracting foreign investment," he explained. An official from the Ministry of Economy and Development laid out it out clearly: the program would be a way to create a "comparative advantage in economic development." Armenia, unlike its neighbors, doesn't have oil or gas to woo investors, he noted, but it does have citizenship, which might lure some foreign money away from its neighbors. Not everyone was on board, and the police and the Ministry of Justice were raising questions. And yet the Ministry of Interior official did not see these objections as insurmountable and thought the program would go through smoothly. Furthermore, the ethnic homogeneity of the country could help it along. "If you have 30 percent foreigners in your country already, there might be some discomfort, but we don't have this." He anticipated uptake to be small—certainly not in the thousands.

The government appointed the firm Arton Capital, a rival to Henley and Partners, to structure the program, which it predicted would generate nearly $150 million over six years—minus operating costs of $20 million.[28] The firm also launched a media campaign to promote the prospective offering and planned to host its next Global Citizen Forum in Yerevan. Yet all of this was cut short. In the spring of 2018, anti-government protests erupted into a "velvet revolution," sweeping into power a new alliance, soldered together by a strong anti-corruption stance.[29] Citizenship by investment was not on the alliance's agenda, and the new government shelved the plans immediately. (However, it had come onto the agenda of the country's new president, Armen Sarkissian, who stepped down from office in 2022 after journalists revealed that he had dual citizenship—not allowed for high public officials—in Saint Kitts.)

The Big Shift: Turkey

If most of these new programs have been small and several of them unstable, Turkey stands apart. Since 2019, it has come to dominate the global market and now accounts for around half of all CBI naturalizations, a stunning feat in just a few years. Its rise, however, was hardly preordained. Indeed, in 2015 when the market was defined by island microstates, few would have expected a country of Turkey's heft not only to get on board but also to take over the game. With a population of over 80 million and a substantial economy and military, it's far closer to the stereotype of a nation-state than the tiny tropical islands. It also didn't rely on specialized service providers to design or implement its program. It just started one on its own, though some sources suggest that business lobbies, particularly among wealthy refugees displaced by turmoil in the Middle East, pushed for the measure.

Ankara rolled out the scheme in 2016 to boost the economy as the housing and construction sectors flagged. The structure was straightforward. Put at least $1 million into property, $2 million into a business, or $3 million into government bonds or a bank, and the investor could naturalize after holding the asset for three years. Alternatively, one could employ a hundred Turkish citizens. The offering was straightforward, but only seventy people applied under this early formulation. Relative to the market, the price was high— comparable to that of Malta and Cyprus—but Turkey didn't have what the two microstates could offer: EU citizenship. It didn't seem to be getting any closer to becoming a member state either as Prime Minister Recep Tayyip Erdoğan increasingly flexed his authoritarian muscle. One service provider I spoke with in these early years said that demand came from those who were already making large investments in the country. As such, citizenship was merely a bonus for the committed rather than a lure for new investors. Plus, as in Egypt and Jordan, most were already living in Turkey. The scheme wasn't doing much to bring in new economic growth.

Two years later, the government dropped the minimum investment amount. A bank deposit, business investment, or government bonds of $500,000 was all that was needed. Most importantly, though, the property investment option was slashed to just $250,000—the cost of a nice house in Istanbul. The change came just as the Turkish lira had lost 40 percent of its value against the dollar and was seeing 20 percent inflation, so for purchasers bringing dollars into the country—the options were priced in dollars, not lira—the investment seemed like a solid money-maker. The program took off like wildfire. Saint Lucia, when it opened its scheme in 2016, received fewer than two dozen applications in its first year. Turkey reportedly received over ten times that number—250 applications—in the first seven months of its relaunched program.[30] Eventually demand grew so great that the government established a separate center for processing the applications to bring the relevant bureaucrats from different ministries under one roof. Where previously files could face long delays, the streamlining shortened the approval process to around three months.

Initially investors from Iraq, Afghanistan, Palestine, and Egypt showed the greatest interest, several service providers told me. Many of them were wealthy people who had moved to or at least set up a base in Turkey in order to escape political turmoil or pressure at home. Among these early adopters were also nearly thirty investors from Saint Kitts—likely "serial investor citizens" who had used citizenship by investment in one country to acquire it in another.[31] After the relaunch, lawyers working with the program said that longtime foreign residents of Dubai drove numbers, alongside new interest from Russia and Pakistan. Turkey was a serious economy right in their backyard, and becoming a citizen there could facilitate business transactions in the UAE, as we will see in Chapter 9. By the 2020s, the Chinese were getting on board as well, attracted by rock-bottom real estate prices that were appreciating by 20 percent per year. As one lawyer in Istanbul put it, people who were buying real estate before "are just getting citizenship on top now."

But why the popularity? The price drop moved Turkey in line with the Caribbean end of the market. Yet in some ways, the Caribbean programs supply a better package. They have visa-free access to the Schengen Area, which Turkey doesn't. More importantly, they don't have military conscription for all male citizens between twenty and forty-one years old, which Turkey does. Yet in practice, these limits and obligations are not as unfavorable as they may seem. Because Turkey is a member of the European Union Association, its citizens can apply for a long-term multientry visa for the Schengen zone with relative speed and ease. Furthermore, there are workarounds to military service. Citizens living abroad are able to gain exceptions, and those within the country serve only fourteen to twenty-one days if they pay the government $7,000. There may be limitations to Turkey's program, but there are also workarounds.

And Turkey offers an extra prize. Like Grenada, the country has a trade agreement with the United States that allows its citizens to apply for an E2 treaty trader visa. As such, investor citizens gain a side door to residence in

America. Capitalize a business at around $200,000, and a US residence visa can be yours. If the annual renewals are onerous—usually the visa is only for twelve to thirty-six months—the tax burden is less so, for unlike green card holders, those on E2 visas don't come under the US tax system for the rest of their lives. Turkey also had a perk no other country offered via the Ankara Agreement. The agreement, signed in 1963 with the European Community, allows for the free circulation of workers between Turkey and the EU. More important, though, has been its British offspring. The agreement became the legal basis of the Turkish Businessperson Visa (TBpV), which enables Turkish citizens to apply for a residence permit in the United Kingdom to conduct entrepreneurial activities. Applicants need only demonstrate the intent to set up a business that could support the investor and their family, as well as sufficient funds to do so. For a wealthy person looking for a foothold in London, access through TBpV via Turkish citizenship is a bargain compared to the more than £2 million price tag for the UK Tier 1 investor visa. The popularity of this perk in the form of third-country access is clear: as the CBI program in Turkey took off, so too did Turkish investors in the UK. Between 2018 and 2019 alone, the number of applications for the TBpV exploded nearly fourfold, from almost eight hundred approvals to nearly three thousand—roughly the same the number lodged in the prior ten years. Beyond these back channels to the United States and United Kingdom, some benefits in the European Union are to be had as well. These may not include derivative residence options or visa-free access, but Turkey has customs relief deals that make it a favorable base for trading with the bloc.

Yet unlike its tiny colleagues, Turkey offers not only benefits outside, but substantial advantages within. Istanbul is a thriving global city that furnishes the luxuries associated with a comfortable elite life. It also serves as a business hub, for both the region and the country, whose economy is ranked around twentieth in size globally. With both livability and serious business options on offer, investors may use Turkey as a second base, which is reflected in the real estate purchase prices. These are often above the minimum investment amount, indicating that investors may be looking not merely to qualify, but to secure a nice place for themselves. As one service provider put it, "you can think of Turkey as a home, as insurance, and as an investment."

In addition, Turkey appears to be more resilient against external pressure than other countries. The United States seems to pose little worry. Unusually for a major program, Turkey doesn't prohibit applications from citizens of countries on US travel-ban or sanctions lists, including Iran and Iraq. In 2022, it didn't fall into line and ban Russians, as did Malta and the Caribbean countries. It also hasn't made any changes in response to the EU. At the same time, Brussels doesn't appear to be turning the screws either. The country doesn't have visa-free access—all Turkish citizens must apply for a Schengen visa—so the leverage the EU has against key microstates doesn't apply. The accession process has been stalled for so long that few see it as ever getting off the ground. Even service providers don't market Turkey as the next new EU member state. Notably Turkey does a lot for the EU, too. For a cool €6 billion from Brussels, it houses over three million refugees who might otherwise seek shelter in Europe. The EU may be reluctant to pressure this neighboring state that has done so much to keep asylum seekers at bay.

By the end of February 2020—just two years after the revamp—Turkey had naturalized over 5,100 investors and their families. An additional 380 were waiting for their documents, and up to 9,000 more applications were in processing. Not only were the application numbers big, the investment ones were as well. The 5,100 new citizens had brought $1.7 billion to the country, and those in the waiting room would deliver over $400 million more. The interior minister estimated that the pending applications together would garner an additional $2.7 billion.[32] By June 2020, the program averaged over 1,300 approvals per month, or about $17 million in daily revenue. With each investor bringing along an average of 2.8 dependents, the total new investor citizenry topped 35,000. The figures are miniscule in comparison to the foreign population of the country: Turkey currently hosts about a thousand refugees for each investor citizen it accepts. Yet as a proportion of the global market, the investor citizenry is huge and likely to grow, now driven higher by Russians and Ukrainians. As Turkey's intake expands, the market's center of gravity will need to shift.

The Global Scene

Most discussions of citizenship by investment have focused on the Caribbean and EU cases, and with good reason: they form the traditional core of the CBI trade. Taking a wider view helps clarify what is distinctive about those in the market and how they operate, and why some programs take off while others never leave the tarmac.

Players in the global market react to rival offerings. As we saw in Chapters 2 and 3, they lower prices, change family dependent rules, and adjust investment options in order to compete. They also get picked up and marketed by service providers, if the private sector isn't deeply involved in creating them in the first place. In contrast, those on the edges simply trot along in their own way. Cambodia serves a regional clientele, North Macedonia rewards its company owners, Egypt nationalizes its foreign wealth(y). Yet none is much concerned about competing in the global market. Some, like Samoa, seem not to bother about attracting investors in the first place. Others, like Jordan, focus on a smaller pool of investors already in the country. Turkey was initially in this group, but more recently has moved from the market's edges to its center. If Turkey's program launched as a relatively unpopular offering that could hardly compete with other options available, it soared once it dropped its minimum investment amount to compare favorably with those in the Caribbean—attracting, too, a large investment migration industry around it.

Failures can be found along the wayside as well. The EU, aided by local political changes, has successfully stymied several attempts to launch programs around its periphery, as Moldova and Armenia can attest. Montenegro held out for a while but eventually folded in January 2023. And there are some, like Vanuatu and the Comoros, that don't entirely square the circle when it comes to formalization. They may raise issues of "sovereign default" when the granting state no longer recognizes the citizenship, or of gross infractions of international law. In practice, the border between discretionary grants and full formalization can remain fuzzy.

When international service providers are not involved in designing programs, CBI offerings typically operate like any other naturalization stream. Places like Jordan and Egypt appoint neither special bureaucratic units to process applications nor private due diligence agencies to vet them. Any kind of person can submit a file, not only a specifically licensed agent. These countries just apply the standard immigration and citizenship assessment process used for any sort of visa or naturalization application, plus some checks by the Ministry of Economy or Finance and the national security agency. Such arrangements may change if the citizenship industry gets involved and turns the option into a product for the global market, as has been seen recently in North Macedonia. Yet as the Turkish example shows, the private sector does not always stand behind the expansion of offerings, even if it remains an important connector that makes a market possible in the first place.

Where's next? With some important exceptions—usually among larger countries—it is service providers who get the ball rolling, or at least plant the idea for new programs. Within the citizenship industry rumors abound about the potential in Azerbaijan, Bahamas, Croatia, Georgia, Greece, Kenya, Maldives, Panama, Romania, Seychelles, and Slovenia, along with a host of islands in the Pacific. In Saint Vincent—long a holdout in the Caribbean—the leading opposition party has made noises about joining the CBI scene should the Socialists ever be ousted. The cabinet of the Solomon Islands has considered launching a program after several years of talks with service providers about design options.[33] The way to implementation can be smoothed if a country has already on hand a provision for granting citizenship for exceptional contributions to it, which can avoid provoking contentious debate when tabling new legislation. Yet even though it is citizenship at stake, states do not have completely free reign when bringing it to market. Instead they jostle against each other and against more powerful players in a complex geopolitics of competition, which we turn to next.

Chapter 5

Geopolitical Maneuvering

THE STAKES ARE clearly high for the small islands that form the traditional core of the market. Yet these microstates are deeply invested in a game over which they have little control. As we have seen, much of investor citizenship's value is determined by powerful third countries or supranational organizations, which can have an overweening influence over the statelets around them. Small states, however, can dodge some thrusts and even push back on occasion, but as they become more invested in the CBI game, they are remade by it as well. How do these countries hustle in the global political economy?

The Big Players: The United States

So far the most formidable player in the field has made only a fleeting appearance. It may not be surprising that the United States is the key power broker, but it does not flaunt its leverage. When it comes to issues of security and mobility, Washington carries much sway among its allies, and other wealthy countries usually follow its guidance, whether that involves altering screening procedures at the border or cooperating over individuals wanted by its secret service. In the CBI sphere, the United States often remains discreet as it keeps an eye on the schemes. The impression that officials give is of parents quietly watching their teenager experiment with smoking: it's better to be aware of what's going on than to outlaw the practice entirely and let it slip from one's control. One former State Department official I spoke to explained that they know the CBI programs provide a revenue stream to poorer countries with few other options. Yet, he added, the United States wants to see transparency in how the programs operate: they want good due diligence checks and no one slipping between the cracks. Another State Department official who monitors the programs explained that initially they kept watch to ensure corruption didn't get out of hand. In recent years, however, they have become more concerned that the schemes may become a conduit for terrorism or other nefarious activities.

Mostly, Washington wants to know who is going through the schemes. Individuals familiar with the origins of the Maltese program aver that the United States met with the government in its early stages and subsequently ensured it was kept in the loop during vetting. Washington's involvement is yet clearer in the Caribbean. In 2017, the US ambassador to the region laid out its position to WINN FM radio: "There are obviously economic benefits to the programs and we have no opinion one way or the other. What we do ask is that people do have due diligence and set up a program that has controls and balances to it to ensure that the people that are getting citizenship through the program are actually the people who you really want to be there." She went on to gesture toward US involvement in vetting, which we saw in Chapter 2: "I think that at the beginning we had a number of questions, and I think that working with the St. Kitts and Nevis government, we have been able to tighten up the controls on the program. I think there are a lot of changes that were made for the good . . . Again, we have worked with various countries and talk to them about what we consider to be acceptable criteria."

The US strategy has been to position itself as the "international partner" of the Caribbean programs rather than shutting them down entirely, as it did in the past. In 2016, the US ambassador to the region made this clear: "The United States does not approve or disapprove individual aspects of the citizenship by investment programs" and added that it was willing to consult with governments on their schemes. It wants to be "confident, beyond a reasonable doubt, that the applicants are bona fide and their identities have been fully validated, and they have no ties to transnational criminal or terrorist organizations, before handing over citizenship."[1] Following—or bowing to— this guidance, several countries run their lists of would-be citizens past Washington before issuing the final approval. An official from one of the islands explained the procedure to me: if a flag comes up, "We consult with our international partners on the necessary course." A tightly run program will always reject a flagged candidate, for too much is at stake. Less tightly run ones may ignore the warning light, perhaps if a generous business deal for a high-ranking politician is involved. Some grumble that the United States does not provide a reason for rejection and does not always get it right when innocent people share names with real crooks or terrorists. However, for rigorous programs, "no" from an international partner means "no." The secondary check serves as an *insurance* policy against bad apples getting through that is also an *assurance* policy to keep the regional hegemon from shutting down the programs. As the prime minister of one of the Caribbean countries told an audience in London, "We want to inspire the confidence of our 'bilateral partners'" when carrying out background checks. The threat is real as well: the United States closed down the early citizenship schemes in Grenada and Belize two decades ago. Few people invested in the current programs want to see this repeated. In the words of one service provider, "The countries are forced to comply with what the US wants because they need the blessing of the US to operate."

Occasionally, however, it fires warning shots when countries play loose, and the Caribbean governments generally fall into line. In 2018, the State Department expressed concern over how Saint Lucia was managing its program, stating in a report that "the CIU does not maintain adequate autonomy from politicians to prevent political interference in its decisions."[2] Within a few months, Saint Lucia revised its system to prevent the prime minister from making fiat approvals if a rejection is appealed.[3]

Why do countries come to heel? If approving final lists provides the United States with a backseat steering mechanism over the programs, it also has a brake pedal. This comes in the form of the greenback. Around 90 percent of all international financial transactions are made in US dollars, which secures for Washington a very long reach abroad. If there is a US "nexus" in any transaction, no matter where in the world it occurs, Washington can claim jurisdiction over it. Sending an email via a server based in the United States can count, but more important is the dollar, which has massive implications for global trade. It is this power that stands behind US economic sanctions against Iran and Russia. If the United States wants to damage a country's economy, it can simply pull the plug on the SWIFT or CHIPS systems that its financial institutions use to make international payments. The US Treasury Department's investigative arm, the Financial Crimes Enforcement Network (FinCEN), enforces this extraterritorial power, tracing the flow of dollars globally to combat money laundering, drug trafficking, terrorism, and financial crimes. The agency's motto is "follow the money"—and so it does, asserting its power wherever dollars move. A critical node in this network is New York. International trade carried out in US dollars must be cleared by a correspondent bank—effectively, a financial institution in New York City that acts as a middleman between the sending and receiving parties. When they carry out extra due diligence checks on the transacting actors or on the money, the exchange freezes until they clear the funds.

Saint Kitts learned about this the hard way. In 2014, the US Treasury reported that illicit actors might be using the CBI scheme to evade sanctions and carry out other financial crimes by masking their identities.[4] Despite the Kittitian government's assurance that it was no longer approving Iranians, such individuals were still obtaining passports, the United States averred. FinCEN then flexed its muscles, recommending that financial institutions globally carry out enhanced due diligence on clients using Kittitian passports to verify their identity. The guidance suddenly transformed a Saint Kitts passport from an easy ID into a hassle and potential liability when banking in any system where US dollars flow. The shift was a wake-up call to the microstate that came just when the field of options was becoming more crowded and it was feeling the heat of competition. Some involved with the program suggested that FinCEN's guidance was an even greater blow than the loss of visa-free access to Canada that came shortly thereafter, which some suspected was actually carried out at the request of the United States. Yet from the perspective of the microstate, the origin of the problem mattered less than the outcome or mechanism for implementation. As one service provider put it, "As long as the US controls the currency, they can tell us what to do."

Within a year, Saint Kitts's prime minister, who had been in power for two decades, was thrown out of office, and the new government undertook a substantial reform of the program. It reached out to professional due diligence firms and Big Four accountancies for audits and advice on how to tighten the system. In response, they increased the staff and training courses for the Citizenship Investment Unit, introduced a new case management procedure, instituted a technical committee to create a more formal and documented process over denials, and integrated the country's "international partners" into the vetting process. By 2017, the IMF carried out a fact-finding mission that praised the program reforms.[5] The powers that be seemed appeased for now.

In 2017, FinCEN issued a wider advisory about the potential for money laundering through real estate transactions. The move was not targeted at specific countries, but it greatly affected CBI programs. If an Egyptian wanted to invest $200,000 in real estate to become a citizen of Dominica, the transferred money would spend weeks on end at the correspondent banks in New York going through additional due diligence checks, leaving the application on hold. Across the region, bureaucrats and service providers described a gummed-up system as they came under ever greater pressure to show that the funds flowing through were clean. The advisory also demonstrated the power of the United States to keep the microstates in check: if it wants to slow the processing of CBI applications, all it has to do is send guidance to New York banks to carry out enhanced due diligence on the transactions. As one service provider told me drily, the only time he has seen some prime ministers sit up and listen is when the correspondent banks pull up the reins.

Facing such delays, some countries and service providers have explored alternatives. Cryptocurrencies are the most obvious pathway to avoid US control over financial flows. Many crypto millionaires, who went in big early on, have a libertarian's suspicion of big states and can gravitate to the off-the-grid citizenship options in microstates. But the United States is quick to pressure governments that begin to move outside its penumbra, and so far only Antigua and Vanuatu allow payments in cryptocurrencies. Yet if Washington saw a reason to do so, it could easily shut things down completely by blocking all dollar-based payments.

The United States has a further weapon in its artillery, though a lighter one. The value of investor citizenship often comes from the benefits secured in powerful third countries, which can lend them some control over its worth. Most significantly, the US could end or revise its E2 treaties with Grenada, Montenegro, and Turkey, which would diminish the desirability of citizenship in these countries as a back door to residence there. It could also follow the EU's example and threaten to revoke visa-free access. However, of all the countries with CBI programs, only Malta has this privilege, and even then a Maltese passport alone does not suffice. All foreigners hoping for admission from abroad must go through an ESTA (Electronic System for Travel Authorization) check, which gives the United States the final say over who can enter. The superpower's own high borders diminish the effectiveness of this threat.

More importantly, the United States can influence who gets through at a general level by transposing its own border control policies onto other countries. When America bans particular nationalities or individuals from entering its territory, or places them on sanctions lists, microstates—particularly those that are reliant on CBI funds—follow suit and prohibit them from applying for citizenship. Malta, with visa-free access to the United States, is the clearest example. After Donald Trump signed the "Muslim travel ban" in 2017, Malta amended its program immediately, prohibiting individuals from the blacklisted countries from applying: it didn't want to put its visa-free access at risk should a suspect person try to use it as a back door to the United States. As of 2022, citizens from Afghanistan, Belarus, Democratic Republic of Congo, Iran, North Korea, Russia, Somalia, South Sudan, Sudan, Syria, Venezuela, and Yemen—a top-twelve list of countries seen as threats to American interests—were ineligible for Malta's CBI scheme.

More striking, however, is that countries that *don't* have visa-free access to the United States also fall into line and change their naturalization policies to square with alterations in Washington's border control regime. Trump's 2017 travel bans had reverberations across the Caribbean and Pacific, with Saint Kitts, Antigua, Dominica, Saint Lucia, and Vanuatu taking several countries off their eligibility lists. The biggest loss came from banning Iranian applicants—a sizeable population and a wealthy one too, including many lifelong expats. As one Caribbean official said about their removal, "I would love to tap into that market, but our international partners are important." Only Grenada, Montenegro, and Turkey continued to welcome applications from Iranians during the height of the ban, shrugging off the pressure.

Most countries also complied with US requests following Russia's invasion of Ukraine in February 2022 and stopped naturalizing Russians and Belarusians. Even if Washington was still granting visas to Russians, it didn't want other countries to enable easier movement. By early March, applications from both countries were no longer welcome in Malta, Dominica, Saint Kitts, Grenada, Saint Lucia, and finally Antigua, regardless of an individual's political allegiances. Even if the microstates hoped to tap into the skyrocketing demand among Russians, almost all fell into line with US interests. Pragmatism carried out the calculation.

As the bans become long-lasting, some countries have issued caveats to their proscriptions. However, they typically don't go off on their own in doing so: the exceptions still operate within the interests and indirect approval of regional hegemons. Saint Kitts, for example, allows those from countries on US banned lists to apply if they are a permanent resident of the US, the UK, or Canada and have lived outside their home country for ten years. Antigua and Vanuatu too maintain similar provisions. When service providers talk lustily about going into banned markets, governments will ask, "What do the Americans say?" It's an enormously powerful mechanism for controlling programs as well, for it turns off the pipeline precisely in areas that are likely to see strong interest. Yet for most CBI countries, the payoff is not worth the risk.

The bans are a powerful mechanism. Yet outside them, US actions over CBI programs have been directed largely at the countries in its Caribbean backyard. It has made few direct moves against those in Europe, the Middle East, or elsewhere. It could, for example, revoke the visa-free access from Maltese citizens. After all, fellow EU citizens from Bulgaria, Croatia, Cyprus, and Romania also don't enjoy the same visa-free entry across the Atlantic. But it has taken no steps, let alone issued threats, in this direction. For the most part, it simply keeps an eye on who gets approved and casts some side glances at the flows of money. Occasionally it pulls a country up by the ears to ensure that everything stays in line with its own interests, as it has done with Saint Kitts. This control it retains by watching from above and occasionally intervening behind the scenes, for turning the screws too tightly might drive it all underground.

The Big Players: The European Union

In marked contrast to the US stance is the approach of the European Parliament and European Commission, which since the mid-2010s has hardened into an incontrovertible "no" to the programs.[6] In 2020, the European Commission called on its member states to "phase out" their CBI schemes "as soon as possible."[7] In 2018, Commissioner for Justice Věra Jourová even threatened to use "all the legal and psychological tools" at the commission's disposal to pressure countries into accepting its recommendations.[8] "We do not want Trojan horses in the EU," she insisted.[9] Thereafter the parliament's Civil Liberties, Justice, and Home Affairs Committee issued a report labeling the programs "objectionable from an ethical and legal point of view," with the head of the committee declaring, "There are no upsides to golden passport schemes. They attract shady business and present a back door to Europe for the wealthy."[10]

Yet such vehement rejections are recent. From 2007 to 2014, Cyprus ran a CBI scheme that naturalized a few hundred individuals with no intervention from Brussels. The only time it entered European Parliamentary debates, then-Commissioner for Justice Viviane Reding declared the point moot: citizenship attribution is not in its domain. Legally, citizenship and naturalization policy remain a "competence"—that is, sovereign right—of member states. This proviso was the result of the near scuttling of the Maastricht Treaty, which established EU citizenship in 1992. Denmark, after a failed referendum, refused to ratify the treaty because its populace was concerned about turning over too much sovereignty to Brussels. To save Maastricht, the EU heads of state acceded to the so-called "Edinburgh Decision." Placating worries that EU citizenship could trump national citizenship, the agreement affirmed that EU citizenship is derivative of citizenship in a member state, and each member state can decide how its own citizenship is apportioned.[11]

In 2014, the European Parliament began to change its position. The history of the EU is a history of the expansion of its control over domains not included in "The Treaties"—those of Paris, Rome, Brussels, Maastricht, Nice, Amsterdam, and Lisbon—that codify its power. Creative judicial ruling stands behind much of this. The European Court of Justice (ECJ) has assured that what the member states didn't agree to when they signed the Treaties can be enacted on them from the outside. Justifying these moves is the concept of *integration,* which can be used to strike down national rules in the reserved domains of member states if they negatively affect the EU's ability to carry out its delegated tasks. Across the 1960s and 1970s, the Court extended EU control over a host of issues internal to states, from domestic labor and unionization to food production and labeling, all by arguing that integration made it necessary.[12] Now ECJ determinations that overrule national law are taken for granted, and it is seen as high rebellion when national courts challenge it, as Germany's Federal Court of Justice does on occasion.[13] In light of the EU's historic expansionary thrust, it is no surprise that part of its machinery would try to claim dominion over citizenship as well—if the opportunity presented itself.

Such an opportunity arrived after the sudden inauguration of Malta's CBI program. Just one year after affirming that citizenship by investment was not a subject that could be debated by the European Parliament, Commissioner Reding declared that countries should provide evidence of a "genuine link" if they are to award citizenship through naturalization. She also questioned whether CBI programs could represent a security threat to the EU or become a channel for money laundering. Her successor, Věra Jourová, continued the stance, maintaining that a genuine link to a country "is something which Europe has to insist on," pronouncing that such a link must be included "as a tough condition."[14]

Throughout the debates in the European Parliament, the issue became a platform for loudly condemning the sorts of neoliberal transformations that the EU advances with little hesitation in other domains. "You earn citizenship by making an effort, not with some money," Green MEP Sven Giegold proclaimed to the body in May 2018. "We need to stop double standards.

Those who come here to work are treated like criminals, but those coming here to park their money are treated like kings," followed MEP Sophie in 't Veld to a round of applause. Meanwhile, nearly as many refugees were dying due to illegal EU pushbacks against boats in the Mediterranean as were gaining citizenship through investment.[15]

Together with the European Parliament, the commissioner for justice has steadily increased pressure on the programs. From 2017, multiple fact-finding missions traveled to Malta and Cyprus, urging the countries to change, or preferably end, their schemes. In response, Cyprus instituted wide-ranging reforms, as already discussed. Ironically, the "constructive criticism" from Brussels brought Cyprus's application and vetting away from its own internally developed system and more in line with the "industry standard," a model designed by the private sector for running CBI programs. Malta, where such checks and balances were already in place, stood by its program.

Even so, reform was not enough. In January 2019, the European Commission recommended that member states end their programs. Cyprus responded that it had already taken on board the commission's suggestions for reform. Malta replied that it would not renew its program once it reached its ceiling of applications. However, as it turned out, it would roll out a new investor citizenship channel in its place, reminding the EU that citizenship is a sovereign prerogative and naturalization policies do not fall under its domain.

By January 2020, Jean-Claude Juncker was no longer president of the European Commission. The financier from Luxembourg hadn't been much interested in cracking down on the privileges that the wealthy secure via the microstates that serve them. This opened the possibility for further EU action. His successor, Ursula von der Leyen, daughter of early Eurocrats, took a much stronger stance against the schemes. In her first State of the Union address, she even declared forthrightly in reference to them—if with tangled logic—that "European values are not for sale." The pressure grew stronger when Al Jazeera exposed several high-ranking Cypriot politicians for running a VIP work-around to its CBI scheme in autumn 2020. The reporters offered clear evidence of what could go wrong around the programs, and the European Commission opened infringement proceedings against Malta and Cyprus. Now the concerns about security and money laundering threats were more real as the commission underscored its fundamental stance: naturalized citizens must have "genuine links" to a country. By the time the letter came out, Malta had already stopped accepting applications to its existing program, though it was planning to launch a new one. Cyprus had declared it would end its scheme on November 1. Nonetheless, the letter signaled that the commission was not going to let up in its attempt to end citizenship by investment.

To date, the EU's main weapon has been merely pressure. It does not have the legal grounds to intervene on naturalization. At least not yet. The programs may give Brussels, following its expansionist logic, the leverage to finally gain control over citizenship. The main concern of substance raised by the parliament and commission is that the programs can serve as a soft spot in EU security and become a conduit for money laundering and criminals. How much of a threat is really posed? As with any visa or citizenship channel, CBI programs carry the risk that some participants have questionable, if not outright criminal, backgrounds. Cyprus, with its known work-around to the formal vetting process, was especially vulnerable. According to Al Jazeera, 97 out of 2,400 investors and family members who gained citizenship through the program between 2017 and 2019 were high risk.[16] By their count, only about 4 percent of approvals went to questionable individuals, even with a corrupt work-around to due diligence screening available to those willing to pay. Whether the scheme represented a greater risk than other visa or naturalization channels remains an open question. Student visas, work visas, and business visas, along with naturalization through ancestry options, offer straightforward access to residence or citizenship in the EU, but without the background checks employed in CBI programs or the anti–money laundering screening the banks use on the qualifying investment funds. However, the amount of funds moving through the CBI schemes is significant. A key question remains: are the standard due diligence procedures applied to individuals and wealth solid and sufficient?[17]

Despite the perpetual concerns about security, no terrorist acts carried out in the European Union or elsewhere have been perpetrated by individuals on passports gained through citizenship by investment. When I asked fixers why this is so, I was told that the program requirements and due diligence procedures are a deterrent: it's easier to find an informal route. There are officials in many countries who will reach one hand over the table with a passport while stretching the other underneath to grasp the money, without looking into the background of the person. High-profile individuals, however, want something else. Those looking for an insurance policy are oriented to a longer timeframe. They may not need a lifeboat today, but they might someday, and so they desire some certitude over the future value and stability of their acquired status. A document secured through a bribe has no formal legal standing, but a full-fledged program backed by law offers the assurance that the deal will remain good.

The European Parliament and European Commission are still trying to find legal grounds for asserting control over citizenship by investment, which is why Brussels has been reiterating the seemingly obscure point that the investors lack "genuine links" to the country where they are naturalizing. The infringement proceedings launched against Cyprus and Malta placed the issue front and center as they declared "the granting of EU citizenship for pre-determined payments or investments without any genuine link with the Member States concerned, undermines the essence of EU citizenship."[18] In legal terms, the genuine link argument is a shaky one. It derives from the *Nottebohm* case of 1955—also an instance of investor citizenship—which is often misread as ruling that "genuine links" are a basis for establishing citizenship or adjudicating between competing citizenship claims.[19] Since then, *Nottebohm* has been frequently ruled over as "bad law."[20] Yet for Brussels, the genuine links argument has supplied the political pretext for extending influence into this new domain. [21] Effectively, it provides a foothold to contend that the programs are incompatible with the principle of "sincere cooperation" among member states established in the Treaty on European Union.[22] If the EU does successfully extend its legal jurisdiction to include the CBI policies of its member states, it may be able to extend its control over other, numerically far more significant, naturalization channels. This would be a remarkable new development in EU power.

The EU has done more than pressure the countries already in its club—it has also successfully exerted influence over those hoping to join. Montenegro, Moldova, North Macedonia, and Turkey are on the list of those in the years-long accession process. For a time, it appeared that governments and service providers could operate relatively freely in designing citizenship options before joining the EU, avoiding the pressure brought down on Cyprus and Malta. Countries and agents could sell the option as an investment in a soon-to-be-member state with future growth potential. It may look like just citizenship in Montenegro right now—so it would be pitched—but in a few years' time, this will mature into full EU membership, with citizenship rights across the entire Union. In 2019, the commissioner for justice began blocking this strategy by declaring that investment migration programs would be monitored as a part of the accession process.[23] By 2020, the European Commission and Parliament were making ever-louder noises against the CBI offerings in hopeful member states. In summer of that year, a new government in Moldova closed its brand-new program to avoid the risk of losing EU funds, let alone visa-free access. In its wake, Montenegro also promised to end its fledgling scheme to avoid derailing accession. In some ways, the EU has been more successful in neutralizing the offerings on its periphery than those inside it—at least thus far—as the carrot it holds is larger. Notably, too, it's made no moves against Turkey, even though it is now home to the largest CBI program by multiples. Its silence is a testament to the stalled accession process and the absence of visa waivers for most of its citizens, with perhaps a nod to the refugee deal with Prime Minister Erdoğan.[24]

The European Parliament, too, has begun to test its influence not merely over member states or candidates in its backyard, but over programs in distant countries as well. Visa-free access to the Schengen Area is a key selling point for the programs in the Caribbean as well as for those in Vanuatu. In 2019, two MEPs penned a letter seeking to remove Saint Kitts's visa privileges, but with little effect. It read like old news, citing cases from five years earlier, preceding the program's operational revamp and its cooperation with "international partners" in vetting. Yet three years on, revocation of visa privileges had become a very real possibility. In early 2022, the European Council cancelled the visa-waiver agreement with Vanuatu for citizens holding passports issued since 2015, when its main CBI programs came into force. By the end of the year, the council had suspended visa-free access to all citizens of Vanuatu. The Pacific archipelago was left scrambling to figure out how to regain this prized privilege, hiring an external firm to help it clean up its process. Members of the European Parliament also proposed that countries with CBI programs should be required to cancel them completely if they wanted to qualify for or maintain visa-free access to the EU.[25] The move was not a warning signal of the sort issued by the United States but a statement that the programs themselves were no longer to be tolerated.

Yet such moves may soon be obsolete, for the European Commission has already planned a 2023 rollout of the European Travel Information and Authorization System (ETIAS), much like the ESTA regime in the United States, which would give it final say on who can enter. No longer will a passport from a visa-free country be sufficient: everyone will need to undergo screening and apply for a waiver, good for five years, before being allowed across the border. With different parts of the EU working toward different goals, the situation is likely to continue to unfold for years.

Other Players

What about other global players who might have a stake? Australia monitors the happenings in the Pacific, but mainly to ensure that its own citizens aren't evading taxes via islands on its periphery, as a civil servant at the Australian embassy in Vanuatu explained to me. China keeps an eye on things as well—easily done in Vanuatu, where the Chinese embassy is the biggest building in the country. Yet to date it hasn't pressured any of the microstates over naturalizing its nationals, even though it's illegal for them to hold second citizenships. One can only speculate on its motives, but it may be that Beijing finds it useful to know who is carrying a second passport. Even sending states like Russia have taken little direct interest. On this score, the main exception is Vietnam, which outlawed the purchase of real estate abroad for its nationals to acquire citizenship elsewhere. It's a move that is difficult if not impossible to police, but still it speaks to Hanoi's frustration with its own businesspeople becoming foreigners in order to avail themselves of better legal protections.

There are also supranational organizations beyond the EU that may take an interest. They can hold some sway, but their leverage is less than that of powerful countries. The OECD has, for the most part, remained silent about citizenship by investment beyond issuing one blacklist. This came out in October 2018 and named and shamed the investment migration programs that it saw as offering a potential workaround to its attempt to crack down on tax evasion though the Common Reporting Standard (CRS). Its main concern was that the identity documents that people obtain could be used to misrepresent a person's tax residence. Some CBI countries balked at the listing, pointing out that the threat is one that exists for any type of residence permit or naturalization channel that does not lock an individual into a country for at least ninety days each year. Since its issuance, the blacklist has faded from importance. The OECD has since faced far more pernicious challenges to implementing CRS from much more powerful countries, such as Switzerland, which has ratified the treaty but neutered implementation, and the United States, which hasn't even signed up. The easiest way to avoid CRS, I was often told in interviews, was to open a bank account in America.

More critical for most states with CBI programs is the IMF, which holds outstanding loans for several of the countries. Overall, the IMF has been supportive of the schemes, which can help pay off debts and build economies. When I met representatives from the fund, they described the schemes as a broadly positive development, if one that must be steered in the most productive way. Predictably, the organization's main concerns are economic: it doesn't want to see macroeconomic destabilization or a race to the bottom in price, but it also wants to make sure that corruption is kept in check. At one conference in London, an IMF representative praised the programs before offering recommendations for improvement—the same recommendations that appear regularly in the IMF reports on the countries: strengthen due diligence and governance, ensure the real estate market is sufficiently regulated, reassess the investment projects regularly, establish a sovereign wealth fund once the national debt has been sufficiently repaid, and improve the quality and frequency of the release of information on the programs. Afterward, he told me that countries are largely using the schemes "in a way that we like," namely for debt reduction and transformative projects rather than recurrent expenses. In 2017 the IMF even recognized Cyprus's CBI program as crucial in enabling its sizeable property and construction market to recover after the European debt crisis, but it also raised concerns the program might generate an overexpansion of the property sector and recommended "decoupling" real estate from the scheme.[26] Caution was the counsel.

Should the programs become part of the economic development toolbox? An IMF representative I spoke with in Switzerland was hesitant: first, they need to see more transparency in how the programs operate. The comment came in the wake of Saint Kitts's "loss of Canada" and other questions swirling about the citizenship industry. A year later, in 2017, the IMF visited Saint Kitts to assess the economic future of the country. In its final report, it praised the island for righting itself: "The authorities are to be commended for the comprehensive reform of the CBI program," it declared, noting that the country's strong economic recovery owed much to the CBI scheme and spillovers in other parts of the economy.[27] Recognizing that the program amounted to around 40 percent of GDP, it recommended that the country broaden its options and direct investment into more sectors, such as education and health, to diversify the economy.[28] From the point of view of global capital, the schemes should be responsibly employed.

Microstates Maneuvering

For microstates, stances like the IMF's are great news; the arm-twisting from northern powers is a different matter. To many former colonies, coercion by the EU or United States is an unwelcome invasion of their sovereignty—and a hypocritical one at that. Caribbean countries often point to the "golden visa" schemes of big states that allow the wealthy to readily gain residence, but not citizenship, as evidence of a double standard. The US background checks for applicants to the EB-5 program, which grants a green card in exchange for an investment, are lighter than those for most CBI schemes. For years, the UK Tier 1 investor visa was known as the easiest way to secure residence by investment: the only background checks were the ones carried out by the banks. If these financial institutions saw a person fit to open an account, the Home Office would take their word as gold. Microstates, however, must run a tighter ship. As one local lawyer put it, "Small countries don't have the luxury of big countries to do what they want." High officials may try to hold their ground against them—at least verbally. The head of Malta's program has declared stridently in the face of EU threats to shut them down, "We are ready to defend the new residency regulations that may lead to citizenship because we believe in our sovereignty in this area, as enshrined in the very laws that regulate the functions of the EU."[29] The prime minister of Antigua has shot back at the United States for "attacking" the Caribbean programs. Leaders will balk at shutting down the schemes, but as we have seen, most bend to US or EU pressure when it comes to how programs are run.

Sometimes microstates parlay these power plays into selling points. One might think that being leaned on to join the US wealth-tracing system, implemented under the Foreign Account Tax Compliance Act (FATCA), would be a demerit for a small country with an offshore sector. Yet a representative from Grenada, speaking to an audience of service providers in Switzerland, proudly quoted praise from the United States for signing up. She went on to affirm that they have been "working with the US consulate to ensure that the process is smooth," referring obliquely to Washington's over-the-shoulder monitoring of application vetting. She even bragged that the country had become a regional site where the United States trains investigative police. Rather than a turnoff to an audience of wealth managers in an Alpine tax haven, such talk signals stability by conveying a strong relationship with global players whose blessing is needed to stay in the game.

In this, Grenada is not alone. At a conference in London, an official from Saint Kitts cited praise from the IMF on the positive reforms the country had made to their citizenship program. Meanwhile, an Antiguan ambassador-at-large reaffirmed that they are "committed to UK, US, and EU concerns" when it comes to how its CBI scheme is run. Even Malta for a time touted its program as the only one "approved by the European Commission," though the commission has forthrightly denied this. Service providers, too, will try to boost their credentials by stating that they "work with the Commission" when advising countries about the best way to design programs. Close ties to global powers are a selling point.

Yet these are just weapons of the weak. When push comes to shove against international giants, what can a microstate do? I spoke with one service provider from Antigua who described relations with the United States thus: "It's like being a small animal in a room with an elephant and trying not to get squashed." Over the years, countries have usually bent to the interests of regional powers, whether Washington or Brussels, making reforms as requested. Typically this has meant sprucing up due diligence and not approving individuals who have had visa applications rejected by the power holders. Caribbean countries even changed their passports, moving to a biometric standard "to be in synch with the EU, Canada, and the US," as a representative of Dominica explained. At the behest of the United States, Saint Kitts recalled thousands of passports issued that did not state the country of birth. And some, like Moldova, have abandoned their schemes under duress from regional powers. Yet even if countries reform, many with programs stand their ground against abandoning them. Cyprus still has its law on the books, even if it is not accepting applications, and the European Commission is threatening to take Malta to court as it refuses to end its program.

When it comes to reforms, most microstates may fall into line, but they can still drag their feet getting there. Malta had long promised to release the names of its CBI participants but did so only at the end of 2017. When the list came out, it was ordered alphabetically by first name and included all people who had naturalized through any means that year. The IMF and the United States have long supported shared regional standards on due diligence in the Caribbean, including a database of rejected applicants to prevent "venue shopping," or applicants rejected by one country trying their luck at another. Though the governments have voiced support for the idea and have met several times to hammer out a regime, years later still nothing is in place.

Microstates can also balk. If an "international partner" red-flags an applicant, a country can always play the sovereign discretion card and naturalize the person anyway, within or outside a formal CBI program. Such a move, however, can endanger a program's survival. When we come across several questionable naturalizations in Chapter 9, it will be easy to wonder whether a lucrative executive override wasn't applied in some of them. As seen in the case of Cyprus, states may refuse to play by the rules, but they also risk getting ejected from the game for doing so.

Remaking States

If countries have retooled their programs over time, the programs have retooled countries too. The hustle they play can have deeper consequences. This shows up not only in their economic dependence on the schemes, but also in their foreign policy. Small states have long leveraged their sovereignty into economic or political gains from bigger players. Moldova and Montenegro swing between the EU and Russia, playing one off the other. Caribbean islands navigate between the US and China, while in the Pacific, China and Australia typically provide the two poles. It's a balancing act in which countries see how much they can get from one or the other beneficiary. Antigua, for example, was the first in the region to establish diplomatic relations with China and was rewarded with a new airport and cricket stadium. Since then, Dominica and Grenada have followed suit, receiving millions in aid and investment in return. Some perform pirouettes, turning from Taipei to Beijing, then to Taipei, and back to Beijing again.

These moves—the bread and butter of international relations for microstates—are refracted in CBI schemes. Saint Kitts and Saint Lucia are among the mere dozen or so countries that continue to recognize Taiwan and not China, which has become a selling point of their programs. Chinese nationals, forbidden to hold multiple citizenships, may prefer options in these places where Beijing has few levers for pressing their new country to release names of their Chinese investor citizens. States that do have diplomatic relations with China, like Grenada, may keep their registry anonymous. Others, like Dominica, may recognize China but avoid signing an extradition treaty with it. The upshot is that politics on one side of the world can transform citizenship policies on the other.

Citizenship by investment also changes the foreign policy of countries that become heavily dependent on CBI revenue. Prime ministers will make the most of the opportunity to boost their product value when they travel abroad. On the CBI conference circuit—trips that may be sponsored by service providers—they might tack on a few days of meetings to negotiate visa-free access agreements, double taxation treaties, or direct flight connections with foreign countries. Caribbean states especially have taken this route, which is visible in their climb up the visa-free access rankings over time. These negotiation successes they then tout at the next round of conferences, refining their product pitches.

The embassy footprint of the Caribbean islands also supports this component of their economy. Countries locate their diplomatic missions in places where it is crucial to maintain their CBI market share (Table 5.1). Their presence in Cuba is an obvious exception: there the outposts are a by-product of history and regional solidarity. Apart from a few unusual choices, like Greece or Jamaica, the placement of most embassies conforms to the demands of the industry. The US, UK, and Belgium, home to the EU, are the powers that sustain the external value of the citizenship. China and the United Arab Emirates are key supply areas. Countries with embassies in Taiwan send a clear statement that they are not aligned with China and are therefore a safer bet for Chinese citizens looking to naturalize. Antigua's embassy in Lebanon is a historical legacy of earlier connections, but it serves as a base in the Middle East in the same way that newer embassies in the UAE do. When Antigua announced plans for an embassy in the Emirates, it also tried to negotiate direct flights between the two places to strengthen the connection. Grenada is the sole country to operate an embassy in Russia, though Dominica has tried as well. Grenada's diplomatic mission, opened in 2017, serves as not only an outpost but also a selling point of its citizenship program.

The new embassies become a base for attracting would-be investor citizens and connecting with them. Recently arrived officials may find the heads of CIUs

TABLE 5.1. Diplomatic missions of Caribbean CBI countries

Embassy or high commission location	Represented country				
	Antigua	Dominica	Grenada	Saint Kitts	Saint Lucia
Belgium	✔	✔	✔	✔	✔
Canada	✔		✔	✔	✔
China	✔	✔	✔		
Cuba	✔	✔	✔	✔	✔
Taiwan				✔	✔
United Arab Emirates		✔	✔	✔	
United Kingdom	✔	✔	✔	✔	✔
United States	✔	✔	✔	✔	✔

Note: The table includes locations where two or more countries have diplomatic missions. Locations with single representation are France (Saint Lucia), Greece (Antigua), Jamaica (Saint Kitts), Jordan (Antigua), Lebanon (Antigua), Russia (Grenada), Spain (Antigua), and Venezuela (Grenada).

organizing meetings to brief them on the needs of their wealthy nationals abroad. When I asked a representative from Saint Kitts about why they chose the United Arab Emirates for their newest embassy, he said that it was a no-brainer. "We thought about doing one in Geneva, but it would cost about 5 million [dollars]. It was clear which place was going to pay off more. It [the UAE] brings in direct revenue to the country. In Geneva, it's about leveraging your connections to try to get benefits for your country, but it's always with strings attached, with too many agencies involved. But the UAE is bringing in direct investment—you get a greater return for the country." Who is doing more for microstates, investor citizens or the United Nations? From the microstates' point of view, it's clearly the former.

Microstates that have thrown their lot in with citizenship by investment have been transformed in the process. It is reasonable to expect that both profit-driven firms in the citizenship industry and pragmatic millionaires se-lecting among options will behave as market actors. Striking, however, is that states too have responded to market demands by transforming their citizen-ship regimes. Once they enter the market, they begin reacting to external influences from three sources—namely, competition, purchaser preferences, and third-country pressure—to protect product value and enhance market share. Not all states with CBI programs play this game. Those processing few claims, like Jordan, Egypt, and North Macedonia, who remain outside the market, resist these pressures, though of course this could change. However, those who put their chips in end up adapting to market demands.

Countries change their programs in reaction to competition, with price cuts a favored tool. When Turkey slashed its minimum investment amount in 2018, it shot to the top of the ranks. This tactic raises concerns about a race to the bottom, however. The risk has been most visible in the Caribbean where an all-out price war broke out in 2017. As Antigua launched its program in 2014, it attempted to jump-start purchases with a six-month "sale"—a new innovation—by dropping the minimum government donation from $250,000 to $200,000, a move that it subsequently made permanent.[30] Saint Lucia matched this price in early 2017 when it launched its new scheme, but within months it halved the amount to $100,000 to compete with Dominica. The rash of hurricanes in the autumn of that year pushed the trend further, and in September 2017, Saint Kitts added a donation option at new low price: philanthropists contributing $150,000 to the country's hurricane relief fund would qualify. Meanwhile, Antigua again lowered its qualifying donation in

October of that year to $100,000. Throughout this period, the issuing governments declared the moves to be merely temporary, but most remained even years later. Service providers, losing commissions as prices declined, met with governments and bureaucrats to attempt to coordinate a simultaneous increase across the region, but to no avail. Though price competition became a recurrent debate at the regional meetings of Caribbean CIUs, no formal agreements on a floor were ever reached: countries just kept undercutting each other.

Similar competitive trends are observable in the Mediterranean. When Malta announced a new program in 2013 priced at about €1 million, Cyprus dropped its lowest investment amount from €10 million to €3 million. Further reductions followed until Cyprus reached a minimum amount of €2.5 million in 2016 to more closely tally with its neighbor. The figures may seem worlds apart, but if one takes into account the end cost to investors, the countries were evenly matched. Malta required a €650,000 donation to the government, which was not recoverable, while the investment in Cyprus—beyond the €500,000 retained in personal property—could be cashed out after three to five years. For investors, the two were competitive.

Malta's €1 million total cost was roughly the level at which Turkey entered the market in 2016, but it saw virtually no uptake: its offering wasn't on par with the benefits secured by EU citizenship. This changed when it dropped its minimum investment amount two years later to $250,000, a move that made it competitive with the Caribbean citizenship offerings as well as the RBI "golden visa" schemes in the EU. Turkey's package effectively combined the benefits of CBI schemes with those of RBI programs in sizeable and "livable" countries and at a price that positioned it between the two types of offerings. Within two years of carving out this niche, Turkey came to dominate the field, accounting for half of all CBI naturalizations globally. Vanuatu too has become more sensitive to global market factors as it expands its options, and the launch of every new program has come with a drop in price—from $350,000 to $260,000 and most recently to $130,000—to keep it in sync with the market.

Countries also compete on visa-free access. The private sector has codified this into a measure of "passport power" by churning out various visa and citizenship rankings, which they use to pitch their offerings. These country scores—frequently touted by governments too—are a selling point for potential buyers looking for mobility options. Countries scrambling for market share do not take these rankings for granted, and prime ministers actively attempt to raise their rank by negotiating visa-free agreements with other countries. Notably, the trend over time is not merely positive: countries with CBI programs are accruing visa-free access at a greater rate than their non-CBI counterparts.

Countries in the market also transform their citizenship products in response to demand, and the preferences of wealthy naturalizers have a discernable impact on policy. Some convey their desires directly when they interact with politicians and bureaucrats, but most pass them on via the service providers, who carry them to the state at stakeholder consultation sessions, periodic reviews, or industry conferences. Requests range from calls for speedy and clear-cut application processes to the reduction or elimination of physical presence requirements, elegant environs and VIP treatment, and an expanded number of family members who can be included on an application.[31] Responses are many. Antigua in 2014, for example, reduced its minimum physical presence requirement from one week per year in the first five years to merely five days total in the first five years, and then dropped it entirely after a rash of complaints. Keeping things speedy, Saint Kitts in 2016 introduced a "fast track" option that guaranteed an approval or rejection within sixty days. Most noticeable, however, are the changes countries make in family provisions, an easy way to tinker with program desirability without attracting the same attention as price drops. In 2018, Grenada began to allow not merely dependent children and parents to be included on an application as family members, but also dependent siblings, such as an unmarried brother or sister of a main applicant. Dominica and Saint Lucia followed in 2019 with similar provisions, and by 2020 all the Caribbean countries had redefined the meaning of "family" in their policies to include siblings. Similar fiddling continues: the maximum age of dependent children ever increases while the minimum age of dependent parents ever decreases as countries tailor their product to meet consumer preferences and expand market share. When the movement goes in the other direction—lengthening the application process, for example, or inserting physical presence provisions, as we saw with Cyprus in Chapter 3—it is due to external political pressure.

This reverse movement brings into relief the third external force: pressure from powerful countries and international organizations. Countries with CBI programs regularly acquiesce to these interests—an unsurprising result given that external parties determine the value of their product. Though not required by law or treaty, Malta nonetheless responded to concerns raised by the

European Commission about whether the investors had a real connection to their new state: it doubled the application time and required evidence of the intent to integrate before issuing an approval. In anticipation of scrutiny from Brussels, Cyprus revamped its program to require a visit to the country while applying and extended the assessment process from three to six months, followed by yet more reforms at the EU's behest. Caribbean countries have brought their passports into line with the biometric standards of the United States. They also run their preapproval lists past "international partners," and have banned individuals from a number of countries to conform with Washington's foreign policy interests. Though these adjustments are undesirable from the point of view of potential buyers, they are necessary to protect product value, which is secured to a large degree by these more powerful actors. Their toleration is crucial for a country to be able to remain competitive in the core market.

Notably, not all states compete in this way. Some, like Cambodia and Jordan, are hardly bothered by the actions of other CBI countries and show little evidence of influence by global powers. Egypt has not lowered its price to gain more market share. Samoa has not consulted third countries when adjusting its channel. Cambodia has not contracted American or European due diligence companies to allay security concerns. The interlinked market for citizenship resides in a more formal and interactive arena. Of course, countries can change: they can enter or exit the competitive market, or inhabit a space at its edges as they consider their options. North Macedonia, for example, had flirted with joining the great competition. On the cusp of 2020, it halved its minimum investment amount from €400,000 to €200,000—a better deal than Montenegro to the north—and by 2021 it was licensing agents to submit applications and, crucially, to promote the program. Yet it held back from going full throttle and remained slow with processing, a major drag against liftoff. The market may have much to offer to those who want to grow their programs, but only to those willing to conform to its demands.

Power Plays

The market in citizenship by investment isn't determined merely by the buyers and sellers: powerful third countries and supranational organizations have significant sway as well. Some prefer to monitor from the sidelines, like the IMF, OECD, China, and Australia, while others take a more active role. The most explicitly interventionist to date has been the European Union. It has demanded that member states end their schemes, pressured countries in the accession process to close their programs, and threatened to revoke visa-free access from countries further away. It has acted on these threats too, most recently taking Malta to court over its program and revoking visa-free access from Vanuatu. Yet for all the EU's moves, it is not the real puppet master. The United States has been more successful in bringing countries to its heel. Unlike the EU, it doesn't want to shut down programs, but to have control when it serves its interest. It has claimed a steering wheel for itself by telling foreign governments just whom they can and cannot accept, whether through vetting their preapproval lists or by imposing bans on particular nationalities. It has also at its disposal an extra brake pedal. Its control over the global flow of dollars allows it to direct the movement of money through the system, slowing or even halting citizenship by investment if desired.

Shutting down programs is a powerful intervention, but it may not end the risks that the EU wants to confront, whether money laundering, security threats, or criminals gaining access to its fortress. Russians, especially oligarchs with ties to President Vladimir Putin, are often decried as the main beneficiaries of investment migration programs in Europe.[32] Yet there are numerous ways for acquiring EU citizenship outside CBI programs, and many oligarchs have made use of them. Aluminum king Roman Abramovich became Portuguese through his Jewish heritage;[33] Arcadi Gaydamak, point man for Angola, naturalized in France, a country without a CBI scheme; oil baron Gennady Timchenko as well as construction magnates Boris and Roman Rotenberg became Finns through standard immigration routes, though without ticking all the boxes.[34] If the EU banned CBI programs, demand would likely shift to other channels. These are more numerous and dispersed, and thus may be harder to monitor and—as is the case with most naturalization streams—would likely have lighter vetting requirements than the formal CBI schemes. The European Parliament's strategy of blacklisting CBI countries, too, may result in the inverse of what it hopes to achieve. Countries once blacklisted may simply go rogue in response. No longer bound by the higher due diligence standards they need to appease global powers, they may develop a "dark web" market. Although such illicit activity may not bring the benefits of a formal CBI program, it might supply maneuverability outside the West's sphere of influence.

In contrast to the European Parliament and Commission's drive to end programs, Washington's strategy of monitoring the flow and closing the taps in a targeted manner may be savvier. Its use of a steering wheel and brake pedal leaves it in a more powerful position because it keeps things in sight, at least in the backrooms. Washington remains in the know about who goes through the programs without losing track of potentially nefarious characters who might try other routes. Its hegemonic position enables it to impose its own border control policy on other countries as well, ensuring that their naturalization rules conform to its interests. Even as the United States continued to issue travel visas to Russians in early 2022, it ensured that all the traditional CBI countries in the Caribbean and EU stopped naturalizing Russian investors. More than a case of extraterritorial migration regulation, the strategy is closer to the command and control that it uses with the militaries of allies.[35] With citizenship by investment, as with the military, the imposition is not total or leakproof—countries may still on occasion disobey—but the influence of the United States is strong. Washington does more than rubber stamp citizenship processes globally—it also molds them.

To date, the big players have coerced only the microstates in their backyard—or ones, like Vanuatu, offering a back door to them. More sizeable countries like Turkey, Cambodia, and Egypt have remained outside the influence of the US and the EU. The microstates that do feel the heat have at their disposal only weapons of the weak against these larger animals: tactics of delay or minor disruption. They acquiesce when it comes to reforming programs. Even their workarounds to the US-obliged bans are crafted to protect the interests of the big powers. When all else fails and they can't hold their ground, they try to rejig foreign pressure into selling points, which contributes to credibility within the market.

These geopolitical games shape the operation of the global market. And in turn they—and the market—reshape the naturalization policies and sometimes foreign policies of states heavily reliant on CBI funds. Players may respond to competition from similar products, purchaser preferences, or third-country pressure, but in all these cases, it is the global market and its geopolitics that recraft a state's decisions about how to employ its sovereign prerogative over naturalization. Whether they launch flash sales, expand regulations for family members, or drop physical presence requirements, countries retool their programs in order to compete. Not all enter the game. Countries may have a policy that enables individuals bringing large amounts of money to a country to naturalize in a standardized rather than individualized way, but that does not necessarily mean that they are players in the global market for citizenship by investment. Being in the market means, to some degree, bending to its forces and reshaping naturalization policies and practices around them as players dodge and dart through. This is a hustle that countries do not undertake alone, for there is money to be netted not only by them. Capitalizing on these opportunities is the citizenship industry, which we will meet next.

Chapter 6

The Citizenship Industry

I F MICROSTATES SUPPLY the good, service providers build the market for it, and a big one at that. In 2019, the annual turnover of citizenship by investment reached over $4 billion globally.[1] At the center of this booming trade is the citizenship industry.[2] This crucial web of intermediaries does more than merely connect buyer and seller. Indeed, the market would not exist, let alone function, without it. Service providers have been key creative drivers of both supply and demand, whether producing policy, assisting with implementation, advertising opportunities to buyers, putting together applications, or encouraging governments to get on board. Around them has formed an interconnected industry of private actors making money off borders.

In most migration streams, intermediaries play a pivotal role, and investment migration is no exception.[3] Applying for visas or citizenship is onerous at best, and even middle-class people turn to visa firms or lawyers to deal with the paperwork and speed the process along. In this, the wealthy are no different and are less likely to bat an eye at paying extra to avoid dealing with bureaucratic hurdles and secure the best service possible. At their call stands the citizenship industry, which will convert their economic gains into citizenship possibilities, reaping profit for their effort. In this complex ecosystem, lawyers, migration agents, application assemblers, real estate developers, due diligence firms, and others interlink to make a buck off the business of citizenship by subdividing and parceling out tasks in the most profitable fashion possible. The result is an extended supply chain, often invisible to the investors themselves, connecting an array of firms involved in getting an application through. A lucrative flow of commissions keeps this hidden world humming. Without it, the market would not function, and states know that too. The co-dependent relationships and feisty power plays between the public and private in this transnational field are a key part of the story as well. What does this look like?

Anatomy of the Citizenship Industry

The citizenship industry itself comprises a motley troupe of business types. At the center stand the investment migration service providers. They come in several forms and have evolved in complex ways, but the heart of what they traditionally do is paperwork: they assist clients in putting together CBI applications. Their key skill—beyond collecting and collating information—is effectively translation: they ensure that the bureaucratic paperwork produced in Country A can be understood and assessed by bureaucrats in Country B. In this they are little different from main street companies that help speed visa applications, or the law firms that help prepare naturalization files and provide a cover letter as an extra insurance that it doesn't get lost in the bureaucratic shuffle. However, the citizenship industry has evolved far beyond this simple client-to-business-to-government model into an international—and internationally networked—industry.

Most service providers concentrate in global cities, like Dubai, London, and Singapore, where wealth and its attendant financial services converge. In some places the businesses are discreet, but in others they do not hold back, sponsoring billboards and advertising campaigns to publicize CBI possibilities widely. Plus not all wealthy people want to work out their membership portfolio under the nose of their own government. Some Russians find Nicosia or Tbilisi a more amenable environment than Moscow for discussing citizenship choices, and some Chinese prefer Singapore or Hong Kong to talking business within earshot of the communist party in Beijing. Dubai can be an easier place to explore citizenship options than India, where dual nationality is forbidden.

Yet whether it's London, Moscow, Hong Kong, Dubai, Istanbul, or Grand Cayman, one player in the CBI scene stands out: the Canadians. The vast majority of the "old timers" in the industry are from Canada. Even in China, many top agents have resident status in Canada, if not also citizenship.[4] All of them cut their teeth on Canada's Federal Immigrant Investor Program (FIIP), a golden visa scheme launched in 1986 that offered residence in Canada in exchange for a passive investment. At the time, it dominated the market among Hong Kongers looking for exit options. "That's where the volume was," as one service provider put it. And the money. These early adopters learned through experience with the FIIP about the search for global mobility among the well-off—namely that demand is big and business is lucrative.

Canada's RBI program was hugely popular, resulting in over 200,000 new residents over its course. It also boosted demand for citizenship by investment, if inadvertently. In 2011, Ottawa announced a moratorium on the FIIP: the economic impact of a few thousand investors annually was unclear in the country's huge economy.[5] The sudden announcement left service providers in the lurch. Many had started the application process for clients, which could take more than two years, but now the files might not see the light of day. "We had a stack of applications this high," a service provider in Hong Kong told me, spreading his arms two feet wide. "I could have retired on that." If he and others didn't want to lose their fees, they had to find a way to "recycle the Canadians," as a lawyer in Dubai put it. Essentially, they needed to offer their clients something similar, and the CBI programs spreading in the Caribbean provided a solution. The price in Saint Kitts was similar, given the discounting and financing available in Canada, and Saint Kitts had visa-free access to Canada as well. The result was a boost to the emerging CBI programs and marked the beginning of a more interactive global market.

But not just any Canadians dominate the CBI field: it's the Montréalais.[6] They became early adopters due to the country's federated system. Since the 1980s, Ottawa has devolved a great deal of migration control to Quebec to stem the rising tide of break-away nationalism. The federal government still has to sign off on its decisions, but Quebec has wide berth in implementing migration policies and approving visa applications. The result was that Quebec developed its own version of the FIIP in the form of the Quebec Immigrant Investor Program (QIIP).[7] In terms of outcomes—securing residence in Canada—nothing distinguished the two offerings: participants in either program would get a visa and could live anywhere they wanted. The crucial difference was the processing times. Whereas it could take years to get an application approved in most of Canada, Quebec offered preapproval within a matter of months. Applicants spent less time waiting and wondering, and consultants could offer faster service and collect their fees more quickly. The profitability of this subnational carve-out made French the backroom language of the original citizenship industry.

Within the industry, however, service providers are not all the same. Businesses run the gamut from an individual with an exclusive client list to massive firms with more than a thousand employees. The most prominent on the scene are what can be termed the *dominant consultancies*. In China they include Globe Visa Group, Delsk, Visas Consulting Group, and Well Trend United. Elsewhere, Henley and Partners, Arton Capital, Apex Capital,

Latitude, and CS Global come under this heading. These firms, which specialize in investment migration services for clients and other companies, are a sizeable presence with massive networks of offices, branches, and business partners. To outsiders, they are the face of the field, not only servicing clients but driving the PR and marketing that have made the programs known across the world. The Western companies in particular have taken a lead in these efforts, advertising the programs in in-flight magazines, granting global citizen awards, publishing global citizen glossies, and hosting networking conferences in major hubs. They also produce various citizenship rankings based on measures of "passport power" that can serve as a marketing tool and spur competition among countries.

Behind the scenes even more goes on. The dominant consultancies include subdivisions and subsidiary companies that specialize in the industry's attendant needs. Some have an intelligence unit that works with think tanks and produces op-eds or press releases for the media as part of the PR battle. More important are the government advisory units. These specialized teams play a key role in developing the citizenship industry itself by advising and lobbying countries, negotiating contracts to run programs, and participating in image management. The most successful have secured spots for their firm as a program's concessionaire or aggregator, ensuring access to a steady stream of profit. Across these cases, the dominant consultancies do much to structure the market and its dynamics.

Standing alongside them are law firms and private client divisions of major accountancies (the "Big Four") and banks that employ lawyers to assist clients with the programs. Some are massive multinational businesses with a footprint in over a hundred countries, far outstripping the dominant consultancies in reach. Others are more modest in size and may have only one large office in a global city. Yet both regularly deal with a wealthy customer base and include investment migration options among their offerings. Some may participate in stakeholder sessions with governments, but they do not try to build or run programs, as dominant consultancies do. Investment migration is not their bread and butter.

Below the dominant consultancies are small- and medium-sized firms that also specialize in investment migration, but on a smaller scale and with little to no international footprint. Many are based in countries or global cities with a pool of potential buyers, and some can be found in CBI countries. Though global mobility is their economic mainstay, these smaller outfits do not shape the industry like the dominant consultancies. Without the rankings, magazines, and government advisory divisions of their bigger counterparts, they focus simply on finding clients. They may put together the citizenship application themselves or feed the file to other businesses for preparation and submission. Smaller players that are connected to wealthy clients may do quite well, for even if they handle only ten or twenty cases per year, they offer "bespoke" attention. "We're a boutique firm" is a line that I heard in Moscow, Dubai, and Hong Kong when talking to smaller offices. Some are even fly-by-night operations, ready to make a quick buck off a tiny footprint, collecting fees from clients and then closing shop before completing the application.

A number of countries require applications to be submitted by service providers licensed by the government. In many cases, these are local firms in the CBI country that pay as much as $10,000 per year for program accreditation. Some may be larger service providers that take on their own clients and prepare their forms directly, while others may be "couriers" that submit a file assembled by another service provider, perhaps after checking it over and running their own due diligence scan to avoid losing their license due to the mistakes of others.

The resulting web of connections—the supply chain enabling the CBI market—is not always apparent to the client. A potential investor may select a firm to take care of their application package and think that only it is on the task. Yet that firm may operate as a mere project manager that organizes and bundles together the services of other firms for the client. It may turn over application assembly to another company before sending it along to yet another business that eventually submits the application to a government. The supply chain can run long.

Beyond the service providers dealing with applications are two attendant businesses that are crucial for the industry. Over the past decade, due diligence screening has taken on increasing importance for CBI programs, as seen in Chapter 2, with a number of countries now regularly appointing specialized firms to check the background of applicants. These are often large corporations, like Thomson Reuters or Exiger, whose bread and butter is running investigations for multinational companies and major banks. Countries will contract with a handful of firms that offer different packages of services at different rates, from searches of publicly available databases through more thorough "boots-on-the-ground" checks that gather information in the applicant's country of origin. Unlike the other private actors involved in the citizenship industry, these firms remain largely insulated from others in the market. For big due diligence companies, hooking into the flow of commissions would be a profit risk rather than a profit gain. Such connections would constitute a conflict of interest that could undermine their core service provision and put in jeopardy their entire business, which extends far beyond investment migration.

Finally, orbiting this field are firms that assist with the investment itself. If an applicant selects a business option to qualify, there are companies that will create and manage the business for them. Other companies will do the same for financial investments, sometimes pooling the money of many applicants to amass hundreds of millions of dollars in capital for specific projects. Most prominent, however, are property developers. For them, investment migration can supply a no-interest loan for building a project or expanding an existing one. This might mean housing, whether a personal residence or a rental unit, or it might come in the form of hotels, resorts, or timeshares that contribute to the tourism infrastructure. Some developers have used CBI money to create marinas and golf courses. If due diligence companies remain aloof from the service providers, real estate developers certainly do not—they need their connections to clients to keep business going and are tied into the flow of commissions that keep the industry humming.

Actual Work

What do service providers really do? The heart of their traditional business is fairly mundane: they fill out forms. If applications in the early days of citizenship by investment were an easy three pages, now they fill reams. For a businessperson, the bank statements, tax receipts, and business filings can expand a file to six inches or more. Most service providers stretch their fingers wide when describing how much paperwork is involved when handling a complex client. One even used a trolley to tote an applicant's file: there was no other way to get the fifteen binders of paperwork—one for each country where he held businesses—to the government for submission.

Effectively, the service providers are the interpreters between bureaucratic systems. They make paperwork generated in one country legible to bureaucrats in another—which isn't always easy. The best, however, know the logic of the bureaucrats on the other side. "We take their language and use it to respond so that they know exactly how to process the client," a service provider in Russia told me. Another in Hong Kong bragged that he knows exactly what sorts of files any specific country will accept or reject. "There's a lot of grey area, but we have a good sense of what they're looking for." It's about knowing the minds of civil servants and making sure that the file is filled out "in a way that they can understand." An agent in China explained, "It's common to have a complicated background in different sorts of businesses." A recent client was a manager at a state-owned enterprise who received shares when his firm was privatized. He used the money to open a restaurant and from there moved into real estate. For him, the challenge was to get the businessman's papers "into a form that foreigners will understand."

Questions about the files can arise from both governments and service providers. What sorts of documents are acceptable? What are available? How are stepchildren to be handled? What about divorce, or complicated company structures? If an applicant lived in a country at age fifteen, is a police background check still needed? And what if the country no longer exists? One lawyer I visited in Cyprus pulled out a three-page clarification the government had emailed in response to a query she had about an applicant's file. Governments can ask for more information when they have a hard time reading an application. Service providers do what they can to head off that threat, and its delays, before it emerges. The art is to take a complicated biography and pack it into boxes that are clear to the government. "Our real work is to help the client move through," explained a service provider in Hong Kong, describing the bureaucratic hurdles of the application process.

Yet sometimes the required documentation simply isn't there. Cash economies remain common in many parts of the world, which can make it difficult to prove the source of funds. Doctors in the United Arab Emirates, for example, may be paid in bank notes and usually have no need to report the income to the government, which charges no income tax. Only recently has Abu Dhabi imposed a VAT tax on medical services, which can supply some paperwork—at least now, but not for previous years. In such a case, patient receipts will reveal more about the source of wealth than a bank statement, but they may not fit the boxes on the form. What to do? Birth certificates are another challenge. Though increasingly common, they were not always available fifty or sixty years ago in many parts of the world. A police clearance certificate too may not be so easy to acquire if one's home state is in the throes of civil war.

In other cases, the documents may exist but not tick the right boxes. One service provider in London showed me a photo of a bank statement from one of his Chinese clients that ran fifteen feet long—and that was for a single year. Tax doesn't always provide a reliable indicator of personal income or company profits. An agent in China explained to me that a tax official could show up every year, demand a lot of tax, and put half in his pocket. It may look as though the businessperson paid substantial taxes, but they may have made no profit. Others working with clients in the Middle East, India, and Africa had similar stories. CBI countries that require income tax statements to check that an individual's wealth is clean face difficulties with applications from such areas. Sometimes even criminal records are not reliable. In places like Russia and Belarus, the court systems are regularly employed by the powerful to take out their competitors or enemies. "Anyone who is worth their salt has a criminal case against them," an NGO worker who deals with the region told me. A criminal conviction in China may in some cases even help an escapee secure asylum in the West. Police records can sometimes muddy the waters for service providers and countries alike.

This raises the issue of background checks. When state infrastructures are not solid and documentation regimes are haphazard, it can be difficult not only for CBI governments to know if an applicant is clean, but for a service provider to know as well.[8] For them, the risk is reputational. In some parts of the world, as a service provider in Dubai told me, "scandals are high and individuals are hard to vet." You have to "pick and choose" whom you take. "I have to think about my reputation," he explained. "If a government sees me submitting a money-launderer or a gangster, that reflects on my business." Another working with clients in Russia explained that he tries to circumvent problems by "drilling down" to get at the source of wealth. "You get to know their families, their personal financial situation." Without this sort of transparency, "it's a risk for me." The largest companies take out paid subscriptions to databases like WorldCheck and carry out their own background scans before onboarding a client. If something is flagged, they ask the person for an explanation and make an assessment about whether the candidate is a risk to their company. Global law firms and accountancies will have even more internal hurdles, including dedicated teams that carry out "relationship checks" and due diligence on wealth before they take on a client.

Yet there are limits. Not all agents probe the backgrounds of those who show up on their doorstep, and clients may successfully hide things from those who look. It can be hard to find hidden assets, should a person shield their wealth with complicated financial structures, and clients rarely disclose their safety deposit boxes. Sometimes "don't ask, don't tell" is the name of the game, which can be beneficial for an agent who thinks a fee-paying client might be able to get through screening anyway. Some service providers give into temptation when a high-risk, high-gain possibility appears. A person with a questionable past might offer top dollar to an agency to help her assemble a convincing file, blind eyes turned to red flags. And there are cases of risky individuals making their way through programs even when hazard warnings flash brightly, as we will see in Chapter 9. The alleged architect of the largest Ponzi scheme in history became an investor citizen of Cyprus. Someone had to help him with his file.

Creating Supply and Demand

The work of service providers goes beyond merely connecting supply and demand; they drive forward both sides of the market too. Making demand means getting the word out and moving into new markets, and agents are always keen to get a corner on a fresh client base. In 2014 this meant Vietnam; by 2016 it was India; and then in 2018 Nigeria and Kenya. Since 2020 and the Covid-19 pandemic, the United States has become the latest frontier market. Usually a few pioneers set up shop, find local law firms or wealth managers to work with, and then carry out a marketing campaign to convince locals that the product is legit. If all goes well, within two or three years, the agents start complaining of market saturation. Advertising and PR campaigns, alongside op-eds, rankings, reports, and other strategies to get the word out, also let people know that the opportunity is there—and could be theirs.

Creating supply is a different story: this means making government connections. First a dominant consultancy will reach out to potential partners in the target country, usually successful law firms, to find allies and feel out the power dynamics. From there they approach the government—both the party in power and in opposition—to assess appetite. At this point, the dominant consultancy's government advisory unit swings into action. The courtship rituals of lobbying are no different from those of other industries: the firms hold meetings with party leaders about the promises of programs, supply generous donations to parties, and appoint lobbying professionals to further their cause. Some may even hire election specialists to help their favored horse across the line.[9] A country that already has a legal provision for granting citizenship for exceptional contributions is a ready target, as it avoids the hassles of passing new legislation. In these cases, a ministerial decree or cabinet order issued behind closed doors may be enough to get a program going. Sometimes governments rebuff the citizenship industry's overtures, as was the case in Cyprus in 2012, or even scuttle public tenders and craft a program themselves, as did Montenegro. If the government reacts positively to a firm's advances, however, several consultancies will move in and compete to secure a coveted monopoly.

What the larger players want are exclusive deals with governments. Those who become the concessionaire, aggregator, or master agent of a program are guaranteed a slice of the pie whenever an application is approved. "That's where the big money is," one agent explained. Though the differences are not hard and fast, *concessionaires* generally help run programs, while *master agents* make their money through guaranteed monopolies over application submissions from specific regions, and *aggregators* market offerings and guarantee bulk numbers. In the case of Vanuatu's Economic Rehabilitation Program (VERP), all applications from China would go through an agency in Hong Kong, which would get a cut from the final submissions. In the Caribbean, the concessionaire has traditionally received 10 percent of the government donations, while Malta turned over 4 percent of its donations to the firm in this role—a tidy €26,000 per application. In exchange, the country gets marketing and promises from the concessionaire to keep the supply chain in line. Where there is no government budget for promoting a program, concessionaries may cover the costs of flying out officials to pitch their countries in key global hubs. With such large payments for so little work, one might wonder if the monopoly fees cover other costs too. Some of those I spoke with who work in the industry speculated that if a concessionaire or aggregator gets $20,000 from each application, it's because government officials want $10,000 of it.

Beyond program design and implementation, service providers also shape supply by pushing governments for alterations that work in their favor. Sometimes this comes through formalized stakeholder feedback sessions; at other times it takes the form of old-fashioned lobbying. A key goal is to build possibilities for extracting commissions directly into the program structure. The standard format is to lobby a government to increase the fees it charges to applicants, which can flow out again as rewards to the service providers if the application is approved. Beyond that is a predictable laundry list of wishes that make it easier to make money: no caps, swift processing times, more family members, straightforward investment processes, financing opportunities, and online oaths.

Service providers may also seek ways to ensure a profit over the short and long term, protecting the future prospects of the market. For citizenship by investment, this has traditionally meant securing legitimacy, particularly in the West where the programs are often met with suspicion, if not outright rejection. The search for legitimacy has led to the creation of two standards boards, the Investor Migration Council (IMC) and the now-defunct Global Investor Immigration Council (GIIC), in an attempt by the industry to self-regulate. Each was backed by competing firms, which left some wondering about how independent they might be. The idea was to clean up the problems that were giving the industry a bad name—weak vetting, bilking clients, false information, noncompletion of real estate projects, and the like—while also forming a networking and lobbying group. The model they looked to was that of the Society of Trust and Estate Practitioners (STEP), the self-regulation group that private wealth managers created to sustain their industry in the face of crackdowns on offshoring. By 2018, the GIIC had collapsed, but IMC remained in the game and boasted a membership of over 300 individuals and firms. Its head described to me their activities "to ensure the sustainability of the industry": track market patterns, provide professional development and networking opportunities, lobby powerful countries and supranational organizations, work with CBI countries to improve program operation and vetting standards, facilitate industry research, and promulgate a code of ethics among its members. Internal regulation may not stop all questionable or dodgy practices—there is always money to be made in playing around rules—but it can possibly reduce them while working on image management. Those concerned with scaling up programs to make them into a profitable mass-market product don't want to see it all come crashing down.

Supply Chain

One of the challenges of regulation comes from the transnational nature of the business. Supply chains run long and across multiple jurisdictions, which makes them difficult to manage. As the prime minister of one of the Caribbean countries told me, "If something goes wrong, people think that we have control over the program, but we really don't—there are too many players involved." What does this look like in practice?

In most cases, prospective investor citizens cannot file an application themselves but must lodge it via an agent licensed in the CBI country. Even when direct submission is possible, most still turn to specialists to reduce uncertainty and bureaucratic hassles. The first port of call is usually a service provider where an applicant is based, or one close enough to facilitate trust and confidence. Local service providers may assemble the application themselves, but many will simply serve as a "feeder" that turns it over to a dominant

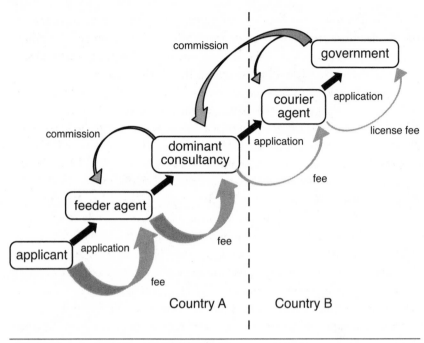

FIGURE 6.1. Basic supply chain

consultancy or bigger firm to do the work in exchange for a commission (Figure 6.1). Of course, larger consultancies may take on clients directly, but many rely on smaller companies to send them applicants. Once the application file is assembled, usually the service provider will partner with an agent in the CBI country who will submit the documents and monitor their progress through the assessment process. Often these agents are just couriers who drop off the file, but if something gets delayed, they can intervene with the local government and try to clear up matters. Some, however, take on clients directly, especially if the investor already has business interests in the country, cutting the intermediaries down to one.

Occasionally the chain has a single link, and the client's service provider assembles and submits everything. But the supply chain often extends much further. Agents whose knowledge is location-specific may reach across borders or seek out more efficient ways to maximize profit. For small businesses, it's not easy to know how to lodge a solid application in a foreign country. A law firm in Lagos with a client interested in citizenship by investment will need, at minimum, to learn how to translate the person's complex situation into a clear case for the application forms and assess which of the various investment options are the strongest—on top of figuring out which country is best for the investor's specific situation. They'll also need to find a licensed agency or law firm in the CBI country to submit the file. Novice agents may use everything from Google searches to word-of-mouth referrals to close the information gaps. Some might make a bigger investment and travel to industry conferences or the CBI country itself to understand what governments expect, search out partner firms, and assess qualifying projects. "I'm here to learn how things work" was a common refrain I heard from smaller service providers attending these events.

Into this breach can step the dominant consultancies that offer business-to-business (B2B) services that profit off borders. If the Lagos lawyer doesn't want to dedicate the resources to dealing with a CBI case, the bigger firm may take on the client in exchange for a referral fee. Alternatively, it can simply take over the file for assembly and processing, ensuring that the application ticks all the right boxes, gets submitted correctly, and its progress is monitored while the Lagos lawyer remains the "face" to the client. An extra fee might attach due diligence checks and investment facilitation to the B2B package as well. Even more specialized firms with experience in the CBI world may use these services if it is more efficient and profitable for them. Some even opt for a "tie-up," a multiyear contract that obliges them to send on clients to the other firm for a set commission. This can be lucrative too: those who "bring bulk" can expect better rates.

Developing transnational connections can also make or break small firms in CBI countries. One lawyer I met in Antigua wanted to expand his business and had recently invested several thousand dollars for a license to submit CBI files. It seemed like a good opportunity, but he was on edge. His legal office was small, and the accreditation costs were substantial. When I asked him about his experiences with the program, he responded plaintively, "How do I reach people?" Several months after gaining a license, he had still received no applications, and he didn't know how to connect internationally. The next day I met another local service provider, who described her relief when she entered into a contract with a large foreign service provider: it secured the future of her small business. "You need to connect with a big firm for a guaranteed income stream—I was fortunate in that."

These disjunctions, however, can be profitable for others, allowing experienced firms to make money by helping other agents to reach out across borders.

Bigger companies might offer training sessions that teach other firms the ins and outs of each national system or coach them through assembling an individual file. The Lagos lawyer may pay for instruction in how to fill out applications for Turkey and handle the filing himself, but hire another business to select and vet a real estate investment. If a client decides on an unfamiliar CBI country, the lawyer may turn over the "back end" application preparation and submission to a firm with greater expertise in that country's offering. The multiple forms these B2B services take can enable big firms to make money, even off of clients who aren't theirs.

Service providers can also turn a profit from the investment options by suggesting particular projects to their clients. Some explain the practice as a way to ensure quality control: with many questionable investments out there, it's hard for an investor to know which ones are solid, especially in a country they may know little about. Principled agents will vet and choose the options that are strongest, even checking into a property developer's history of completion. Others, however, may just recommend those that offer the largest commissions—which can be doubly lucrative if the service provider is invested in the real estate project itself.

Within this global scene, China requires separate discussion. It's home to the oldest, most developed, and most complex ecology of migration businesses, and it remains a subsystem of its own. Foreign companies, despite their best efforts, are rarely able to overcome the challenge of breaking into it and usually end up partnering with a local company. Yet "China drives the market" was a sentiment I often encountered, even outside China—and one with much truth to it. Before Covid-19, the country accounted for about half of global demand, and now that Beijing has lifted its draconian anti-Covid measures, it will likely resurge.

Mainland China did not always predominate in the search for options abroad, however. Beijing had long imposed exit restrictions on its populace, rendering it difficult to leave without government approval and mooting the acquisition of additional travel documents. The turning point came in 2001, when China joined the World Trade Organization. As a condition of membership, it was required to relax exit controls on both goods and people. The result was a bubbling market in migration advisories. Initially this centered in the southern province of Guangdong, home to flourishing IT and manufacturing sectors. It was also next door to Hong Kong, where the migration firms had seen business boom before its return to China in 1998 and then freeze thereafter. Once controls lifted, many of them moved to Guangdong, and in 2001 Beijing licensed two hundred such "immigration consultants." As interest grew, firms expanded northward to Shanghai and Beijing, and farther out to other provinces. Government regulations enabled only Chinese nationals to own such businesses, which had to be registered with the police for a substantial fee, on top of payments for each office opened in a different district. Regulation resulted in a market without foreign intermediaries, and one that was divided between first-tier, second-tier, and third-tier agents, depending on the size of their operations and the city where they are based. In 2014, Guangdong Province deregulated, followed by Shanghai in 2016 and the entire country in 2018, producing additional growth in agent numbers, now freed of heavy licensing fees.

The resulting field of migration service providers is substantial, with at least 5,000—as many as 20,000 by some estimates—in operation.[10] Yet just a half-dozen leading firms dominate the market. These massive companies are national in reach, with twenty-five to thirty-five offices in both major and medium-sized cities, employing at least 500 and sometimes more than 1,000 workers. The biggest operate as franchises, with the mother company selling its name to a local bidder who sets up shop under its framework. Most have much more on offer than citizenship by investment: they also supply student and employment visas, along with a range of additional services, including visits to the CBI country to assess investment options, relocation assistance, and help with securing places in schools abroad. At these "supermarkets of immigration," as an agent in Shanghai described them, "You just go there and pick the country that you want and they get you the visa." Typically their foreign footprint is small. Unlike their counterparts elsewhere, even the biggest firms often do not have branches abroad. Still some have been involved in program design and government advisory, including iterations of Vanuatu's various CBI programs, as well as Hungary's RBI scheme. Most will have a "patch," either by city or by program, and then jostle for market share around it. Traditionally, too, they maintain factory-style back offices of hundreds of people dedicated solely to application assembly. "They're like a machine," an agent in Hong Kong put it.

Below them are the far more numerous small players that concentrate on local clients and lack the national reach of the dominant firms. Most have one or two offices, sometimes in more than one city, staffed with a handful to a few dozen employees. Contrary to appearances, their mainstay isn't processing applications but supplying the bigger companies with customers, as seen elsewhere. "They just collect clients," a service provider in Guangzhou explained, and then send them on to a bigger agent with the resources and the know-how to reach abroad, assess the options, carry out due diligence, and understand its bureaucratic procedures. Yet this does not mean lazy service: agents have an added incentive to make sure a client gets through. Outside China, most intermediaries charge fees in stages, with a set amount collected as the application process advances. In China, by contrast, all the fees must be paid up front. This may seem like a risk, but if an application fails, the customer can expect a full refund. The performance-based system puts pressure on the service provider to ensure that a client is approved, in contrast to the "advisory model" elsewhere, where fees are piecemeal and refunds unheard of outside of gross negligence.

Since the mid-2010s yet a new layer has appeared, extending the chain further: the application specialist firm. Even the behemoth dominant consultancies have begun to cut down on their back offices and turn to their services, outsourcing application assembly. As an agent in Guangzhou explained to me, it makes financial sense because the application specialists take care of the hassles of paperwork. "Going through them slows everything down and increases the price for the client, but it's easier for the company." Even under the new configuration, the dominant consultancies still receive the bulk of the commission—usually about 50 percent—and remain the face of the industry. They are the ones advertising the production and interfacing with their clients. The application specialist, by contrast, is solely "business-to-business" in its connections. "We just move a lot of people through, getting volume," one employee explained.

The application specialist firm can also become the connector abroad, bridging countries as it takes care of everything required overseas. This can include inspection trips and "after-sale" care, in addition to real estate options, including ones they may be invested in themselves. The bundle can be tied up as a package that guarantees a supply of tenants and a minimum rental income, on top of fully managing the property. As a worker at an application-assembly company described the setup drily, "We're kind of an immigration-funded real estate developer."

Seen from above, the market in China is narrowly national, even if the product on offer is anything but. Few Chinese firms have established offices abroad and developed an international presence of the sort common in the citizenship industry elsewhere. Their clientele remains largely Chinese. The largest firms are most likely to reach across borders and maintain partnerships with companies or lawyers abroad, which submit the final file. It's mainly the application specialists that have crafted a sizeable overseas footprint, but one largely invisible to those outside the industry. These arrangements, emerging from the market and feeding into market changes, can be readily reconfigured in the endless search for profit.

Commissions

Tying the whole system together is the flow of commissions—and sizeable ones at that. Top service providers can make out like bandits. A London-based lawyer described the choicest position: the government pays a commission to the agent, the applicant pays a fee to the agent, and the real estate company pays a commission to the agent—and the agent owns part of the real estate development.

How do these flows break down? What a client pays often depends on where the client is. A small agent or basic lawyer in a city like Dubai may charge as little as $5,000 or $10,000 to take on a run-of-the-mill case for the Caribbean. A local lawyer in Malta or Cyprus who works with a client directly—a chain with only one link—might levy a flat fee of €20,000 that also covers five years of "aftercare," including any annual documentation governments may require. Boutique firms or dominant consultancies dealing with very wealthy individuals will extract significantly more—from $30,000 to $80,000 for a straightforward case. A family of four applying to Malta through a high-end firm might expect to foot a bill of over $100,000 for its services, in addition to paying over $1 million for the program. The wealthiest, though, are unlikely to bat an eye, or even notice. "They don't even ask about fees," as one service provider operating in this stratosphere put it. "They just go for it because their banker referred them," working off trust. And trust is key, for a large amount of personal information is exposed in the files.

Of course, some of the money flowing into the larger firms can end up flowing out again in referral and courier fees. In China, these can be as low as $1,000 for the small firm that feeds the client onward and rise to as much as $20,000. On the other side of the supply chain, a local lawyer in a Caribbean country can expect about $2,000 for bringing the file to the right office and monitoring its progress. In other markets it can reach around $10,000.

In between these two ends are the commissions that agents gain from real estate developers in exchange for bringing clients to their projects. For a large Chinese firm, these can run as high as 30 percent or more of the entire investment amount. These commissions are crucial: "The programs that don't pay well, don't become popular," one Chinese agent explained flatly. Both in China and elsewhere, a big service provider with a broad clientele can demand higher commissions from property developers in exchange for a steady flow of investors—and may do doubly well off the deal if invested in the property development too. Yet developers who pay commissions out of their incoming funds are left with less money to pay for construction—sometimes with substandard consequences, as we will see in Chapter 7.

If these fees seem exorbitant, they may still come off as a bargain, particularly if financing is involved. If, for example, a real estate investment of $200,000 is required to qualify for a program, the agent might simply charge a client a flat fee of $120,000. In such cases, the agent will retain control of the investment, or offer a "guaranteed buy-back" after five years, while the client puts out only $120,000 to qualify for citizenship. To the savvy businessperson, this is not a loss of $120,000 but a gain of $80,000 that can be invested in other markets over the next five years where it might make a higher return. In places like China, some agents will extend their financing services to include assistance with getting the money out in the first place. If currency controls block financial flows—in China, for example, an individual can take out from the country only $50,000 each year—a service provider may partner with financial institutions such as shadow banks to make sure the money keeps moving.

Governments are well aware of the economic calculus of agents, and those looking to attract more applicants will build commissions into the structure of their program itself, typically by padding out application fees. Across the Caribbean, governments offer between $10,000 and $20,000 in commissions to agents for each approved application—in addition to what they may pay a concessionaire. The bonus will go to the local agent who submits the application or to an aggregator. Either way, the bulk of the commission will leave the country, oiling the supply chain as it departs. One way to build a CBI business is to negotiate an even higher guaranteed commission from a government—for example, an additional $10,000 for each approved file—in exchange for a minimum number of submissions each year. The firm might keep $5,000 for itself while topping up the commission to a feeder by $5,000, adding an incentive to insert a new link in the supply chain—though at a loss of funds that might otherwise be kept in the country. Still everything keeps flowing as fees from clients move up the chain and commissions from governments move down it.

If each link in the chain brings additional costs, why wouldn't individuals do the application themselves and take it straight to the government—or else, if needed, find their own courier to drop it off? Trust and poor information are the mundane answers to this conundrum of globalization. How does one know what the government is looking for when assessing the application, especially if the bureaucratic systems are different? What are the best investment options in an unfamiliar market? And what does one do if there is a problem? Investors reveal much personal and business information on the application files, which can leave them wary about going to an unknown agent half the world away in the CBI country. Often a word-of-mouth recommendation closer to home is the chosen route. They will also need advice they can trust to guide their investment strategy in an unknown business or property. The fees that agents charge are costly, but people are willing to pay because "we supply a lot of convenience and security," explained one in Shanghai. It's not always easy to know how things operate in a different part of the world. Agents save time and effort, always in short supply, and offer the assurance that everything will go well. The borders that investors seek to cross and that fuel the citizenship industry, are also the ones that separate systems, which are not always easy to bridge.

There are exceptions to the extended supply chains as well. Global law firms and Big Four accountancies are an example. Their in-house legal teams stand on the lookout for conflicts of interest that can emerge when, for example, a company is making money off real estate in two directions. Some firms specializing in investor citizenship prefer to leave out as many intermediaries as possible. "Keeping things in-house is less risky," one agent explained to me. The largest firms taking this route can have multiple subcompanies and interlocking boards that enable them to provide "integrated services." These package deals supply everything a client might need from under the same umbrella. This can include the qualifying real estate properties, financial services for setting up the investment, health and life insurance for the frequent traveler, and even aftercare, including property management or passport renewals. Those offering a full concierge service may help with opening bank accounts and moving businesses and other assets into the country. "When a client signs up, they're not forced into the package, but it's there if they want it," a service provider in Hong Kong explained. But if it becomes more lucrative to subcontract some elements, the logic of profit maximization will usually win the day.

Power Plays between the Public and Private Sectors

The citizenship industry is powerful and lucrative, yet service providers do not hold all the cards. At the end of the day, governments determine who will become investor citizens. If bureaucrats are slow, lose documents, or don't respond to emails, agents may take their business elsewhere, but there is not much they can do to change decisions. States become reliant on the citizenship industry to both positive and negative effect. The result is a complex interplay between public and private that may be conflictual, is often codependent, and can even be collusive.

For service providers, close relationships with governments are a key selling point. They give the appearance, if not actual proof, that should anything go wrong, they can get into the bureaucratic black box and solve it. "Connections to a government," a service provider explained at a conference in Switzerland, "can give you a good sense of whether a file will go through or not." In Cyprus, a lawyer echoed the sentiment: "you need to be on the good side of the government." If there is a question about the documents submitted, they need to be able to pick up the phone and ask for clarification, she explained. An advisor at a major accountancy told me that they get to know the civil servants running the programs so that they can go straight to the government with questions: "'Is this the sort of profile you want to see?' And the government might say 'Go away and do this before I can say yes.'" Some service providers even put such links proudly on display. One of the grandest I came across was in Guangzhou, where an agent had covered his office walls with photos of him standing alongside the prime ministers and CIU heads in several countries. Some decorate their websites with such snaps, while others keep them in a file on their phone to bolster their credentials with potential clients.

Governments that want to compete for market share do not remain aloof from the industry that supplies them with buyers. Those hoping to develop their programs will hold consultation sessions with agents, lawyers, due diligence firms, and developers to gather input, which they may or may not take on board—sometimes to the private sector's chagrin. Some service providers come away with stories of the major reforms they influenced, while others offer a litany of complaints about ignored advice on topics that range from processing times to whether additional fees should be required for new children. "They take feedback and make their own decisions," described one accountant flatly.

A consultation session between the public and private is unlikely to raise eyebrows, but can these relationships become too close? Connections to high government officials can be of particular concern, especially if a service provider is able to go straight to the top—to a high-level politician or the prime minister—and get a "yes" where the standard vetting process would produce a "no." Such practices have been exposed in Cyprus, as we saw earlier, but that doesn't stop them from remaining a possibility elsewhere. Service providers may even blur the boundary between company and country entirely, as has happened in Vanuatu. There firms have effectively commandeered the state at times. Sometimes cooperation moves into collusion and then further corruption, as we will see in Chapter 8.

Rumors of favoritism are common, particularly if a single agent has a monopoly in running part or all of a program. In the first version of Malta's scheme, the concessionaire could not only file applications but vet them too, on top of handling the money coming through. Their office was even situated alongside the government, and Malta's head of state was also obliged—schedule permitting—to attend promotional events hosted by the concessionaire, raising queries among the public about just who was in control. The country's leading blogger posted leaked email exchanges between the two and railed at their buddy-buddy informality and casual first-name basis. By the time I visited Malta in 2018, the concessionaire was not involved in application processing or vetting and had moved its office to another part of town. The questions raised about the close relationship between the public and private were hardly worth the political risk, and the government distanced itself from the private sector. When the program reached its cap and Malta launched a new iteration, it did away with the role entirely. The word was now out about the program, and the government had acquired substantial experience of its own: there was no clear need for a concessionaire.

There can be infrastructural issues as well. Microstates may not have the wherewithal to carry out many international activities on their own, and specialized private firms might be better positioned, or better resourced, to do so. "How can a little Caribbean island know what's going on in China?" a London-based service provider asked me rhetorically. Officials in microstates also recognize their limits when it comes to such assessments. A panel of CIU heads at a conference in Dubai laid out their concerns and dilemmas. The representative from Dominica explained, "I need you to vouch for clients," aiming his words at the service providers in the room. "If I'm not clear on an application, I talk to the agent, and sometimes I decide based on the agent's word. I'm in Dominica and you are in Dubai and know the client. You need to be able to tell me whether it's a good applicant or not." The representative from Saint Kitts continued, describing what's at stake for the microstates: "We are under pressure from international partners and banks—under pressure to prove where the funds are coming from." Therefore, he stressed, "It's important for agents to know and assess the source of funds before it gets to us," noting that their work eases the burden on the state. Yet governing the entire length of the supply chain presents difficulties, as the representative from Saint Lucia acknowledged. "We have access only to the agents who are the face of the applicant," meaning those in the country who submit the application. "But how can we control the international ones?"

The question he raised is crucial. The country borders that produce supply and demand also produce barriers to keeping the supply chain in line. Borders enclose not only states but also jurisdictions, and this limits a government's legal reach for regulating the industry. Allowing only licensed service providers to submit applications is one option—especially if those who break the rules lose accreditation—but that works only in the state's backyard. One way to extend the pressure is to require agents to submit their own due diligence reports, as some countries have done. The point is not to substitute for the government's screening, which is carried out anyway, but to shake the supply chain into ensuring that only strong cases are submitted. In 2017, Saint Kitts began registering not only the local agents but also the international ones, demanding due diligence reports on all the companies involved before they can be approved. "We want to know who is marketing our product, their AML [anti–money laundering checks], their KYC [know-your-client checks], and who their subagents are," the head of the CIU declared. Four years later, he told me that the initiative had worked better than expected: they had a blacklist on the government website, naming and shaming about a dozen agents abroad whom they had banned for violating rules. Complete control is impossible, he explained, but this was a start. Still, the chain's transnational nature makes regulation hard to enforce. How would an official know if a banned service provider halfway around the world changed their company name and started up again? The borders between countries can be convenient and profitable for bad apples too.

Chronic limited resources can send microstates into the arms of service providers. With populations smaller than that of some multinational companies—and far less in capitalization—they may lack the capacity to carry out some standard state functions. One worker at a due diligence company described his job as akin to serving as the country's de facto FBI or Department of Homeland Security. "They just don't have the infrastructure." When he met the prime minister for the first time, he was taken aback: "The country is the size of my little town, but without the resources." In his view, it is the private sector and international actors that are critical for getting small places up to standard. If a country is the size of a city, even locals can wonder if they have it in them to deal with a wealthy and powerful clientele. One Caribbean woman who had just joined a CIU from an international job in finance doubted the skills of her compatriots. "They're not going to know how to handle these people," she said flatly, predicting that application assessment would end up a slow mess. "They won't be able to keep up with cases like these." Especially when programs are new, the private sector may know what it takes to run a scheme better than the government.

Even funding can be a challenge. A former CIU worker I spoke with expressed his frustration that the unit didn't have a viable operating budget, which left them reliant on the private sector for promotion activities. If they want to compete in the market and champion the program on the conference circuit, he told me, service providers must pick up the bill: there are no separate government funds for it. Prime ministers, too, can end up traveling abroad on an agent's dime. They might spin these overseas gigs into further business and governmental meetings, piggybacking off the CBI trip to stump for other sorts of investment or further diplomatic relations. A popular option is to negotiate greater visa-free access in the region they're visiting in order to boost their country's position in the passport rankings. Still, the situation is one that can easily raise eyebrows. Why are officials being flown about on a private company's tab?

Sometimes it's private actors that are most effective at getting governments in line when things go wrong. When Saint Kitts lost visa-free access to Canada, as we saw in Chapter 2, it was an international due diligence firm that cleaned up and redesigned the program while a Big Four accountancy carried out an audit. It's not a role a foreign government could play, and the stables were too Augean to rely on locals in a place where everyone knows everyone. Private actors have also been intimately involved in regional coordination efforts. How else to get a handful of competing states to sit down and cooperate? It was again a due diligence firm that was able to bring the Caribbean countries to the table to form a regional organization that would put together standards, develop a regulatory framework, and share best practices. This is not always easy. Once the firm stepped aside from its role as umpire and overseer, in-fighting and competition among the countries took over, and within a few years the organization was defunct.

On occasion, governments have turned down overtures from service providers, preferring to go it on their own. Cyprus is the most prominent case, where foreign firms tried to woo the state and create a concessionaire position, which it flatly rejected. Montenegro, when approached in a similar manner, decided to appoint not a single concessionaire but a consortium of three to help get the program going. Antigua, after allowing a foreign firm to come in and design their program, backed off from creating a concessionaire position and assumed the role itself. Copying the private sector's promotional techniques, it established a marketing budget for the program—the first in the Caribbean—and approached the huge Chinese market directly. It even launched a CBI magazine and hosted its own conference in Dubai. "[One of the dominant consultancies] said we wouldn't be able to do it, but we pulled it off," cheered a civil servant at the end of the event. Breaking the contract and taking the program in-house, however, came at a $4 million cost—a sizeable burden for a small government. Where a concessionaire position is fixed, some countries have maneuvered around it rather than risk such fines. Saint Kitts, for example, developed a way to channel funds into ear-marked government projects without going through the donation option. The bypass comes at significant savings to the country, which is contracted to turn over 10 percent of the donation money to the concessionaire. Sometimes a creative government can reclaim the upper hand.

Making Markets, Making Money

There would be no CBI market without the citizenship industry: it generates and implements supply, crafts and channels demand, and connects the two sides, enabling the market to run. For these businesses, state borders are opportunities. This is clear in the industry's most basic function, namely to translate between two bureaucratic systems. In putting together a file, agents ensure that the documentary evidence produced in one country is sufficient and legible to bureaucrats in another.

But there is far more to it. Borders also lengthen the supply chain and multiply the actors involved. It's often a challenge for local service providers to reach across jurisdictions and get a solid grasp of how things operate elsewhere—whether it's a medium-sized agent in China seeking out programs or a small law firm in Malta looking for files to submit. These information asymmetries create business opportunities for service providers, who capitalize on differences between national systems to sell their services to both clients and other businesses. Specialization, too, can extend the supply chain yet further, as service providers carve out profitable market niches. The front-facing business that meets the client may be a mere project manager that links with other firms to complete the naturalization journey. There are, of course, exceptions, particularly on the boutique side of the market where a single firm may handle everything, yet it's often the larger players that are best equipped to connect the two ends. The result is that naturalizers typically join their new country via a complex web of citizenship industry agents that is at least two, if not three or four, levels thick, even if most of it remains invisible at the surface.

For buyers, the network produces convenience. It helps with the hassle of paperwork and application assembly, but it does more. A service provider may offer a package deal that simplifies complicated business decisions and clears bureaucratic hurdles in a country where the investor is unlikely to know the scene. Buyers usually prefer agents close to them, whom they can trust, for a large amount of personal and business information is exposed on a citizenship application. Yet if something goes wrong on the ground in the CBI country, they also need someone there who can follow up. The resulting chain can be extended still further if a service provider outsources application assembly, investment maintenance, or other tasks. Even if the client must pay for every link in the chain, few will decline the convenience it supplies. For the client, the industry resolves conundrums of trust, information asymmetries, and control that emerge in cross-border mobility.

Keeping all the parts moving are commissions, and hefty ones at that, which are extracted from both the supply and the demand sides of the market. In the first instance, these are taken from client fees and then parceled out along the supply chain. But they can also be culled from governments that try to gain market share in a competitive environment by offering commissions. Their overall impact depends on the balance between applications and investment amounts. In some cases, it may be money well spent by the government, securing higher numbers of applicants. But tipped in the wrong direction, the lucrative nature of the citizenship business can also eat into the economic benefits for the country.

If there are clear reasons for the extended supply chains—trust, convenience, and a lack of information—there are clear consequences as well. The first is an increase in costs from both sides: fees from the clients and commissions from the governments.[11] The second consequence is the challenge posed for regulation. The country borders that the investors hope to cross and that the service providers profit from are the same borders that present great hindrances to keeping everything in line. They enclose both states and jurisdictions, thereby circumscribing a state's reach. As such, countries are limited in what they can do, and regulation ends up partial and indirect, relying on pressure feeding down the supply chain.

What does this all mean for the relationship between public and private actors in the citizenship business? Migration industries can be found alongside nearly all forms of international mobility, and CBI programs are no exception. In some cases, the relationship is symbiotic, hinging on a division of labor and third-party oversight in which the private sector is crucial, as we saw earlier. In others, the private sector is paramount as service providers substitute for limited state capacity. Due diligence companies stand in the place of law enforcement, agents lobby foreign governments for visa-free access, and standards boards do what they can to win the PR war over what in some countries is a main revenue source. Some private actors—due diligence firms and regulatory boards in particular—may also be well positioned to intervene and get governments in line when things go wrong.

The upshot is a co-dependent relationship between the public and private spheres. The partnership can function well in some areas, making for stronger program structures, but it can undermine them, too.[12] Conflicts of interest can emerge if a state becomes too reliant on private actors, and the division of labor is not clearly maintained. The large financial flows running through the programs can make it easy for a business to offer a politician a cut of the pie, compromising integrity at best, fueling corruption at worst. The twinned relationship is one that needs to be monitored.

In the end, who is in control? The answer depends on the case—and in some instances, such as Vanuatu, it's been unclear just where the government ends and the private sector begins. Many states do not so easily bend to the industry's will. Governments can nullify public tenders, delay in getting a program off the ground, get rid of concessionaires, slow application assessment, and ignore the industry's entreaties to start programs in the first place. However, limited state capacity can give service providers the upper hand elsewhere, and the politics of borders can work in their favor. A state may have sovereign control—to a greater or lesser degree—over what goes on within its territory, but outside it is another story. Name-and-shame blacklists for companies abroad and revoking licenses of companies at home are unlikely to end all bad practices. Businesses can play the geographic limits of state control to their own advantage. If a service provider halfway around the world produces misinformation, facilitates financing even when it is banned, or violates a code of conduct, there's not much that a state can do to hold it to account. Most countries, however, find it hard to compete without working with the citizenship industry. What do they gain in the end? If the business of citizenship is profitable for the private sector, is it for states as well?

Chapter 7

Do the Programs Pay Off?

W HAT DOES IT take to become an investor citizen? Moldova's now-defunct program offers one example. People looking to naturalize could purchase a property in a housing complex, run by a German company, called the "Heart of Europe." However, the real estate development wasn't actually in Moldova, or even Europe for that matter. It was in Dubai, or just off the coast of it on a series of manmade islands designed to evoke an image of Europe when viewed from an airplane.[1] The project is a part of the World Islands, started in 2008 as a second-home area for the Dubai-based elite—something like what the Hamptons are to Manhattan, except with "the world" on offer.

Even within a rather fantastical floating reproduction of the planet crafted out of artificial sand bars in the Persian Gulf, the Heart of Europe's take on the continent is imaginative. Sweden Island is to be covered with exotic jungles that surround beach palaces designed to look like Viking boats. The Germany Island, by contrast, provides the elegant austerity of Bauhaus-style mansions. For those who find life on land passé, the Floating Seahorse Villas offer a "signature edition" opportunity to subsist underwater, with windows looking out to engineered coral reefs and marine life.

Yet even with such once-in a-lifetime opportunities on the block, sales of the seahorse villas and Viking boats were up and down for many years. At one point, the company was offering free yachts to lure buyers across four kilometers of Persian Gulf to the new and improved World. And then a solution appeared: the Heart of Europe became a qualifying investment project under Moldova's CBI program. According to the company's chairman, the phones were "ringing all the time" once they started promoting the offer.[2] Buy a jungle-surrounded Viking ship palace and become a citizen of Moldova. Sounds even better than a free boat.

The Heart of Europe's special offer didn't last long; the company dropped the option after less than a year. Moldova, too, closed its program shortly after opening. It is easy to wonder if CBI programs, touted as economic panaceas for struggling countries, bring the benefits promised. In some cases they do, I found, but not in all. In fact, a lot can happen on the ground to enhance or mute the benefits. To fully assess the economic outcomes requires looking at how the programs work in practice.

The Macroeconomic Picture

In citizenship by investment, a lot is at stake, for the potential economic impact of the programs is substantial for microstates. The most common way to calculate revenue is by multiplying the minimum investment amount by application approvals. Though a rough-and-ready estimate, it still gestures at the magnitude.[3] Globally, the market saw a turnover of approximately $4 billion in 2019, before the Covid-19 pandemic disrupted application numbers (Figure 7.1).

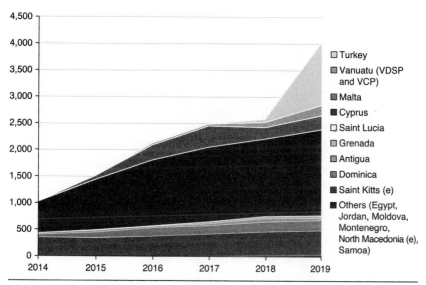

FIGURE 7.1. CBI donation and investment revenue (in millions USD)

Note: (e) indicates estimates based on statements by government representatives

Data source: InvestMig database

A glance across the global scene shows that the Caribbean and EU microstates account for the bulk of the proceeds. Cyprus, with its high minimum investment amount of €2.5 million, dwarfed its competitors in revenue accrued, even though it maintained significantly lower naturalization numbers—typically no more than 600 applications approved annually—than the powerhouse countries in the Caribbean. These small islands can approve thousands of applications each year, but their lower price reduces their economic take. Vanuatu in the Pacific also has enough turnover to appear in global figures and compete with Caribbean counterparts. Yet all have been dwarfed by Turkey's sudden rise since 2018. Its huge approval numbers, even at a relatively low minimum investment amount of $250,000, raised in 2022 to $400,000, are enough to make it a competitor with Cyprus in overall revenue intake. Since Cyprus froze its scheme in 2020, Turkey has become the clear leader.

The other programs—Montenegro, Samoa, Egypt, and the like—are so small, both in approval numbers and investment generated, that they do little to shift the needle globally. Approval figures for Pakistan, Mauritius, and Romania are unavailable, but my investigations suggest that they have few to no investor citizens. Including Cambodia may add more to the global total, but approvals are uneven—ranging from none to a few dozen to a few hundred each year—and accurate data are unavailable.[4] Adding these cases does little to change the global picture. Accordingly, the focus here is on the schemes that are large enough to register an impact: Cyprus, Turkey, Malta, Saint Kitts, Dominica, and Vanuatu, while bringing along a few of the smaller Caribbean vendors, where the economic injections can make a difference to the country.

Even as a proportion of GDP, itself a very wide-scale view of an economy, the annual revenue from the programs can be huge (Figure 7.2). Over its five-year course, Malta's first CBI scheme brought in more than €1.4 billion to the country, accounting for around 2.1 percent of GDP. Between 2017 and 2019, citizenship was the country's third largest export, behind petroleum and technology, attracting nearly €300 million each year. With a state donation constituting the bulk of the investment, the sizeable intake enabled the government in 2016 to post its first budget surplus since the 1980s.[5] The IMF even praised the scheme as one of the key drivers of economic growth and the reduction of national debt, fueling a Mediterranean tiger economy.[6]

In Cyprus, the intake of its more costly scheme was even greater, amounting to a sizeable 4.5 percent of GDP. Netting a massive €1.4 billion annually before the Covid pandemic, citizenship could be considered the country's top export, far outstripping the closest contender, petroleum, at a mere

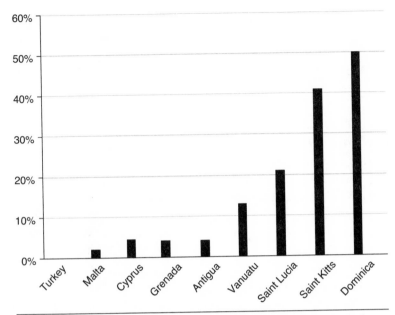

FIGURE 7.2. CBI donations and investments as a proportion of GDP (2017 to 2019 average)

Data source: InvestMig database

€570 million. This moneymaker has even been credited with rescuing the country's real estate and construction sector—17 percent of its economy— after the 2008 financial crisis.[7]

We also see that for a country with a sizeable economy like Turkey's, even approving hundreds of applications per month, as it did in 2019, leaves no impression on the macroeconomic picture. A finer-grained analysis may reveal economic significance in specific domains, especially local real estate markets in Istanbul and Izmir. Still, CBI programs, typically small, don't pack the same punch in a big state. Turkey would need to approve about 50,000 applications per year (over new 150,000 investor citizens, including family members) if it were to see an impact on its GDP to rival Cyprus. It's in microstates where citizenship by investment can change the economic picture significantly.

In the Caribbean countries and Vanuatu, the macroeconomic numbers soar through the roof. On the lower end are Antigua and Grenada, which collect around 5 percent of GDP through their programs. Even if it takes a mere

$100,000 to qualify and they approve only a few hundred files each year, that is enough to make a remarkable difference. Elsewhere the numbers climb even higher. Vanuatu draws in over 10 percent and Saint Lucia over 20 percent of its GDP from the programs. Yet they are no match for Dominica and Saint Kitts, where citizenship sales account for a whopping 40 to 50 percent of GDP. According to the IMF, the positive impact of citizenship by investment on Saint Kitts has been substantial, with the program enabling the microstate to emerge from a deep recession. In 2010, its debt-to-GDP ratio was nearly 160 percent, and two years later it was close to defaulting, but by 2016 it had brought its debt-to-GDP ratio down to an enviable 68 percent.[8] Notably, both Dominica and Saint Kitts are on the small side of microstates, with only 72,000 and 55,000 inhabitants, respectively. Though their options are comparatively cheap, the governments approve thousands of applications each year, driving the numbers skyward. In these two countries, citizenship is the number one export.

Even the government receipts from citizenship by investment amount to a significant proportion of state revenue in the Caribbean and Vanuatu (Figure 7.3). In Antigua's smaller program, the effect is more muted, yet the revenue the government gains from CBI equals about 20 percent of its tax

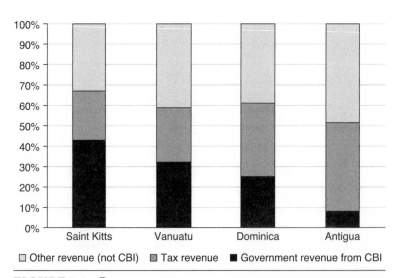

FIGURE 7.3. Government revenue sources

Note: CBI revenue is calculated based on the line item given in the government budget report.

Data source: InvestMig database

intake. In Dominica, the proportion is still higher, with CBI revenue alone equating to 70 percent of tax receipts and over 25 percent of the government's entire revenue. In Saint Kitts and Vanuatu, it is greater still, with governments collecting more in CBI revenue than they do in taxes. Indeed, in Saint Kitts, it amounts to nearly half of all government receipts. The state could not run without it.

Relying heavily on the investor citizenship programs for government revenue, however, brings some risks. After all, much of what investor migrants seek lies in the benefits that citizenship secures outside the granting state—a situation over which it has little control. When Canada revoked visa-free access from Saint Kitts and Antigua, sales declined in both countries. The IMF monitors the programs when it assesses countries holding loans and consistently raises the possibility of economic destabilization if the programs are not carefully managed. There could be "sudden stop" effects should the inflow suddenly dry up. In places where the programs account for a substantial portion of GDP, the economic reverberations would be great. Such vulnerabilities are common in microstates, where diversification and economies of scale are nearly impossible. Many of the islands are already heavily dependent on tourism and subject to hurricanes and the vagaries of climate change. At the same time, well-managed programs, the IMF notes, can enable states to build up needed fiscal buffers, reduce debt, and stimulate growth.[9] As a local developer I spoke with in the Caribbean put it plainly, "This is a way for us to bring capital into our own economies." Without it, "What else is there for locals? Emigration?"

Offshore Worlds

It doesn't take a sharp eye to notice that all of the classic CBI countries are former British colonies with an offshore financial services sector. There are good reasons for this, but they are not as straightforward as one might think. Partly it is due to the nature of British decolonization. Unlike the French and Dutch, the British encouraged many of their smallest colonies not to remain dependencies but to become fully independent—and, crucially, to cut ties to the public purse.[10] To help them along, the former rulers also supported the development of offshore financial sectors, sometimes complementing the services offered by the City of London. The legacy of common law and its useful devices, such as "intent" or "domicile," which allow legal persons to be present and not-present, proved advantageous as well.[11] Tax isn't so much about where one is, but where one isn't. Offshore centers permit people and corporations to hang a plaque that enables them to circumvent regulations and obligations where their actual business takes place.

Notably, the distinction between an "offshore center" and a "financial center" is often a political one. The term *offshore* usually conjures an image of tropical islands of ill repute that serve as a luxurious home for tax evaders. *Financial center*, on the other hand, more readily brings to mind the skyscrapers of Manhattan and the hum of London. The reality, though, is more complex. Some of the biggest offshore financial hubs, like the City of London, the state of Delaware, and the canton of Zug, are in major wealthy countries.[12] Furthermore, offshore is not tangential to global capital but central to it.[13] Every major multinational corporation makes use of offshore structures, and virtually all very wealthy people employ similar provisions to protect their assets. As one expert in the field estimated for me, "There's no one with more than $10 million who isn't 'structured'"—that is, employing offshore possibilities to protect their wealth. Furthermore, the vast majority of the tools and mechanisms they use are perfectly legal. Indeed, their legality is precisely what makes them desirable because it gives their wealth the protection of law. As one lawyer put it to me, "Big players want serious regulations and rules." It's just too risky not to have recourse to courts.

However, the connection between offshoring and citizenship by investment isn't automatic. For those looking to "structure their wealth," virtually everything is possible without picking up membership in a microstate. If there were clear advantages, demand for citizenship by investment would be far higher—and there would be many more wealthy Americans and Europeans making use of the options. Instead, service providers supply the link between the CBI offering and the offshore sectors: they are the ones connected to wealthy individuals who may be interested in expanding their citizenship options.

A CBI program can turn into further financial benefits, if of a trickle-down sort, going into a country's financial services industry or other areas. The ideal investor for most governments is one who doesn't stop at the initial injection to qualify for the program but moves some of their business and financial interests to the country and even spends a bit of time—and additional money—there as well. These moves don't do much to stimulate the productive capacity of the countries, but for a microstate, the service sector may be a more promising way forward than volatile sectors like agriculture or manufacturing in which a tiny island is unlikely to achieve the needed economies of scale to compete.

Particularly in Turkey, Malta, and Cyprus, agents described clients shifting financial structures or businesses into the countries after gaining citizenship. They might set up a parallel family office to manage their wealth or move some of their portfolios to the country, lending a boost to the banking, insurance, and financial sectors. A service provider at a Big Four accountancy in Malta said that most of their clients spend more than two weeks on the island and about half end up extending their investments into other areas or making use of other services within the financial industry. As a Cypriot lawyer related, the CBI program helps bring people, and once they have a hold on them, it's important not to let go. "We're talking about very wealthy people, very successful people. We need to keep them in so that they keep doing more for Cyprus." Do the business interests in the country encourage people into the citizenship program, or is it the other way around? "Who is to say?" a financial advisor at a Big Four accountancy responded rhetorically, "It's more or less a package."

In the Caribbean and Pacific, however, the secondary impact is smaller. Investor citizens are less likely to visit or ever set foot in the country and are less likely to move other business interests into and through it. Financial services are available, but people shifting large sums typically want the reassurance that the institutions and legal provisions involved are solid. They want to trust the bank, and with the delays the countries have faced with correspondent banks, discussed in Chapter 2, other offshore centers are simply more appealing. In some ways, a body of naturalized citizens who remain at a distance is convenient. Outside the country, they don't become a flashpoint of xenophobic or class conflict in the way that immigrants might. At the same time, their contributions remain largely one-off injections, and further connections often never appear. Several countries would like to see this change, shifting the relationship to one that invites a more continuous revenue stream. "The truth is, less than one percent actually come to the island and spend time. We want to turn our citizens into tourists," the head of one Citizenship Investment Unit told me.

The goal of "turning citizens into tourists" is on the agenda of many bureaucrats who wish to get more out of their new members. But it's not easy. Some consider sending annual Christmas cards on the off chance that when the next hurricane comes through, a wealthy long-distance citizen will donate to relief funds. Representatives from Saint Kitts, Grenada, and Antigua issue open invitations to their investors, hoping they will visit the place with open wallets. "We want to see them create some businesses and put more into the island," the head of a CIU explained. Malta has seen some success on this score, with Valletta becoming a touchdown spot for globally mobile elites. In 2016, the city had virtually no boutique hotels, but by 2021 it offered over forty. Between 2020 and 2021, it gained five Michelin-starred restaurants, though before 2020 it had none. As a Maltese financial expert explained, the CBI program "put Malta on the map of very wealthy people." The Caribbean countries and Vanuatu, smaller and more disconnected, find it harder to make the sell. How does one run an international business, parent children in top-notch schools, and stay connected to friends and family from a remote island? As one Caribbean bureaucrat put it to me dryly, "Do you think rich people want to come and live here? Even the locals don't want to live here," referring to the large emigration numbers. "We're too small to sustain much." It may be easy to create investor citizens, but it's harder to keep them.

Investment Choices

Instead, countries rely on the qualifying investment to bring in funds and offer would-be citizens a range of possibilities. Real estate purchases, government donations, and business investments are the most common, followed by bank deposits and government bonds (Table 7.1).

In most cases, a single investment suffices, but some countries require a combination. In 2019, for example, Cyprus mandated that its investor citizens put at least €2 million into real estate, businesses, or investment funds, donate €75,000 to support research and innovation and €75,000 to social housing projects, *and* purchase a residence worth at least €500,000. Malta's first program required a €650,000 contribution to the state, an investment of €150,000, and the purchase or rental of a private property. Countries, too, can tweak the combination. Antigua, for example, added an option for donating to its local branch of the University of the West Indies in 2020, while Saint Lucia included a government bond option in 2017, removed in 2022. Cyprus permitted bank deposits from 2011 to 2015. Such alterations may seem to enable the economic contributions to be channeled into the sectors of the economy with the most need, but often they don't, for if given a choice, investors gravitate to government donations or real estate purchases (Figure 7.4).

There is also some variation in selection. In Cyprus, where a government donation was not an option and the economy is more substantial than elsewhere, real estate was the most popular pick, accounting for 40 percent of cases. Business investments were a close second at 30 percent. In the Caribbean,

TABLE 7.1. Minimum investment amounts and types of investment options

Country	Total minimum investment or donation (single applicant)	Investment or donation types
Antigua	$100,000	GD, RE, B, O
Dominica	$100,000	GD, RE
Grenada	$150,000	GD, RE
Saint Kitts	$150,000	GD, RE
Saint Lucia	$100,000	GD, RE, B, GB
Cyprus (2020)	€2,650,000	Required combination: GD, RE Selected: RE, B, SF
Malta (MEIN)	€740,000	Required combination: GD, RE, O
Moldova (2020)	€100,000	GD
Montenegro	€350,000	Required: GD Selected: RE
North Macedonia	€200,000	GD, RE
Romania	€1,000,000	UI
Russia	$1,360,000	B, O
Egypt	$250,000	GD, RE, B, BD
Jordan	$750,000	B, GB, BD, SF
Turkey	$250,000	RE, B, GB, BD, O
Comoros (2018)	$45,000	GD
Mauritius	$500,000	UI
Seychelles	$1,000,000	UI
Pakistan	$25,000	BD
Cambodia	$250,000	GD, UI
Samoa	$1,500,000	B
Vanuatu (VDSP or VCP)	$130,000	GD, RE

Note: Government donation (GD), real estate (RE), business (B), government bond (GB), bank deposit (BD), unspecified investment (UI), stocks and funds (SF), other (O). The amounts and types are from 2022 unless otherwise noted. Russia requires an investment of 100 million rubles; this was converted to USD using the 2021 average exchange rate.

however, government donations have been extremely popular. Over half of the investors in Grenada and nearly 80 percent in Antigua have made this choice. In Dominica, the results are more muddled. There investors are offered three choices. The first two are a straightforward government donation or real estate investment. The third straddles them. Applicants can invest in a social housing project aimed at rebuilding a village destroyed by a hurricane. Yet unlike most social housing developments, this one is run entirely

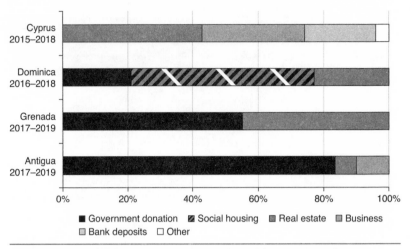

FIGURE 7.4. CBI investment option selected (proportion of main applicants)

Note: The graph includes only the optional component of the qualifying amounts. Therefore data for Cyprus does not include the required purchase of a minimum €500,000 residence or the loss of bank deposits in the 2013 haircut.

Data source: InvestMig database

by the private sector. From the point of view of both the investor and government, it resembles a real estate investment more than a government donation in its operation and financing. By this reading, Dominica also sees over 75 percent of investors choose real estate.

Those who select government donations generally regard the option as quick and easy, leaving them unencumbered by an asset they may not want. Real estate may be seen as a safe bet for diversifying assets and growing them through the broader global property market boom. It may also be the cheaper option—even if the sticker price is double the donation amount—for in many cases financing or guaranteed buy-back possibilities reduce the cost to investors. The viability of other alternatives, like starting a business, usually requires some familiarity with the local economic environment, and thus they are usually limited to a select few. Cyprus is the exception: the Russian community has had a foothold there and is more familiar with its business potential.

In certain countries, some investment types are not optional. In Cyprus and Malta, participants must make a specified array of contributions on top of a few chosen components (Figure 7.5). Malta's first program was the most rigid, requiring a €650,000 government donation, €150,000 in shares or funds, and

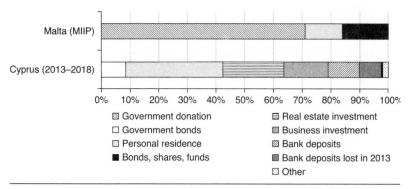

FIGURE 7.5. Proportion of revenue by investment type

Note: The numbers for Malta are based on the required investment combination, with real estate calculated based on the minimum rental and purchase amounts multiplied by the number of people selecting each option.

Data source: InvestMig database

a rental property of at least €16,000 per year for five years or a purchased personal property of at least €350,000. Renting rather than buying proved the more popular pick for 85 percent of participants in Malta. Cyprus required all investors to purchase a personal residence worth at least €500,000, in addition to mandatory donations to government programs. An additional €2 million could go into an investment option of choice, such as businesses, real estate, or funds.

Notable in the array is how little of the money went into saleable real estate, despite perennial concerns that the programs distort the housing market. In Cyprus, the property sector was the biggest beneficiary of its scheme, reaping about 55 percent of the revenue, but about 35 percent of this went into a personal residence that the investor citizen was required to hold in perpetuity—a momentary boost for the construction sector more than a transformation of the secondary housing market. Next door, a mere 15 percent of program revenue in Malta went into real estate, while the bulk went straight to the government.

Yet the real estate market is the prime beneficiary of most CBI programs, apart from the direct injections into state coffers. How this works depends on the way the program is structured. Turkey, since June 2022, requires that a qualifying property be worth at least $400,000, but it can be anything on the market. As long as an external evaluator confirms that it's worth what is put down, anything goes—from a private house to a hotel investment, from a new build to a resale. Cyprus operated along similar lines, but at a higher price. In these cases, the real estate sector is an open field.

Others, like Vanuatu, Montenegro, and the Caribbean countries, take a more focused approach and channel money into specific projects, usually in new tourism infrastructure. Some keep the range tightly drawn, such as Montenegro, which provides only three options: a ski resort, a coastal resort, or a spa area. Others approve all and sundry. Antigua has about forty real estate investment options on offer, and the buyer is left to select the most viable. Saint Kitts has over one hundred. Choosing from the list, investors typically acquire a time-share or rental unit, such as a resort condo or a hotel room. They may be able to stay there a certain number of days each year, but otherwise the property is rented out to tourists, usually with a small commission for the investor.

For the developers, the funds serve as a low-cost bridging loan that covers expenses during key points of the construction. Usually resort projects are built in phases, and the company raises funds or takes out loans to cover each step rather than footing the whole bill up front. However, the 2008 financial crisis wiped out the capital markets in the Caribbean and Cyprus, making it difficult for developers to secure loans for their piecemeal work. Without the crucial reserve supplied by citizenship by investment, people in the Cypriot and Caribbean real estate industries explained to me, it would be impossible for them to keep their projects going.

What does this mean for locals? A number of commentators have sounded the alarm at the potential for investment migration programs to price locals out of housing.[14] However, the reality may not be so dire.[15] Antigua, for example, has long zoned almost the entirety of its coastline for tourist developments. The result is a bifurcated real estate market that has relegated most locals to the center of the island. Few have beachfront residences, but they can still find affordable inland housing outside the holiday-home market. The same holds in Cyprus, where the impact on real estate has been concentrated mainly in a luxury segment along the coast with limited spillover effects on the wider real estate market.[16] Malta has seen only about 300 new rentals per year through the program, a tiny number even in a microstate. In Turkey, the huge investor citizenship numbers leave little mark within its sizeable real estate sector. Even if its estimated 12,000 new investor citizens each year purchase a home to qualify, this is still less than 1 percent of the 700,000 new homes built and over 1 million secondhand homes sold annually.[17] More fine-grained studies of each real estate market are needed, ideally looking at neighborhood-level data and including local home ownership rates. Yet the general picture suggests that it may be premature to sound the alarm bells regarding local housing costs.[18]

Evaluating the Investments

Do these investments provide an economic boost that justifies the programs? Because the preponderance of funds goes either into real estate or to the government, assessment can focus on these two domains. A full analysis would require peering into the economic structures of nine countries, an in-depth undertaking not attempted here. However, understanding how the programs operate on the ground offers a solid starting point for evaluating their purported economic benefits.

In terms of positive economic impact, some real estate cases stand out. Perhaps the best example is found in an ecotourism resort on Dominica. The holiday destination is a self-described labor of love by a local developer who made it big abroad in finance. When the country was forced to abandon banana exports, its economic mainstay, the prime minister approached him about developing a project back home. The nudge provided the opportunity to pursue a long-harbored "crazy fantasy," as he put it, of developing an ecotourism getaway: something that combined sustainable development with community building. If he was convinced of the value of the project, the banks were not. The idyllic location in the country's undeveloped north was simply too remote, so he turned to citizenship by investment for a bridging loan to get the project started. Construction began in 2000, and five years later, the resort was open for business. And to great success. Travelers rated it among the top resorts in the region on Tripadvisor, Forbes named it among the top ten best luxury eco-resorts, and Condé Nast Traveler Magazine granted it the World Saver Award for poverty reduction by a small resort.

Driving the project was the principle that, where possible, everything would be locally sourced in an environmentally sustainable manner that developed local communities. The resort workers, including those in managerial positions, are almost all from the island. Yet the multiplier effects are far more important, the developer told me. The resort secures its foodstuffs from local farmers and fishers, supporting forty agricultural families. It runs a local literacy initiative, several entrepreneurship programs, a facility to care for severely disabled children, and a scholarship fund for secondary education, in addition to training local farmers in organic food production and providing piped water to underserved areas. The list of interventions and local initiatives goes far beyond the standard corporate social responsibility box-ticking.

When I met the developer in 2015, however, it was all gone: the resort had just been wiped out by a hurricane. Yet he wasn't ready to close up shop and was already working on plans for fifty eco-villas on a new site. Again, citizenship by investment was the best option he had for funding it, he told me. The properties would be sold as freeholds for $200,000, which are then leased back to the resort. The investor receives 50 percent of the profits, plus citizenship. "CBI is a tool," he explained, taking stock of the scene. "I don't have negative feelings about it. . . . From a nation-building standpoint, it's good." He went on to clarify that any property development needs to be "bankable"—that is commercially viable on an open market—for it to really work. "But in reality, this isn't always the case." It can still be challenging to get loans, he said, and even with a record of successes and awards, CBI money has remained a key source of funding.

The Dominican eco-resort above is not the only award-winning holiday spot to have been completed on the CBI dime. One in Saint Kitts even made Condé Nast's list of the Best New Hotels in the World—and given its location, perched on the very end of the island's long peninsula, it feels as though it's at the end of it. Until a few years ago, only a dirt and gravel road with several precarious hairpin turns linked the largely untouched peninsula to the rest of the island, but new resort developments have vastly improved the connection to the area. Not all the projects are in top shape, and several boondoggles litter the scene, but the latest hotel has proved a success. Keeping the place going are four hundred employees, over 90 percent of whom are local. When I met the co-owners, they spoke of their investment in skills training for new hires, which they saw as crucial for developing the country. They lamented that the island's agricultural systems weren't geared for restaurant production—at least not yet—and hoped to develop local sourcing. Though their project was complete, the CBI opportunity was too good to let rest. When we spoke, they had another hotel in the works, this one on a different island and also funded through citizenship sales.

Another notable case is the marina area in Cyprus's Limassol. A combination of public boardwalk, shops, harbor, and housing, the area has become a hub for both locals and tourists, with an estimated 4,000 people visiting daily.[19] Beyond the public parks, cafes, and promenades are the upscale housing units sold to investor citizens. "It's a marina and it's also property, so you can park your yacht in front of your house," as one lawyer pitched the project to me. The idea was to capture not only the investment money but also the secondary benefits of retail sales from investors who shopped, ate in local restaurants, played golf, stored their yachts, and made use of the barrage of financial services offered. They may not spend the whole year in Cyprus, but they might be lured into spending enough time there to qualify for generous tax provisions, producing trickle-down effects for financial advisors as well. And many actually do come. In contrast to the Caribbean, where very few investor citizens have made much of a footprint, let alone set foot, Cyprus, and in particular Limassol, has become a touchdown spot for many of its new members, particularly Russians.

The broader impact of the CBI program in Cyprus is striking. In the early 2000s, the British were the main foreign buyers of property and drove a bubbling market. By 2006, more foreigners than locals were acquiring real estate (Figure 7.6).[20] The 2008 economic crisis ended British demand, leaving developers with half-built projects, no sales, and no new loans.[21] Citizenship by investment, stepping into the breach, fueled the return of the real estate and construction sector by supplying a much-needed stream of funds.[22] Even in 2018, when I visited the island, most people told me that without the program, the construction industry would still be hurting. However, it wasn't producing the same imbalance seen before the global economic crisis. By 2019, the

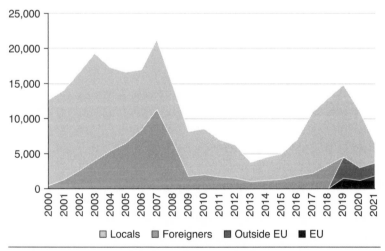

FIGURE 7.6. Total number of properties with registered contracts of sale in Cyprus

Data source: Cyprus Department of Land and Surveys

foreign proportion of property purchases had risen to 40 percent, but EU citizens—not the CBI market—accounted for over a third of them.[23] The CBI program was important, but it wasn't the whole story of a transforming market.

Still, how citizenship by investment is used for development has changed over time. In 2016, the Cypriot government relaxed regulations on building size, and soon builders started high-rise projects up and down the Limassol coast. Advertisements made the area look like a new Dubai, with designs that stood out of alignment with the low-slung buildings that defined most of the area. The new towers were funded by buyers making purchases "off-plan" during construction, and so developers needed a constant flow of new investments to finish. "It could be a disaster," an accountant at a Big Four agency told me at the time. The government is being optimistic, he said, but the situation "is fragile" since regular Cypriots have no means or desire to purchase such a property. A steady stream of foreign buyers would be needed to see a high-rise tower to completion. Two lawyers I spoke with said that they never advise clients to go for the towers, estimating that they'll lose half the investment because the market is saturated. "Just do the numbers," one said. The internal demand for such a building isn't there, and the CBI program may not be big enough to sustain them, they feared. The end of the program in 2020 left many developers stumbling. They have since revised their marketing strategies to attract capital through golden visas. Apartments once pitched as CBI properties have now been recast as a part of Cyprus's still-running RBI program.[24] For developers, the invasion of Ukraine was a godsend, with the exodus from Russia driving numbers skyward. So far, the patch seems to be working, but it certainly wasn't the initial plan, and local residents complain about the proliferation of high-rise eyesores as the building rolls on.

Deeper problems can emerge as well. Projects that are started but never completed are the most common. An early example from the Wild West scene of the 1990s can be found in Dominica's Shangri La Hotel. It was planned as the country's first five-star resort, a flagship venue that would lure high-spending tourists to the island. Funding was to come entirely from investors, who would receive citizenship in return. The program was managed by the country's honorary general consul in Hong Kong. The government held the controlling stake in the project, though the honorary consul owned a considerable portion as well—a good incentive to get the word out. Investors were coming in and citizenships were issued, yet building progress was remarkably slow, and people started wondering where the money was really going. Six years after the project started, it was still nowhere near completion when a flood wrecked the construction site and brought the whole thing to a halt. Over $100 million was reportedly lost in the fiasco that left the people of Dominica as 51 percent owners of a decaying heap that, over a decade later, was still the center of court battles.[25]

Dominica is not alone in project failures. Elsewhere governments have become major investors in qualifying projects that never finish—and may even bail them out—leaving the country with nothing to show from the program. In many cases, the private sector owns the whole site but never finishes building, leaving a form of "real estate blight" that mars the landscape. Even so, computer-generated images can continue to attract investors to the decaying skeletons. Such projects can linger for years as cash cows for insiders, both funders and politicians alike, just as long as they're never completed.

Other real estate projects are simply overpriced. One that I visited in the Caribbean was a buzzing construction site right on the water in a stunning location. Wandering around, I came across several dozen workers busily mixing cement and assembling prefabricated condo units. The progress was promising, but the economic benefits for the small island were unclear. The development company was based in China, the materials were imported from China with zero tariffs levied, and even the workers were from China. Rental units were going up, but their design was cramped and had the feel of a cheap motel in comparison to the spacious cottages with private gardens that dominated the area. One wondered if they were worth the minimum investment amount, yet eight had already been sold to individuals acquiring citizenship. In the end, the development was finished, but remains largely unused.

In concept, the real estate projects are to be in the country granting citizenship—how else would it benefit? But this is not always the case. The Sweet Homes project is one example. It enabled investors who purchase a property to qualify for citizenship in Antigua. But setting it apart was that the development was literally apart—not in Antigua, but in the United Arab Emirates. The plans for the massive complex were grand: advertisements showed a hospital, school, mosque, health club, hotel, and the requisite shopping mall. When ground was broken in 2007, the gated community was scheduled to finish in 2011, but when I visited in 2016, the site was a half-built, dusty skeleton, nowhere near completion. One official I spoke with said that the area wasn't slated to get electricity for another six years. It took a bit of geographic magic to arrange the deal as well. Legally, the qualifying investments for Antigua's program must be in Antigua, so the Antiguan cabinet passed a special motion extending the country's territorial reach. A stretch of sand in Ajman was to be "treated as if it were in Antigua and Barbuda."[26] Investors who found this a good deal would pay $400,000 for qualifying residence, but Antigua would see only half of it in a convoluted play that somehow didn't quite square the circle.

Even a country like Vanuatu that, until recently, didn't have a real estate option can fall victim to such problems. Rainbow City is one such example, where a developer managed to create a property possibility in a country that accepted only government donations—at least formally. Filling an expansive peninsula, the development is to be more than a holiday resort. It's a full-on city, with architectural plans showing schools, churches, hotels, medical centers, shopping areas, sports facilities, and an open-air theater. The set-up arrives on the island as prefabricated flat packs from China—or at least it was supposed to arrive in this way. When I was there in 2018, a few units had been put together, but most of the expansive site was still barren dust and brush, a far cry from the spectacular computer-generated images on the company's website. When I asked locals about the fenced-off fields and whether it was generating any employment, I just got headshakes. "We've become a dumping ground for rubbish. It's really not good, and it's not good for the future or for our children." Four years later, little had changed.

Such failures aren't unusual. Sustainable aquaculture, airports, yacht harbors, race courses, film production ventures, and more have all been pitched through CBI programs, then never finished—and sometimes they never even get off the ground. Saint Kitts's government website lists many approved real estate projects, but officials admit that only about five or six are really getting built. A ten-megawatt solar panel project for Antigua sounds like a promising foray into environmental sustainability. Yet after the first part was installed at the airport—at what some say was a substantial markup—the rest never came through. The supplier has been in and out of courts on fraud allegations, and the Antiguan government is contemplating a lawsuit against the company for nondelivery of over $4 million for the venture.[27] When the deal was first set up, the prime minister promised that the country would be on 30 percent green energy by 2020, and it would offer scholarships to all qualifying students to enable them to study abroad. All easily said, but nothing done.

If real estate investments can go either way in their benefits and risks, the same holds for government donations. These financial injections to state coffers can be a significant source of revenue, as we saw at the beginning of the chapter. But the economic upshot may not always be as promised. It can also be hard to trace the outcomes because the movement of donation revenue is often less visible than money going into flagship real estate projects. Sometimes the funding is well spent but unseen. If a country uses CBI capital to pay off IMF loans, as Antigua and Saint Kitts have done, the money is drained from the island, but it leaves the country in a stronger macroeconomic position. More difficult to assess are cases where the donations get rolled into the general government budget and mixed with other revenue sources, which makes it impossible to say with any accuracy how the revenue has been used. This happens in Vanuatu, where the department of finance, which controls the budget, decides how the revenue is spent. When I asked officials where the money went, I was told that much goes to pay the civil servants—a source of continuous complaint by locals—whose salaries and pensions are one of the biggest budget items.

Some governments earmark part or all of the revenue for special projects, as did Cyprus from 2019 when it required investors to put €75,000 into a research and innovation fund and a similar amount into a social housing fund. Such strategies can facilitate monitoring and ensure that the monies are employed in a targeted and productive way. Without such safeguards, the cash may become a slush fund for the party in power—an accusation often lobbed by opposition parties but one that raises real concerns. Alternatively, the money may just be poorly spent. The government in Saint Kitts, for example, used donations to bail out a failed project in 2010.[28] In such cases, those backing the project are saved while regular citizens are left with little to nothing.

Antigua offers some insights into how CBI income is spent. The government has used its program to make essential purchases, including medical supplies, power generation equipment, and books and broadband for schools, on top of providing support for local festivals, athletic events, and school boards. Yet some of the expenditures raise queries about prudence: $8,000 for a dinner, $50,000 for a dinghy championship, $150,000 for a chartered flight. The most interesting expense is the largest: pensions. In 2019, for example, 55 percent of the money disbursed—$6.3 million out of $11.4 million—went to pension payments.[29] Such expenditures have an important impact on local lives, wedding the CBI program to social care systems. But the choice leaves one wondering why the pension system—something designed to accumulate capital for future expense—doesn't have its own funds to cover these costs, and if it does, what is happening to them.

Given these promises and pitfalls, some countries have taken a page from the IMF's recommendations on how to handle windfall income and have established sovereign wealth funds. These, too, can create the appearance of money that has disappeared, though clearly it has not—the economic benefits simply remain unseen as they quietly move through the system. This has been the case in Malta, where a government donation of €650,000 constituted the bulk of the qualifying investment under the original program.[30] Of that, 30 percent was rolled into the government budget, which drove the government into the black in 2016 for the first time since the 1980s.[31] More substantial is the National Development and Social Fund (NDSF) built from the program, which collected 70 percent of the donation money. By the end of 2020, it held nearly €600 million. Thirty percent of NDSF funds are managed by the Central Bank of Malta and the rest go into a directed portfolio. There the money is held in government bonds, government stock, and equities, but the portfolio is tagged to support social and economic initiatives. For years, the government was cautious about dipping into it. When I visited in 2018, I was told that there was no point in being "reckless" about the opportunity. But slowly it has begun to move. First it purchased stocks in the Bank of Valetta—an action that would have been publicly palatable, as most of the bank is owned by citizens through their pensions. By the end of 2020, around €110 million was earmarked to contribute to the "wellbeing of society," with €66 million set to be released in stages to support the construction of social housing, and a further €10 million directed to upgrading health clinics. Additional grants amounting to €27 million went to support athletics, urban greening endeavors, and other social projects. Though it took several years, the donations began to have an impact.

Sometimes the programs work, but other times not, and surveying an uneven terrain can leave one wondering: Where has all the money gone? A complete economic picture in any of the countries under examination isn't easy to piece together. As we have seen, real estate investments can build tourism infrastructure and generate significant employment in some cases but fail in others. Yet donations are not a silver bullet either, and the substantial flows going into the government can yield questionable results too. Those that arrive without earmarks or remain untracked can end up as a magic wallet for the party in power. It's not uncommon to find accusations across the political spectrum about misappropriation.[32] Developers looking for sweetheart deals may offer gifts to government officials and attempt to work out profit-sharing arrangements with them as well. The testimony in the Royal Courts of Justice decision handed down in *Virdee & Trutschler v. NCA* gives a flavor of how these negotiations can run. The case revealed important issues around the possible misappropriation of funds and pointed to a strong desire among high-ranking government officials in the Caribbean for acquiring luxury goods.[33] High-end watches, however, are a pittance compared to the possibilities for skimming money from programs. Problems like kickbacks aren't unique to CBI schemes—they're common in developing countries, as well as outside them—but because the CBI programs are fiscally large, such opportunities abound.

Even without such manipulations, which is the better structure, one like Cyprus's where the bulk of the investor's money is put straight into the economy, or one like Malta's, where it is gifted to the government to spend how it sees fit? The answers I encountered in the field followed local choice. Service providers in Cyprus sang the praises of attracting people with real business interests. By putting their money at risk, one lawyer explained, "People invest in the country, become invested [in] its future, and get a tangible benefit. It's a win-win situation for them and the country." In contrast, officials in Malta tout the strength of using a donation-based system. It show a commitment to the country, I was told: "It's not just a three-year investment that can be pulled out afterward. They are actually saying goodbye to their money."

Assessing Economic Outcomes

What about the economic impact? As we saw at the beginning of this chapter, usually the macroeconomic benefits of the programs are calculated by multiplying the number of approved applications by the minimum investment amount. After examining what happens on the ground, however, it becomes clear that such rough-and-ready estimates leave much to be desired. A fine-grained assessment must take into account the potential pitfalls: projects that never complete, funds that are misspent, and simply bad decisions that are made, alongside leakages in commissions and kickbacks. Given how localized an accurate assessment must be, comparing across countries becomes enormously challenging, leading one back to the rough and ready. However, the standard estimate can be improved by incorporating two additional elements that reflect the actual operation of programs in a competitive market.

First are the basic program costs. Part of the funds coming in through a CBI program will go out again to keep it—and the citizenship industry—running. Some of the money will support the bureaucracy behind the program, but a sizeable chunk will leave the country. A portion, ear-marked in the application process, will go to international due diligence companies. Countries that appoint concessionaires will allow them take a larger slice of the money intended to enter the country, often between 4 percent and 10 percent of all government donations.

Second is the cost of competition. The most mundane example is commissions. As discussed in Chapter 6, governments that want to increase their market share may offer bonuses—sometimes amounting to $10,000 to $20,000—to service providers for each approved application. These outflows are taken from application fees and may be seen as a loss to the country. Yet if they succeed in raising application numbers, the overall money coming into the country might be greater.

More dramatic, though, are discounting strategies, which can be found in the Caribbean as governments—and developers—seek to increase their market share. These operate by dropping the actual cost to the naturalizer below the minimum investment amount. For example, a country might set its required real estate investment at $200,000, and in addition, an investor might expect to pay government fees and due diligence costs of about $60,000. To attract customers, a developer building a new resort may advertise a qualifying property at far less than the going rate: say, for example, a flat $120,000 for the entire citizenship package, including the investment, all fees, and any additional costs. If the real estate project has been approved by the government for the program, the developer can readily fudge the details: no matter how the money moves, the investment will still qualify the investor for the program. If the deal is made abroad, it's difficult for the government to know just how it's being advertised and what is going on. From the $120,000, the developer will cover the government fees of $60,000. He will also likely pay a commission, perhaps $10,000 to $20,000, to the agent who brings their client to the project. In addition, there will be marketing, conveyancing, and escrow expenses, which might amount to $10,000. The result leaves the developer with a mere $40,000 to build with—or even less if the advertised cost is lowered yet further.

Are buyers shafted in the process? Not really. In the end, they're not left holding an asset worth $40,000 that was advertised at $200,000 and cost them $120,000, but instead are offered a guaranteed buyback or allowed to walk away. In these scenarios, the investor returns her shares to the developer after holding them for the minimum required length of time, typically five years, and the developer ends up fully owning the property. For clever investor citizens, paying out $120,000 today rather than locking away $200,000 for five years in what might be an overvalued asset is the savvier move, for it allows them to invest their money elsewhere for higher returns. The result for them is similar to financing methods, which remain popular. The resort, too, will be built if everything follows through, potentially bringing profit to the developer and employment to locals. Of course, the country is left with an asset of lesser value in its territory: a property worth around $40,000 rather than the advertised $200,000.

Caribbean governments are aware of these practices, and some have devised strategies in response to them in order to compete for market share. Many countries, when approving a development for the CBI program, will estimate how much investment will be needed to complete it and will cap the number of investors—effectively, citizenship slots—allowed to qualify through the project. To operate in a scene where commissions drive sales, however, they may over-allocate citizenship slots to developers. If it costs $160,000 to build a property that gets sold at $200,000, then the government may grant a developer who is advertising at $120,000 and getting just $40,000 from a client four times the number of citizenship slots they would otherwise need. The guaranteed citizenship slots are critical because they give the developer room to maneuver when deciding what to charge and how the funds are allocated: no matter what happens to the real estate project, investors will still qualify for citizenship if they put their money into it. The guaranteed slots are known as "passports" in the parlance of the trade but are the equivalent of approved main applications. In terms of actual documents, more total passports will be issued because most applications include family dependents under the same investment. For countries, this is a risky practice. Developers may simply collect the revenue for their allotted slots and then halt production.[34] Countries, too, will need to naturalize more citizens to bring in the same economic benefits, increasing the possibility that a bad one might make it through. However, it does allow countries to compete by driving costs below the going rate. The practice also keeps the official price high, suggesting a quality good.

The cost of competition can be used to shroud a further cost: that of private gain. Developers and others on the back end of the deal, including politicians, can make out very well for themselves through markups and by releasing several times the number of citizenship slots needed to build a project. Of course, the excessive profits, drained through side flows, mean a loss for the country. In the example above, the commission structure cut the value of the property constructed by 75 percent.

Because of these dynamics, estimating program revenue from the minimum investment amount and approval numbers can be a poor approximation of

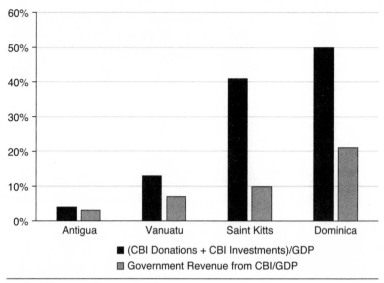

FIGURE 7.7. Citizenship by investment contributions as a proportion of GDP (2017 to 2019 average)

Note: Government revenue from CBI is calculated based on the line item given in the government budget or treasury report. Government figures for Grenada and Saint Lucia are unavailable.

Data source: InvestMig database

the funds coming into the country. Discounting, guaranteed buybacks, and "walkaways" mean that the country may not see much of the actual investment prescribed as sizeable commissions are extracted from real estate investments. Such business strategies are seen less in Turkey and Malta, but are common in the Caribbean and Vanuatu. For these cases, it is possible to estimate the minimum revenue entering the country by including only what governments declare in their budgets as CBI program receipts, a figure that encompasses application fees, agent licensing fees, and qualifying donations, while excluding due diligence costs going to foreign firms (Figure 7.7).

The actual intake is likely to be somewhere in between the two measures, but even a cautious estimate of the revenue entering the country shows that CBI accounts for over 20 percent of GDP in Dominica and 10 percent in Saint Kitts. By either measure, the impact of the programs is still outsized in microstates with few other sources of revenue.

The economic story of citizenship by investment, if rarely straightforward, is one fraught with the realities of capitalism. Examination of the practices on the ground adds some important caveats to enthusiastic cheers for the development potential for the programs. The schemes do not always work as well as they might, especially when it comes to benefits that impact the lives of locals, for along the way service providers, politicians, financiers, developers, and others can do well off leakages. The actual amount of money entering into a country may be significantly less than the number gained by multiplying the minimum investment amount by the number of approved applications.

That commissions and kickbacks lubricate many programs should come as little surprise. There is a lot at stake in some places and the market is competitive, which keeps the money moving. Some of these flows can be considered simply the cost of business. Others, like kickbacks, are more detrimental. Even if corruption is bad for an economy, not all corruption is bad in the same way: different types have different impacts, as political scientist Yuen Yuen Ang has shown. Petty bribes leave a different dent than "grand theft" by elites stealing from the state coffers. In CBI programs, there have been some cases of grand theft, but the most common mode of misconduct takes the form of "access money" in Ang's terms: cash that assures special deals. Even if it acts, in the long term, as "more sludge than grease" by creating distortions, risks, and inequality, access money can still facilitate short-term economic growth. A successful resort built through discounting still brings money and employment to the country. The result is something like a shot of steroids for an economy: it expedites growth, but with negative side effects.[35]

These, of course, must be monitored, for the downsides of access money appear mainly in times of crisis. Especially in the Caribbean, economic dependence on the programs has become substantial. During my visits, many in the region asked me rhetorically, "If not CBI, what else do we have?" Ending the programs would likely bring "sudden stop" effects, as the IMF continuously warns. Yet it would not be the first time these microstates, buffeted by hurricanes, both climatic and financial, have faced such issues. They would just have to find another way to hustle.

Chapter 8

Local Perspectives

WHAT DO LOCALS make of these developments? Whenever I traveled to a country with a program, I took the opportunity to gauge local opinion when not investigating the scheme itself. Whether sitting on a park bench, getting a SIM card at a telecom shop, buying a ticket to a museum, or standing at a cart and ordering juice, I would introduce myself and my research, and ask those around me what they thought. Never very long in any one country, I wasn't able to access the deep debates that people might have, but—as with many political issues—many had their own opinions that they were willing to share with a curious researcher.

The answers I encountered ranged widely. People in countries with a longer history of citizenship by investment generally took it as a given, and few of them saw it as something that should be abolished. In places with new programs, the buy-in was less, if there at all. Sometimes the programs were politicized: those supporting the party in power also supported the program, while adherents of the opposition party hoped to see it out the door. Yet many of the people I spoke with were not alarmed by the concept of investor citizenship. "We need the money," I was often told, even if there might be problems with program management, where the money was going, how it was being spent, and who was naturalizing through these means. The variety of opinions I encountered points beyond the often one-sided media coverage and political debates in wealthy Western countries to reveal much more happening on the ground.

Microstates in particular are diaspora societies. Their small size means that, by nature, bigger and more diverse opportunities are available only abroad. If one wants to be a doctor or an engineer or a scientist, the top prospects aren't to be found in a country with a population of only 100,000 or so. The best and brightest, and even the mediocre, head outside for opportunities, and in many cases do not return permanently. The result is that often more nationals live outside the country than within them.

The dynamics are perhaps most starkly drawn in the Caribbean, though Malta and Cyprus also produced mass emigration through the 1970s. For these islands, London, New York, New Jersey, Atlanta, or Miami are the prime destinations for anyone looking to build a better life. A local family might have half its members living in the United States or the United Kingdom. Most don't come back, I was often told, and instead are replaced by intra-Caribbean migration. CARICOM offers mobility opportunities across the region, allowing citizens of member states to reside anywhere as long as they are employed. Typically it's those from the more impoverished countries, like Haiti, who take up the offer of better jobs elsewhere in the region. The dynamics are known to everyone but are controversial enough to keep governments from taking censuses and exposing the real numbers of population loss and gain. Without such counts, exact figures are hard to come by, but Antigua can be taken as a case in point. Officials estimate that anywhere between 30 to 50 percent of the population of 100,000 is foreign, largely migrant workers from elsewhere in the Caribbean who are known immediately by their accents. Double that figure, about 200,000 Antiguans, live abroad, according to UK and US figures. The upshot is that the nation does not live in the state and the state houses those who are not the nation. This, too, was clear when I spoke to locals and found that many had spent several years living abroad or were even migrants themselves. What do they make of investor citizenship?

Saint Kitts

In Saint Kitts, one of my first stops was at a local radio station, where I met two deejays known for dropping Afro-nationalist beats. One was on break and gave his thoughts under posters of Patrice Lumumba and Malcolm X. When I asked for his opinion on the program, he replied, "Personally, I don't have a problem with citizenship by investment. It provides a much-needed economic boost. After colonialism, we just had sugar and a bit of early tourism, but that was fragile. [CBI] offsets the financial burdens and challenges that we have, and in that, I'm all for it." He went on to question the moral high road that critics in the United States and Europe often claim when it comes to the programs, situating them within a longer history of imperialism, colonization, and exploitation. "Why do we have citizenship? It's from Europe. Europe came into Africa and colonized it. Europe came into the Caribbean and started the slave trade. Europe came into America and stole it. They murdered, maimed, and raped their way to great economic success. So now there is Saint Kitts and it has citizenship. How can you say that it [citizenship] is sacred when you steal lands for your own benefit? We're not doing that. We're not murdering and raping and exploiting people to get rich. It's all above the board and in accordance with our laws. No country has moral authority—and especially not countries that have become wealthy by stealing and exploiting. And they haven't even paid any of it back. They expected us to pay for our own freedom after slavery. These small islands have heavily indebted economies and only tourism to keep them afloat."

For him, citizenship by investment isn't a desperate measure but an innovation of which he is proud: "We're a progressive nation. We pioneered it, developing the whole concept from scratch. And now people from overseas want to see it flop." He went on to rail about the hypocrisy of big states, clear to a person on the receiving end of imperial force. "I feel like the larger countries have issues with small countries gaining wealth and trying to become equal to them. Look at Canada. It's pulled back visa-free access out of jealousy. They think: 'You're making money by getting visa-free access to me.' But they do it as well. They have their own program [the FIIP, discussed in Chapter 6]. Do you want all the financial wealth and benefits going only to you?" he asked rhetorically of the richer power. When I queried the negative coverage by the foreign media, he responded, "I suspect that the US is trying to kill off our thing. They have their own program [the EB-5 residence by investment program] and are jealous of the success of ours. They never speak about the hoodlums that are attracted to the US through their program. They're just trying to take down our thing."

If the deejay was one of the more expressive individuals I spoke with regarding power and politics, he wasn't the only person in Saint Kitts to voice such concerns. Negative media coverage of the program, a young man working at a telecom shop told me, is simply power politics. "The US is just jealous of us now. England—all those places want to dictate to us what we can do. It's like FATCA telling us what to do. But look at the big countries. The US has more tax loopholes than anyone." For him, and others, the program was a way to attract much-needed revenue. As a small business owner in his forties described, "The program is good. It's designed to help people. Since sugar was phased out, people have been struggling, and CBI offers the opportunity to have money flow into the economy."

On Saint Kitts in 2018, I asked twenty locals who were not employed through the CBI industry what they thought of it. Several took the casual approach of a young man selling fresh juice from a pushcart. As he handed me my drink, he answered, "It's terrific—it brings money in. Why don't you buy our citizenship too?" Of everyone I asked, only one was firmly against citizenship by investment, both in practice and in principle. This older man had retired back to his home country after living in the United Kingdom for several decades and was completely against the concept. "It's not a good idea at all. There are other means for bringing money into a country than selling passports. It's like prostitution . . . I just don't like the idea of CBI, period. I just can't feel comfortable with it. There are other ways to generate money. Gaining citizenship is the highest honor a country can give—money shouldn't be able to buy it."

He was hanging out at a cabstand near a beach area. After listening to this tirade, one of the young cabbies responded, "I think it's been one of the better programs over the years, but it's diminished over the last few years. Saint Kitts should be the premium program in the Caribbean, but now they've lowered the price, which is like going around and begging. But a big plus is that it brings in investment, and that's important." He continued, "Since the sugar industry went into decline, we've needed alternatives. But you have to do it right. You need to make it like 'I'm giving you an opportunity' and then don't let the people get away with anything." The young man, however, wasn't happy with everything. "All the beaches in the country have to be public, but it no longer appears to be that way. [One of the hotels] has been trying to get locals off the beach. We don't want to end up like Barbados, where foreigners own everything. Or like Saint Martin, which is just a concrete jungle. Here you can have your house right on the beach," he said with some pride. Questions of foreign ownership in Saint Kitts often carried an echo of resentment against colonization, yet he had no problem with the program per se. "I always mention it to the people I take on tour. If you want to stay, you can invest and become a citizen. I think the price of $400,000 is good—it's more exclusive."

Reacting against the young man's defense, the critical retiree responded with a deep concern about program management. "The money is misappropriated. There's no accounting of it. They're just selling passports and not thinking about the prosperity of the country itself . . . And you have to wonder about where the money is going. It goes to lawyers and developers, the 'five percent.' [A former government leader] wasted the money he brought in through it. There was no transparency—just his cronies getting rich."

Others on Saint Kitts, if supportive of the concept of citizenship by investment, would also question how the program was run and raise concerns about misappropriation. A woman who works in the country's heritage industry lamented, "There isn't any money for the national trust. Why can't they take 1 percent of the SIDF [government donation] funds and use [it] for the national trust? I'd like to see the program run better." A recent college graduate who found work at a museum echoed the sentiment: "We're giving too much away and not getting enough back. We're not seeing the impact ourselves. We need schools; we need textbooks. Money may be coming in, but the locals are not seeing it." She went on to clarify, "I'm not against the program per se, especially if the money went to fixing the schools, creating extra training, doing music programs, getting computers in schools. But there are a lot of problems here. It's too hard for millennials to own land and start off on our own. If the money were trickling down and our cost of living were less, then it would be fine." She added some hypothetical concerns that weigh on her mind: "What would happen if all the CBI citizens were to come to Saint Kitts? We would be sunk, the people would rebel. I talk a lot with my friends about what's next after tourism. What will we do?" A librarian I met also had doubts about how the funds were being used. "I don't know about the money from the program, it's not really explained to people." She added with some bitter sarcasm, "The real estate developers seem to be getting money, though. Hotels and the Chinese have gotten millions." Many who are supposed to be feeling the economic benefits of the programs clearly aren't.

Political loyalties run deep on the island. Elections are hotly contested, and in a small place, they run close to the ground. (Some even joke that they run underground and include active participation from cemeteries.) The signage of key businesses reads like an electoral ballot—the big names in town are repeated over and over. "People cheer for their [political party's] color," I was told, and these alignments also channel criticism too. All the main parties support citizenship by investment—the utility of the revenue source is all too clear. This has meant that its management, rather than the existence of a program itself, comes under fire.

Another local, a young man with a part-time job, explained to me, "It can help small countries, but it depends on how it works. You need transparency, good government, and accountability for it . . . But then there are also a lot of issues around perceived corruption, and a lot of propaganda around the program. It has become a political football." A gritty-voiced radio manager complained that the opposition party used a few failures to cripple what had been an economically beneficial program. His comments included a sentiment I ran across repeatedly in Saint Kitts and elsewhere: either the former government did a terrific job with the scheme while the current government is on the take and has completely destroyed it, or the current government is making positive changes to the program after the former government, totally corrupt, made a mess of things. Political affiliation determined where anyone pinned the blame.

Many people saw citizenship as something that could be sold because it is a legal status that is separate from nationality. For them, it's not "Kittitian-ness" that's on offer—just passports. The distinction between membership in the state and membership in the nation was starkly drawn by two large events the government held in spring 2018. In June, Basseterre hosted a massive Caribbean Investment Summit, a regional conference organized by the countries with CBI programs to showcase their offerings. Three weeks later, the signs were changed to welcome the participants for a second international bash: the inaugural Diaspora Conference. Aimed at mobilizing Kittitians abroad to boost the country's development, the speaker lineup and target audience were notably different: not the investor citizens, but the native sons and daughters who had left the islands to make it big in the metropole. The event contained more rituals of nation-making than pitches of nation-branding. All stood when the national anthem was solemnly played to open the event, reminding Kittitians of their roots, followed by an incantation of the Lord's Prayer.

Cyprus

In Cyprus, too, the opinions I encountered were broadly supportive. If accounts in the foreign media were often scathing, locals were rather nonchalant about the offering. That was in 2018, three years before Al Jazeera broke the big corruption scandal discussed in Chapter 3, yet it was just a week before a presidential election when I visited the island. Though political statements and images were all over the cityscape and the media, the well-established program appeared in neither the news nor the political debates—in great contrast to the highly contentious scene across the water in Malta. Indeed, within hours of my arrival, a cab driver volunteered to sell me a piece of scenic coastal land that he owned, should I want to become a citizen. "The thing is, the coast is on the Turkish side," he told me up front. But that shouldn't be a problem, he explained, since now you can cross the border. "It's a beautiful country, you should become a Cypriot."

A young yoga teacher told me that she supported the program. "It was really bad here after 2009, and it's helped to rebuild the economy out of that, bringing money in." However, she wasn't sure about the future trajectory. "They're building a lot of luxury residences," she observed, referring to the massive high-rise condominiums under construction along the coast in Limassol, "but will these people really live there?" she queried, expressing doubt about the long-term benefits. "I read about a street in London where rich people from the Middle East bought all of the houses. But they stayed empty and now the neighborhood has nothing in it. I don't want that to happen to Cyprus." She complained, too, that her fellow Cypriots "just chase after money," a stereotype I heard more than once. Several others I spoke with echoed the sentiment. In the tavern of a small mountain village, two local women found no problem with the concept of investor citizenship, but questioned how the money was used: "What does it do to preserve village life and culture?" They went on to complain about conglomerates displacing local production and hollowing out the countryside.

On the coast, a bar owner, a tall and proud member of the communist party (AKEL), was in support. "Sure, it's alright," he told me. "I think we're just beginning to see the economic benefits, though it might take some time." I asked what he thought about the sale of citizenship in principle: "Look, it's very loose here," came the response. "You can figure out ways to do anything." It was this "flexibility"—which Al Jazeera would document a few years later—that some people I encountered found to be the most problematic. They were concerned about the nature of the government and the transactional approach to everything within society more broadly, as well as possibilities for corruption. It was a sentiment of general dissatisfaction—even exasperation—with the way things are done in the country, of which CBI was a mere symptom. One former businessman who worked between the United Kingdom and Cyprus for most of his life complained, "Why should they get residency just for investing? If they start paying taxes, contributing to the pension fund, that's different—that's what a citizen does. I suspect that all these Russian oligarchs and Chinese are using the citizenship as a stepping-stone to get somewhere else."

Antigua

When I visited Antigua in 2016, the CBI program had been operating for just two years and was still making the news in ways unimaginable in Cyprus or Saint Kitts, with their long-standing offerings. The papers were covering every move, from minor changes in program operation to announcements of new projects it was funding, along with controversies over the revocation of citizenship and questions about the flow of money. In the tiny country, it was a big topic. A dreadlocked man who had recently moved back from Brooklyn said he thought the program was a good idea. "What other options are there for a small country?" he asked me rhetorically. But it's unclear where the money is going, he noted. "If it's coming in, I don't see it." A retired pilot I met while waiting for the local minibus said that he thought the concept behind the program is fine. "I don't have a problem with it," he stated, but added that he too didn't know how the funds were being spent to build the country. "Look at this place. Do you see a massive investment?" A few other locals voiced the same concern: the idea is fine, but where is the money? The government would argue that the program was still in its early days, and most of the funds were earmarked for paying down an IMF loan taken out in the wake of the 2008 global economic crisis. Yet several years down the road, the same questions might still be raised, especially if the funds are not spent well. If locals have problems with citizenship by investment, they haven't made themselves heard at the ballot box so far. In 2018, Prime Minister Gaston Browne, who has done much to tout the program, was reelected in a landslide win.

Others would speak from within—or about—the party divides. A man who runs a small beauty salon thought the program would address real economic need and supported it as long as the due diligence is thorough. "I think they need to be careful about who applies and give every person the proper scrutiny." He praised the program administration under the previous party in power, but he didn't like the way the current prime minister was running it. Under the old government, he said, "It was very transparent. When there was a new citizen through the program, we all knew about it. I think the present government is using it only for its own financial benefit. It hasn't done anything for the people, like creating job opportunities. . . . It needs to be better structured and managed." A woman on the cleaning staff at the airport said that she thought the program was a good idea, but that it's highly politicized.

"Those who are against it are those who prefer the previous administration," she said as she confessed that she supports the current government. "I'm not going to say they're not corrupt, but it's not as much as the past administration. And they don't make things hard for the locals—they try to make it easier."

Some locals complained that the program has made it more difficult to secure short-stay tourist and business visas for the United States, with the consulate in Barbados rejecting their applications in higher numbers than before due to CBI issues. The concern is important given how many have family who have emigrated, and visa approval data show that the United States is indeed refusing higher numbers now than in comparison to ten years before. However, it is rejecting people from Caribbean countries without CBI programs at higher rates than ones that have them.[1] Still, this does little to change the impact of the loss of visa-free access to Canada, which now has everyone queueing for permission to enter.

Malta

On Malta, sentiments were starkly divided along political lines, and voices against the program—and even the concept of investor citizenship—were far stronger than elsewhere. In contrast to the Caribbean, where greater economic need generated wider acceptance of the idea in principle, many in Malta wondered why the program was even introduced in the first place, given that the island had weathered the global economic crisis quite well. A recurring concern was that citizenship should not be granted to those with no ties to the country—a controversy since the program's launch and a key point of debate within the EU. Around the lunch table at a university, one professor complained that the naturalizers should be required to spend more time in the country. "It's ridiculous that 'residence' means just having a flat," she said, and added that the apartment above hers has been rented out for the program, but it just stands empty. It used to rent for €500 per month, but now the owner makes €2000 off the absent investor citizens, she said. Her neighbor agreed that people should spend more time in the country, but she supports the program if it brings in "real investment." For her this meant "building factories" and the like: she was skeptical of the utility of a government donation. A third professor said that he was initially dubious, but now thinks "Why not? We sell land, we sell labor, we sell everything. Why not citizenship?" At a small restaurant in Valletta, an older man I met voiced a concern, repeated by others, that the new citizens don't really want to be Maltese. He had been following coverage in the newspapers and complained that people "just fly in and fly out, covering their faces for journalists because they don't want to be known as a citizen of Malta." The main gripe of a local writer was the two-tier nature of the system, which supplies a smooth process for the wealthy and many delays for anyone else. He explained that anyone who tries to naturalize after living in the country for five years will face long waits, as the minister must approve every application. "Many people never get an answer—just a request for more documents."

I met several people who rejected citizenship by investment straight out. A retiree who had worked most of his life in the United States and returned to Malta a few years ago said frankly, "I'm totally against it. You shouldn't sell something like citizenship to people who have no connection to Malta. Who are these people?" He complained that there was corruption before, but now it's been taken to new levels. He's become so sickened by it that he no longer supports any of the parties. The sentiment was similar to that of other life-long Nationalist Party supporters. "I don't like it, to be honest," a middle-aged man I met on a pier told me. "But if you are Red [Labour Party], you say it's good, and if you are Blue [Nationalist Party], you say it's bad. It's just politics that determines opinion. That's the problem." His observation was supported by a public opinion survey: only 10 percent of Nationalist Party voters supported a program, while over 60 percent of Labour voters did the same, and nearly 50 percent of swing voters who had moved from the Nationalists to Labour did so as well.[2]

I didn't meet anyone who was virulently against the program in the limited time I had on the island, but I was relying on the encounters that came my way rather than actively seeking out both sides of a contentious issue. Given the repeated public protests and long-standing vigils in the wake of the murder of Daphne Caruana Galizia, there is clearly strong public mobilization against it from certain factions of the population. Even in 2021, protestors continued to organize demonstrations against government corruption that would shift into criticism of the CBI program. Pressure from Brussels to close the scheme was heartily welcomed in many sectors, even while staunch Labour supporters, as well as the professional layer of lawyers, accountants, and wealth managers, defended it. Settlement or settling down looks far from the horizon should the program survive EU pressure.

Vanuatu

Vanuatu was the only place I went where most people I met hadn't heard of the CBI programs on offer, even though they had been around for several years when I visited. It was also a place where national-level politics are largely self-referential and penetrate little into the daily lives of people, especially outside the capital island of this far-flung archipelago. At the local level, customary law—*Kastom* in the national language of Bislama—is a holdover from colonization and remains the most important legal system for most people. Everyone is a member of a tribe, and its chief is the principal political leader for most as the person who deals with issues that emerge on the ground.

Standing apart from this local system is the parliament, which is housed in what is for many a very distant capital city of Port Vila. In its fifty-two seats are politicians from thirty different political parties, a tremendous diversity that necessitates rule by coalition. When I was there, the ruling party had just six members and cobbled together its coalition from there. Such groupings are famously unstable, as "grasshoppers" jump from party to party, even in the same session of parliament. Some parties even have members sitting in both the government and the opposition. The result is a continuous flotation around cabinet positions, portfolios, and even governments. I visited when the parliament was in session—they were about to hold a vote of no-confidence against the prime minister—yet the building was largely deserted. It was easiest to find politicians in the local restaurants or resorts. Few people in Port Vila offered kind words about them or their civil servants. The major complaint, supported by newspaper headlines, was that most of the government money goes to pay the bureaucrats, and they continuously implement pay raises for themselves.

As such, the government's citizenship by investment was a nonentity for many people. Outside the capital, no one I spoke with had heard of it. A number of people offered a response similar to the one given by a woman who used to work on a cruise ship but now was just tending her garden. She smiled shyly when I asked what she thought about the program and admitted that she hadn't heard of it. "It's just a government thing. The government does its own thing, and we do our thing. Maybe we have a job and we work, or maybe we just have our garden. The government and those sorts of things don't really matter—we don't think about them." Not thinking about them means turning a blind eye when there is little that can be done to change the situation, and virtually everyone I met from across the socioeconomic spectrum complained about the politicians. A single mother who scrambled to-gether a living from odd jobs didn't know about the program but immedi-ately complained about the government, "They just take our money and don't do anything. The village chiefs are a bit better," she sighed. A youthful man who had gone abroad for university whom I met at a local kava stand said that he thinks the program is a good thing if the government is in control, if it's transparent, and if the money is injected into the local economy to create more employment opportunities and benefit the general public. "But," he complained, "there's too much corruption, so there has been no reporting about how the money has been spent." Another young man beside him added, "We are moving like a crab, very slowly and sometimes sideways."

Asked about what they thought of the concept of selling citizenship in gen-eral, some, like the young man above, were supportive, but it quickly became clear that they imagined the program would bring immigrants to the country. On this, most were tolerant, as long as the foreigners were willing to adapt. Typical was the response of three women at a fruit market who welcomed new citizens if they chose to live there. "You should marry a ni-Van [person from Vanuatu] too. You need to want to be here and a part of the commu-nity," one opined. "And maybe learn to dance," another added with a smile. A local man who worked along the promenade in the capital city told me, "It's a good way to bring money into the country. But they need to make sure they give it to the right people." Complaining about the recent influx of Chinese shop owners, he went on, "It's not good if they sell citizenship to people who open businesses and then just send the money back home rather than con-tributing locally." When I noted that many people purchasing citizenship rarely visit their new country—often they're looking for an insurance policy—he responded, "So they just want to protect their family just in case? That's fine, or even better." He then added the common refrain of complaints about the government. "Politicians here are all corrupt. They start a lot of projects but never finish them. They just take part of the money for themselves and then go on to the next project."

In a minivan, the equivalent of a local bus, I struck up a conversation with a middle-aged man in the seat behind me. Like many, he hadn't heard of the program but was surprised to learn how expensive it is to naturalize through it. "I'm ni-Van [from Vanuatu] already," he told me. "Is my citizenship really worth that much to someone?" he queried incredulously. He had labored as a seasonal agriculture worker in Australia and knew very well what the differ-ence between Vanuatu and Australian membership meant. "How much does citizenship in Australia cost?" he asked, taking me for an Aussie. "I want to move to Australia and was told the best way to become a citizen was to marry one, so now I'm looking," he said half-jokingly. Not only the wealthy seek out alternatives.

Montenegro and Beyond

In Montenegro, the feeling of stasis and corruption in politics was stultifying. When I was there, the country was already in its twenty-sixth year under the political influence of Milo Đukanović, who had dominated the country from one political position or another since the breakup of Yugoslavia. In 2017, most people I talked to were simply jaded about the government. If I asked about what they thought about selling citizenship, the first word out was typically a variant of "Oh, the government is so corrupt." Some had heard of a few headline cases. Others didn't know about the fledgling program at all, but even they were not surprised when I brought it up. One young, sporty man I met who had moved to the coast in search of work told me straight off, "Oh, the government is so corrupt," before going on to explain, "Even if the president says that the Russian mafia and money laundering are gone, everyone knows it's not the case—it's just talk for NATO." He knew about people like Thaksin Shinawatra getting citizenship, but it didn't matter much to him in the grand scheme of things. All of this had little bearing on his life, he said.

Another man I met, in his early thirties and with a university degree, said that he ended up working in tourism because everyone in the government is corrupt. "You don't get anywhere without passing money," he told me. "I don't want to be like a banana republic, but this government is terrible." Yet he was supportive of the concept of investor citizenship in general. "If you want to invest in Montenegro, it's okay to get citizenship too, I think. But if you don't really invest and just provide a bunch of euros in a government bribe, then it's a problem." Still, he didn't have much hope for the way that the program might operate in practice. "We've had the same government for thirty years and it's a big problem. I hope that NATO states will push our government not to sell citizenship to criminals."

A third young man who worked at a boating company said—after telling me about how corrupt the government was—that he was okay with the concept. When I asked if he would support an offering, he replied, "I don't care. If you want to invest and if you hire some Montenegrin people, then it's good. I finished university, studying for three years in business and tourism, and now

I want to find a job. But there are maybe a thousand people who are qualified and only fifty job places. It's not good. So when someone comes from another place to invest, then it's okay if they get citizenship. It's fine. I don't care. Why not if they do something for the economy?" But he also didn't have much hope for how a program might operate in practice. "To me, a citizenship program is suspicious. Everything here is suspicious, because for everyone who wants to invest, there is always someone from somewhere who is the intermediary. And he gets the job but never finishes the job. He just steals the money and goes. In Montenegro, nothing gets finished." He ended up asking me how he could get citizenship in the United States to try to create a better life abroad. A woman working in a café in the capital city gave a similar view. After explaining government corruption to me, she said rather pragmatically, "I'm not against giving citizenship to people who invest in the country, but those investments will turn into payments to politicians. Sure, if you create a business, you can be Montenegrin. But the problem is that the money will end up only with the government."

Across the cases, the locals I met during my travels voiced a range of opinions about the programs, from decisively for to clearly against. In places with older schemes, people had become acclimated to the option and the buy-in was often greater. In Saint Kitts, some even spoke with national pride about their citizenship innovation that dated back to independence. No matter the country, often knowing a person's political affiliation was the easiest way to guess their stance. Yet apart from Malta, even if people disagreed with how the party in power was running the program in their country, it didn't necessarily mean they were against the concept of investor citizenship itself. Especially for microstates, options are limited, as anyone on the ground knows well. If people in Vanuatu, where the program wasn't much known, seemed genuinely welcoming of new foreigners, those elsewhere, where the programs were a topic of public discussion, were not terribly concerned with being overrun by investor citizens—they know that few come, and some even regretted that. Yet many had no problem with absentee investor citizens, whom they saw as doing little to destabilize the content of their national identity. Some rolled out the welcome mat while others rolled it up.

Chapter 9

Who Wants to Buy a Passport?

W HO WOULD WANT to become an investor citizen in a place like Saint Kitts? The coastline is beautiful and the weather difficult to beat, but it's hardly Paris. Yet a register of the most prominent investor citizens there and elsewhere reads like an invitation list to a charity dinner in Monaco. There is the heir to the Nestle fortune, Patrick Liotard-Vogt, who became a Kittitian in 2013, a few years after buying ASmallWorld, a social networking site for the super-rich, from Harvey Weinstein. Malta has welcomed the founder of the largest media company in the Middle East, Waleed al-Ibrahim, as one of its own, and recently courted PayPal founder Peter Thiel. Peter de Savary, British real estate mogul and sailor, became a Grenadian through its investor program. The erstwhile Speaker of the House in Afghanistan, Mir Rahman Rahmani, naturalized in both Cyprus and Saint Kitts, which may have been useful once he fled his country following the Taliban takeover in 2021. Yang Huiyan, a real estate scion considered the richest woman in Asia, naturalized in Cyprus, along with Khaled Juffali, heir to the Juffali conglomerate, Saudi Arabia's largest private enterprise. Pham Nhat Vu, brother of "Vietnam's first billionaire," is Cypriot too, along with a string of Russian oligarchs, including Oleg Deripaska, president of the massive energy company En+ Group and aluminum firm Rusal; Alisher Usmanov, owner of steel giant Metalloinvest; and Vadim Moshkovich, chair of the farming conglomerate Rusagro.[1] And there are cases only whispered about. One service provider I spoke with described being approached by a sibling of Kim Jong-un, Supreme Leader of North Korea, for a new state membership.

Among the famous are not merely the rich. Even the most spiritually pure can seek out citizenship solutions. Ogyen Trinley Dorje, one of highest lamas in Tibetan Buddhism, has long had difficulty crossing borders. In 2000, he fled his native Tibet by crossing the Himalayas on horseback to arrive in India, where the government granted him refugee papers that did not allow him to leave the country. Kept under close surveillance and denied an exit visa for years, he was finally granted permission to go to the United States for medical treatment in 2017. Outside India for the first time in nearly two decades, he used the opportunity to shed his stateless status and gain citizenship—and his first passport—in Dominica.[2]

The trend in second citizenships has taken off among American tech billionaires as well. Those who do not negotiate directly with a government, like Evan Spiegel of Snapchat, can go through formalized programs. Service providers describe an unexpected explosion of interest from this pool of elites who found during Covid-19 that their US documents no longer secured the mobility advantages they were accustomed to. If you're riding out a global pandemic on a yacht in the Mediterranean, what do you do when a child has a medical emergency and no one wants to let you in? For these elites, an extra passport is small change for an insurance policy. Google's longtime CEO Eric Schmidt slid in an application for Cypriot citizenship just before the government froze its program. However, PayPal founder Peter Thiel may not have been so fortunate. He posted his required personal residence in Malta—not to be rented out—on Airbnb, potentially botching his application for investor citizenship in the country.

Russian techies too have gravitated to these options. Pavel Durov, the founder of VKontakte, Russia's equivalent of Facebook, naturalized in the Caribbean after Russian security services pressed him to release personal information about opposition activists who use the site. Unwilling to bend, he became a citizen of Saint Kitts and went into self-imposed exile in Dubai.[3] Service providers I spoke with in Russia described a small exodus of techies in his wake, including Arkady Volozh, the founder of Yandex—Russia's version of Google—who became a citizen of Malta in 2016.[4]

Other elites leave one wondering about their motives. In 2022, Armen Sarkissian resigned from the presidency of Armenia after the media exposed his citizenship in Saint Kitts, violating a ban on dual nationality for high office holders. Why was Armenia not enough? Eased cross-border mobility was probably not the motive for naturalizing—an inadvertent mistake, he claimed—because he also had diplomatic papers as Armenia's ambassador to the United Kingdom.[5] It's similarly unclear why family members of Cambodia's iron-fisted ruler, Hun Sen, have naturalized in Cyprus. Social media posts show them gallivanting across Europe in the lap of luxury.[6] But did they become Cypriot merely to smooth the trip between Capri and Ibiza? One might wonder, too, why European elites, like a German billionaire or French philanthropist, listed but unnamed in Al Jazeera's Cyprus Papers, would become investor citizens in Cyprus given that they, as EU nationals, would already have similar rights across the Union.[7]

There is also the curious case of the former prime minister of Saint Kitts, Denzil Douglas, who stood behind the formalization and great expansion of the country's CBI program before he lost the general election in 2015. Two years later, newspapers reported that he had acquired a diplomatic passport from Dominica at the same time he lost his Kittitian diplomatic credentials.[8] Travel ease might be the excuse, but the new passport also listed his nationality as Dominican. The case worked its way through the courts as the politician, still the leader of the opposition party, was constitutionally bound not to show "allegiance, obedience, or adherence to a foreign state." In the end, the Eastern Caribbean Supreme Court determined that he had indeed broken the law and should step down from the National Assembly.[9] Yet none of the proceedings addressed why he might want such a passport (and additional nationality) in the first place.

Perhaps the most spectacular case to date is Jho Low, an international fugitive at the time of writing. Allegedly the mastermind of the 1MDB scandal that defrauded the Malaysian government of $4.5 billion, Low is a citizen of not only Malaysia but Saint Kitts and Cyprus as well. He acquired Kittitian documents in 2011 during the early phase of the massive fraud but before warning sirens were ringing. Cypriot citizenship, however, he picked up in September 2015, six months after reports of the misappropriation began to emerge. Even with flags on his due diligence report, he was still approved, and he expedited his way to a passport by making a generous donation to the archbishop of the country's autocephalous church.[10] Since 2019, the country has been bogged down in the courts trying to revoke the membership.

These high-profile figures easily capture the attention of the media, and if one goes by the newspapers, they are the long and short of demand for citizenship by investment. They also raise important questions about how second citizenships can facilitate second identities, and what people might be doing with them. But in the great majority of CBI cases, the reality is far more mundane. The program in Cyprus had a work-around that enabled those with problematic backgrounds to bypass the formal vetting procedure and get approved straight from the top—for a hefty contribution of bribes and kickbacks. Yet Al Jazeera, whose undercover reporters broke the story, found that only about 4 percent of the applicants raised red flags—including those who were only potentially of concern.[11] Although the lives of the famous, powerful, and even dirty are intriguing, these headline-grabbing types are hardly the main constituency that drives the programs. The reality of most investor citizens is far more ordinary—though no less interesting, especially if one is used to seeing the world from the position of a privileged Global North citizen.

The Global Scene

At first glance, demand for citizenship by investment may seem underwhelming. Each year, around 50,000 individuals gain citizenship through it—a tiny figure in comparison to the nearly 8 billion people on the planet. However, its significance increases when placed in context.

First, naturalization itself is relatively uncommon. Comprehensive statistics are not available, but one can gain a sense of its rarity as a human experience by looking at the places where one might expect to find it: countries with large migrant populations. The United States, home to nearly 45 million foreign-born people, naturalizes only 750,000 people per year. The next five largest migrant-receiving countries—Saudi Arabia, Germany, Russia, the United Kingdom, and the United Arab Emirates—naturalize a mere 400,000 individuals each year combined. The rate is similar to that of the EU member states, where liberal democratic norms, if uneven, may make for more open naturalization policies. Simply very few human beings ever naturalize.

Furthermore, the pool of people likely to participate in CBI programs is relatively small. Demand comes largely from three areas—China, the Middle East, and Russia—places outside the North Atlantic where economic and geopolitical transformations have produced a growing set of wealthy individuals (Figure 9.1). In Saint Lucia and Dominica, half or more of all reported naturalizers hail from the Middle East. In Antigua, the proportion of Middle Easterners is less, but still significant, coming just behind China, the other key source area. Though government numbers for Saint Kitts are unavailable, officials told me that before the Covid-19 pandemic most of the citizenships went to Chinese and a substantial portion to Middle Easterners. In the Mediterranean, the numbers of Russians is much greater, accounting for over 60 percent of the Cypriot program and about half of the Maltese scheme, with Middle Easterners taking second position.

Though interest in additional citizenships is strong, citizenship by investment is not cheap. Service providers confirm that those who are serious about the programs are usually willing to spend no more than 10 percent of their assets on them. They also tend to be the first generation in their family to

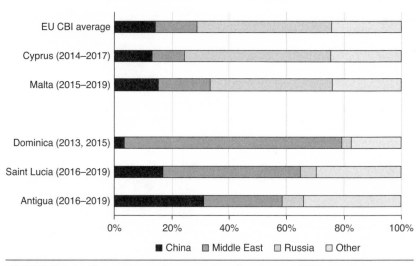

FIGURE 9.1. Key regions of approved applications to CBI programs

Note: The figure covers cases where data on the country of origin is available. The data for Dominica are estimated based on the names recorded in the National Gazette.

Data source: InvestMig database

have substantial wealth since "citizenship solutions" of any sort are inheritable. Figures for the size of this population are imprecise, but wealth reports gesture to the scale. According to Credit Suisse Research Institute, over 4.3 million "new millionaires" emerged outside North America and Europe between 2000 and 2018.[12] The figure is likely to be low, but even so, it yields an annual naturalization rate of about 1.2 percent for this population, a sizeable proportion. These broad-brush estimates point in the same direction as the limited survey data available. Based on interviews with 500 private bankers and wealth advisors, Knight Frank has reported that 34 percent of individuals with at least $30 million in assets hold more than one citizenship, and 29 percent are thinking of acquiring an additional one.[13]

The population of possible investor citizens may be broadening. Service providers I spoke with across the geographic spectrum described a general fall in their average wealth as the programs have become more accessible. "We see a lot of middle-class professionals who want mobility because of unstable political regimes back home," as a service provider in Dubai put it. Yet "middle class" should be taken with a grain of salt: such individuals usually earn six figures if calculated in US dollars. "They're 'poor millionaires,'" as another agent described the population to me—people with between $1 to $5 million in assets who may be doing well off small businesses. In some parts of the world, such as the oil-rich Gulf states, it is not unusual for a university graduate from, say, Sri Lanka to work as an upper-level manager in an international firm and earn a generous, tax-free salary that would make the cheapest CBI programs readily accessible. Though oligarchs and billionaires grab headlines when making these purchases, most of the memberships go to people who are economically successful on a much smaller scale.

Motives

Why would someone spend so much on a passport? The price may seem high, but as one service provider put it, "It's not a lot, especially when you come from a country with a lot of geopolitical instability. Someone always wants your money, you want to do business internationally, you want to get your children educated, you want a place to go if it all goes wrong." The laundry list he gave would be reiterated in my interviews across the world. Breaking them down reveals some intriguing patterns.

Many people are reluctant to talk about their citizenship strategies to a stranger—and for good reason. Several countries, including China and India, don't allow dual citizenship. In the Middle East, a number of people explained that it's common for everyone to protect their privacy, whether from nosy family members or from governments they don't trust. In Russia—the demand center where I spent the least amount of time—intermediaries explained that their clients were worried about getting on the wrong side of the regime. As such, much of the material I amassed came from agents describing clients. Yet during my travels, I met eleven investor citizens and nine people shopping for options who were willing to share their stories with me. Few in this field—whether journalists or academics—have listened to their voices. Most fixate on the high-profile cases that confirm their moral suspicions that the business is bad news. The stories of more ordinary people who have gone through the programs reveal a different side.

Mobility

The most common response to my "Why?" question was simple: mobility. Crossing borders can be a challenge, particularly for people from the Global South. Some individuals "simply have a useless passport," as one lawyer explained. "They're not necessarily looking to relocate, but to just do business or go on holiday." For those without the right passport, applying for visas is onerous and time-consuming. Samira, an Iranian businesswoman who grew up in Dubai, described the frustrations. Her parents had relocated in 1979 after the Iranian Revolution. Three years old at the time, she knows no other home than the United Arab Emirates and has developed several successful businesses there. I met her at an investment migration fair where she was browsing the booths for citizenship options. "A passport is my number one priority," she explained. "I want to be able to travel or live wherever I want, without worrying about the visa." She went on to detail the hassles of getting a visa to visit family in the United Kingdom. To go anywhere, she explained of Iranians, "We have to show everything, even our bank accounts, to show that we are not laundering money." She went on: "All the money in London is from money laundering. It's ridiculous. Why do you punish regular people?" she asked rhetorically. When I probed further, she emphasized that I wouldn't understand as an American. "Where are you from? The US? See, you have many more choices—you can go wherever you want. You have visas everywhere. For us, it's much worse." An agent in Dubai elaborated on what this might mean, describing a recent client's travails when applying for a visa. "All the documents are correct, but they [at the embassies] still think, 'You're Iranian, you're a terrorist.'"

These hurdles, interviewees across the world would tell me, are debilitating. "Time is everything for the very wealthy," as one lawyer described. "Everything happens at the last minute in my life," explained an investor citizen from China. Even if he readily obtains visas, a hassle in itself, they are often only for ninety days and single entry. As such, the visa-free travel his Caribbean citizenship supplies "really makes a difference." In Jordan, a lawyer set out the mobility issues plainly: "If you're a businessperson and you have to go from Dubai to Paris for a meeting, you don't want to have to submit your passport to the embassy and then wait three or four weeks for a visa. You need to be able to get on a plane and go." A service provider in London offered the case of a Pakistani client with business deals in Europe. "He has got a passport this thick," the agent said, spreading his fingers an inch wide. "He gets his visas, but it's a hassle." The client wanted to know, "How much will it cost to get this monkey off my back?" Demand in Russia, when I visited in 2018, had grown among young tech entrepreneurs for similar reasons. "They're in Hong Kong one week and London the next, always moving, and don't have time to apply for visas," described a service provider. In some cases, the travel challenges are perceived as a stigma. A Hong Kong–based lawyer set out the motives of one of his clients from the subcontinent who runs an international business: "He may be rich, but if he can't travel to London whenever he wants, he will always be second class." To be "high class," he explained, "you must have the freedom of movement to go wherever you want, whenever you want."

Sometimes an additional citizenship can enhance one's career through improved mobility, a motive common in the Gulf region where oil wealth has attracted large populations of highly trained expats from places like India, Pakistan, Philippines, Iran, and Syria. They may attain top positions in global firms but face difficulties traveling to company branches or headquarters, often in the West, because of their passport. Whether they're working in cosmetics, telecoms, automobiles, or travel—I came across cases in each domain—the top employees in the Gulf do well financially and can afford the expense. An Iranian manager of a major American firm in the United Arab Emirates is indicative. She was tired of being unable to travel like her colleagues because she's Iranian, her lawyer told me. "So, she said that she's ok with not buying one more Mercedes and got a passport instead." Tariq, a young Pakistani whom I met as he was shopping for options, explained that he has no problems getting visas and has never been refused, but it can take one or two months to receive them. He is a university graduate who has risen high in the telecom industry and often flies internationally for work. "I want to get a better passport because it's very hard to travel on mine," he said plaintively. A service provider I met in Dubai thought she had discovered an untapped market when she was surrounded by Iranian medical professionals in a hospital where she was tending to her father. She started touting the benefits of a second citizenship but found no takers: most of the doctors already had second passports. They told her that they must update their credentials in the US or UK every few years, and it's difficult if they travel on Iranian documents. "It's easier to get a US visa or a UK visa with a Caribbean passport. They see it as an investment to save their time, to give them peace of mind."

After they receive their new papers, the first stop for many isn't a foreign country but the local American embassy, where they "complete the passport" by applying for a ten-year multientry visa to the United States. Many countries will more readily issue a visa if an American one is already in the passport. The stamp of approval indicates that the person passes muster: if she is good enough for Uncle Sam, then she is good enough for us. A new passport can lower the waiting time for visas as well. An Iranian who applies for a visa to the United States may have to wait several months to secure an interview while other nationalities sail through. A former State Department official told me that such bottlenecks can also be deliberately crafted through under-staffing. The result, in a place like Dubai, is a six-month backlog at the US consulate, which has dedicated only two staff members to deal with a heavy caseload of Iranians. This onerous wait, however, can be circumnavigated with documents from somewhere else.

Even individuals from relatively "high-ranked" countries may seek out al-ternative mobility options out of political and geopolitical considerations. US citizens are the largest group with such concerns. "Americans aren't always the most welcome people in the world, depending on where you travel," a ser-vice provider in the United Arab Emirates explained to me, listing the high rates of kidnapping in some parts of the globe. When they get a passport in a place like the Comoros, they think, "I'm taking that target off my back." Another in Lebanon described his US clients as looking for a "peaceful" travel document. Robert, an American-turned-Kittitian whom I met on a plane, had similar concerns. Donning a black hoodie set off against bleached blonde hair, he had a casual friendliness that didn't betray his wealth. He had done well for himself as an extreme photographer and expanded into other travel businesses. The job meant that he spent very little time in the United States, where he was born. Even in Singapore, where he is currently based, he spends only two months per year. When I asked why he naturalized elsewhere, "per-sonal safety" was his immediate answer. In his line of work, he often goes to countries where US citizens may get kidnapped or even shot. After one inci-dent, it was just getting too dangerous, he said. "In Mumbai, they took one of the luxury hotels and whoever was around, and if you were American, they just killed you." Though it's common to hear about such cases from service providers in Dubai, even in Hong Kong I encountered an agent whose last case was for a US client. He was being dispatched to Yemen for work and sought out a Caribbean passport for safer business travel.

The strength of these boundaries, however, is not fixed: geopolitics deter-mines fluctuations. It was once relatively easy to travel on a Middle Eastern passport, but since the 2000s, heightened tension with the West has thrown up barriers. The movement can also go in the other direction. After China negotiated ten-year multientry visas for the United States and the EU's Schengen Area, service providers noted a decline in Chinese clients looking for second citizenships to secure mobility. However, the approval of multiple-entry visas is not guaranteed, which leaves many still searching for solutions. Even if one has a valid visa, border guards may police certain citizenships more strictly than others, particularly when geopolitical tensions flare, a story I often heard from service providers in the Middle East and Russia.

Sometimes mobility doesn't mean smoothing frequent travel but rather simply getting out in the first place. One old-timer in the industry told of clients from the Middle East who seek out a "one-use passport." They use it to get into Europe or North America, "and then they rip it up and apply for asylum." If their case isn't approved, he said, they'll be deported to an island country rather than back to their authoritarian regime, where they'd end up in jail. For the most part, however, it's the moneyed stateless rather than asylum seekers who go for this option. The cases I came across were of Palestinians, Kurds, and Bidoons—literally, those "without papers," whom we met in Chapter 4. Though many have been allocated Comoros documents, some seek out citizenship on their own. A lawyer in the region offered an example when I asked about recent clients. One was a Bidoon businessman who had purchased citizenship in a Caribbean country for his teenage daughter so that she could go on a school trip abroad.

Do these "citizenship solutions" for improved mobility really work? Problems crossing borders on their new passports were rare among those I spoke with. One of the most frequent travelers I met, Robert, fills a passport every year and was pleased with the border-crossing experiences on his Saint Kitts documents. Some might think it foolish for a person in the travel business to give up a US passport and all its mobility privileges, but Robert was blasé. "So there's 140 countries versus 180 countries visa-free travel, so what? It's not a big deal. Saint Kitts has been good to me." He simply gets ten-year visas for the countries he cannot enter visa-free, he said nonchalantly. "There's lots of visa-free access, even to places like Russia. China is the only sticking point." If most travel is smooth, sometimes problems can emerge, and a few service providers described clients facing occasional issues at the border. One investor citizen from the Middle East said that the only issue he encountered was in Pakistan, where the border officials had never heard of the small Caribbean country. A lawyer at a Big Four accountancy said that immigration officers, as they see more of such passports, have become concerned and check them more carefully. "People find that they are being held up in queues and being examined closely, which isn't what they're looking for" when they sign up for a new citizenship. Another reported that border agents at major hubs sometimes ask, "So where is Saint Kitts on a map? Don't you know?" It's a question that can lead to delays at the border rather than a smooth ride across it.

Moving and Not Moving

Yet it's not all about moving. Some naturalizers want to stay where they are. In the United Arab Emirates, for example, 90 percent of the population is foreign and needs a work visa to live legally in the country. However, the visa must be housed in a valid passport. This can raise problems if, for example, political turmoil impacts a home country's ability or desire to renew documents. In recent years, Syrians who decamped to Dubai have sometimes turned to citizenship by investment to plug the gap when their embassy was unavailable. Venezuelans working in the Middle East oil industry have faced similar challenges. An agent in the region noted a substantial uptick in interest after Venezuelan president Nicolás Maduro began to restrict emigration. "You send in your passport and it sits with the government for ten months, and then it comes back not renewed and you don't know why." As a result, a stream of oil engineers with expiring documents applied for quick Caribbean passports to hold their work permit.

One place that investor citizens typically do not look to move to is the country issuing the passport. "Businesspeople don't want to immigrate. Their businesses are here," a service provider in Dubai explained. Another in Shanghai put it plainly, "They don't want to leave China permanently since here is where all of their business interests are." A service provider in Russia set out the same issue: "Not everyone wants to relocate. Business in Russia is done through connections, and so you must be there to retain control of the business. Otherwise, someone else will take it. The government might even take it." One investor citizen with companies across three continents explained, "I want UK citizenship, but I just can't do it. I can't be there nine months a year for five years." Even when things get really bad, business owners remain reluctant to move. An agent in Dubai offered the stark case of a client in Lebanon during the country's financial meltdown in 2021. Though there was a run on the banks, a run on fuel, and finally a run on food, producing what the *New York Times* termed a "humanitarian catastrophe,"[14] he kept his Dominican and Turkish passports in a drawer and remained in the country to oversee his businesses and properties, afraid that he might lose them.

Many naturalizers will visit their new country once or twice to see the investment, but most do not transform it into a second physical base, with some exceptions. Russians picking up holiday homes in Cyprus are the most notable, but a few can be found elsewhere, too. In Malta, for example, investor citizens are required to buy or lease a residence, and those who buy usually buy big. They spend on average over €850,000 on the purchase—far above the minimum amount of €350,000—to acquire something "livable" and select the upmarket areas of Saint Julian's and Silema, where they might like to spend time.[15] However, only 15 percent of applicants purchase rather than rent, suggesting that most remain unanchored in their new state.

Yet for the countries involved, it may not be such a bad deal. "These programs wouldn't work if people actually moved," as one lawyer told me. If all the investor citizens of Saint Kitts actually relocated, they would increase the country's population by about 50 percent, with dramatic repercussions for society. Places may claim that they want the talent that investors carry with them, but it's mainly the money that matters.

Investors who did talk about relocation typically used the future tense. Some who had invested in property described possibly retiring to their new country. One example was Tariq, whom we met earlier. "Everyone here [in Dubai] is thinking about the future," he explained, "since there is no security." He had lived in the United Arab Emirates since he was a teen and now finds it "more of a home than my home country," but he knows he can't retire there due to the country's strict requirements regulating foreigners: only workers, and sometimes their family members, are allowed to live there. Europe is Tariq's big love, and his ideal would be to move to Sweden or Switzerland in his old age, but the Maltese program is outside his budget. As such, he's focusing on the Caribbean options. "They're the fastest, too," he said with a smile. They would take care of his current travel hassles and, he mused, they might offer entry into Europe so that he could retire there. He went on to explain, "If you look at developing countries, there's a big issue around the very well-educated middle class. We have three degrees, we're successful in our jobs, and we want to improve the quality of our lives." For those who made it out and became successful abroad, what happens after retirement remains unclear. "We can't go back. It's hard to go back and reconnect. This is an issue across the developing world." As he summed up, "I'm just looking for a better life and the possibility to travel." Ahmed, an Egyptian citizen but longtime resident in Abu Dhabi, told me a similar story. He chose to invest in real estate because it could serve as a retirement home or at least remain an asset he could sell in his old age. "There's no retirement here," he explained, gesturing to the country's strict visa regime. However, the time horizon is long in these cases of forward planning, and much can change as well: the property anchors only a hypothetical future.

The main exceptions are the CBI programs in sizeable Middle East countries with large economies, where applicants are more likely to have already relocated. Most naturalizers in Jordan and Egypt, for example, are Palestinians and Iraqis who been living in the country for years but have few other chances of acquiring citizenship. "They already have their businesses there and they just apply," a service provider in Jordan explained. "Only Palestinians want an Egyptian passport," another told me, which is marginally better than their own documents. "Really, who would want an Egyptian passport? They [Egyptians] have trouble getting visas in the first place." With a limited pool and limited benefits, uptake in these cases remains comparatively small.

Turkey, though, stands apart. "It has livability," as one lawyer put it, before rattling off the high-end neighborhoods and restaurants, as well as attractive business possibilities. "You can have a real life. A driver costs only $1000 per month." Another service provider explained that Turkey's high demand among Middle Easterners is because it's close, easily accessed, and livable. "With a Turkish passport, you can't go to the UK or the EU," she observed, "but in comparison to an Iraqi or Syrian passport, it's very good." A lawyer in Turkey noted that interest was initially limited to the wealthy refugees from the region who were already in the country, such as Syrian or Iraqi businesspeople. Once the price dropped to $250,000, demand diversified to include foreigners abroad. Still, the country has its own allure, and many investors purchase homes well above the minimum price, setting up a house or a second base where they can comfortably spend time.

Insurance Policy

Though many seek present mobility, future mobility may have an even greater allure. People usually aren't thinking of moving immediately, one service provider explained. "They don't want to use the passport now," but to have it "just in case." In these instances, the second citizenship serves as an insurance policy or a Plan B. "People do it for risk management or risk hedging," as I was told in Hong Kong. This may mean simply ensuring that all possibilities remain on the table. A service provider in East Asia clarified with circular precision: "There's mobility and there's mobility." It's not just about flying around the world but saying "I can move there if I want . . . It's options, not migration. They want a real, unlimited option." Often buyers desire an additional passport "just in case," a lawyer at a Big Four accountancy told me, and what this means can be taken to the extreme. "They may have three, four, or five passports lined up just in case." Ahmed, an Egyptian naturalizer I met in Abu Dhabi, described his new Caribbean citizenship as "like having a backup generator." He naturalized—"took out a second passport," as he put it— during the extended political upheavals following the Arab Spring.

Especially for the "ultras"—the mega super-rich—"having options is key," a lawyer in London explained, and went on to describe their thinking. For the wealthy, "certainty is important, and now we have a lot of uncertainty." In this context, "Many people are trying to hedge their bets in a time of uncertainty, based on what they know about the known unknowns." Samira, whom we met earlier, explained that the situation is precarious for long-term expats in the United Arab Emirates. "No one can be certain in Dubai. There's no security. You don't know if you will be told, 'Ok, now you have to go back to your home country.'" For her, this would be Iran, a place her family left when she was a baby. "I've been here for 43 years. It should be one hundred percent my home, and I do feel at home, but in the end it's not. My companies are here, my investments are here, my life is here, I should have some security here too, but at any point, they can tell me 'Good bye, pack your things.' I'm thinking about security."

The result, for some, is a portfolio of passports: multizenship. One lawyer I met described the paranoia of a Saudi "zillionaire" client who had been locked up in the Ritz-Carlton in Riyadh under Mohammed bin Salman. After spending several weeks in the exclusive prison, "He wanted everything— Canada, a European golden visa, and a second passport." Ling, a Chinese investor citizen whom I met, already had permanent residence in Australia, Hong Kong, and Singapore when her family decided to acquire Maltese citizenship. They had done very well in technology and real estate in China and had amassed assets over $50 million. "We want a place to go in case anything goes wrong—a backup plan," she explained. "In China, there's a lot of arbitrary confiscation of wealth," she said. "We were making a lot of money at once, but there was no legal way of protecting it." Fear and uncertainty drove the choice. "The government could decide to take everything you own, in addition to capital punishment or locking you up forever."

Some go for programs sequentially, becoming "serial investor migrants" as they use a citizenship acquired through investment to acquire investor citizenship or residence in yet another country.[16] Others will apply for multiple programs at once. This may mean selecting a CBI program to quickly acquire a travel document while applying for residence and citizenship in a place they consider livable, like Canada or the United States. "If they're coming from a country with a crappy passport, they need something while they wait," a service provider in Dubai put it plainly. He gave the example of a Pakistani national in the United Kingdom waiting for permanent residence, which takes five years. Until then, "they're still stuck on their Pakistani passport." The solution? "They get a Caribbean citizenship to allow them to travel while they wait."

Historically, this has provided an opportunity to game the system. Canada, for example, traditionally required its investor residents to spend several years in the country in order to qualify for naturalization. Until the 2000s, this was rarely policed, but as checks became more frequent, investors found that they could enter Canada on their original passport and then exit and return at leisure on the one gained through citizenship by investment. If officials looked only at their home country's passport, it would appear that they had been in Canada the entire time.

A portfolio of options may represent the luxury of choice, or it may supply much-needed alternatives under more difficult circumstances. In such cases, a second citizenship can offer a fallback to returning home. We saw this earlier with Tariq, the young tech professional in Dubai who doesn't want to go back to Pakistan. Another long-term UAE resident from India voiced a similar concern. Going back to his home country isn't an option, he told me. "Either the pay isn't as good or there is too much competition or there are no jobs." Caught between the UAE's policy that excludes retirees and the country's near-impossible naturalization regime, he was looking for a second passport to secure a place to go as a pensioner. The situation, though, can get more dire. A service provider in Cyprus explained that he had several Syrian clients who are against the regime and may never be able to go home. In many cases I encountered across the Middle East, the uncertainty of the future in a person's homeland was a strong driver. "When things go bad in your country, you want to be able to take your family somewhere safe," as a Dubai-based agent explained.

In some emerging economies, authoritarian regimes or the weak rule of law can provide lucrative business opportunities to those who are well connected, but this is double-edged.[17] A service provider in Russia described the local scene: businesspeople like "working in the gray"—there's money in it. "But they want it backed up in black and white." Everything needs to be very clear for them, I was told. Distrust of the government—whether in Vladimir Putin's Russia or Xi Jinping's China—frequently emerged as a motive for future planning, with autocratic leaders a great source of uncertainty and anxiety. "In Russia, businesses can easily be taken by the government," leaving people simply frightened, a service provider in Moscow told me. In China, an intermediary explained that her clients know that Beijing cannot be trusted and that their emails and phones are monitored. "One simply doesn't know what the government will do in the future," noted an agent describing a boom in people searching for CBI options after Xi changed the constitution to enable himself to become president for life. In such uncertain circumstances, a lawyer in London told me, "the thing is to retain flexibility." In Hong Kong, the risk-hedging opportunities may even be outflanking "mobility enhancement" among the Chinese. In the estimation of one China-based agent, 80 percent of his clients are seeking out an escape option. Another whom I met in Russia gave an even higher figure: 90 percent of his clients are looking for "a Plan B, purchased for the family."

Even democratically elected leaders can furnish enough distrust and unpredictability for some to seek out a Plan B citizenship. The United States is the clearest case, where successive and highly divisive presidential elections have produced ever greater numbers of people seeking a lifeboat. In London, intermediaries told me stories of the 2016 wave of "Armageddon Americans," who became interested in European citizenship options after the election of Trump. "They're not looking to leave the US," as one lawyer described, "but they want to have Europe as an option." Another in Malta explained, "Americans come because they hate Trump, or they are afraid that with Biden they'll have to pay more taxes." One former US citizen whom I met in London was a part of the trend. A longtime foreign resident with substantial wealth from real estate investments, he shed his US membership and became Kittitian just before Barack Obama took office. "I could see the writing on the wall" when it came to enforcing taxes on global income, he said. Robert, the photographer mentioned earlier, expatriated after the 2008 presidential election. "It was class warfare," he told me, complaining about the rise of political correctness. "This idea of the elite dictating what's best for everybody else is just total crap." In the end, he decided, "I didn't want to play that [game]."

Not only internal politics but also external politics can drive demand, particularly in geopolitical hotspots. A service provider in Hong Kong explained that his Taiwanese clients seek citizenship options in case something goes wrong between Taiwan and China. "It would leave everyone in the lurch," he said, "but the rich have more at stake." In Russia, US-led sanctions stoked worry within the business community about future growth, even before the invasion of Ukraine. One service provider described an in-or-out logic in 2018: entrepreneurs with largely Russia-based companies are pivoting inward, while those that rely on foreign markets are shifting out of Russia and looking for other options. In the Middle East, sanctions in addition to conflict and war have left people anxious to acquire a Plan B elsewhere, with Syrians supplying good business for many agents.

As an insurance option, citizenship comes in different grades, and buyers seek what they can afford. For those with fewer resources, the Caribbean offers a way out. As a service provider in Dubai described, citizenship in the Caribbean is "a ticket so that they can go somewhere and then move on." He explained that investors don't see themselves relocating to the Caribbean, but "if something happens in Iran, what can they do with an Iranian passport? No one will give them a visa." At least with Caribbean documents they can go to the United Kingdom and figure out what to do next. Others, however, want gold-plated protection. As a service provider in Russia told me, "For a Plan B to work, you have to be able to live there as well." Most people described the Caribbean as lovely for a holiday but unlivable in the long run. Those looking for a "serious Plan B," as service providers from London to Russia to China put it, will select the European programs, which leave open the possibility of residence anywhere in the EU. Some even start out on a Caribbean passport and then "upgrade their options" to an EU one, a lawyer in Cyprus described. "Europe offers more security—it's a question of the strength of the passport."

Yet passports that are largely Plan Bs may never leave the deposit box in which they are stored. Particularly in China, where dual citizenship is illegal, naturalizers are likely not to use their documents but to hide them away. "Once they get it, they just put it in a safe. They don't really talk about it either. Sometimes their family members don't know," an agent explained. I met him in Shanghai, though he is based in southern China, and he said that clients prefer that: working with someone from a different region means that the secret will remain secure. "They don't want others to know about their residency planning or second passports." Another service provider based in China agreed: "People won't talk about it. They won't even tell their friends if they have a second passport," and went on to note the impact on his own business: "You don't get personal referrals with passports." The result, in some cases, is that testimonials can be hard to come by, as investors don't want to expose themselves publicly. Interest in secrecy, which I regularly came across in China, stands apart from the accounts of the Plan B citizenships acquired by middle-class naturalizers who make use of—far more public—ancestry options.[18]

Lifestyle

Improving one's quality of life can also lead a wealthy person to the local citizenship service provider, but usually this does not end in moving to their new country. The EU is clearest on this score: get a passport from Malta or Cyprus and reside freely in your villa in Italy. Less well known, though far more popular, are residence opportunities in Anglophone countries that a new citizenship can secure. As we saw earlier, citizens of Grenada, Turkey, and Montenegro can easily gain a residence permit for the United States through the E2 business visa program. Before Brexit, Turkish citizens could gain the same in the United Kingdom through its Turkish Businessperson Visa (TBpV).

Chinese nationals in particular are drawn to the education advantages that a new citizenship can open. "The number one motive is to move the kids to a Western country for schools," as one service provider in China put it, an assessment I would hear over and over. Of course, citizenship by investment is hardly a necessity to study abroad—a mere student visa suffices. Yet privileged families may look for the greater flexibility that citizenship secures. As a Russian service provider described, "They want to put their kids in foreign schools and have the option to visit them too." After university, it keeps the door open for employment opportunities. Intermediaries will push for this package, which brings in higher fees. An agent in Hong Kong explained the financial strategy behind it: "Convince the client to become an investor so that school costs go down, and then say that the price you pay will be the same as the saving on the tuition fee—and you are a citizen at the end!" Mostly, though, it's schools outside the country granting citizenship that are an attraction. Before Brexit, some sought citizenship in Cyprus and Malta to make it easier to enroll their children in the UK's top schools—a strategy that still works for elite schooling in Switzerland.

The utility of foreign citizenship for improving education access is not limited to schools abroad. In China and Taiwan, international schools are in high demand but can have strict quotas on the number of local students allowed to enroll. The result is a pool of eager parents in search of ways to make their children appear to be foreigners. In China, the success of using a second passport as a workaround depends on the school, and I was told that fewer institutions are accepting such documents now, though I met two service providers who still received inquiries. Taiwan appears to remain more relaxed, and parents still seek extra citizenships to turn their offspring into, as one agent put it, "real international kids."

One South Korean investor citizen I met, Jihun, had recently gained Maltese citizenship. As a child of international businesspeople, he grew up in a peripatetic world, living first in Hong Kong, then Bangkok, and later China. His family on both sides had done well, and he was the beneficiary, with combined assets running into eight figures in US dollars. Yet even with such a safety net, his motive for naturalizing was "employability." Or at least that was the motive of his father, who wanted to see his son maximize his job prospects after graduating with a law degree. "There's an unspoken hierarchy for employment," he put it plainly. In London, employers "want UK citizens the most, followed by EU citizens, followed by everyone else." Even after Brexit, "it's still quite nice to have an EU citizenship because there are so many opportunities in the EU," he noted. Even though it's common to include several family members on an application, his parents did not pick up citizenship for themselves, which surprised Jihun. His father told him, "We're past our prime and you have your future ahead of you." Even reduced university fees in the United Kingdom for EU citizens were not a motive because the parents had already paid in full. "It's not really about taking advantage of the welfare system," Jihun said. Nor was it about mobility. "I can get to more places without a visa using my Korean citizenship anyway." Job prospects were paramount. "My parents have just been adamant on my employability. It's been very black and white."

Often family concerns stand at the core when considering the quality of life. Wealthy people "don't want their children to have to worry about the same things they've had to worry about," a Big Four lawyer described to me. This was the main motive of a South Asian couple, Sanjay and Meera, whom I met during my travels. They had three children now studying at US universities. Sanjay moved to the Gulf region at eighteen in search of a job and built a successful business in medical equipment. Frequent travelers, he and his wife managed the company by splitting their time between Dubai and South Asia. When I came across them, they had just spent a week at the Caribbean resort where they had made their investment and reported that they had enjoyed the hotel and were happy with their choice. "It's a good addition to our overseas portfolio," Sanjay found. Their motive, however, was their children. "With our passport, you can't travel many places," Meera explained.

"I wanted to open up more opportunities for them," Sanjay continued. Yet rather than embrace the gift, their children rejected it, telling their parents, "Take those things away!" For them, it was a shock. In Dubai, where the couple is based, investor citizenship has become normalized. "Everybody in Dubai knows about these options," Sanjay said, which is why he looked into them. But his three children, all living in the United States, saw it quite differently. "There's a perception of funny business involved, that you're hiding something," he lamented. "I just wanted more travel opportunities for my family and kids, but they don't want it."

Whether family members want it or not, countries cater to familial interests by expanding the definition of a household, sometimes quite generously. Among Caribbean CBI programs, competition has turned virtually anyone over the age of fifty-five into a dependent parent and under the age of thirty-five into a dependent child, and some even allow "dependent siblings" to join. As one official joked, "Some say, 'I have a wife and two kids, two brothers with three children, and they each have a parakeet and a dog.'" Of course, few will raise an eyebrow at excluding the animals, but it's not always clear what might happen in the cases of polygamy or children born after naturalization—an area of lively debate among the countries offering citizenship options.[19]

Family arrangements affect how an application is lodged, and it is not unusual for a spouse—most often a wife—to serve as the main investor and applicant. A businessman who deals with large government contracts, for example, may not want to put his connections at risk by looking like a turncoat. His wife then can include the rest of the family as dependents. However, there can be more nefarious reasons for applying through a family member. If a country runs background checks on only the main applicant, a person with a questionable past may slip under the due diligence radar though a "family workaround": that is, having a spouse or child submit the file and then tagging on as a dependent.[20]

Occasionally, too, the citizenships are used to facilitate "second families." A wayward spouse may employ the new membership to travel unbeknownst to their partner, set up an inheritance plan and manage assets for children born out of wedlock, or obtain papers so that a lover with a "bad passport" can travel. Sometimes this can backfire. A London-based lawyer cited a few cases concerning "very strategic partners who then extricated themselves from the relationship." That is, once the lover was gifted the funds to invest in a new citizenship so that the couple could be together, the person took the money and ran.

Changing nationality can also improve how a person is regarded, shifting them up a hierarchy of citizenships. Ahmed, the Egyptian naturalizer long based in the United Arab Emirates, confided that he puts his Emirati residence permit in his Caribbean passport: it gets him better treatment than his Egyptian document. Similarly, a Moscow agent listed clients who prefer to enter the United Kingdom on an EU passport because it offers "a better level of service" when they cross the border. Samira, the Iranian expat in Dubai, spoke of the far-reaching quality-of-life issues that can affect individuals even at home. In the Emirates, everything from salaries to schools is channeled by citizenship: wages are set based on what workers might earn in their home country, and state-sponsored education is open only to the national few. "It all depends on where you are from. It's the first question that everyone asks. Everything depends on it." Citizenship is virtually inescapable. But, she continued, "we shouldn't care—it shouldn't matter. We're all human. I just want to expand my possibilities. I've been here for 43 years and I will never get the passport." In such circumstances, "These [CBI] programs become a way of accessing everything. Over the past 50 years, it has become really important that you have a good passport here in the Middle East. A passport is something that gives you more options."

If investor citizenship is something only the wealthy can afford, is it also a status symbol? In places where demand runs strong, such as Dubai and Hong Kong, everything from public advertisements to dinner conversations ensures that the programs are common knowledge. Certainly advertisements for "citizenship products" project images of a high-status life in which a second passport is a luxury good, and some service providers I encountered adopted this language as well. Yet the investor citizens themselves whom I met were more reserved, and generally did not discuss their new membership with those around them. It's not surprising that they might be reluctant to parade about their future hedging strategies or possibly illegal second citizenship.[21]

To the extent that status was important in the cases that I encountered, it was largely in association with a cosmopolitan and international lifestyle, rather than a second passport itself. As a service provider in Hong Kong described, many of his clients "simply want to be more international or want their kids to be more international." For them, this meant naturalizing in Malta or Cyprus in order to spend time with their children in UK schools. When I asked an agent in Moscow about status issues, he explained that his clients "enjoy thinking of themselves as cosmopolitans." They have a house here or there and kids in schools in the United Kingdom—possibilities foreclosed during Soviet times that are now chic. A Chinese investor who was shopping for options when I met her in Shanghai described sporadic status competition among her friends. Having a passport—or, more often, a residence—from a prestigious country like the United States or Australia, she said, is something that can impress others. "It gives you access to a lifestyle that they don't have." Yet the concrete examples she gave were not of citizenship by investment but residence programs in Anglophone countries. A stronger exception to the general rule of downplaying the choices was voiced by Robert, the American-turned-Kittitian. Dropping his US membership had garnered the highest praise from his business friends, he said. It was right before Barack Obama took power, and the wealthy were concerned about the threat of tax increases. "Oh you lucky sonofabitch. Your timing was great, you did the right thing!" they praised.

Business Opportunities and Wealth Structuring

Finally, business opportunities may be a draw, but usually it's not the qualifying investment that is the allure: more important matters are at stake. Even as money flows across borders with incredible fluidity, a businessperson's nationality can still be consequential, affecting their legal rights and ability to engage in certain forms of trade. A new citizenship can make it easier to own land, list a company on a stock market, access international arbitration courts, or even open a bank account and acquire lines of credit. "If you have a nationality that's very restricted, you can't do much," a service provider in Dubai explained. He gave the example of a recent client who came to him complaining, "the banks are killing me." His business is in construction, and so he has numerous international transactions. With an Iranian passport, "he has a really hard time" since most banks are unwilling to open accounts for Iranians.

The EU offers the clearest case: gaining citizenship in a member state facilitates business activities across the entire Union. "If you're doing business between the EU and the Middle East," a Dubai agent explained, "it makes your life much easier if you're holding a European passport while you are banking, getting lines of credit, setting up a business . . . It's much easier to be European. It's much more efficient." Another listed several cases of clients who face problems when transacting with Europe. "If they are signing a business contract, people don't want to work with them because they are Iranian or Iraqi or Syrian or Lebanese. It's just because of their nationality." Geopolitics recasts their standing as a business partner. But, she went on, "if they have any other nationality, it's not a problem." One lawyer described securing citizenship for a group of Russian investors who planned to buy a European bank and become its board of trustees, an activity, I was told, that was possible only if they were EU citizens. Turkey, too, can offer business benefits: its citizens receive a reduction in customs tax when importing goods to Europe. "People see Turkey has a bridge," one service provider explained: it can be a base for connecting to markets in the Middle East, Russia, and Europe.

In the Middle East, a different citizenship can be used to circumnavigate the barriers to business erected by geopolitical conflicts in the region. Especially in Cyprus, I came across cases of people who naturalized after using the country as an international business platform. One was an Egypt-based exporter who employed Cyprus as a business hub to meet and work with individuals who cannot travel to Cairo. Following years of running business through—and occasionally investing in—Cyprus, he decided to add citizenship to his local activities as well. Service providers described cases of citizens of Arab countries using Cyprus, and sometimes Cypriot citizenship, to facilitate business transactions with Israeli partners.

Occasionally, the new citizenship can smooth business activities not abroad but in an investor's home state. The motive? Protection against one's own government. The past decades have seen a great expansion in bilateral investment treaties and other tools for international arbitration that take disputes out of national courts, which may not be trustworthy, and into arbitration. The catch is that only foreign investors can avail themselves of these stronger legal protections. Citizens carrying out business in their home country cannot: for nationals, national law holds. Yet if a national becomes foreign, a pathway is opened for shifting to international arbitration. I came across one such case in Dubai. A businessman from South Asia with a global network of companies had built a fortune in soap and was interested in doing more to help his home country. Yet there were challenges. "He's got a lot of businesses outside, but it's a pain for him to bring those businesses back," his service provider explained: he is concerned that the government will take them. Even if the paperwork is fine, I was told, the government could easily invent an excuse to seize his assets. They might claim that he didn't file the right form five years ago and then leave it to the unreliable courts to decide the outcome. A second citizenship is a way to circumnavigate the risk: "He's getting a passport to get more protections as a foreigner so he can bring his money back home." His case is not a one-off. Indeed, such strategizing became so common in Vietnam that, unusually, the government reacted. Vietnamese business-people in search of stronger legal protections would simply naturalize in Cambodia by purchasing real estate and then turn to international arbitration courts should any problems arise. By 2020, the government of Vietnam was so worried that the trend might undercut its power that it banned its nationals from purchasing property abroad in order to acquire citizenship.

Yet *homo oeconomicus* is ever on the prowl. Sanjay, whom we met earlier when he and his wife visited the resort in which they had invested, said he kept an eye out for other business opportunities during the trip. He thought of expanding his export of medical supplies, but the problem, he explained, is one of size. The Caribbean microstate "is simply too small for an economy of scale"—the same reason it was selling citizenship in the first place. Other investors, new passport in hand, will do more, and larger service providers usually had a few stories of secondary spending and further business development. Occasionally these were in the Caribbean, but more common were Malta and Cyprus. However, none can compete with Turkey, whose massive population and economic heft supply far more attractive opportunities than those in microstates. Service providers often spoke of clients who had built factories or farms or extended their entrepreneurial activities into the country. As one based in Turkey explained, "we have the population, we have the demand, we have the internal market." He elaborated with an example of a recent client based in Dubai, who naturalized and set up a cosmetics production factory in Turkey. "He'll be employing fifty to sixty people here."

More common, though, is to move additional financial assets to the country. A wealthy naturalizer in Malta, living in Dubai, might set up a parallel family office to manage her accounts, for example, or shift some financial structures to it. In this way citizenship sales can work symbiotically with a country's financial service industry, as discussed in Chapter 3. "It's all about protecting their money, expanding their banking options, and ensuring the safety of their capital," a service provider in Shanghai told me, a strategy that folds into CBI's insurance policy function. Agents in China described how their clients diversify their assets into multiple currencies—dollars, pounds, euros, and yen—to mitigate risks. They may set up some trusts in Hong Kong to shade their holdings from Beijing, I was told, but they know these won't last forever and therefore may use their new citizenship to set up foreign accounts outside Xi's watch. Russians, meanwhile, will incorporate their businesses in Cyprus to keep them at arm's length from Putin, a service provider in Moscow explained in 2018.

All of this merges into more complicated issues around taxes. Mobility may come with tax implications, but these are rarely straightforward. Typically physical presence determines one's tax residence: spend more than 183 days in a country and it becomes your tax home. For anyone mobile enough to stay under that number, a combination of factors comes into play. These vary from country to country—there is no set formula—but they generally include the location of one's homes, family, businesses, "center of vital interests," and even where one spends the most time. Citizenship may enter the equation, but it's generally low on the list.

Still, most countries offering citizenship by investment have low or zero income tax, which can make naturalization look like an easy way to scam the taxman. However, utilizing such provisions to lower one's taxes is complicated, even under the most favorable circumstances. For example, if one spends less than 183 days in any single country and can produce enough "substance" to make the claim that Malta is one's tax home, but remains "domiciled" in another country, then it may be possible to benefit from Malta's preferential tax regimes for the non-domiciled.[22] Yet success in this still depends on whether another country is able to claim the person for tax purposes and whether the two countries have signed a treaty preventing double taxation. The result is good business for lawyers.

Furthermore, very wealthy people are usually "structured." That is, they receive their income not as paychecks but as capital gains or loans, which are typically subject to much lower tax rates, if taxed at all. By one estimate, wealthy Americans pay only 3.5 percent in taxes annually, although the top income tax bracket is 37 percent.[23] Even if countries with CBI schemes have low tax regimes, the vast majority of tax avoidance and evasion goes on outside them. Structuring wealth usually means putting assets into trusts or foundations, or even more exotic legal instruments like the Liechtenstein Anstalt. Once wealth is wrapped in these cloaks, wealthy individuals no longer own it outright and thereby avoid taxation or seizure of their assets even though they can still benefit from them. These legal structures, a dime a dozen in the offshore world, are all readily available and easily used without citizenship by investment. Indeed, if CBI offered an easy "solution" for lowering tax burdens, the uptake of the programs would be much higher.

Yet countries offering citizenship by investment will often tout their low tax rates. They are still relevant to most investor citizens, for tax is involved whenever a person acquires an asset. There might be property taxes, corporation taxes, title and deed fees, and the like that are due when the qualifying investment is made. Some countries make this more palatable for investors. A citizen of Saint Kitts, for example, will pay no capital gains tax when selling a property and will be subject to a mere 0.2 percent property tax. For others, the rates can make a difference internationally. If a British national invests in North Macedonia and takes the profits back home, she must pay UK taxes on them. Yet if she becomes a North Macedonian citizen when making the same investment, she can simply open a bank account in Skopje and move the money through it, paying only Macedonian tax. In most cases, a country's low to zero tax rates are not a product of the citizenship trade. They're usually developed for the financial services industry rather than handcrafted to support the sale of citizenship.

US citizens and permanent residents are the important exception. They are taxed on their income no matter where it originates and no matter where they are in the world. For them, membership always matters. If Americans groan in early April every year when their tax filings come due, the situation is worse for their internationally mobile compatriots. Even if they never set foot in the country, they are still responsible for taxes on income over $100,000 or so. Indeed, it can be so complicated that most accountancies in global cities have a special division for US citizens and green card holders.

The upshot is that, as a Maltese lawyer put it, "the US client is a different animal than other clients. He doesn't worry about security, but tax." Some are libertarians who take a principled stand against the state seizing what does not belong to it, but most cases I encountered were of long-time foreign residents or "accidental Americans" who had spent most of their lives abroad. One introduced himself to me by his US city of birth rather than his new nationality and told me proudly that he expatriated to become a citizen of Saint Kitts in 2006. The United States was going to more seriously enforce taxation on global income, and he wanted out. He had moved to Europe years before and developed several property businesses, but he didn't want to continue to pay tax in a place where he spent no time. He naturalized in Saint Kitts because it was the only program on offer, he told me, and even maintains a residence there, though he rarely visits. He had no complaints about the process or the scheme: ten-year multientry visas to the United States and to the Schengen countries in Europe are easy to obtain, and he has never had a problem at the border. There's little else that he asks of his citizenship, he explained. One might wonder why an American would give up a "good" citizenship, yet the status can become a burden for those who shift their lives outside the country. A service provider in Hong Kong captured the logic when he described an American client, based in Asia for many decades, who was considering expatriation: "Even if a Saint Kitts passport is weaker, it doesn't really matter since he doesn't live there [in the US] and doesn't need it for Hong Kong and Bangkok," where his homes are.

Getting out, though, isn't easy, and the United States has made it increasingly hard to expatriate. It now requires multiple interviews and the process can take well over a year. Americans who renounce their citizenship must also pay tax on all assets over $2 million, held anywhere in the world, and show that they have filed their taxes in the previous years. As a tax dodge, it's not very straightforward. Lawyers taking on such cases told me that if the US government suspects that a person has expatriated in order to avoid tax—like Roger Ver, the CEO of Bitcoin who made a big show of it on social media—it is unlikely to give an entry visa to the individual afterward. Even an ex-American has no prima facie right to enter the United States, and as a hedge, some former citizens keep a few businesses in the fifty states to maintain a good reason for receiving a visa. The rollout of the Foreign Account Tax Compliance Act (FATCA) in 2010 also stimulated expatriation among long-standing emigrants. Under the act, the United States obliges all non-US financial institutions across the world to report on the assets of clients who are US citizens or green card holders. The requirement has left foreign banks skittish about taking on US customers, even for mundane requests such as mortgages. Service providers in places like Hong Kong had stories of long-term American residents who sought to finally expatriate because day-to-day financial transactions had become too onerous, and many banks uncomfortable with the invasion into their client relationships simply stopped taking on US citizens. As one lawyer put it, Americans are now "toxic" to foreign banks.

FATCA proved to be a useful tool for tracking financial flows abroad, and other wealthy countries did not want to be left out. Following the US's lead, the OECD in 2014 developed a similar mechanism with the Common Reporting Standard (CRS). To date, around one hundred countries have signed this agreement, which facilitates the exchange of information about assets and accounts held globally. The immediate result, particularly in China where Xi Jinping combined its launch with a crackdown on tax evasion, was a burst of interest in cheap "banking passports" as a tool for "serious tax planning." Some service providers I encountered in China at the time were loudly touting passports as the best way to avoid CRS. "A second citizenship is the only way to protect yourself," as one in Guangzhou explained. CRS meant, as a lawyer in London put it, "the bank is no longer necessarily on your side."

The CRS rush in China highlights a crucial characteristic of the relationship between citizenship by investment and taxation: it is only when governments become serious about collecting taxes that workarounds proliferate. For this reason, tax evasion is not a motive for many wealthy people hailing from and making their money in developing countries, where the state often does not have the infrastructure to enforce tax collection. Some have begun to do more, like China, which in 2019 started to tax its citizens on their global income if they spend more than 183 days each year outside the country. Before the reform, it was perfectly legal for Chinese citizens to avoid paying taxes by using shell companies to hold their assets; now it's not—or rather, it depends on how it's done.

Though the CRS boom generated extra business for service providers, in practice the passports have not proved to be a silver bullet. Mainstream banks, responding to their legal departments, demand evidence of "substance" beyond the passport—documentation indicating long-term physical residence in the country—to establish one's tax home. A Hong Kong service provider indicated that Switzerland, for example, now requires a host of additional justifications and documentation if a client wants to open a bank account with a Caribbean passport. A second citizenship can be a liability in these cases. An agent in Vanuatu lamented that two clients had international banks close their accounts after they had acquired documents from the Pacific archipelago—the move just raised too many warning flags on their risk profiles.

Yet, as a service provider in Russia told me, "If a client wants to lie, he will lie." It may be the bank's obligation to check, but the bank may also just tick the necessary boxes without investigating thoroughly. In countries where it's relatively easy to change one's name—Dominica requires only a small fee and a short form—it's even easier to obscure one's identity. You just get citizenship, file a form, and secure a passport with a new name. Is that any different from getting a new identity? The Comoros, too, has seen demand from Americans looking to open a bank account outside the watch of Washington and the long arm of FATCA. With a different name, it becomes possible to set up accounts and create companies that keep the connection between the person and the money invisible to one's adversaries, whether governments, divorcing spouses, or others bringing lawsuits.

Additional workarounds to CRS exist. A straightforward one is to open a bank account in the country where one is a citizen: countries only report to foreign governments, not to themselves. As Cypriot lawyer explained to me that a Cypriot citizen banking in Cyprus is "invisible" under CRS. The situation is the same in any state, whether or not it offers citizenship by investment, though Malta in 2021 gave in to EU pressure to report to home governments on its investor citizens. In its wake, yet another workaround has emerged: a form of "serial investor citizenship."[24] Become a citizen of, say, Saint Lucia and then naturalize in Malta. In such cases, Malta will report only to Saint Lucia if that is the original citizenship declared on the bank account. Yet the existence of these possibilities doesn't mean that they will always be used. For strategizers, the main question is whether they trust a country's banks. Vanuatu may produce a working travel document, but can its financial system be counted on?

This is why the easiest workaround for CRS is the United States. The global behemoth hasn't—and is very unlikely to—sign onto an agreement that is an offspring of its own FATCA regulations. All a person has to do to avoid CRS reporting, one service provider explained to me, is to set up a shell company in a place like Delaware, Nevada, or North Dakota. These internal workarounds are the best way to keep wealth anonymous or invisible. No investor citizenship required.

What about the qualifying investment itself? Does it add to the business opportunities opened to the investors? In most cases, it's not a key driver. "A means to an end," is how one lawyer in London described the investment. "As long as the client breaks even and doesn't lose money, it's a good outcome." In Shanghai I was warned, "If any Chinese say that they're looking only at the real estate [and not the possible passport], it's because they already have their exit option taken care of. Everyone secures an exit option first." Though these channels have come to be called citizenship by *investment*, naturalizers rarely see these opportunities as a substantial moneymaking venture. The double-digit returns that typically produced their wealth are available in emerging markets but not in investment migration projects. They are aware that their money would be making more money elsewhere: citizenship is the premium for the low or zero return on the investment. Of course, citizenship is for life, and once it is gained, investors can sell their qualifying assets after a specified number of years, usually three to five. The result transforms the investment into, effectively, a savings account. Because it's possible to cash out, investing in a country is like "putting money in a bank," as one service provider phrased it. In these cases, the end cost of citizenship is the difference between the amount invested—and then divested—and what the money might have otherwise earned over three to five years (plus, of course, fees).

Indeed, investors try to avoid putting money into a country with a lower rate of growth than what they could find elsewhere. Financing makes this possible, and in some countries, like Saint Kitts and Dominica, it's perfectly legal. As a would-be investor citizen I met in Shanghai explained, she's looking only at options that can be financed since she doesn't want to tie up her money for five years. Some, however, find it more straightforward simply to gift the money to the government. One naturalizer who chose a donation option in the Caribbean asked me rhetorically, "Why would I pay that much for a piece of property that I probably can't sell for the price of the donation anyway?"

Still, *homo oeconomicus* would prefer not to lose money if possible. "Smart business people don't just write a check—they like to get a bit of return," a service provider in the United Arab Emirates observed. Another in London noted that as economies cool off in developing countries, her clients are increasingly interested in what their money is going into, as well as the performance of the asset class. If it looks like an investment might pay off, it can be a deciding factor. This possibility is strongest in Turkey, which has seen a 20 to 30 percent appreciation in property values in recent years. Though demand has been largely from the Middle East—people in the region who already have a foothold in Turkey—service providers note a growing interest from Chinese investors. "Brick and title" have long been perceived in China as a safe way to watch one's money grow. Since the government in Beijing limited the number of properties that an individual can own in China, people have looked even more fervently for options overseas. In an exception to the rule that citizenship rather than investment is the draw, one lawyer in Turkey said that he's seeing a growth in clients from China interested first in the real estate opportunity and second in the passport. "They're looking for portfolio diversification," he explained, describing the desire to move assets overseas and into different currencies. "And now they are getting citizenship on top."

Even if the qualifying investment is not always seen as an investment, sometimes the citizenship itself is. The result transforms "citizenship by investment" into a "citizenship investment." With that comes a concern about its future value. Investor citizens can take a personal interest in how things are going in a country, raising concerns, for example, if the EU presses down on them. When Cyprus closed its scheme in 2021, service providers in Malta faced applicants worried about their own future: would the citizenship itself retain its value? Sanjay and Meera, the investor citizens from South Asia whom we met earlier, voiced similar fears to the prime minister of their new country at a feedback session the head of state hosted for the investor citizen community in Dubai. "We made the investment with a certain set of expectations about what we were getting in terms of mobility," Sanjay told him, "but if you compromise the country, it can compromise us as well." He also cautioned the prime minister not to bring down the price, which can "attract a much less desirable level of people, which is a risk." Looking at the lay of the land, he said, "If they are not careful, they could lose a lot." As with any asset, the value of citizenship can sink or soar.

Picking a Country

How do people decide which country to invest in? Not all citizenships are the same—which is why there is demand for the programs in the first place—and neither are all investor citizenships. That is, the market is segmented. In the first instance, a citizenship's cost and benefits channel demand. Membership in Malta comes with rights across the EU and fetches a higher price than that of Saint Lucia, which brings merely visa-free access to the EU. Geography can matter too. Places like Jordan and Egypt cater to populations already in the country. Cambodia sees most interest coming from Chinese and Vietnamese nationals doing business in the region. Others with small programs, like North Macedonia, may attract a clientele looking for a "boutique" option that is off the radar, where exposure is less likely if something goes wrong.

In the end, choice comes down to a person's situation and preferences—if they are not swayed by an agent's entreaties to follow the route offering the most lucrative commissions. Even service providers operating outside such financial incentives will always have work as they lay out the benefits of an E2 visa in Grenada versus swifter processing and a "legacy product" in Saint Kitts versus readily changing one's name in Dominica. Others—especially those from countries under US sanctions—may find the menu of options narrowed for them. If an Iranian seeks citizenship in the Caribbean, there is only one choice: Dominica.

Others simply follow personal advice. Ling, a Chinese investor citizen whom we met earlier, decided on the Caribbean after looking at European possibilities. Even though money wasn't an object, she still preferred the proximity to the United States. A recent university graduate, she had started to take over parts of the family businesses, and her father advised that the US rather than the EU was where the economic action was. Jihun, who became a European citizen due to employability concerns, chose Malta over Cyprus because Maltese friends of his father in Hong Kong had mentioned the opportunity. Plus, he added, "Malta is the most well-known and it's got a decent reputation. It's a nice country. It's got good banks, it's quiet ... I'm sure my parents would consider it as a retirement country too." He elaborated, "even though it is about my employability, if you have the option between different countries, you might as well go for the one where you think you'll enjoy living there, just in case." When Robert began looking at options, it was 2009 and choices were few. There was Austria, where membership can be negotiated, but this was expensive. Dominica had an option, but it had a "bad reputation," he had heard. Then a friend who worked at a bank recommended Saint Kitts. "It was the best choice out there at the time." And he's remained happy with the selection even as new programs come into the market. As a travel document, "it's terrific."

Covid-19

The Covid-19 pandemic, however, has changed some key calculations around citizenship by investment. The pandemic was great for the super rich, who saw their wealth increase substantially. But for people in the 0.1 percent rather than the .01 percent—the "poor millionaires" with less than $5 million in assets—times were tougher. The economic slowdown impacted the businesses of many, eating into liquidity they may have otherwise used for a citizenship-based Plan B. At the beginning of the pandemic, many in the market feared that, like flights, the citizenship trade would be grounded. Sudden new travel restrictions meant that the easy border crossing, once in high demand, was unavailable. The pandemic looked like it might be even more effective than the EU in closing down programs.

Instead, demand soared.

For the microstates that were heavily reliant on citizenship income, the developments were a godsend since their other economic pillar, tourism, had shut down. With airports and hotels closed and tourists blocked from entry, Caribbean countries quickly retooled their citizenship processing to online workflows, online application submissions, and even online oaths. Assessment took a bit longer, but applications kept moving down the pipeline. Countries in Europe that required the in-person submission of biometric information couldn't give full approval, but they kept accepting applications, their programs simmering on the back burner. The result has been backlogs and delays, depressing annual approval figures, but overall demand has kept climbing.

Covid has raised the stakes. It has also reconfigured the calculations of many would-be investor citizens. The travel bans meant that some people, for the first time, couldn't readily go where they wanted to go. US citizens, accustomed to easy mobility across borders, suddenly saw barriers thrown up left and right. Their blue booklet was, in many cases, no longer a VIP pass into Europe. The actual operation of travel restrictions on the ground varied across countries and across time, and with a great deal of unevenness even within the EU. There were some stories of US citizens using the United Kingdom as a back door until Brexit took effect, or landing in Portugal to access private medical care in Switzerland. If some side doors stood ajar, the uncertainty alone was enough to drive many to apply for full citizenship in an EU country to make sure that the gate remained firmly wedged open. "It's been a big reality check for Americans," as one service provider recounted. "They're being told that Europe doesn't want you, Canada doesn't want you, a lot of places don't want you. You can't even get into the Bahamas!" Agents around the world described surprise at how many wealthy Americans they were seeing for the first time. A service provider with a global footprint summarized his shock: In 2018, they had two US clients, rising to fourteen in 2019, then thirty in 2020. "And this year [2021], it's about 400." Another, whom I met in Dubai, explained "Americans don't like being told that they can't do something," and for them Covid was a wake-up call. "It's great if you have a great passport, but if you can't use it, what good is it?" Many I spoke to described "smart money"—people who made a fortune in tech—driving interest among US nationals. "Most of them are discreet but they all have friends they hang out with. It's a new status symbol for them. It's not just what watch or car you have, but what passport is in your pocket." If the world is your oyster, you want it to stay open.

There were not only people who couldn't get in during the pandemic, but also those who couldn't get out. From April to August 2020, Russia blocked the exit of citizens. The great fear of being trapped in the country, as under Soviet times, was realized once again for the first several months of the pandemic, with an important exception: those who already had a foreign residency or citizenship could leave. Anyone with a Plan B passport had an exit ticket, encouraging those who hadn't already secured a life raft to find one. (And some who did may have counted their blessings two years later when Russia invaded Ukraine.)

Plus, there were people who couldn't stay where they were and didn't want to go home. During the pandemic, job losses were heavy across the Gulf and businesses took a hard hit. Even top-level managers and tech talent were left high and dry. Yet under the region's draconian visa regimes, anyone without employment has only one month to find a new job or else return home. Successful professionals from places like India, Pakistan, and the Philippines watched how their home governments handled the pandemic with alarm, and many were wary of returning. "Just look at what a mess the government made of it," a shopper from South Asia living in Dubai said about the Covid situation back home. "I have to make sure that my family is ok. It's just not safe there." After making it through the continuous lockdowns, he said he wants to find a country "that's more secure, where the government helps its people." As a service provider in the region put it, "With Covid, going home was not an option." Not only were flights cancelled and return blocked, but it was also clear that the Emirati government wasn't doing much to help people during the pandemic. Even those who maintained their jobs began thinking more carefully about future options with a medium- to long-term perspective. Agents suddenly started fielding queries about government efficiency and the medical sector. "I could have gotten into Europe before the lockdown if I had done it [CBI] sooner," lamented one applicant I met in Dubai.

Finally, there are those who waited for years to exit easily. Until January 2023, China was still enforcing some of the toughest quarantine rules under its no-Covid policy. Before then, anyone who left the country needed to self-isolate in a government hotel for two weeks upon return, followed by a third week of isolation at home under police surveillance, on top of continuous testing. Gone were weekend business trips to Singapore or Tokyo, let alone to places farther afield. Travel was just too onerous. With in-person application requirements, Malta and Cyprus have been out of the question, and who needs a Caribbean travel document if travel is impossible? Some appetite remained as the lockdowns continued, but it wasn't like the pre-Covid days when China accounted for half of the global market. Yet service providers suspect that it won't last. Too many people are frustrated at how the government had handled the crisis, especially if they were trapped, for example, in Shanghai for weeks on end without even reliable access to food. Most predict that as the barriers come down, pent-up demand will explode.

Across the spectrum, Covid produced many people fearful for their health and dissatisfied with how governments handled the pandemic. Americans were upset with Trump, Indians with Modi, Pakistanis with Khan, Russians with Putin. As one service provider in the Middle East described, "Covid-19 left people looking for countries that can manage a crisis." Even if they didn't—or couldn't—leave their home state, they began thinking of ways to keep their options open. Many of the ultra-rich hunkered down on their yachts. Yet this was no clear solution either: an American tech tycoon on his floating palace in the South Pacific still needs a way to get into New Zealand should a family member need urgent medical care. Wellington can be negotiated with, as wealthy techies have shown, but the uncertainty brought on by Covid still left many seeking to hedge their bets. But their calculations were different to those before Covid. It wasn't just an exit option or life raft for a distant and uncertain future that they sought. Now the medium term was more pressing. Investors began looking for "livability"—somewhere one could go for several months or half a year. Somewhere with a good health-care system—or easy access to one. Places like Turkey, which has services that cater to an elite set, did well off these calculations, while the Caribbean tried to compete by pitching its medical credentials and low infection rates. If anything, the pandemic only diversified the risk-aversion strategies of the elite, adding investor citizenship to the set.

Identity and Connections

In the end, what does this all mean? Citizenship may be for sale, but it is an important locus of identity for many people as well. This is due to the historic welding of state and nation into the double-barreled amalgam "nation-state," or what most people think of simply as a country. In the contemporary world, a state's legitimacy comes not from divine right or a mandate from heaven, but from the people—the nation—in whose name it rules. "We, the people . . ." begins the founding constitution of not only the United States, but also India, South Sudan, Nigeria, South Korea, and elsewhere. Even non-democracies conform to the modern norm of anchoring the legitimacy of political rule in the nation. The Democratic *People's* Republic of North Korea or the *People's* Republic of China are just two examples. It is the nation side of the hyphen that is filled with identity, and it is as members of a nation that our identities are coupled to states. It is "our" national anthem that we sing solemnly at sporting events. It is "our" national history that we learn in school. It is "our leader" whom we read about in the papers. The transformation is, of course, not absolute, and many people do not identify with nations at all, but national identity is still a powerful device that has spread across the globe over the course of the twentieth century, marked by the willingness of people to sacrifice their lives in war for something as abstract as the nation.[25]

For investor citizens, however, the identity side of membership in a country is—as one might expect—thin at best, if not entirely absent. They are members of the state and not the nation. Naturalization connects them to the government and the legal benefits that its sovereignty secures, but not to the people in whose name it rules. Service providers mostly responded with a version of "people are pragmatic" when I asked if identity issues mattered to any of their clients. The wealthy naturalizers I spoke with also replied along pragmatic lines when I asked about the decision and any identity issues that might arise. Several lived international lives and had only thin attachments to any one country in the first place; others still felt strongly connected to their country of birth. In either case, when I asked where they were from, the answer was always their original nationality, sometimes qualified with a complex response about a peripatetic upbringing.

Robert, the American-cum-Kittitian, touched on the matter when he told me how he took the CBI plunge. "I finally just thought, 'Screw it, I'm outta here. The world's a big place and a passport is just an ID,'" he said, describing an existential shift. For him, citizenship and national identity are two separate things. "My culture is American. I spent most of my life growing up there. If people ask me what I am, I say I'm American, and that doesn't change. I feel American, but I'm not American and that doesn't bother me. It doesn't bother me to have renounced my passport because a passport is just an ID." When I asked if he feels Kittitian, he said that he didn't until he started facing various passport hassles. (However, as he said this, he pronounced the nationality not as the locals do, namely *ki-TI-shan*, landing squarely on the middle syllable, but as a reader new to the word on a page might be inclined: *KIT-ti-an*.) When he was standing in line to renew his document, he began joking with the others around him. "Kittitian people like to play," he recounted. "They just tease each other, which is something that I like doing too. I realized that we all have that in common." It's a thin basis for a sense of national belonging, but for a person who travels to the country only to renew his passport, it's hard to expect there would be much more.

Jihun didn't identify as Maltese, but he didn't identify with South Korea either, having grown up in Hong Kong, Bangkok, and Shanghai. "For me [Korea] is just another country. I feel attached to people there, yet I don't feel attached to the country itself." As such, it doesn't seem strange to him to be Maltese but not live there. Still, he thought that his new citizenship could be useful on a personal level: it might mitigate the racism he faces in the United Kingdom. The British "are more respectful of naturalized Asians, as opposed to full-on Asians, which is what I am." He went on to explain, "I feel like being from some kind of western country plus Asian, like British-Asian, just seems to be more . . . I don't want to say acceptable, but it seems to be more acceptable to be a European-Asian." Despite his new citizenship, he's worried that he might not seem to be a real EU citizen to an employer and could end up being treated as a third-tier "full-on Asian," as he put it. "If they see 'EU citizen,' then maybe they'll consider me more seriously. But if they know about the program, then maybe they'll think that I'm not a real Maltese citizen who has lived there, and then maybe it will be back to just the usual," he said with a sigh.

When I asked Ling what the new citizenship meant for her identity, she was nonchalant. When she moved abroad to go to university, people warned her that "you'll always just be Chinese in the UK." Though it bothered her at the time, she doesn't think about it anymore. If people ask where she's from, she avoids being pigeonholed. "I usually end up giving them a long story about how I grew up in China, lived in a lot of places, and now I'm here." She went on, "I don't see my identity as being based in a country. If I were to put my identity in a country, where would it be? China? Not after all the things it's done to my family. The UK? I live here, but I don't have a permanent place here. And now I'm from [the Caribbean] too." When I asked if the programs devalue citizenship, she responded that she's been wondering that herself and didn't have an answer yet. "People tell me that I will always be Chinese, but I don't take that view . . . I don't feel a sense of obligation to a country. I'm not patriotic." Drawing a distinction between Chinese culture and the Chinese Communist Party—the nation and the state—she added "You can be a part of a culture but not a supporter of the government."

If the media are eager to label investor citizens as criminals and corrupt, how do investor citizens themselves respond to the impressions of others? Usually the reaction is dismissive, but with some variation. Jihun said that he knows some people in the West who think of citizenship by investment as "a cheating way to get citizenship." They look down on it. "It's almost as though you haven't put in the effort to be rewarded with citizenship. . . . People can be like 'You don't deserve it, that there is no moral backing.'" He was also worried that people—if they knew he gained EU citizenship through investment—would treat him with even more slights than he receives as a citizen of an Asian country. "If they find out, maybe they will disrespect me even more." Sanjay admitted that in South Asia, people are suspicious of investor citizenship. "Why are you doing that? It's such a small place, it's nothing . . . it's barely a state," are the reactions he gets from others. But if it were citizenship in Canada or the United Kingdom, the response would be completely different, he told me, well aware of a hierarchy of belonging. "The perception is much better because they are large and wealthy countries." Robert found a more welcoming response. Those around him—"successful businesspeople, professionals" as he described—were supportive: "Nobody says, you shouldn't do that. They say, 'good decision.'" He thought he may have produced some converts among his American friends, who are in full support of his choice. Only a British colleague queried his selection, asking if he really wanted to give up the opportunity to live in the United States. But for Robert it's not a concern. "If I ever decided that I wanted to live back in the US, I'm sure that I would be able to do that. People move every year to the US under different investment schemes. If I wanted to do it, I could."

Some investors found that reactions were often different depending on where people are from. When I asked Ling about how her friends have responded, she broke them down into two sets: the British and the Chinese. "My British friends will say, 'Oh that's so dodgy.' But there's nothing dodgy about it. It's not a loophole. It's a law—it's completely legal." However, she went on, they don't really need to think about citizenship issues. "If I had a British passport, I wouldn't think about them too." But talk of investment migration and various mobility options is "big" among Chinese expats, she said. "All of my father's friends talk about it, and a lot have done it as well." She listed off the RBI programs in Canada, the United States, Australia, and Singapore as popular choices. The motives? "Usually political," she responded. Jihun's schoolmates were also split in their reaction. His friends in the United Kingdom query the matter when he mentions it. "It's like 'Oh?! You're buying citizenship?! Hmm, interesting . . . ,'" he narrated to me, emphasizing a note of doubt. They think that it could be dodgy and are worried that his family could be getting ripped off. However, his schoolmates back in Hong Kong are unfazed. "My international friends are just used to weirder stuff. It's like, 'Oh, you're buying citizenship? Ok, good luck!'"

The programs hardly change the investor citizens' identities, but they do change their identification. As some of the intriguing cases of high-fliers that opened this chapter suggest, a new set of documents—especially if they are not linked to the old ones—can prove useful. Because evidence of who we are lies outside us, in documentary form, it is possible to sever the link between ourselves and our IDs. People can deftly dissemble and connect to— or disconnect from—bureaucratic systems and legal regulations to their advantage. Particularly if a new passport carries a different name (a simple procedure in some countries), the possibilities are many. Serial investor migrants who skirt CRS reporting might take out several new citizenships to obscure their history or identity. These strategies work only as long as systems rely on passports as the definitive document for identification, and the rise of biometric systems, which identify our bodies rather than our papers, may have already limited the life span of such tactics.

If some investor citizens are coolly instrumental when naturalizing, others are emotionally overwhelmed. One Egyptian I met said that he was so happy that he wept when he was approved for a program in the Caribbean: the sense of liberation and possibility was too much. Especially for those without documents, finally gaining papers can be existentially profound. Service providers and government officials described cases of stateless people, often Palestinians, who were elated, even crying, when they were approved.

As members of the state but not the nation, investor citizens are hardly part of a diaspora. In 2018, I went to Saint Kitts for a conference the government was hosting on citizenship by investment. Three weeks later in the same venue, it held a similar meeting, but this time for the diaspora—meaning native-born Kittitians who had left the country and made it big abroad. The intent was to enhance their connections back home in order to encourage remittances, investment, and any other kind of wealth or skills transfer they might be able to muster, reversing a brain-drain decades in the making. Yet no mention was made of the large body of investor citizens, also living abroad, who might be well placed to contribute significantly to the homeland. "Kittitian" meant something else.

Countries offering citizenship by investment may do well to avoid being swamped by wealthy naturalizers, who could easily bring with them gated communities, resentment, and xenophobic tensions. This isn't to say that the governments, especially in the Caribbean, don't want to strengthen ties to their new members. At a conference in Monaco, the prime minister of Saint Lucia declared that he hoped that their investor citizens would have a strong "transactional relationship" to the country and continue to give back to the island. "We are looking for people who will be genuine partners in development," as he put it, who can take the place of supranational organizations like the IMF and its strings-attached loans. At another event in London, a representative from Saint Kitts declared that the government was trying to do more to get investor citizens to come to the island, stay longer, and spend more. By this he didn't mean immigration, but "turning citizens into tourists."

More recently, Antigua has explored ways to transform the one-time investment into stronger ties. In 2021, the government appointed a representative to hook into the "investor citizen diaspora" and encourage a continuous engagement through philanthropic contributions. "Right now, it's just transactional. It's just a one-off exchange and people don't come. They don't even know where the country is," he explained to me. However, his job hasn't been easy. The investor citizens connect to the country only through the intermediaries, he complained. "Even when they renew the passport it's through the agents." He wanted to change that and make the link direct. "Once they're citizens, they're ours. They're a part of us too. We have a direct connection to them . . . and we can get them to invest more to build the country." However, it wasn't national belonging in a traditional sense that provided the leverage. What he aimed for was something along the lines of an alumni association. In reaching out, his strategy was similar to that of any organization trying to attract donors: a get-to-know-you meeting followed by more serious discussions of investment or donation opportunities. He had even found a potential partner in a wealthy longtime foreign resident in the United Arab Emirates who had given up his citizenship of birth to become Antiguan and was even thinking of retiring to the island someday. If the initiative bears fruit, it might look like a member's club, providing networking, camaraderie, and connections to encourage a newly minted "investor diaspora" to keep giving to, or investing in, their country of passport. The result might turn what were once one-off injections of foreign direct investment into a more steady stream of, effectively, remittances.

A Future of Global Citizens?

Citizenship by investment enables the wealthy to transform their economic advantages into citizenship solutions. As we have seen, the goal is often to open possibilities unavailable to them because of their country of birth: visa-free access, faster processing of visa applications, respectful treatment at borders, business offerings, and opportunities for their children. Sometimes they are closing the gap between their own options and what citizens with "privileged passports" can enjoy.[26] In other cases, they hope to avoid the liabilities that a good citizenship can bring. US nationals sometimes find membership in the global hegemon disadvantageous: they may face kidnapping risks, problems with banking, and continuing tax responsibilities in a country where they spend no time. Others seek to maximize options—an orientation to the future set on ensuring that the world remains their oyster. This could include students using a new membership to access prestigious international schools in their home country, "multizens" collecting several golden passports just in case, businesspeople making money as nationals at home but wanting to back it up abroad "in black and white." Some are maneuvering in a world of shifting geopolitical tensions—such as Arab-Israeli friction, China-Taiwan conflicts, or changing US sanctions—and becoming a different kind of foreigner can ease transactions across these boundaries. Sometimes even being foreign at home brings more benefits too, as with Vietnamese becoming Cambodian to invest in Ho Chi Minh City under the protection of international arbitration and trade agreements.

For the most part, it is the combination of differences *between* countries in what citizenship secures and differences *within* countries in the distribution of wealth that produces rich people with limited options and in search of solutions. That is, the confluence of interstate and intrastate inequality shapes demand.[27] If all citizenships were the same and treated interchangeably—what might be seen as "global citizenship"—there would be little need to replicate what one already has. It is because some countries are authoritarian while others are democratic, some are rich while others are poor, some supply generous benefits while others provide very little, and some treat the nationals of other countries as irredeemably suspect or as privileged outsiders that people look to expand their range of options.[28]

What is the impact of investor citizenship on inequality within the countries of origin? Does it, contra T. H. Marshall, reinforce class disparities rather than upending them? It might seem that when elites use citizenship by investment to circumvent the state borders that enabled their wealth accumulation in the first place, they might impede economic growth. Indeed, some evade foreign exchange controls to pay for their new passport, draining resources from a country that might otherwise be reinvested in it. But given the small numbers and relatively low costs involved, the effect is largely negligible. Chinese nationals, for example, have traditionally constituted around half of the global market in citizenship, investing an estimated $2 billion abroad for such programs in 2016. What appears to be a sizeable figure, however, represents less than 1 percent of the more than $150 billion in overseas investments that left China in that year.[29] Foreign transfers are even more endemic among Russians: oligarchs hold about as much wealth outside the country as the rest of the population does inside the country.[30] Within these great disparities, CBI funds are a drop in the bucket.

Are the investors "global citizens"? Most of the wealthy naturalizers I spoke with were uneasy with the term. One shopper in Dubai confessed, "'Global citizen' is a very heavy word—it's not for me." Images of environmentalists on bicycles or NGO workers in Africa came to his mind. Another naturalizer said that he's not concerned about being a global citizen at all and feels most comfortable in his hometown. Jihun shunned the phrase: he thought that if he embraced it himself, then people would think, "Oh, he's really pompous." Robert listed all the countries where he feels at home: "So I guess you could call that a global citizen—I don't feel attached to anywhere." When I asked Samira if she thought of herself as a global citizen, she found the question ridiculous. "Because you're from a different background, you don't see the pressure on me because of my passport. If I want to travel anywhere in the world, if I want to live in a different way, if I want to make a business, I can't." Then she said pointedly to me, "You can go to many different countries. You can invest wherever you want. You can move freely. But I can't. This is my life. I want more choices, I want more options."

It was the service providers who most frequently invoked the term *global citizen,* sometimes with different nuances. The "global citizen" awards given out by various firms are meant to honor the internationally minded, risk-taking, self-sacrificing, agenda-setting, entrepreneurial heroes, who are often quite privileged themselves. People in the citizenship industry sometimes describe it as the "right to live wherever you want." One lawyer in London talked at length about the uneasy relationship between hypermobile people and the state: "For the wealthy, the world is truly global. They can be anywhere. What stops them is tax." That is, states trying to claim people. Clients come to him saying, as he put it, "I want to be a global citizen. I don't want anyone to pin me down." But—barring Elon Musk's adventures in the stratosphere—one has to be somewhere, in some country, for the planet is divided up into these units. Even those going the "peripatetic route"—deliberately allocating their time among different countries in order to secure the most advantageous tax situation—still have citizenship. "I don't think you can escape it," the London lawyer admitted in the end.

Chapter 10

Citizenship in the Twenty-First Century

W ORLD EXPOSITIONS ARE a curious phenomenon, a nineteenth-century product of the spread of capitalism and overseas empires. Yet somehow they have survived into the present, perhaps a testament to the economic and political priorities of the powerful. At these grand displays, countries show off their achievements in industry, science, and culture, effectively pitching their competitiveness. The most recent iteration was Dubai's Expo 2020, which the Covid-19 pandemic pushed into 2021 and 2022. Never shying away from grandiose expression, the Emirati government transformed a swath of the Arabian desert larger than Monaco into a massive celebration of the countries of the world. To visit was to wander through a great outdoor mall of country pavilions surrounded by spouting fountains, leafy trees, and coffee carts. Christmas even brought the standard accessories of capitalism's biggest holiday to the desert: decorations and light shows featuring snowmen, reindeer, nutcrackers, decorated trees, and stockings over fires. Very Instagramable.

In the pavilions, countries put on their best show of what they can bring to the table, both culturally and economically. For the United States, it was Elon Musk's SpaceX rocket and Bud Light. The quasi–tax haven of Luxembourg touted its "sustainable finance" to visitors who wandered along a path that, like a Möbius strip, folded in on itself. Turkmenistan welcomed guests with a 360-degree cinematic tour of the country led by four horses galloping around a circle of glowing wheat. Bangladesh flaunted its manufacturing prowess in a pavilion that looked like the inside of an Ikea store.

Within this setting it should come as little surprise—particularly if citizenship is a country's number one export—that several microstates in the Caribbean, as well as Vanuatu, included citizenship by investment in their exhibits. Between the costumes from Carnival festivals, celebrations of cricket prowess, and the advertisements for beach holidays stood displays of their citizenship offerings. Saint Lucia ran with its strong reputation as an ideal wedding destination, but alongside photos of happy couples stood a huge sign that asked, "What does global citizenship look like?" Flanking it were the keywords "access," "security," and "identity" that glowed above images of planes, passports, and triumphal people. In Vanuatu's pavilion, an agent had joined with a local coffee grower to put up a small internal display. Beside a one-cup espresso machine offering visitors a taste of its local brew, a poster proclaimed, "Experience global freedom with Vanuatu citizenship" and listed passport options. The barista was happy to serve up both.

Saint Kitts went all out. It had a large section on its greatest celebrity export—US founding figure, now Broadway star, Alexander Hamilton—followed by a chronicle of the country beginning with its Indigenous people through colonization, sugar production, slavery, and independence. The historical tour ended with the island's most recent achievement: a celebration of "the longest running citizenship by investment program in the world." After wandering through, I spoke with a representative from the country's Chamber of Commerce who was working at the pavilion. When I inquired about the program, his first response described frustration. "People come in and ask, 'Do you sell passports?' I say, 'We don't sell passports. We provide investment opportunities, just like any other country. You invest and you can get citizenship.'" He went on to explain about the history of the program with some pride. "We needed investment, and we developed a competitive strategy." But he wasn't happy with the way people project it. "If you look on the internet, service providers say that we are selling passports, but we're not doing that. It really makes me angry. No one can just sell the passport. This is my country. Don't devalue it. What I wish is that some of these people will come and see the country, see the people, get to know it too. Just to deepen their connection. To get to know it—it's a really special place." The legitimation that he offered was the government's standard line, and one that I heard occasionally among locals in Saint Kitts as well: the program is not a form of prostitution but a reward to those who help support the country. Whether or not one agrees, the economic picture is clear. Topping 40 percent of GDP by most calculations, the scheme has become the country's lifeline.

A Global View of Citizenship by Investment

Of course, Saint Kitts would be struggling far more if it were on its own and the global citizenship market did not exist. Yet creating and sustaining this market has hardly been straightforward. Joining together its different parts—supply, demand, and the connective tissue of the citizenship industry—reveals the mechanics of its operation and the power plays that run through it.

Supply

Building a market around citizenship is not easy, as we saw in Chapter 1. The state not only sets the rules of play but is also the sole producer of the product. As such, the basic mechanics of the market generate conflicts of interest, which increase risks for others in it. How can one be sure that the sovereign will not "default" on the citizenship if a new government comes in, erasing the memberships and canceling the passports? Such moves were common in the 1980s and 1990s, when discretionary economic citizenship channels proliferated, as detailed in Chapter 2. At that point, the world of citizenship sales was much murkier and turned more on passports than formal state membership: application and vetting processes weren't always clear, due diligence was rare, one hand of the government might not know what the other was doing, and buyers could be left wondering if the documents would really work.

Shifting sales out from the shadows required broader credibility and greater reliability. In this space, private actors working with the Saint Kitts government refashioned its economic citizenship scheme into a formal program. This became the model for others—both countries and service providers—to follow. Even places with previous experience in citizenship sales emulated the new standard. The result was not cash-for-passports, but an extended and elaborated application process with clear stages, prices, and investment options. Prospective naturalizers submit applications via licensed service providers, which then vet and turn them over to an independent bureaucratic unit for further consideration and additional background screening by international due diligence companies, and sometimes third states, before going to a final panel for approval. The division of labor and external oversight created distance between the state's two roles, as rule maker and product producer. Citizenship by investment became standardized and straightforward.

The resulting formalization enabled market expansion, transforming citizenship by investment from a mere legal provision into a scalable product: it was now routinized, calculable, and offered a more secure future, as seen in Chapter 3. Applicants want to know what to expect and when they can expect it. The same holds for the citizenship industry, which also needs stability and predictability to navigate market uncertainties.[1] As they grew, the programs replicated each other in design and operation: countries borrowed from established models, and service providers touted a standard form that had served them well. Formalization doesn't necessarily mean that all problems were solved and that programs achieved buy-in from everyone. Yet overall the division of labor, external oversight, and increased transparency supplied enough credibility to assure other market actors that the sovereign would not default—cancel the citizenship by fiat—and that they could trust the product. The result was credibility within the market, and with that came future calculability. The value might fluctuate—depending in particular on the actions of powerful third states and supranational organizations—but still there would be a longevity and durability to the status.

For some countries, the programs became a huge moneymaker, laid bare in Chapter 7. Citizenship is now the top export of some microstates, and can bring in more government revenue than all taxes combined. Analyses by Big Four accountancies and the IMF have credited citizenship by investment with rescuing ailing property and construction sectors, revitalizing tourist infrastructure, and moving government books from red to black. Yet they are not a silver bullet: projects may never finish, money may be misspent or flow out from the side, and overdependence brings its own risks. What is the true benefit? The answer is somewhere in the middle. In many cases, the actual financial intake is less than the rough-and-ready estimate generated by multiplying the number of approved applications by the minimum investment amount. The costs of market competition and program operation, including greased hands, can diminish the actual inflows. Yet even using conservative estimates, the contributions can be substantial—topping 20 percent of GDP—and a number of countries have become economically dependent on the programs.

If countries have changed their schemes over time, the schemes have changed many countries too, as Chapter 5 revealed. This appears not only economically, in an over-heavy reliance on this income stream, but also in foreign policy and embassy footprints abroad. Countries can respond to market demands arising from competition from similar products, purchaser preferences, and third-country pressure. Those that get caught up in the game can succumb to price wars, races to the bottom, and other competitive forces. They also get entwined in tussles with powerful third countries and supranational organizations. Some even transform their offerings to appease them, handing to a foreign power a measure of control over background checks and the decision of who can become a new member. In these power plays, the United

States remains decisive: it readily transposes its border regulations and political interests onto the naturalization policies of other states.

Local opinion, as we saw in Chapter 8, ranges widely, from national pride or pragmatic acceptance to embarrassment or disgust. Older programs tend to have more buy-in than newer ones. In a number of places, partisan politics determines opinion. People support their own team and criticize not the program but how the other political party had made a mess of it. If they had no problem with selling citizenship—"What else can we do?" was a common refrain in the smallest countries—they would raise questions about how the money is spent. Newer programs were more often controversial and could even become a political football, with Malta providing the clearest case. As time has passed, many of the countries have seen a turnover in power, yet new governments rarely end the formalized CBI programs of their opponents: they are too big a cash cow to slaughter.

Much of this book has focused on the heart of the citizenship market: the programs that have defined the field, that compete against others, that naturalize large numbers, and that have become a crucial revenue source. These are primarily the Caribbean and EU cases, around which the market coalesced, and they still have great impact on the scene even as it changes. In the past few years, Vanuatu has risen in prominence as a less formalized variant. However, Turkey now soars over all of them, accounting for around half the global market. It shot to prominence just before the Covid-19 shutdowns, and the pandemic's impact continues to work its way through and reconfigure the market. Still, Turkey represents a shift in the citizenship industry away from microstates, where investor citizens spend little to no time, toward bigger countries, with bigger economies and "livability." It remains to be seen how this will reshape the game.

Yet not all other countries have followed suit, as Chapter 4 showed. Surveying the wider scene reveals a broad range of variation in CBI possibilities outside the core market. Other big countries, like Egypt and Jordan, have rolled out schemes, but they focus on "nationalizing" wealthy foreigners who have long lived in the country. Like Turkey, they set them up largely outside the influence of foreign service providers. Yet without the independent due diligence checks, a dedicated unit to process applications, and other bells and whistles, their programs operate like other nationalization streams. Some countries, like Samoa and Russia, have promulgated provisions but haven't yet transformed their options into a marketable good, perhaps preferring, like Mauritius, to remain small "boutique" possibilities. They offer a channel, but their tiny numbers raise less ire among the populace. Others, such as Cambodia and, historically, North Macedonia, use their programs to facilitate active foreign business investment in the country. States like Armenia and Albania have set out on the path to a program only to close it before it gets going—or, like Moldova, shut it down shortly thereafter. On the edges of the scene are options that raise questions about the legality, solidity, and reliability of the programs, as seen in the Comoros and Vanuatu. Citizenship by investment is much more widespread than is often thought, and a great deal of variety is visible on the margins. Most of this diversity has little demographic or economic significance, and these offerings stand outside the competition with other states for investors. From a bird's eye view, the global market for CBI programs is elsewhere.

Demand

Driving demand for citizenship by investment are the triple engines of inequality, uncertainty, and geopolitics, exposed in Chapter 9. For all their wealth and privilege, elites from outside the global core do not possess automatic access to a full range of possibilities when it comes to international mobility, business opportunities, or lifestyles. For them, a second citizenship is a ticket. Increasingly, too, wealthy people from powerful countries are seeking to hedge their bets with additional memberships. CBI programs enable them to convert their economic resources into legal benefits as they open alternatives and safeguard themselves. In many cases, the divisions they seek to overcome are conditioned by geopolitical tensions, which themselves shift patterns in demand as they fluctuate.

For the most part, investor citizens seek the privileges that citizenship secures not in the granting country but outside it, whether in eased cross-border mobility in the present, the future mobility options of a "Plan B," lifestyle improvements, or business opportunities. A Pakistani CEO may get citizenship in Antigua to travel readily around Europe. A Chinese real estate baron may naturalize in Malta to more easily visit children in Swiss schools. A Vietnamese businessperson may go for Turkey to take advantage of import opportunities in the EU. An Indian doing well in the tech industry may become Grenadian to pick up an E2 residence visa in the United States.

Yet third-country privileges are not always about getting into the West. A second citizenship can secure key benefits elsewhere, too. Chinese businesspeople may purchase citizenship in Cambodia in order to own the land under their factories in Phnom Penh. The most prominent cases, though, are found in the Gulf, where "nationality is everything." In places like Qatar, Kuwait, and the United Arab Emirates, upwards of 70 to 90 percent of the population is foreign, and a nonnational workforce carries out almost all private-sector work. Western media have focused on those laboring on construction sites, but foreign workers are found at all levels of the job spectrum, including doctors, bankers, accountants, and lawyers. With salaries often tagged to citizenship—a carryover from pay hierarchies during British colonial penetration—a Bangladeshi tech engineer will earn less than a French colleague doing the same job. In such cases, ethnicity matters far less than the documents. An Indian with Maltese nationality will earn more than an Indian with Indian nationality, and the new citizenship can pay for itself through the increase. In the region, Iranians have a particularly difficult time, especially in Dubai. After 1979, many moved across the Persian Gulf and did much to build the city. Yet since the global financial crisis of 2008 and subsequent geopolitical tensions, they've faced a number of challenges to carrying out everyday activities. Most banks refuse to open an account or extend a loan due to sanctions, making it challenging to do business or even get a mortgage. In such cases, a second passport simply makes life more livable, not in the West, but in Dubai.

Sometimes being a foreigner is advantageous, even at home. For businesspeople uncertain about the intentions of their home governments, taking on a foreign citizenship can open access to international arbitration, should a conflict arise, and foreign investment incentives and protections as well. Countries like Vietnam have even tried to prevent their nationals from finding a way around such regulations—or risks, as businesspeople might see them. Others become foreign to open education possibilities, like Taiwanese who may pick up an additional passport to make their children "foreign enough" to circumnavigate the quotas on the number of nationals who can apply to international schools within their country.

Even individuals with ostensibly top nationalities may seek "citizenship solutions" in countries lower down on the citizenship ranks.[2] Most common are Americans with lives based outside the United States, whose nationality has become a liability as pressure from Washington on international banks has rendered simple transactions, like taking out a mortgage, extraordinarily onerous. Since FATCA was rolled out in 2010, the number of Americans renouncing their citizenship has skyrocketed from a few hundred to over 5,000 annually since 2015.[3] They may also see no reason to pay taxes to a country where they haven't resided in decades, or to face the dangers of being American in parts of the world where they are unwelcome. Changes in the presidency too can leave some feeling no longer at home and lead them to search for exit options. Though less common than citizenship "up-grading," such cases expose the complexities of state membership and extraterritorial influence. For citizenship is not only ubiquitous (cases of statelessness, relatively small in number, notwithstanding), but necessarily portable, and obligatorily so: even outside the United Kingdom, a British citizen is still a British citizen. Citizenship by investment offers options for escaping a status that may have become an impediment internationally.[4]

Furthermore, one never knows what's around the bend. People also want options—a portfolio of options—and an additional passport can furnish that. Some have learned the hard way through the Covid-19 pandemic. US citizens saw once-open doors suddenly closed in their faces. Others, like Russians, were trapped inside and could not leave without a second citizenship or residence. There were also those, such as unemployed foreigners in the Gulf states, who suddenly found they could not stay and were reluctant to return home. Across the board, individuals began searching for not merely a travel document but also a destination—someplace to go in the event of another lockdown.

Political instability, insecurity, and violence condition demand as well. Citizenship, after all, is about a legal connection to a state, whether one likes the government or not. Authoritarian regimes, by nature, generate uncertainty about the government's future moves, encouraging the search for a lifeboat or Plan B. The spread of capitalism within formerly communist states, still often authoritarian, has generated substantial wealth among the few, facilitated by weak legal structures, within a setting of political precariousness.[5] Geopolitical tensions, particularly when translated into sanctions and travel bans, also generate risks and liabilities. Politics, of course, can change, moving in either direction. It was relatively easy to travel on an Iranian passport in the 1970s; now it is far more difficult. Chinese nationals, by contrast, have become more warmly welcomed. The country's broad acceptance into the global capitalist economy has enabled Beijing to negotiate ten-year multi-entry visas with sought-after places like the United States. But the US is not insulated from these trends either. Though a relatively stable democracy, its electoral convolutions have produced a rash of so-called "Armageddon Americans" wanting to secure exit options.

Demand for citizenship by investment, however, is premised on the absence of other options. Naturalization based on ancestry or ethnic heritage, if available, is far cheaper and more popular.[6] But such opportunities remain out of reach for many in the Global South who lack genealogical connections to countries at the top of the citizenship hierarchy. Notably, demand for CBI programs is low in South America, where many wealthy people with the right heritage make use of Spanish or Italian ancestry to gain a European passport, and for far less than the nearly €1 million required for the Maltese program. Russians aside, nonwhite wealthy individuals are the most likely to seek citizenship by investment.

Investor citizenship depends on a separation of state and nation. Wealthy naturalizers seek the benefits the state secures—and largely those it offers not within but outside its borders—and show little to no interest in its imagined national community. The result is hardly a mushrooming international diaspora of, for example, hyphenated Saint Lucians. Unlike their new fellow citizens "at home," these absent members are attached to the state but not the nation. However, the governments of these countries might count themselves lucky if the affluent did see the nation-state boundary as one worth crossing. At present, a one-off contribution is enough to make an investor citizen. Harnessing communal ties might transform this momentary injection of foreign direct investment into a more continuous flow of, effectively, remittances. Such a scenario remains hard to imagine for those involved, though. With the exception of Turkey, the governments hope that, at best, a few of these "expats" might come and spend time—and money—on the islands.

Citizenship Industry

Connecting the two sides of the market is a complex, multilayered citizenship industry that turns a profit off borders and connecting people to countries. As seen in Chapter 5, the rise of CBI programs is inseparable from this business. It is middlemen producing policy, implementing programs, and advertising opportunities who have driven the schemes forward. They have been crucial to the formalization process and division of labor that established the calculability and credibility needed for the market to grow. They also needed predictable products—box-ticking and straightforward—to advance their businesses. Since service providers helped establish a standard model, it's become easier for states to roll out programs on their own, but most that have popular programs still rely on the citizenship industry to reach customers. At base, the private sector's role is mundane: agents act as a translator between bureaucratic systems, ensuring that the documentation from one country ticks the right boxes for another in the application process. Effectively, they transmute an investor's economic capital into state membership for a handy fee. Yet they do much more.

There is money to be made off borders and inequalities, and this pushes the industry forward. The citizenship industry generates substantial profits off flattening borders for clients, but it is structured by these barriers as well. It can be a challenge for a firm to extend beyond its own jurisdiction and do business in other parts of the world, whether it sits on the "demand" side, working with clients, or "supply" side, submitting files to governments. An extended supply chain results as companies connect across borders and collect fees off the differences on both sides. Within the chain, businesses are specialized: feeders, application handlers, dominant consultancies, couriers, and others have carved out niches. They populate an elaborated ecology of mobility specialists that operate in connection with run-of-the-mill law firms, international accountancies, private wealth managers, and others who also funnel clients though the system. The front-facing agent of this complex web may be merely a "project manager" for a deeper division of labor. The most prominent citizenship consultancies, particularly in the West, may present themselves as the face of the industry, but in reality many more layers and divisions are involved. The long supply chains provide convenience, close information gaps, and facilitate trust in a market that is fundamentally international. However, they also produce regulatory challenges as they span multiple jurisdictions ruled by separate authorities. States' attempts to keep actors in check are often incomplete, for in many cases their direct influence ends at their own border. Keeping it all spinning are commissions—and hefty ones at that. These are reaped from clients, but they may also come from the state and even the investment itself. Their flow can diminish a CBI program's overall economic contribution to the country, but in a competitive environment, they may be the cost of doing business.

The result is that powerful firms and microstates are often co-dependent. Agents need governments to start programs, and they need good connections if they want to know what is required to get a file through. They will also lobby for program changes and offer feedback in consultation sessions. Governments can acquiesce, brush them off, or take a position in the middle as a cooperative or recalcitrant partner. Those with limited resources are more likely to become dependent on the private sector to carry out what the state cannot. Due diligence companies may stand in the place of national law enforcement, service providers may take up foreign policy and lobby other governments, and standards boards might fight a PR war for a country's main revenue source. In some cases, it's even the private sector that has brought governments into line when things go wrong with a program. Sometimes the co-dependence can function well, making for stronger program structures. But it can also undermine them, opening up possibilities for conflicts of interest, kickbacks, or other questionable activities, such as ensuring a rejected file gets through anyway. The scale of the money moving through the programs can make such temptations too tempting for some, compromising integrity at best and leading to corruption at worst. The interface between public and private around these sizable flows of funds, if unavoidable in some cases, should not go unmonitored.

Citizenship in the New Millennium

The rapid spread of citizenship by investment programs since the early 2010s is striking. What are the implications for citizenship in general? If taken at face value, they can hardly be said to be changing citizenship as we know it. The schemes, nearly all in peripheral countries and servicing a small population of wealthy individuals, don't pack the punch to move mountains. They may periodically mesmerize the media and irk EU politicians, but they're far from shifting everyday understandings of citizenship outside the countries hosting programs, let alone on a global scale. Yet they are not trivial either. The programs are best viewed as exemplary expressions of pervasive dynamics that are not unique to them but may otherwise go unnoted. As such, they supply an opportune site for unpacking broader transformations in citizenship in terms of inequality, extraterritoriality, neoliberalization, and strategic action.

Inequality

Citizenship, in T. H. Marshall's foundational account, is the great equalizer. In a society divided by class and status, citizenship serves as a weapon against entrenched powers by enabling disadvantaged segments of the population to obtain basic rights. Prompting his foray into citizenship was a deeper concern with transformations in inequality. Marshall asked: How can capitalism, reliant upon inequality as an incentive, exist together with modern citizenship, an institution that turns on the equality of members? The answer he found was partially damning. Citizenship, effectively, "provided the foundation of equality on which the structure of inequality could be built."[7] Within this configuration, though, lay a moment of hope, for citizenship in its increasingly elaborated form—particularly with the addition of social welfare rights— simultaneously provided a more equal footing for people to escape the class distinctions of their birth. The end result was a still-stratified class system within high capitalism, but one more flexible than before: citizenship made economic inequalities more difficult to sustain, unsettling once firm class differences.[8]

Yet does this social democratic utopia still hold, if it ever did in the first place? Even if the equalizing potential of citizenship loosens class dispari- ties, enabling those at the bottom to secure better life chances (if social wel- fare is available), migration controls still prevent people outside a state from accessing such opportunities. State borders are powerful exclusionary mech- anisms. According to one estimate, international migration to wealthy OECD countries would increase fivefold if they removed entry visa requirements.[9] Immigration regimes and border controls do not merely reflect unequal rights, but actively produce inequality both within and between states. These, too, are a pillar supporting capitalist social relations, dependent on expropriation and exploitation.[10]

No matter the country, much of immigration policy is about economics. States are loathe to give ready access to citizens from places that are on average much poorer than they are. Today, visa regimes screen out the unwanted, playing the role that head taxes did in the past.[11] They categorize people based on where they stand in the labor market and decide which workers with de- sired skills will be given access. They also readily permit members of wealthy countries to enter and spend their money, if on a temporary basis as tourists. Even much family reunion migration is economic, contingent on proof that one has the means to support the additional kin. Often it's the preserve of only those higher up on the economic ladder anyway, as many countries forbid foreign workers in the lowest jobs from bringing their family with them. Sending states are not immune from the economic strategizing. Scholars of diasporas have tracked the ways that countries latch on to emigrants, ex- tending political rights and other benefits, in order to capture a greater share of remittances.[12] Hierarchies of worth channel mobility and membership through naturalization, not just in cases of citizenship by investment.

Beyond the question of how the wealthy buy privilege, CBI programs pro- vide a unique window into global inequality today. They remind us that it's not merely inequalities within states that matter. Disparities between states also play a crucial role in producing the value of citizenship.[13] Countries are not all equal, and neither are all citizenships, and it's these differences—lost in debates about democratic participation and inclusive rights—that transform citizenship into a preferred product for both its wealthy consumers and its microstate producers. The implications go beyond the well-known story that global inequality fuels migration among those seeking to improve their life chances: in this case, it is not immigration itself but present and future mobility options, as well as business and lifestyle benefits, that define the stakes.

Thus a double layering of inequality formats the demand for CBI programs. Not all citizenships are the same when it comes to mobility options and the package of rights they guarantee, nor are all citizens equal in wealth. Those on the prosperous end of *intrastate* inequality strain against the limits imposed by *interstate* inequality—and feel the effect more than others.[14] It's not the poorest of the poor who move internationally, but those with some financial resources, and the very wealthy are the most mobile of all.[15] In the face of these barriers, many people act strategically: they acquire a second citizenship to increase their possibilities and hedge risks.[16]

Are the wealthy naturalizers, often born in countries with authoritarian regimes, perhaps under a weakened rule of law or even torn by war, simply the victims of an unjust system of unequal nation-states? Some fit this pattern. Think of the expat Iranians trying to get a mortgage in Dubai and being declined simply because of their passport. Or of Russians who have been denied entry to numerous countries since the invasion of Ukraine, even if they stand against Putin's regime. Or of stateless people who cannot find a country willing to take them on as a member.

However, others have done well precisely because of their citizenship at birth. A cursory examination of the Chinese and Russian cases suggests that the borders that many investment migrants attempt to work around may also be the very ones that enabled them to amass great wealth in the first place. Many members of the entrepreneurial or oligarchic elite in these countries would not have accumulated their vast financial resources had they not been born there at a particular point in time—one marked by mass privatization, marketization, and increasing economic inequality. It's not Kenyans or French or even Chinese Americans who made money when the Chinese Communist Party shifted to a more capitalist mode of production. Instead, it was Chinese nationals—frequently well-connected ones—who profited enormously. The same holds in post-Soviet countries and other places where capitalism has spread. For the winners, the accrued capital becomes a resource to transcend the political borders that encased their great wealth accumulation in the first place. As such, there's more to it than simply drawing a bum straw in the birthright lottery. Not all such jostling is about compensating for perceived deficits in one's original citizenship.[17] In many CBI cases, the drive is more expansionist than compensatory. The super-privileged often seek out unlimited options that allow them to untether themselves from the limits imposed by states. It can be a great hassle to be unable to travel to one's Italian villa during a global pandemic. Yet the inequalities between countries can still play a role. State borders still define—and circumscribe—opportunity. It is this division of the world, which affects all within it, on which players in the citizenship market seek to capitalize.

If much of the discourse on citizenship in the Western world celebrates its promise of equality, access remains fundamentally unequal. The porosity of borders varies based on the value ascribed to different human beings—whether labor migrants, refugees, family reunifiers, or investors. As countries screen entry into their territory or their membership club, they reinscribe class boundaries. Those deemed less worthy are left waiting on the doorstop while the skilled, the ethnically connected, the talented, or the wealthy move to the head of the line, securing benefits beyond those available to their less fortunate compatriots. In this world, citizenship continues to sustain capitalist inequalities not by leveling but by riding on them.

Extraterritoriality

Conventional accounts of citizenship focus on the relationship between a sovereign and subject and reduce its benefits to the rights it secures within the granting state. However, consideration of citizenship by investment underscores the often-ignored privileges that citizenship can furnish outside the granting country. The EU is perhaps the most well-known example, where being a citizen of one member state secures extensive rights across the Union. Other regional alliances, like CARICOM, the Nordic Union, and the GCC provide similar advantages of mutual recognition in a range of domains.[18] On this score, it is the Icelander, with full access to forty-one countries and territories, along with rights on par with those of local citizens, whose citizenship packs more punch than that of the Canadian, whose citizenship carries far fewer external benefits.[19] If the international treaties, alliances, and bilateral agreements that secure these rights were initially intended to encourage the free flow of capital and goods, they now facilitate the free flow of people as well. These extraterritorial advantages, a strong draw for investor citizens, are of course available not only to them but to any national—something typically forgotten when considering the advantages of citizenship.[20]

As the proportion of the world's population crossing international borders steadily grows, and as regional and bilateral agreements proliferate, the significance of extraterritorial rights increases as well. What is the upshot for citizenship? Extraterritorial citizenship is, in philosopher J. G. A. Pocock's terms, Roman, not Athenian. The political participation that Aristotle extolled is increasingly episodic and fades over time for those who are absent—if ever fully there at all. (Aristotle's Athens was, of course, a slave-based oligarchy.) Distance presents difficulties for participating in civic life when a citizen is away. Laws may prevent it as well: slightly under half of all democracies do not allow citizens living abroad to vote.[21] Instead, Cicero's plea, *civis romanus sum*—I am a citizen of Rome—which was used to appeal for protection when traveling within the empire, is the essence of citizenship by investment. To be a citizen of Ancient Rome did not hinge on participation in the rule of the polity: it was a privileged legal status, and just one of many in a multiplex empire. Furthermore, Roman citizenship was akin to a possession and therefore transportable, following the individual across the imperial domain.[22] Its bearer was a member of a community of law and subject to those laws, and could invoke them even when away. Jurisdiction, rather than democracy, stood at its core. It is this version of citizenship that is ascendant in the contemporary world. *Legalis romanus* is not a *zoon politikon*, but in an age of de-democratization even among the nonmobile population,[23] it can be argued that political animals are already a species in decline. Investor citizenship epitomizes the shift away from mythical Athenian conceptions of citizenship to a more Roman version: a territorial yet portable legal privilege.[24]

Are these new state members merely "offshore citizens"?[25] In the realm of money, offshoring grants privileges by treating its beneficiaries as if they or their activities were resident in the locale: in the eyes of the law, they are present, even if physically absent.[26] On this score, citizenship by investment is very different. Most investor citizens are both physically absent and treated as such. Indeed, if they were regarded as legally present nonetheless, investor citizens would be able to make easy use of low and zero tax provisions without setting foot in the country, and demand for CBI would be through the roof. There would also be extraterritorial voting, which most CBI countries do not allow, though their national diasporas might appreciate the move. Rather, nonresident investor citizens take the penumbra of the state with them when they are abroad. There they access extraterritorial benefits that the state has secured through treaties. Some, like those shifting from Syrian to Saint Lucian documents, may even enjoy the advantages of a less stigmatized membership than they carried before.

In this regard, citizenship by investment operates rather like imperial modes of organizing mobile populations. The Ottoman Empire had protégés, or foreigners who rendered extraordinary service to another state and could therefore rely on its protection.[27] A Greek ship captain operating within Ottoman domains, for example, could become a protégé of Russia and thereby travel on Russian documents, availing himself of Russian rights and protections within Ottoman territories. Originally, protégé status supplied a mechanism to deal with the practicalities of diplomacy, but over time it came to be had for a price. For many it was worth it: if any problems arose, they had access to the consulates, as well as the courts and legal system of their guardian country, and often fell outside Ottoman tax obligations to boot.[28] Such extraterritorial protections—long fundamental to empires[29]—are one of the most desired aspects of citizenship among the globally mobile, past or present. During the great wave of global mobility in the nineteenth century, foreigners who were not racially stigmatized could have a better deal than locals. Many were able to claim extensive domestic privileges within their new state—far more than would be available to resident aliens in the next century—and benefit from the protection of foreign powers as well.[30] Across North and South America, picking up an additional state membership was comparably easy for many who sought an insurance policy for travel, settlement, and business.[31] Within the Ottoman Empire, it became such a common strategy among merchants and others that French, US, and British consular officials chafed at the added burden, even as their governments benefited from the extension of their hand into new areas of foreign trade.[32]

Similar are the nationality strategies of foreign corporations today as they try to secure the best legal protections possible. A web of over 2,500 bilateral investment treaties (BITs), most signed between the 1980s and 2000s, produce the grounds for states to protect the investments made by their citizens or corporations abroad. If a state decides, for example, to nationalize or expropriate a corporation, it can do so readily if the company is one of its own. Yet if the corporation is foreign and protected by a BIT, it has more rights and can even take the government into arbitration and challenge for compensation. A company might have been founded in Indonesia and have an

Indonesian board of directors, but savvy "corporate nationality planning" can transform it into a foreign entity at home. Once the firm's board becomes foreign and acquires extraterritorial membership, it gains far greater protections against its erstwhile government.

Extraterritorial benefits supply a significant part of the value of investor citizenship in otherwise peripheral microstates. However, they also bring fragility, for they provide foreign states with leverage over what is otherwise a sovereign prerogative. Here we have seen two ways in which third parties wield influence over citizenship policies. In the economic realm, international service providers proactively craft policy templates and advise governments in a search for profit that drives the industry forward. In their case, extraterritorial possibilities are the prize that transform citizenship in minor countries into a valuable commodity. The outcome is that not merely immigration policy but citizenship policy too has become swept up in the broader trend toward public-private partnerships. In the political realm, global core states and regional alliances wield reactive influence over the design, implementation, and existence of programs. Here the extraterritorial benefits of citizenship render it vulnerable to extraterritorial power plays. As a result, citizenship policy is more susceptible to external influence than is often presumed. The hierarchy among states means that the countries naturalizing the investors do not always have the only word on approvals. Powerhouses like the United States have even been able to transpose their own political interests and border control policies onto weaker countries and gain a say in who gets approved. Washington, as we have seen, has the greatest control: a brake pedal in the form of the US dollar and a steering mechanism in the form of influence over vetting. Others, like the EU, have persuaded countries to make fundamental shifts in how they organize schemes. And both have successfully pressured countries to end programs. Not merely a politics of legitimacy but a geopolitics of legitimacy—ensuring that more dominant third states countenance the offerings and are involved in program operation—influences the market's continued operation.

The extraterritorial dimensions of citizenship turn upside down traditional assumptions about who gets to naturalize. In conventional accounts, naturalization is intimately tied to immigration: to become a citizen of a new country, one must first move to it. Of course, there are many cases that fall outside this pattern. China, Saudi Arabia, Vietnam, and the United Arab Emirates are but a few that naturalize virtually no immigrants, while others like Hungary, Italy, and Romania naturalize more co-ethnics living abroad than they do foreign residents. Yet even if one takes the immigrant-into-national trajectory as the gold standard, CBI schemes do not fit the mold. Rather, they reconfigure it: it is not the person but their money that must be resident for a defined period in the territory, contributing to the economy in the same way that labor might.[33] As with migrant workers from abroad, the state welcomes individuals outside its territory to reinforce its capacity for achieving economic projects within it.[34] In the case of citizenship by investment, however, they usually remain outside the country. If the modern nation-state is often seen as welding together the state as a territorial unit with the nation as a membership unit,[35] this transformation suggests that a disjuncture between the two may be increasing as states strive to draw desired populations into their orbit, though not always their ambit.

Neoliberalization

Is the state's reliance on private actors symptomatic of growing neoliberalization? Citizenship is, at its core, a relationship between the sovereign and subject, a status conferred at the prerogative of the executive. As such, it may be surprising to find private firms playing decisive roles in the formation, implementation, and continuation of citizenship by investment. Yet this involvement is demanded in part by the nature of the commodity. When a sovereign prerogative like citizenship goes to market, it brings its own challenges, for the government does not merely set the rules and legal system that the market needs to operate,[36] but is the sole direct producer of the good being traded. This "multiple hat problem" generates conflicts of interest and the threat of sovereign default. To mitigate these risks, governments turn to third parties to supply the credibility needed for the market to operate. Private actors may simply facilitate market development, or they may drive its expansion into new domains—which often gets branded "neoliberalization"—but their presence is required to vouch for the sovereign if its character is in doubt.[37]

These dynamics can be observed in the long history of third-party involvement in sovereign debt. As with citizenship, the state wears multiple hats as both the key market regulator and sole direct producer of the good, raising questions of credibility and reliability, particularly against sovereign default. The dilemma emerged in the early sovereign bond market of eighteenth-century London. To solve it, joint stock companies became involved in the issuance of government debt, underwriting the transactions. The reputation of these third-party actors, standing behind the sovereign debt sales, was a vital indication to investors that the deal was solid and the government was good for its liabilities.[38] By the nineteenth century, buyers offered premiums for "big name" underwriters—firms that would have more to lose if their brand were sullied by sovereign default—to certify the debt and guarantee the return.[39] Today credit rating agencies perform a similar function, evaluating a state's ability to make good on a loan and indicating the riskiness of default.[40] Such co-dependence between the public and private sectors may be cast as a symptom of neoliberalization, particularly when markets expand into new domains like citizenship, but it is characteristic of plain old capitalism as well.

Divisions of labor also mitigate the conflicts of interest that arise from the multiple hat problem. In the case of sovereign bonds, states now commonly establish debt management offices that separate debt administration from monetary policy, which could otherwise be used to lower the amount owed through inflation.[41] Creating separate spheres bolsters integrity because the chain of actors involved distances the sovereign from the product: countries with checks and balances, as well as independent judiciaries, are deemed more creditworthy than others.[42]

Similar dynamics are visible in the evolution of the CBI market, if with some different contours. Here, too, its development has been inseparable from powerful firms from inception. It is they who advertise the schemes, drawing the attention of the very rich and their wealth planners, and they who connect the array of primary and secondary businesses involved into a networked citizenship industry. The upshot of their engagement has distanced the sovereign from the grant of citizenship and supplied external oversight to the process. These shifts, as we have seen, facilitated the credibility that other actors in the market needed in order to know that the deal would be good. The formalized process also made it more difficult for the sovereign to "default" by canceling all the passports and erasing the citizenships if a new government were to come to power. With formalization came industry expansion as pioneer firms, legal templates and best practices in hand, promoted CBI programs in new countries. It is they who are the market-makers advancing the programs, capitalizing on the global inequalities that drive demand.

Of course, it is not unusual for private actors to implement migration policies: airlines carry out border control checks, security companies run detention centers, independent firms collate visa applications.[43] However, their participation in CBI programs goes much further. Major companies in the citizenship industry design policies, formulate law, and work closely in program implementation, while due diligence firms serve as a check on the rigor of vetting. The result goes beyond the client politics often involved in much immigration policy formation and is more akin to the close relationship between Washington policy makers and K Street, where think tanks and lobbying groups, to an ever-greater extent, produce policy blueprints that lawmakers may implement whole cloth—and then subsequently delegate the program's execution to private agencies. Indeed, private actors have amassed great influence over decisions and responsibilities in many areas once considered to be core state functions, including military intervention, the provision of public goods, and migration management.[44] The European Union may be little different, with 25,000 lobbyists now working in Brussels, where an estimated €1.5 billion is spent annually to influence EU decisions.[45] Examining the CBI scene reveals that citizenship is not insulated from these trends, and it too has become subject to the growing efforts of private actors to shape and implement policy.

Yet the private sector doesn't always win out, for it can be challenging to move into an area traditionally controlled by the state. If the government wants to throw out all the applications in a public tender, delay a program launch, or end a business partnership, it can readily do so, as several countries have shown. It may also find workarounds to contractual obligations. In its worst-case scenario, the private sector can sue, but more often this does not happen as the firms know they need the government on their side to do their business. States can flex their muscles and retain the upper hand.

But states can also be transformed by the market as they bend to its demands. Countries that want to compete may adjust their foreign policies, embassy footprint, and naturalization regimes to grab more market share. They may take on the traditional functions of the citizenship industry by hosting promotional events, publishing CBI magazines, and even rallying the prime minister to pitch the product. The enormous economic importance of citizenship by investment in several countries means that the market in investor citizenship has the power to reshape state functions too.

Strategic Action

Many people today regard citizenship in almost hallowed terms as an inviolable bond between subject and sovereign. To be "a citizen of nowhere," as former British prime minister Theresa May once put it, is more often a slur than an accolade. However, this development, recent and partial, may already be on the decline. The rise of the nation-state as the predominant political form from the late nineteenth through the mid-twentieth centuries saw governments and populations strengthen their mutual embrace as they both convey and return identity, responsibility, privileges, and duties.[46] In the early twentieth century, new laws armored the singularity of the relationship: individuals who left their home state for an extended period could be automatically denaturalized, as were women who married men from a different country. Matrilineal citizenship inheritance was prohibited, limiting the reproduction of dual nationals. The League of Nations even established committees to deal with the great "threat" of multiple citizenships. Yet in the past decades, these once rigid prohibitions have become far more flexible. The number of countries allowing for multiple citizenships has increased more than tenfold since 1959 and doubled since the 1990s.[47] A recent survey of over a hundred countries found that fifty-one allowed dual citizenship and fifty-eight took a restrictive approach to it.[48] Toleration of dual citizenship is becoming the new normal.

If dual citizenship once evoked the menace of divided loyalties, now it yields options. Individuals with multiple citizenships have more to choose from: they can select from an array of rights and benefits that best fits their needs—a sort of "citizenship à la carte."[49] Turkish American dual citizens may strategically maneuver between the two countries to avoid military duty and improve their tax status and education possibilities.[50] Middle-class Argentine Italians might leverage a second passport to expand travel and labor market access. As they extend their menu of options, "multizens" can more deftly adjust to changing circumstances.[51] Indeed, many people, not merely the rich, are great strategizers when it comes to leveraging citizenship possibilities. However, it is those who have the most to gain economically from a second passport who tend to naturalize.[52] Studies show that people from less developed countries are more likely to acquire a new citizenship, if given the option, than are those from more prosperous ones, and they do so to hedge economic risks.[53] Members of the middle classes seeking economic opportunities and mobility options may employ ancestry routes and "birth tourism" to secure access to wealthier states.[54] Those in a wealthier stratum, opting for CBI routes, may not be so different as strategizers.

States, too, are strategic when it comes to citizenship.[55] Indeed, their embrace of external investors resembles a tactic common among countries with large emigrant populations. Many extend dual citizenship possibilities or grades of nationality to those who leave in order to encourage remittances.[56] By keeping them in the nation, they hope to keep them economically connected to the state. If the continued membership of a transnational diaspora of emigrants stretches the nation-state's hyphen past the borders of a country, investor citizenship, by contrast, slices the hyphen in two. Wealthy naturalizers show no interest in their new national communities, and the issuing states aren't fostering multicultural identities for them. Unlike their compatriots, these absent citizens are members of the state but not the nation. For them, citizenship does not carry the baggage of identity. On the positive side, such nonnational investor citizens may be less likely to contribute to xenophobia within their new country; on the negative, they may be less concerned with building it up through resource redistribution. Fundamentally, citizenship's substance is reduced to documents: it is access to the passport that matters.

These trends are both a consequence and a cause of the thinning of citizenship, what sociologist Christian Joppke has termed "citizenship light."[57] Stripped away are concerns with identity and a sense of belonging. Gone are expectations of social welfare benefits, social protection, and resource redistribution. The obligations of membership, already on the decline across the board, are nonexistent as well.[58] No military service, no jury duty, and of course no substantial taxes are expected of the new nonresident citizens.[59] These trends, which Joppke identified as characteristic of twenty-first-century citizenship more broadly, find crystalline form in citizenship by investment. Where T. H. Marshall charted the progressive "thickening" of citizenship through a cumulative enrichment of rights, the direction of development is now inverted. Citizenship by investment is indicative of the most recent stage in citizenship's "thinning." The rights that investor citizens claim are those of the most limited sort: foremost, travel, possibly business benefits, and perhaps residence. Citizenship is a tool, both for states seeking to embrace possibly profitable populations, and for migrants leveraging options.[60] Investor citizens are merely a part of this, if a privileged tier within it.

Yet even lightened citizenship has not lost all color. Sacred or moral elements may soften the dominant pragmatic and instrumental orientation. Antigua requires an oath that—until the Covid-19 pandemic—was sworn in its capital city. Malta has all its new incumbents parade down a red carpet in a formal citizenship ceremony. In his promotional speeches, the prime minister of Saint Lucia declares his hope that new investor citizens will develop a genuine connection with the island. A residential property can become a planned retirement spot, imagined with fondness by investor citizens, even if they never end up going there. The industry, too, is replete with moral justifications for its instrumental action. Prominent service providers point to the unjustness of the "citizenship penalties" that their clients face and donate to refugee and statelessness causes. Yet overall, it is instrumental rather than affective action that structures many citizenship choices. If the elite have the most levers at their disposal, the middle and lower classes, particularly when the stakes are high, can be just as instrumental.[61] In a world of borders, memberships have their privileges, and the significance of this is rarely lost on those who cannot take it for granted.

Conclusion

In our globalized world, capital moves across borders with far greater ease than people. For those with the means, however, citizenship by investment provides a solution. It releases individuals from the weight of "bad passports." It provides an insurance policy against an uncertain future. It furnishes lifestyle benefits, better legal protections, and even improved business opportunities. In an unequal world, the desire for these advantages is unlikely to fade.

Citizenship by investment has seen remarkable growth over the last decade, but it has faced headwinds too. Pressure from the EU or United States can shut down individual programs, but now that the market is well established, such efforts are unlikely to stop the phenomenon altogether. Things could change, however, if there is a radical transformation in the link between citizenship and proof of identity—improbable in the present, but possible in the future. If powerful states police borders and opportunities based not on a person's passport but their individual biography, a second citizenship may do little on its own to multiply options. Biometric records and identification systems, now proliferating, facilitate this transformation, as who we are is increasingly read from our bodies rather than attested by documents. This hyper-individualized mode of tracking could also moot the importance of state belonging to identification systems. If France wants to limit the entry of individuals deemed more likely to overstay their visas as they seek out a better life—the principle now used to deny easy entry to, for example, Nigerian nationals—it may be more relevant that a person has a PhD and is employed as a professor than that she was born in Lagos. The same might be said for entire populations who come under sanctions or go through tougher checks on the premise of terrorism control. Utopian or dystopian, a world in which profiling is carried out based on individual identity and through biology, rather than state membership attested through documents, could render numerous extraterritorial benefits of citizenship by investment useless.

Increasingly, our world is one of mobility rather than migration, in which people move—or seek movement options—with greater flexibility and on a shorter time horizon than captured by the heavy notions of immigration and settlement. This should remind us that, far from obsolete, citizenship continues to hold force even outside the granting state. A doctor who moves to a different country may lose her credentials, but the same does not hold for citizenship: you take it with you wherever you go.

For this reason, even in an age of mobility, citizenship still has fundamental importance, and its implications for global inequality are profound. Citizenship is about far more than a valued bond between sovereign and subject. It is the differences between citizenships that define their worth. The CBI market turns and capitalizes on this uneven terrain of interstate hierarchies, but their perniciousness is well beyond its control. Golden passports are but a small part of a wider global economy of citizenship in which people and countries are valued—and evaluated—differently. An example can be found in the struggle to attract globally mobile talent, whether scientific, artistic, entrepreneurial, or athletic.[62] Rich countries compete for the best and brightest by offering deals and special provisions that poorer countries cannot hope to match. In this contest, the countries that are already on top win, while those far below them are left looking for alternatives. For them, CBI programs are one way to compete for a trickle of funds from the wealthy, though there are others as well. Refugee protection, for example, has become lucrative for states like Jordan, Lebanon, and Turkey, which take payments from powerful countries for containing the unwanted who might otherwise seek refuge in them. The outcome is the monetization of the most vulnerable populations—to keep people out rather than, as with citizenship by investment, to let them in.[63] The most extreme case is perhaps tiny Nauru, which now earns half its revenue processing asylum seekers repelled by Australia. Within the global economy of citizenship, the rich—whether countries or individuals—do what they can, while the small look for alternatives.

In recent years, globalization and growing inequality have met a strong backlash in many places, manifested by the rise of autocrats, xenophobia, and social instability. The turbulence has fundamentally transformed politics. The major divide is no longer between capitalism versus socialism or right versus left, but between those who see globalization as an opportunity and those who see it as an existential threat. Surveying the scene, Donald Trump offered a pithy prognosis to the United Nations General Assembly: "The future does not belong to globalists. The future belongs to patriots." Making a nation great again may not address the key issues, but his forecast still points to the uneasy position that countries occupy within a globally connected world. Nation-states remain fundamental to capitalist-driven globalization. They delimit and preserve the opportunities that companies and individuals profit from, whether by exploiting cost differentials or trading on comparative advantages. More crucially, they furnish the legal backing and regulations that markets require to operate—and that facilitate the juridical jiggering which unfettered capitalism embraces.

Nation-states, however, do more than cordon off jurisdictions and labor cost differentials. They cordon off populations as well, divvying up nearly all of humanity among themselves and regulating movement between them. A globalized world does not come with global citizenship. Instead, the status divides, affecting where we can go, how we are treated, and what rights we have not only at home, but across the planet. For some, it supplies possibilities and privileges; for others, it brings down penalties and limits. Whether we like it or not, we are stuck with the status as much as it is stuck to us. The world of golden passports reminds us just how foundational it is—and inescapable, too—even in a highly interconnected world. As long as countries anchor capitalism, citizenship will anchor global mobility.

METHODOLOGICAL APPENDIX

NOTES

INDEX

Methodological Appendix

The research for this book was enormously fun. How often does one get to go to Vanuatu? One of my key contacts there was not only a service provider but also a village chief, who on occasion ritually sacrificed wild pigs. In Saint Kitts, I carried out archival work on the origins of the program in an aging auto parts shop. It was run by a similarly aging gentleman who was one of the leaders of the country's independence movement and served as a minister in the government for many years. I was allowed to go through his files, which were in much better shape than those in the actual government archives, while perched between stacks of old car parts.

I began fieldwork almost by accident in 2015 while pursuing a project on guestwork programs. These schemes bring low-paid workers into a country, but most face steep barriers to naturalization even after years of labor. CBI programs, in the news at the time, appeared as the exact opposite: wealthy people buying citizenship in countries they had never even visited. Around that time, I had the opportunity to attend a professional conference for the citizenship industry and was hooked. There was much more going on in this complex sphere than merely cash for passports. Within a few years, I had traveled to sixteen countries on four continents to trace the market. I did so with the generous support of a Leverhulme Research Fellowship, and while writing, I benefited from a Fung Global Fellowship at Princeton University. Grants from the London School of Economics Research Support Fund and the Suntory and Toyota International Centers for Economics and Related Disciplines supported the construction of the InvestMig database discussed below.

Between 2015 and 2021, I attended over twenty-five professional conferences organized by the citizenship industry in cities around the world: London, Zurich, Geneva, Monaco, Sveti Stefan (Montenegro), Athens, Moscow, Abu Dhabi, Dubai, Frigate Bay (Saint Kitts), Bangkok, Shanghai, and Hong Kong. At these events, prime ministers and ambassadors made country pitches, bureaucrats and lawyers answered questions about programs, real estate developers advertised investment opportunities, due diligence companies discussed the importance of clean records, and tax specialists reviewed options for wealth planning. Filling the audience were lawyers, private bankers, personal wealth managers, family office representatives, bureaucrats, and the occasional prospective client. The frequent coffee breaks provided the opportunity to learn about the contours and concerns that structure the field from an array of actors—a conference benefit not only for its professional participants but for an academic researcher as well. Meeting people meant exchanging business cards or inquiring into the institutional affiliation on the name badge, and I used the opportunity to introduce my research. As I picked up small talk, I found that many in the field spoke with relative frankness to a professor—a situation supported by the industry's growing interest in legitimation. Around a third of the participants at any conference attend several such events each year in pursuit of business connections and the chance to keep abreast of transformations. Becoming a part of the conference circuit helped to establish rapport as I encountered the same people multiple times and pursued follow-up questions. After the Covid-19 pandemic shut down such travel opportunities, I moved to online interviews.

To understand the industry outside the space dominated by international firms, as well as the history of the programs and how they operate on the ground, I conducted fieldwork in countries with CBI programs, including Antigua (2016), Saint Kitts (2016, 2018), Cyprus (2018), Malta (2018), and Vanuatu (2018). In all places, I visited government offices, service providers, and real estate developments, and talked to locals about their impressions of the program. In key global hubs, including London, Dubai, New York, Montreal, Moscow, Shanghai, Guangzhou, and Hong Kong, I conducted over 100 formal interviews typically lasting between thirty minutes and two hours with industry players, including lawyers, service providers, bureaucrats, government ministers, due diligence providers, real estate developers, and private wealth managers. I also carried out over 400 informal interviews with people involved in all aspects of the programs. Unless otherwise noted, I use pseudonyms when referring to interviewees. In many cases, particularly with the investor migrants from countries that do not allow dual citizenship, I apply additional levels of anonymization, such as changing gender or making a slight shift in location—for example, from Shanghai to Shenzhen—while maintaining the person's general set of characteristics.

Because of the controversies in the West around the programs, I'm some-times asked about how I'm able to investigate such a prima facie illicit trade that deals only with criminals and money launderers. I found in my research, however, that most of what goes on is far more mundane yet still intriguing, and that many people enjoyed the chance to talk about their work. Interviewees will, of course, present cases and perspectives that they think an academic will find sympathetic, but what this means varies from person to person and from country to country. In China and Vanuatu, for example, I found many who were surprisingly frank about practices that those in the West would find improper and rarely mention. I also got a sense of how things really work by asking individuals about the business methods of their rivals. Especially when competition is fierce, people may be eager to expose the questionable practices of their opponents. Without supporting evidence, such claims must be viewed with caution, but they can sensitize a researcher to the pos-sible range of activities in the field, including more nefarious ones, and to what might go wrong but remain under the surface. Of course, not every-thing in the citizenship industry is squeaky clean or operates as it should, and I have discussed ways in which this occurs as well. Most of the market, however, is far less sensationalist, though no less compelling.

In addition, I interviewed twenty people who had either received citizen-ship through investment or were shopping for programs. Many of them I encountered at industry conferences, which they visited to learn about the options available. Others I met through introductions from acquaintances or service providers. One approached me after a university lecture I gave on the topic; he attended the public talk out of curiosity about academic work in the area. Traveling to Saint Kitts, I encountered one investor citizen on the plane and three on the island itself. Of the eleven investor citizens I spoke to, eight had gone through programs in the Caribbean and three in the Eu-ropean Union. Three were from North America, three from East Asia, three from South Asia, and two from the Middle East. Of the shoppers—who were usually looking at both CBI and RBI options—four were from South Asia, three from East Asia, and two from the Middle East. Some had as-sets of around $50 million while others were in the lower millions, and none reached the billionaire stratosphere. However, some service providers spoke about billionaire clients, lending a sense of the concerns and interests of people at that level of wealth. Many of the service providers I met had also picked up the citizenship of the countries they worked with by going through the programs themselves, but I excluded them from the pool of investor citizens as a particularly niche subset, unlikely to have naturalized through these schemes if they weren't in the business.

When I started work on the book, there were seven countries with citizenship by investment that defined the market: Antigua, Cyprus, Dominica, Grenada, Malta, Saint Kitts, and Saint Lucia—plus Vanuatu was making new moves. Turkey, which opened a program in 2016, now accounts for half of all approvals globally. This development I have followed as best I could despite travel restrictions around the Covid pandemic on top of professional obligations. Travel plans stymied, I investigated Turkey's operations through online interviews. These have their own benefits and limitations, and I have included the Turkish case to the best extent possible. Still my greatest familiarity remains with the original seven, which form the historical core of the market and provide a longer timeframe for assessment. I have supplemented my work on these cases by bringing in other programs, such as those in Jordan, Egypt, and North Macedonia, where citizenship is for sale but the scale is far smaller.

Many academics in the West remain fixated on the West as well. Even though China has historically represented about half of global demand and has an investment migration industry that dwarfs that of any other region, Western researchers often set it aside as geographically distant or linguistically inaccessible. However, it cannot be overlooked. Notably, my trips were before the onslaught of Covid-19, which China addressed with stringent and long-lasting travel restrictions. Two years into the pandemic, it was still nearly all but impossible for foreigners to enter the country, and it remained so onerous for nationals to leave and return that travelers had to carefully weigh their movements. Even after the most stringent border controls were lifted, re-entry still required a minimum two-week quarantine in a no-frills government-run hotel room, followed by a week of continued surveillance, which even the wealthiest and most powerful could not avoid. Passports were for many not a key priority in that moment, and traveling to give biometric data, required by the European programs, was no longer an easy option. Demand did not die out completely, but the service providers I spoke with who had previously dealt with the Chinese market described a drop-off in sales. Most, however, expected demand to resurge once the quarantine restrictions were lifted and people, disgruntled with the government's response, looked for options elsewhere.

To substantiate and expand on the interviews, I also assembled the InvestMig database, which is the basis of the quantitative figures in this book.

The collection is the most comprehensive assemblage of statistics on both CBI and RBI programs.[1] In the case of CBI schemes, it includes annual numbers on applications submitted, approvals, family dependents, country of origin, investment amount, and investment type where available. It also incorporates information on policies and laws, as well as financial data from government budgets. In the first instance, the figures were acquired from government reports and through government information requests. If government figures were unobtainable, numbers published in major newspapers or news sources (often gained through government leaks) were used, along with figures from NGO and private sector reports. Multiple sources were triangulated where possible. Complete information was not available for all countries with programs. For example, a country might have a six-month gap in official reporting, list only the top countries of origin and not the complete set, or not release figures on total investments. However, in most cases, the data gaps can be managed to provide a broad overview of trends. Covid-19 had a significant impact on governments, slowing application review in many cases and leading to delays in the publication of reports and numbers. These lags were still not completely resolved at the time of writing. The pandemic has also been configuring demand patterns, a process that is still unfolding. For these reasons, several graphs map trends only through 2019 or take the average from 2017 to 2019 to establish a basis for comparison.

Along the way, I became a dual national myself. After nine years of living in the United Kingdom, I added a—post-Brexit and therefore greatly diminished in value—British passport to my US one. While carrying out research, I was often asked where I was from, and when I confessed to being a US national, service providers would frequently say, "I can help you with that," with their thoughts gravitating to the global tax burden that Uncle Sam imposes on its own. As a UK university professor, however, I don't earn the minimum income required to pay US taxes from abroad. Even though I have a privileged nationality and a secure job, my own "citizenship journey" through an immigration route was bumpy. At one point the British government changed its residence requirements, and it looked as though I might lose my work visa, and with it my job and my ability to stay in the country: I had spent so many days traveling internationally for research and on fellowships that I could no longer renew my work permit. I ran into the same problem when I applied for citizenship. Again, frequent work travel meant that I had been out of the country too long to qualify. I was too global to become a citizen. The Covid pandemic offered some respite and—after paying sizeable legal fees—I was able to make the case that I should still be admitted as one of the (then) queen's subjects. (Swearing allegiance to her, her heirs, and her successors was required; involving a god was optional.) A private company, headquartered in France but outsourcing to India, handled the application submission and vetting on behalf of the government. The process was incredibly slow. It took eight months before I could naturalize and another five before I received my passport, and I was unable to leave the country for nearly half the time I waited. Even if far more inefficient than any CBI program, my UK citizenship "journey" cost just over $10,000 in bureaucratic and legal fees—a bargain!

Notes

1. Selling Citizenship

1. Roberto Patricio Korzeniewicz and Timothy Patrick Moran, *Unveiling Inequality: A World-Historical Perspective* (New York: Russell Sage Foundation, 2009), 100.
2. "Indicators," World Bank Data, https://data.worldbank.org/indicator. Unless stated otherwise, all dollar currency mentioned in the book is USD.
3. Branko Milanovic, *Global Inequality: A New Approach for the Age of Globalization* (Cambridge, MA: Harvard University Press, 2016), 131–134.
4. Kwame Anthony Appiah, "Citizenship in Theory and Practice: A Response to Charles Kesler," in *Immigration and Citizenship in the 21st Century*, ed. Noah M. J. Pickus (Lanham, MD: Rowman and Littlefield, 1998), 41–48.
5. Ayelet Shachar, *The Birthright Lottery: Citizenship and Global Inequality* (Cambridge, MA: Harvard University Press, 2009).
6. "Unholy Alliances and American Interest," *Organized Crime and Corruption Reporting Project*, 2009, https://www.occrp.org/en/unholyalliances/.
7. Jelena Dzankic, *Country Report: Montenegro* (Robert Schuman Centre for Advanced Studies: EUDO Citizenship Observatory, 2012), 15.
8. The government did the same in early 2019 when it ended another public tender, this one to select due diligence agencies, by rejecting all thirteen applications on technicalities.
9. International Monetary Fund, "Montenegro" IMF Country Report No. 19/293 (September 2019), 2.
10. In July 2018, the government announced an opening date of October, which came and went. In December 2018, it promised to launch the scheme in early January 2019. When February arrived, both the guidelines and the application forms weren't ready. A month later, the program was still far from leaving the ground: thirty businesses had applied to become "mediation agents" who could submit applications on behalf of clients, and the government had approved just three. The private sector pushed for the opening, but the government delayed over and over.
11. Andrew Byrne, "Montenegro Counts Cost of Becoming NATO's Newest Member," *Financial Times,* June 2, 2017.
12. Jean-Arnault Derens and Laurent Geslin, "Balkans Are the New Front Line," *Le Monde Diplomatique,* July 4, 2015.

13. For the sake of readability, I use "citizenship industry" as a replacement for "CBI industry" throughout the book.

14. Naomi Klein and Alleen Brown, "Robert De Niro Accused of Exploiting Hurricane Irma to Build Resort in Barbuda," *The Intercept,* January 23, 2018. See also Linda Pressly, "Why I Don't Want to Own the Land My Business Is Built on," *BBC,* August 15, 2019.

15. Barbuda Land Amendment Bill, Antigua and Barbuda, 2017.

16. Locals also sued over electoral anomalies in the referendum that approved Paradise Found. Afterward, the prime minister passed the Paradise Found Act—overriding the law that enshrined communal landholding and democratic decisions on development—to enable the resort to build infrastructure, like a super-yacht port, for resort members' sole use. Klein and Brown, "Robert De Niro Accused of Exploiting Hurricane Irma."

17. Gordon Rayner, "Princess Diana's Favourite Caribbean Resort at the Centre of Legal Battle between Robert De Niro and Islanders," *The Telegraph,* December 28, 2016.

18. Gemma Sou, "Barbudans are Resisting 'Disaster Capitalism,' Two Years after Hurricane Irma," *The Conversation,* July 17, 2019, https://theconversation.com /barbudans-are-resisting-disaster-capitalism-two-years-after-hurricane-irma -119368.

19. Klein and Brown, "Robert De Niro Accused of Exploiting Hurricane Irma." Asha Frank, a member of the Barbuda Council, stated plainly: "You can't just expect you can go somewhere and then decide 'this is how I want to do it—it doesn't matter who's there, this is how I'm going to do it.' It's neocolonialism."

20. Peter John Spiro, "A New International Law of Citizenship," *American Journal of International Law* 105, no. 4 (2011): 694.

21. Dimitry Kochenov, *Citizenship* (Cambridge, MA: MIT Press, 2019).

22. Economist Intelligence Unit, "Democracy Index 2021: The China Challenge," https://www.eiu.com/n/campaigns/democracy-index-2021/.

23. The term "genuine link" reaches back to the *Nottebohm* case of 1955. This, however, is a ruling that has been frequently misinterpreted and often rejected as effective precedent. See Peter J. Spiro, "Investment Citizenship and the Long Leash of International Law," in *Citizenship and Residence Sales: Rethinking the Boundaries of Belonging,* ed. Dimitry Kochenov and Kristin Surak (Cambridge: Cambridge University Press, 2023).

24. Yossi Harpaz, *Global Citizenship 2.0: Dual Nationality as a Global Asset* (Princeton: Princeton University Press, 2019).

25. See also Kochenov, *Citizenship.*

26. See Christian Joppke, "The Inevitable Lightening of Citizenship," *European Journal of Sociology* 51, no. 1 (2010): 9–32.

27. Peter John Spiro, *Beyond Citizenship: American Identity after Globalization* (Oxford: Oxford University Press, 2008), 97–99.

28. Thomas Humphrey Marshall, *Citizenship and Social Class: And Other Essays* (Cambridge: Cambridge University Press, 1950), 77–80.

29. Yasemin Soysal, *Limits of Citizenship: Migrants and Postnational Membership in Europe* (Chicago: University of Chicago Press, 1994). Even with some counter-vailing movements, the overall trend is expansionary.

30. Kochenov has written trenchantly on this point. See Kochenov, *Citizenship*.
31. Christian Joppke, "Transformation of Citizenship: Status, Rights and Identity," *Citizenship Studies* 11, no. 1 (2007): 37–48. Kochenov, *Citizenship*.
32. See also Kochenov, *Citizenship*.
33. Even if citizenship is nearly universal, activating it is a different matter, particularly when bureaucracies look for paper trails as proof of membership. See Kamal Sadiq, *Paper Citizens: How Illegal Immigrants Acquire Citizenship in Developing Countries* (New York: Oxford University Press, 2008).
34. It is perhaps the overweening presence of the United States and Canada as the key models in migration studies and policy making that has transformed this immigrant-into-citizen trajectory into the unspoken standard.
35. Yet one might wonder about Thiel's diligence on this score as it took him six years to make his new membership public. Thiel has since also applied to Malta's citizenship by investment program.
36. More questionable cases can be found as well. Belgium, for example, naturalized several powerful Kazakhs who were under continuous investigation by European authorities after they invested state funds through Belgian companies in the "Kazakhgate" scandal. Open Source Investigations, "A Failure of the Belgian State: The Story of Naturalization and Punishment," https://www.opensourceinvestigations .com/corruption/failure-belgian-state-story-naturalization-punishment/.
37. In my research, I came across cases of people who had acquired citizenship through such connections in a range of countries, including the United States and Japan.
38. The total is calculated from the InvestMig database, discussed in the Methodological Appendix.
39. Though RBI programs are not the subject of this book, I have carried out extensive research on these schemes as well. See Kristin Surak, "Citizenship and Residence by Investment Schemes: State of Play and Avenues for EU Action," European Added Value Assessment, European Parliamentary Research Service, European Union, Brussels, 2021. Kristin Surak and Yusuke Tsuzuki, "Are Golden Visas a Golden Opportunity? Assessing the Economic Outcomes of Residence by Investment Programs in the EU." *Journal of Ethnic and Migration Studies* 47, no. 15 (2021): 3367–89. Kristin Surak, "Who Wants to Buy a Visa? Comparing the Uptake of Residence by Investment Programs in the EU," *Journal of Contemporary European Studies* 30, no. 1 (2020): 151–169. Kristin Surak, "Investment Migration: Empirical Developments in the Field and Methodological Issues in Its Study," in *Citizenship and Residence Sales: Rethinking the Boundaries of Belonging*, ed. Dimitry Kochenov and Kristin Surak (Cambridge: Cambridge University Press, 2023).
40. The golden visa program in the United Arab Emirates is one such example.
41. If citizenship equaled passports, then states could readily get rid of their investor citizens simply by refusing to renew their travel documents. Indeed, this happened more than once in the 1980s and 1990s, before an elaborate bureaucratic process of assessing applicants became *de rigueur*, eliminating such easy erasures. Now a formal denaturalization process is required to revoke the membership, and it can be challenged in courts.

42. U.S. Passports, Reports and Statistics, U.S. Department of State, Bureau of Consular Affairs, https://travel.state.gov/content/travel/en/about-us/reports-and -statistics.html.

43. The naming challenges extend further. Such programs may be called citizenship by *investment*, but an investment is not always involved. Donations to governments, low-interest deposits in banks, the purchase of zero-interest government bonds and the like are commonly found in qualifying channels that result in a guaranteed financial loss—at least for the applicant.

44. Kristin Surak, "Marketizing Sovereign Prerogatives: How to Sell Citizenship," *European Journal of Sociology* 62, no. 2 (2021): 275–308.

45. Branko Milanovic, *Global Inequality: A New Approach for an Age of Globalization* (Cambridge, MA: Harvard University Press, 2016).

46. This figure is based on the available data from 2017–2019 and excludes the legally questionable case of the Comoros.

47. The multiplier is calculated from the InvestMig database. Statistics are available from the programs in Antigua, Cyprus, Grenada, Malta, and Saint Lucia.

48. Steffen Mau, Fabian Gulzau, Lena Laube and Natascha Zaun, "The Global Military Divide: How Visa Policies Have Evolved over Time," *Journal of Ethnic and Migration Studies* 41, no. 8 (2015): 1192–1213. Roberto Patricio Korzeniewicz, "Trends in World Income Inequality and the 'Emerging Middle,'" *The European Journal of Development Research* 24, no. 2 (2012): 205–222.

49. See Harpaz, *Global Citizenship 2.0*, on the growing use of ancestry options by middle-class naturalizers. Dimitry Kochenov and Justin Lindeboom, eds., *Kälin and Kochenov's Quality of Nationality Index* (London: Bloomsbury, 2020).

50. Marshall, *Citizenship and Social Class.*

51. Of course, economic calculations lay behind both moves: the EU was paying Turkey billions to keep refugees from entering its domain, and Turkey was gathering millions off its investor citizens.

52. Pierre Bourdieu, "The Forms of Capital," *Handbook of Theory and Research for the Sociology of Education*, ed. John Richardson (New York: Greenwood, 1986), 241–258.

53. David Cook-Martin, *The Scramble for Citizens: Dual Nationality and State Competition for Immigrants* (Stanford: Stanford University Press, 2013).

54. Marilyn Grell-Brisk, "Eluding National Boundaries: A Case Study of Commodified Citizenship and the Transnational Capitalist Class," *Societies* 8, no. 2 (2018): 35; Ayelet Shachar, "The Marketization of Citizenship in an Age of Restrictionism," *Ethics and International Affairs* 32, no. 1 (2018): 3–13; Jelena Dzankic, "Immigrant Investor Programmes in the European Union (EU)," *Journal of Contemporary European Studies* 26, no. 1 (2018): 64–80; Owen Parker, "Commercializing Citizenship in Crisis EU: The Case of Immigrant Investor Programmes," *Journal of Common Market Studies* 55, no. 2 (2017): 332–348; Michael Walzer, *Spheres of Justice: A Defense of Pluralism and Equality* (New York: Basic Books, 1983).

55. Ayelet Shachar, "Citizenship for Sale?" *The Oxford Handbook of Citizenship*, ed. Ayelet Shachar, Rainer Bauböck, Irene Bloemraad, and Maarten Vink (Oxford: Oxford University Press, 2017), 789–816. Luca Mavelli, "Citizenship for Sale and

the Neoliberal Political Economy of Belonging," *International Studies Quarterly* 62, no. 3 (2018): 482–493; Jelena Dzankic, "The Pros and Cons of Ius Pecuniae: Investor Citizenship in Comparative Perspective," EUI Working Papers (Robert Schuman Center for Advanced Studies: EUDO Citizenship Observatory, 2012), 14. Ana Tanasoca, *The Effects of Multiple Citizenship* (Cambridge: Cambridge University Press, 2018). Margaret Somers, *Genealogies of Citizenship: Markets, Statelessness and the Right to Have Rights* (Cambridge: Cambridge University Press, 2008).

56. Shachar, "The Marketization of Citizenship," 13.

57. Manuela Boatcă, "Commodification of Citizenship: Global Inequalities and the Modern Transmission of Property," in *Overcoming Global Inequalities,* ed. Immanuel Wallerstein, Christopher Chase-Dunn, and Christian Suter (London: Routledge, 2014), 3–18.

58. Viviana Zelizer, *Pricing the Priceless Child: The Changing Social Value of Children* (Princeton: Princeton University Press, 1985). See also Didier Fassin, *Life: A Critical User's Manual* (London: Polity Press, 2018). Javier Hidalgo, "Selling Citizenship: A Defence," *Journal of Applied Philosophy* 33, no. 3 (2016): 223–239.

59. Rene Almeling, *Sex Cells: The Medical Market for Eggs and Sperm* (Berkeley: University of California Press, 2011). Indeed, a decrease in the utilitarian value of an item and an increase in its sacralization may, counterintuitively, correspond to an increase in the price attached to it, as economic sociologist Viviana Zelizer demonstrates occurred with children in the early twentieth century. See Zelizer, *Pricing the Priceless Child.*

60. Keiran Healey, *Last Best Gifts: Altruism and the Market for Human Blood and Organs.* (Chicago: University of Chicago Press, 2006). Sarah Quinn, "The Transformation of Morals in Markets: Death, Benefits and the Exchange of Life Insurance Policies," *American Journal of Sociology* 114, no. 3 (2008): 738–780. Simon Mackenzie and Donna Yates, "Collectors on Illicit Collecting: Higher Loyalties and Other Techniques of Neutralization in the Unlawful Collecting of Rare and Precious Orchids and Antiquities," *Theoretical Criminology* 20, no. 3 (2016): 340–357. Adam Dalton Reich, *Selling Our Souls: The Commodification of Hospital Care in the United States* (Princeton: Princeton University Press, 2014).

61. Viviana Zelizer, *Morals and Markets: The Development of Life Insurance in the United States* (Princeton: Princeton University Press, 1979).

62. Arjun Appadurai, ed., *The Social Life of Things: Commodities in Cultural Perspective* (Cambridge: Cambridge University Press, 1986).

63. Neil Fligstein, *The Architecture of Markets: An Economic Sociology of Twenty-First-Century Capitalist Societies* (Princeton NJ: Princeton University Press, 2001); Frank Dobbin, "Why the Economy Reflects the Polity: Early Rail Policy in Britain, France, and the United States," *The Sociology of Economic Life,* ed, Mark Granovetter and Richard Swedberg (Boulder, CO: Westview Press, 2001), 63–85. Greta R. Krippner, *Capitalizing on Crisis: The Political Origins of the Rise of Finance* (Cambridge, MA: Harvard University Press, 2011).

64. On the impact of state regulation, see also Karl Polanyi, *The Great Transformation: The Political and Economic Origins of Our Time* (Boston, MA: Beacon Press, 2001). Jens Beckert, "The Social Order of Markets," *Theory and Society* 38, no. 3

(2009): 245–269. On state influence over the type of goods exchanged, see also Neil Fligstein, *The Transformation of Corporate Control* (Cambridge, MA: Harvard University Press, 1990). Healy, *Last Best Gifts*. On illegal markets, see also Jens Beckert and Matias Dewey, eds., *The Architecture of Illegal Markets: Towards an Economic Sociology of Illegality in the Economy* (Oxford: Oxford University Press, 2017).

65. On the state sustaining trust, see also Carol A. Heimer, "Allocating Information Costs in a Negotiated Information Order: Interorganizational Constraints on Decision Making in Norwegian Oil Insurance," *Administrative Science Quarterly* 30, no. 3 (1985): 395–417. On state capture, see also Lee Drutman, *The Business of America Is Lobbying* (Oxford: Oxford University Press, 2015).

66. Polanyi, *The Great Transformation*. Colin Crouch, *The Strange Non-Death of Neoliberalism* (Cambridge: Polity, 2011).

67. For a depiction of what a secondary market of citizenship swaps might look like see Kit Johnson, "A Citizenship Market," *University of Illinois Law Review* 2018, no. 3 (2018): 970–999.

68. The state's monopoly over citizenship or flags of convenience stands apart from other sovereign claims, such as land titles or natural resources, where secondary markets are not only common, but even dominant. In these cases, the state does not generate the product in the same way: land and natural resources can exist without it, but contemporary citizenship or flags of convenience cannot.

69. A reader of the *Financial Times* undertook this thought experiment in a letter to the paper, writing "it seems unfair that I am not allowed to sell my citizenship and right of abode to a foreigner. I have no wish ever to live in the UK again, and I'm sure many others feel the same. Thus the immigration and emigration figures would cancel each other out, and no net immigration would result. As a bonus you get rid of us disaffected folk with all our negative views on the way the country is going." Peter Verstage, "I'd Be Willing to Sell My Citizenship," *Financial Times*, March 1, 2014.

70. Mark Aguiar and Manuel Amador, "Sovereign Debt: A Review," *National Bureau of Economic Research*, working paper 19388, 2013.

71. Bruce G. Carruthers and Arthur L. Stinchcombe, "The Social Structure of Liquidity: Flexibility, Markets, and States," *Theory and Society* 28, no. 3 (1999): 353–382.

72. Marc Flandreau and Juan H. Flores, "Bonds and Brands: Foundations of Sovereign Debt Markets 1820–1830," *The Journal of Economic History* 69, no. 3 (2009): 646–684. However, countries still frequently defaulted until the twentieth century. Jerome E. Roos, *Why Not Default? The Political Economy of Sovereign Debt* (Princeton, NJ: Princeton University Press, 2019).

73. Christopher M. Bruner and Rawi Abdelal, "To Judge Leviathan: Sovereign Credit Ratings, National Law, and the World Economy," *Journal of Public Policy* 25, no. 2 (2005): 191–217; Marion Fourcade, "State Metrology: The Ratings of Sovereigns and the Judgment of Nations," *The Many Hands of the State: Theorizing Political Authority and Social Control*, ed. Kimberly Morgan and Ann Shola Orloff (Cambridge: Cambridge University Press, 2017).

74. The Bantustan policy of apartheid South Africa revealed that the opposite is possible as well: Black South Africans were assigned citizenship in a Bantustan to strip them of rights within greater South Africa.

75. On citizenship à la carte, see also David Fitzgerald, "Rethinking Emigrant Citizenship," *New York University Law Review* 81, no. 1 (2006): 90–116. David FitzGerald, *A Nation of Emigrants: How Mexico Manages Its Migration* (Berkeley: University of California Press, 2009). On citizenship constellations, see Rainer Bauböck, "Studying Citizenship Constellations," *Journal of Ethnic and Migration Studies* 36, no. 5 (2010): 847–859.

76. A notable exception to the general rule that multiple citizenships secure more benefits is the increased risk of denaturalization that they bring. Under international law, states should not denaturalize citizens if it renders them stateless. As such, it is easier for a law-abiding country to denaturalize a dual citizen than a person with only one citizenship. On this, see Patrick Weil and Nicholas Handler, "Revocation of Citizenship and the Rule of Law: How Judicial Review Defeated Britain's First Denaturalization Regime," *Law and History Review* 36, no. 2 (2018): 295–354.

2. A Product Is Born

1. David Richardson, "The Slave Trade, Sugar, and British Economic Growth, 1748–1776," *Journal of Interdisciplinary History* 17, no. 4 (1987): 739–769.

2. Marc Aronson and Marina Budhos, *Sugar Changed the World: A Story of Magic, Spice, Slavery, Freedom, and Science* (New York: Clarion Books, 2010).

3. Peter Richards, "Trade: Collapse of St Kitts Sugar Sector Leaves Bitter Aftertaste," Inter Press Service, April 2005.

4. Saint Kitts and Nevis, "Medium Term Economic Strategy 2003–2005," http://www.sice.oas.org/ctyindex/KNA/MTESP2003_05_e.pdf.

5. Saint Kitts and Nevis, "Medium Term Economic Strategy."

6. Eric Hobsbawm, "Some Reflections on the Break-up of Britain," *New Left Review* 105, no. 1 (1977): 3–23.

7. Godfrey Baldacchino, *Island Enclaves: Offshoring Strategies, Creative Governance, and Subnational Island Jurisdictions,* vol. 14 (Ithaca: McGill-Queen's University Press, 2010).

8. Geoff Bertram, "The MIRAB Model 12 Years on," *Contemporary Pacific* 11, no. 1 (1999): 105–138. Harvey W. Armstrong and Robert Read, "Microstates and Subnational Regions: Mutual Industrial Policy Lessons," *International Regional Science Review* 26, no. 1 (2003): 117–141. Jerome McElroy and Katherine Sanborn, "The Propensity for Dependence in Small Caribbean and Pacific Islands," *Bank of Valletta Review* 31 (2005): 1–16.

9. Baldacchino, *Island Enclaves,* 44–45.

10. In 1987, Turks and Caicos offered themselves to Canada, with 90 percent of the population favoring some sort of special relationship. Anguilla voted to remain in association with Britain, seceding from Saint Kitts in 1980 after a long struggle, with only 5 percent of the population voting against it. Saint Martin and Saint

Barthelemy voted in 2003 to become a *collectivité d'outre mer* of France rather than a subpartner to Guadeloupe. Baldacchino, *Island Enclaves,* 58.

11. Baldacchino, *Island Enclaves,* 164.

12. If the population is under 1 million, the likelihood of becoming a tax haven increases by nearly 40 percent. See Dhammika Dharmapala and James R. Hines, "Which Countries Become Tax Havens?" *Journal of Public Economics* 93, no. 9–10 (2009): 1058–1068.

13. On the history of the concept of equality within theories of sovereignty, see also Ronnie Hjorth, "Equality in the Theory of International Society: Kelsen, Rawls and the English School," *Review of International Studies* 37, no. 5 (2011): 2585–2602.

14. Even if principles of sovereign equality were readily applied within Europe, they did little to convince the empire-builders that polities outside the West held equivalent forms of sovereignty. Susan Strange, *States and Markets* (London: Bloomsbury Academic, 1988).

15. Stephen Krasner, *Sovereignty: Organized Hypocrisy* (Princeton: Princeton University Press, 1999).

16. Baldacchino, *Island Enclaves.* Helen M. Hintjens and Malyn Newitt, eds., *The Political Economy of Small Tropical Islands: The Importance of Being Small* (Exeter: Exeter University Press, 1992).

17. Vanessa Ogle, "'Funk Money': The End of Empires, the Expansion of Tax Havens, and Decolonization as an Economic and Financial Event," *Past & Present* 249, no. 1 (2020): 213–249. Statistical analyses have also shown that places with common law are more likely to become offshore financial centers. Donato Masciandaro, "Offshore Financial Centers: The Political Economy of Regulation," *European Journal of Law and Economics* 26, no. 3 (2008): 307–340.

18. Rafael La Porta, Lopez-de-Silanes, Andrei Shleifer and Robert W. Vishny, "Legal Determinants of External Finance," *Journal of Finance* 52, no. 3 (1997): 1131–1150.

19. Brooke Harrington, *Capital without Borders: Wealth Managers and the One Percent* (Cambridge, MA: Harvard University Press, 2016).

20. Harrington, *Capital without Borders.* Ronen Palan, *The Offshore World: Sovereign Markets, Virtual Places, and Nomad Millionaires* (Ithaca: Cornell University Press, 2006). Ronen Palan, Richard Murphy, and Christian Chavagneux, *Tax Havens: How Globalization Really Works* (Ithaca: Cornell University Press, 2013). Vanessa Ogle, "Archipelago Capitalism: Tax Havens, Offshore Money and the State, 1950s–1970s," *American Historical Review* 122, no. 5 (2017): 1431–1458.

21. Oliver Bullough, *Moneyland: Why Thieves and Crooks Now Rule the World and How to Take It Back* (London: Profile Books, 2018). See also Mark Yeandle and Mike Wardle, "Global Financial Centres Index 26," China Development Institute, September 2019.

22. Tax Justice Network, Financial Secrecy Index Results 2022, https://fsi.taxjustice.net/.

23. Bullough, *Moneyland,* 142–143.

24. Government records preserved by a former minister (see the Methodological Appendix).

25. Bullough, *Moneyland*, 146–147.
26. Compare Bullough, *Moneyland*, 149.
27. For the emigration figures, see also Ronald Skeldon, "Emigration and the Future of Hong Kong," *Pacific Affairs* 63, no. 4 (1990): 502–594. Cait Murphy, "Hong Kong: Culture of Emigration," *Atlantic Monthly*, April 1991.
28. Peter Fredenburg, "Controversy Played Up as Brute Honesty," *South China Morning Post*, March 11, 1990.
29. David Ley, *Millionaire Migrants: Trans-Pacific Life Lines* (Chichester: Wiley-Blackwell, 2010).
30. Aiwah Ong, *Flexible Citizens: The Cultural Logics of Transnationality* (Durham: Duke University Press, 1999).
31. David Ley and Audrey Kobayashi, "Back to Hong Kong: Return Migration or Transnational Sojourn?," *Global Networks* 5, no. 2 (2005): 111–127.
32. "Passport Scheme Rejected," *South China Morning Post*, February 21, 1990.
33. "Belize Consulate First Step in Passport Plan," *South China Morning Post*, January 20, 1991.
34. Freddy Cuevas, "Honduras Foreign Minister Under Investigation in Passport Scandal," Associated Press, May 20, 1997. William Branigin, "INS Veteran Is Sentenced to 40 Months," *Washington Post*, August 17, 1996.
35. "Caribbean Passport for Investors," *South China Morning Post*, May 14, 1983.
36. "Jamaica Attracts Investors with Tax Breaks, Passports," *The Emigrant* 1, no. 6 (1989): 49–51.
37. Anthony Van Fossen, "Citizenship for Sale: Passports of Convenience from Pacific Island Tax Havens," *Commonwealth and Comparative Politics* 45, no. 2 (2007): 138–163.
38. Danny Gittings, "Ronald Li in Passport Deal," *South China Morning Post*, March 17, 1991.
39. "Tongan Passport 'Gave no Trouble,'" *South China Morning Post*, March 2, 1991.
40. Beryl Cook, "Inquiry Call on Tongan Passports," *South China Morning Post*, July 3, 1993. Tad Stoner, "Passports Scheme Rejected by Tonga," *South China Morning Post*, February 21, 1990. "Tonga Alarm at Abode for HK Chinese," *South China Morning Post*, February 14, 1991. Glenn Schloss, "Tonga Prepares to Put Passports Back on Sale," *South China Morning Post*, August 7, 1996.
41. Gittings, "Ronald Li in Passport Deal."
42. "Prague Studies Passport Deal," *South China Morning Post*, September 26, 1990. "Small Step Toward Eastern Investment," *South China Morning Post*, April 27, 1991. "Passport Seekers 'Swamp' Bulgaria," *South China Morning Post*, June 25, 1991.
43. "Foreign Passports for the Rich," *South China Morning Post*, May 29, 1994.
44. See, for example, "Passport to Nowhere," *South China Morning Post*, February 22, 1992. "Nations Ready to Offer Passports for Sale in HK," *South China Morning Post*, July 26, 1993.
45. W. G. Hill, *The Passport Report* (Hants: Scope International Limited, 1995).
46. "Sackings May Help Passport Victims," *South China Morning Post*, November 11, 1992.
47. "Nations Ready to Offer Passports for Sale in HK," *South China Morning Post*, July 26, 1993.

48. "Kenya Denies 'Passport in Four Months' Claim," *South China Morning Post,* August 12, 1993.

49. "Passport Probe Lands HK Barrister in Manila Jail," *South China Morning Post,* November 20, 1998.

50. See, for example, "Mystery of Missing Millions in Lesotho Passport Case," *South China Morning Post,* June 22, 1992.

51. "Island in Uproar Over Passport Row," *South China Morning Post,* September 6, 1992.

52. Assembly of Ireland, Adjournment Debate—Non-National Passport Holders, October 15, 1998, https://www.oireachtas.ie/en/debates/debate/dail/1998-10-15/.

53. On the numbers in the Pacific, see also Van Fossen, "Citizenship for Sale," 141.

54. Senate of Ireland, Adjournment Matter—Investment Based Naturalization Scheme, December 19, 2002, https://www.oireachtas.ie/en/debates/debate/seanad/2002-12-19/.

55. Saint Kitts Cabinet Submission No. 195/2006.

56. Saint Kitts Cabinet Submission No. 195/2006.

57. Saint Kitts Cabinet Submission No. 195/2006.

58. Saint Kitts Statutory Rules and Orders no. 52 of 2011.

59. The new rules also stipulated that anyone who sold the qualifying real estate in less than five years would have their citizenship revoked (Section 5 (10a)). In an unusual move, the effect was to tie the ownership of property to the validity of one's legal status, a formulation that Cyprus and Antigua also employed in their CBI programs.

60. Notably, the United States did not pressure Saint Kitts to end the program, as it did with Grenada and Belize in 2001.

61. Atossa Araxia Abrahamian, *The Cosmopolites: The Coming of the Global Citizen* (New York: Columbia Global Reports, 2015), 80.

62. St. Christopher and Nevis Budget Address 2019, 8.

63. Oliver Bullough, "Is St Kitts and Nevis' Passport Scheme Lucrative for All Involved?" *GQ Magazine,* July 2018.

64. The concessionaire received 10 percent of each government donation but nothing from applications moving through the real estate route.

65. Abrahamian, *The Cosmopolites.*

66. Ann Marlowe, "How Cambridge Analytica Fueled a Shady Global Passport Bonanza," *Fast Company,* January 2018. https://www.fastcompany.com/40571052/how-cambridge-analytica-fueled-a-shady-global-passport-bonanza.

67. Testimony before the Digital Culture, Media and Sport Committee, UK, June 6, 2018.

68. Reportedly, Marshall Langer, a libertarian known for his advice on how to avoid the "eight tentacles of tax," assisted in designing the original program.

69. Marilyn Grell-Brysk, "Eluding National Boundaries: A Case Study of Com-modified Citizenship and the Transnational Capitalist Class," *Societies* 8, no. 2 (2018): 35.

70. The government revoked and replaced the law with a similar formulation in 2014 that continues as the legal basis of the present program.

71. The program, however, would not be launched until January 1, 2017, when the country began accepting applications.
72. Ed Pilkington, "Islanders Count Cost of Billionaire's Collapsed Empire," *Guardian,* February 21, 2009.
73. Patrick Barkham, "The Banana Wars Explained," *Guardian,* March 5, 1999. Malcolm Bothwick, "Peace Finally Breaks out on the Banana Export Front," *BBC,* November 9, 2012. Ronald Sanders, "Dominica: Poverty and Potential," *BBC,* May 19, 2009.
74. Sarah Ryle, "Banana War Leaves the Caribbean a Casualty," *Guardian,* November 24, 2002.
75. Associated Press, "Hurricane Ivan Devastates Grenada," *Guardian,* September 9, 2004.
76. Based on the Saint Kitts model, the company was also to become the concessionaire for Antigua's program, but the government decided to do away with the position shortly before the program's launch and run it on its own. Grenada and Dominica, however, retained the role.
77. The ceiling was revoked in 2017.
78. Grenada adopted the term "Citizenship by Investment Committee."
79. Antigua, for example, moved decision-making from the prime minister to the board a year after the program opened. By 2016, all mention of the prime minister within the law was amended to necessitate his or her consultation with the cabinet.
80. However, in 2014 the Grenadian government deleted the requirement to print the names, addresses, and nationalities of those approved through the program.
81. Compare Manuela Boatcă, "Commodification of Citizenship: Global Inequalities and Modern Transmission of Property," in *Overcoming Global Inequalities,* ed. Immanuel Wallerstein, Christopher Chase-Dunn, and Christian Suter (London: Routledge, 2014).
82. FinCEN report FIN-2014-A004.
83. Previously Canada had raised concerns about Rustem Tursunbayev, a businessman wanted for massive embezzlement in Kazakhstan who attempted to enter the country on a Saint Kitts passport. See "In St. Kitts, Passport 'Sales' Lead to Escalating Political Drama," *Toronto Star,* January 16, 2014.
84. "In St. Kitts, Passport 'Sales' Lead to Escalating Political Drama."
85. These included reviews of the regulations, escrow accounts, and approved applications, as well as a changeover of staff in the CIU. More than 1,600 applications had piled up, with some waiting more than a year for adjudication. The recommendations led to a revamped workflow to prevent backlogs and to a new external committee tasked with reviewing all files before approval.
86. Other CIU heads have described similar vetting procedures of running applications through checks by INTERPOL, the JRCC, and even the US Department of Homeland Security.
87. Hugo O'Doherty, "Canada Enforces Visa Requirement on Citizens of Antiqua and Barbuda," *CIC News,* June 26, 2017.

88. See, for example, how corruption works in China in Yuen Yuen Ang, *China's Gilded Age: The Paradox of Economic Boom and Vast Corruption* (Cambridge: Cambridge University Press, 2020).

3. EU Citizenship

1. Thomas Edward Smith, *Commonwealth Migration: Flows and Policies* (New York: Macmillan, 1981), 148.
2. The top UK tax rate was nineteen shillings and six pennies to the pound. One pound equaled twenty shillings, and one shilling was worth twelve pennies, thus yielding the "six pennies" rate.
3. The Permanent Resident Scheme ended in 2010 and was replaced in 2011 by two variants of a High Net Worth Individual Visa, one for nationals of the EU, EEA, or Switzerland, and another for everyone else could also employ the tax benefits. This was superseded in 2013 by the Global Residence Program, aimed at non-EU nationals, and the Residence Program, aimed at Europeans. In 2015, the Malta Residence and Visa Program was added to the mix as a variant of the CBI option aimed at Chinese investors, who are not allowed to have dual citizenship.
4. Even in 2011, less than 10 percent of the 1,143 people who naturalized were foreign-born residents of Malta. Matthew Vella, "The Keys to the EU for €650,000: How Malta's Golden Passport Scheme Will Work," *Malta Today*, October 17, 2013.
5. Jurgen Balzan, "PN, AD Express Fears over New Permanent Residence Scheme," *Malta Today*, June 4, 2013.
6. "Malta Not for Sale?" editorial, *Malta Today*, October 13, 2013. Frank Salt, "EU Passport: Citizenship for Sale," *Malta Independent*, October 10, 2013. "Citizenship at What Cost?" *Malta Independent*, October 20, 2013. James Debono, "Cash for Citizenship," *Malta Today*, October 9, 2013. Vella, "The Keys to the EU for €650,000."
7. James Debono, "*Malta Today* Survey: Malta Says Yes to Budgets and No to Sale of Citizenship," *Malta Today*, November 11, 2013.
8. The election also saw the rise of swing voters for the first time. These "switchers" who moved from the Nationalists to Labour were split down the middle with 45 percent supporting the program.
9. "Malta 'Not Consulted' on Amendments to Citizenship Law," *Malta Independent*, October 8, 2013.
10. "Government 'Surprised' by Opposition's Criticism of Citizenship Scheme," *Malta Today*, October 19, 2013. "Malta Not for Sale?"
11. The shadow minister of finance was in the meetings where the concept was floated, and had even been offered a position with Henley. "Golden Passport Concessionaire Henley Says Opposition Was Informed of IIP," *Malta Today*, October 31, 2013. Jurgen Balzan, "Tonio Fenech Was Offered Consultancy Role with Henley and Partners," *Malta Today*, December 30, 2013.
12. However, Identity Malta could take the final decision if a person presented a sound justification.

13. In the original contract, the division of labor was clearer but raised more conflicts of interest. The concessionaire was to operate and manage the scheme, including vetting applications and overseeing due diligence, and it could submit applications too. Identity Malta was to be in charge of the last stage of application approval. In the final version of the legislation passed, this division of labor became blurrier. "Public Service Concession Contract" between Malta and Henley, Government of the Republic of Malta, September 24, 2013, https://parlament.mt/media /90506/dok-105-l60.pdf. See also Matthew Vella, "Golden Passport Concession-aire Henley to Take 4% Commission," *Malta Today*, October 30, 2013. Miriam Dalli, "Opposition Insists There's No Investment in Citizenship," *Malta Today*, November 8, 2013. Tim Attard Montalto, "Golden Passport Concessionaire Henley Has Conflict, Says Mario De Marco," *Malta Today*, October 25, 2013. Balzan, "Tonio Fenech Was Offered Consultancy Role."

14. Government of Malta, ORiip's First Annual Report 2014, 5, 20. Government of Malta, ORiip's Second Annual Report 2015, 12. This was confirmed to me again when I visited Identity Malta in 2018.

15. Matthew Vella, "In London, Muscat Says Maltese Citizenship Is Based on Collective Relationship," *Malta Today*, October 31, 2013.

16. Miriam Dalli, "Mario De Macro: Opposition Will Not Support Prostitution of Malta's Identity, Citizenship," *Malta Today*, November 9, 2013. Jurgen Balzan, "Contentious Citizenship Scheme Approved," *Malta Today*, November 12, 2013.

17. Dalli, "Opposition Insists." Jurgen Balzan, "Citizenship Scheme Should Serve to Create Jobs—Tonio Fenech," *Malta Today*, October 14, 2013.

18. Matthew Vella, "Citizenship Row: PM Publishes Fenech's Praise for Henley," *Malta Today*, November 13, 2013.

19. Chris Mangion, "PM Warns It Will Withdraw Golden Passports, Refuses to Publish Legal Advice on Revocation," *Malta Today*, January 27, 2014.

20. The requirement was to rent a residential property for at least €16,000 per year for five years or purchase one for at least €350,000, which would be held for five years.

21. In addition to 4 percent of the donation, the reforms gave the concessionaire an additional 4 percent, typically €6,000, of the investment requirement. Matthew Vella, "IIP: Henley's Commission Is 10 Times What Stockbrokers Get on Sale of Government Stocks," *Malta Today*, November 16, 2016.

22. Sergio Carrera, "How Much Does EU Citizenship Cost?" CEPS Paper in Liberty and Security in Europe, no. 64, Centre for European Policy Studies, April 25, 2014.

23. James Debono, "Inglorious Attack, Inglorious Retreat," *Malta Today*, February 4, 2014.

24. Most significant is the Micheletti case from 1992, which held that Spain must recognize the Italian citizenship of a dual national. Mario Micheletti was an Argentinian who naturalized at an Italian consulate in his home country based on ancestry provisions. Though he had never lived in Italy, he used his newly acquired Italian citizenship to move to Spain.

25. Article 4(2) of the Treaty on European Union. The notion that citizenship attribution depends on a "genuine connection" to a country derives from the

Nottebohm case, which in 1955 was one of the first lawsuits heard by the International Court of Justice (ICJ) and is itself an instance of citizenship by investment. The person in question, Friedrich Nottebohm, had lived most of his life in Guatemala after leaving his native Germany in his early twenties. In 1939, he naturalized in Liechtenstein through its CBI option—*Finanzeinbürgerung,* as it was known—that operated from 1919 to 1950 based on a set government donation. Once Nottebohm gained another nationality, the German state expired his citizenship. Nonetheless, the ICJ ruled that he should be considered German for the purpose of the case, and as such, Guatemala had the right to seize his assets as a national of an enemy country. The ICJ supported the ruling by arguing that Nottebohm had no "genuine link" to Liechtenstein. The shaky legal reasoning behind the ruling is well known, and the case has often been labeled "bad law." Peter J. Spiro, "*Nottebohm* and 'Genuine Link': Anatomy of a Jurisprudential Illusion," IMC Working Paper IMC-RP 2019/1, Investment Migration Council, Geneva, January 23, 2019.

26. For example, MEP Kinga Göncz on the Left worried that it might "undermine the whole of the European Project," finding it "neither fair nor equitable that the richest get citizenship in a privileged way." On the Far Right, MEP Morten Messerschmidt declared that "becoming a citizen of a country is to become part of a family" and that, of course, "it's not something to put up for sale." The MEPs from Malta's Nationalist Party stressed that citizens have "a full and deep connection" to their country. For naturalization, "there has to be a real link, there has to be a real connection for you to get a passport." European Parliament Debates, CRE 15/01/2014 -17, https://www.europarl.europa.eu/doceo/document /CRE-7-2014-01-15-ITM-017_EN.html.

27. European Parliament Resolution P7_TA(2014)0038, adopted January 16, 2014, Strasbourg.

28. European Parliament Resolution P7_TA(2014)0038, Section L. The resolution stated that "the foreign investors concerned will not be required to pay taxes" and thus "it is not clear whether Maltese citizens will really benefit from this new policy."

29. In addition, the government contribution that investor citizens make is much greater than what an average Maltese citizen, on an annual income of €20,000, ever pays in taxes. See also Kristin Surak, "How COVID-19 Will Transform the Market in Investment Migration," blogpost, Global Citizenship Observatory, Robert Schuman Centre, European University Institute, Florence, June 5, 2020, https://globalcit.eu/how-covid-19-will-transform-the-market-in-investment -migration/.

30. For many of them, the additional citizenship serves as an "insurance policy" against an uncertain government and economic future, similar motives to those seeking citizenship by investment. Guido Tintori, "The Transnational Political Practices of 'Latin American Italians,'" *International Migration* 49, no. 3 (2011): 168–188, 172–173. Yossi Harpaz, *Citizenship 2.0: Dual Nationality as a Global Asset* (Princeton: Princeton University Press, 2019), 31. Similarly, Spain and Portugal have granted citizenship to people with a Sephardic Jewish ancestor in recognition of the violence of the Inquisition of the fifteenth century. Initially,

there was little uptake, but once the residence requirements were lifted, application numbers skyrocketed, and by 2019, more than 130,000 had applied. Henry Chu, "Welcome Home, 500 Years Later: Spain Offers Citizenship to Sephardic Jews," *Los Angeles Times,* October 1, 2015. Simon Romero, "Some Hispanics with Jewish Roots Pursue an Exit Strategy: Emigrate to Spain," *New York Times,* November 6, 2018. Sam Jones, "132,000 Descendants of Spanish Jews Apply for Citizenship," *Guardian,* October 2, 2019.

31. In the Italian, Spanish, and Hungarian cases, for example, there are no limits on how many generations the connections can go back when applying for ancestry-based naturalization.

32. "Citizenship by Exception," Parliamentary Question E-006519/2011, European Parliament, June 24, 2011, https://www.europarl.europa.eu/doceo/document/E-7 -2011-006519_EN.html?redirect.

33. Richard T. Ford, "Law's Territory (A History of Jurisdiction)," *Michigan Law Review* 97, no. 4 (1999): 843–930, 905.

34. Some may relish the chance, for the successful are ushered down a red carpet that runs along the entrance hall of a five-hundred-year-old fortress constructed by the Knights of Malta. Ancient suits of armor stand at attention as the country's VIP inductees parade past on their way to swear allegiance to their new sovereign. Plebeians find their immigration and naturalization needs met in a more mundane government building around the corner.

35. See also, for example, Government of Malta, ORiip 2015, 99–103.

36. It began with assembling a sizeable application package that would include police checks, income verification, identity verification, translations, official certifications, apostils, and more. Once Identity Malta received the application and a deposit, it verified the documents and ran background checks via government databases and INTERPOL. Meanwhile the Financial Intelligence Analysis Unit checked the sources of wealth and the invested funds for money laundering. If all was clear, the file was passed on to the board of Identity Malta for approval, completing a nearly four-month journey through the bureaucracy. Next, the applicant received an approval-in-principle and would then move forward with paying the contribution to the government and securing a residential property. Finally, they submitted biometric information, given in person, along with confirmation that the investment has been made and sufficient health insurance acquired. After twelve months of building residence connections to the country, approved applicants returned to Malta to swear an oath of allegiance and receive their naturalization certificate.

37. When I asked the head of Identity Malta about the refusal process, he explained that—beyond the obvious like money launderers or those terrorist links—they turn down individuals with unclear sources of wealth or with information gaps on the forms, along with anyone with substantial adverse media coverage due to the negative impact on the country's reputation.

38. Some service providers too have complained about an unfair advantage. Government of Malta, ORiip 2014, 134–139.

39. As the prime minister told an audience at an investment migration conference in 2015, "Let's face it, these are controversial programs. When it was introduced a

year and a half ago, this was a big topic of conversation locally." Yet since then, he explained, they have found a consensus with the EU, and the result is that the program is "the first time that citizenship-by-investment has been endorsed as a concept by the European Commission." The European Commission has denied that it endorses the program.

40. See "Malta: Concluding Statement of the 2019 Article IV Mission," International Monetary Fund, January 16, 2019. "Malta: 2020 Article IV. Consultation-Press Release and Staff Report," Country Report, International Monetary Fund, April 10, 2020.

41. Kristin Surak, "Citizenship and Residence by Investment Schemes—State of Play and Avenues for EU Action," Annex II, to M. Fernandes et al., "Avenues for EU Action on Citizenship and Residence," European Parliamentary Research Service, October 2021, 34.

42. For assessments of her reportage, see Raisa Galea and Michael Grech, "The Death of a Journalist," *Jacobin,* November 13, 2017, https://www.jacobinmag.com /2017/11/malta-daphne-galizia-corruption. Andrew Higgins, "Brutal Killing of Journalist Exposes 'Something Darker' in Malta," *New York Times,* October 21, 2017.

43. See Galea and Grech, "The Death of a Journalist."

44. "Who Murdered Daphne Caruana Galizia?" *Atlantic,* December 16, 2019.

45. "The Rule of Law in Malta, after the Recent Revelations around the Murder of Daphne Caruana Galizia," European Parliament Resolution, December 18, 2019, https://www.europarl.europa.eu/doceo/document/TA-9-2019-0103_EN.html.

46. "Daphne Caruana Galizia: Malta Suspect Will Not Get Immunity," *BBC,* November 30, 2019.

47. On the European Court of Justice, see Perry Anderson, "Ever Closer Union?" *London Review of Books,* January 7, 2021.

48. Money doesn't only flow out through Cyprus—it also flows back in. By 2011, Cyprus had become the second largest source of foreign direct investment entering Russia. Effectively, it was a base for "round-tripping" that enabled Russian companies to utilize a less corrupt and more effective legal system. See Alexander Michaelides, "Cyprus, From Boom to Bail-In," *Economic Policy* 29, no. 80 (2014): 641–689.

49. European Construction Center Observatory (ECSO), Country Fact Sheet of Cyprus, European Commission, 2018, 3.

50. Between 2007 and 2013, 420 people were naturalized through the program.

51. At Laiki, the levy was 100 percent on all uninsured deposits over €100,000, and at the Bank of Cyprus, it was 47.5 percent of all deposits over €100,000. For a history, see Alexander Michaelides, "What Happened in Cyprus?" Imperial College Business School, University of Cyprus, March 15, 2014.

52. Evie Andreou, "Haircut Five Years After: The Long Road through the Courts," *Cyprus Mail,* March 25, 2018.

53. Cyprus Audit Office Report 2020.

54. "Total Number of Acquisitions of Citizenship, 2018–2019," Eurostat, March 24, 2020, https://ec.europa.eu/eurostat/statistics-explained/index.php?title=File :Total_number_of_acquisitions_of_citizenship,_2009-2018.png.

55. The figure is based on the InvestMig database and uses an estimator of family dependents to extrapolate total individuals.

56. In practice, this was a mere box-ticking exercise: a permanent residence certificate was issued within days of filing the application if the applicant passed muster.

57. The definition of investment migration program used by the 2018 European Parliamentary Research Service report included citizenship by investment, residence by investment, and some entrepreneurial programs, and found them to be present in eighteen member states. For a more rigorous definition of RBI programs, see Surak, "Citizenship and Residence by Investment Schemes."

58. See, for example, European Commission, "Report from the Commission," January 23, 2019, https://commission.europa.eu/system/files/2019-01/com_2019 _12_final_report.pdf.

59. Elias Hazou, "Archbishop Testifies Only Briefly Met Wanted Malaysian Businessman," *Cyprus Mail*, January 26, 2021.

60. "Al Jazeera Cyprus Papers Web of Lies Revealed," *Cyprus Mail*, August 27, 2020. Matthew Bodner, "Russian Tycoon Oleg Deripaska Stripped of Cyprus Citizenship in Clampdown on Cash-for-Visa Scheme," *Guardian*, November 27, 2019. "Treasury Designates Russian Oligarchs, Officials, and Entities in Response to Worldwide Malign Activity," press release, US Department of the Treasury, April 6, 2018, https://home.treasury.gov/news/press-releases/sm0338.

61. Al Jazeera Investigative Unit, "Cyprus Sold Passports to Criminals and Fugitives," *Al Jazeera*, August 23, 2020.

62. Kimberly Hoang exposes how this works. Kimberly Kay Hoang, *Spiderweb Capitalism: How Global Elites Exploit Frontier Markets* (Princeton: Princeton University Press, 2022). Instances, however, are not limited to the developing world. See, for example, the dubious links between business and government in contracts worth billions of pounds that the United Kingdom awarded in response to Covid-19. Jane Bradley, Selam Gebrekidan, and Allison McCann, "Waste, Negligence, and Cronyism: Inside Britain's Pandemic Spending," *New York Times*, December 17, 2020. See also Yuen Yuen Ang, *China's Gilded Age: The Paradox of Economic Boom and Vast Corruption* (Cambridge: Cambridge University Press, 2020).

63. "Cyprus Abolishes Citizenship through Investment Programme," *Al Jazeera*, October 13, 2020.

64. George Psyllides, "Last-Minute Citizenship Applications Number 416 Ministry Says," *Cyprus Mail*, November 6, 2020.

4. Beyond the Core Market

1. Muhammad Ghazal, "18 Investors Apply to Obtain Citizenship, Residency under Incentive Scheme," *Jordan Times*, March 5, 2018.

2. The required amount for Egyptian citizenship was EGP 7 million.

3. Sonia Farid, "Egypt's Multi-million-pound Citizenship to Foreigners: Who Gets It?" *Alarabiya News*, September 1, 2018.

4. The amounts are 1.25 million Cambodian riel and 1 million Cambodian riel, respectively.

5. Mauritius Citizenship, Act 45, Section 9(3).

6. Ministry of Commerce, Industry and Labour, Samoa, Investment Promotion, https://www.mcil.gov.ws/services/investment-promotion-and-industry -development/investment-promotion/. Ministry of Commerce, Industry and Labour, Samoa, Infographic, https://www.mcil.gov.ws/storage/2017/12 /Infographic.pdf.

7. Ministry of Commerce, Industry and Labour, Samoa, *Annual Report 2018,* https://www.mcil.gov.ws/storage/2020/10/Annual-Report-2018-2019-MCIL .pdf.

8. BBC News, "Kuwait's Stateless Bidun Offered Comoros Citizenship," *BBC,* November 10, 2014. Camilla Hall and Michael Peel, "UAE's Stateless Acquire Foreign Passports," *Financial Times,* June 4, 2012. Atossa Araxia Abrahamian, "Kuwait Offers Stateless Group Citizenship—From Comoros," *Al Jazeera America,* November 10, 2014.

9. On the legal questionability of this practice, see Peter J. Spiro, "Investor Citizenship and the Long Leash of International Law," in *Citizenship and Residence Sales: Beyond the Boundaries of Belonging,* ed. Dimitry Kochenov and Kristin Surak (Cambridge: Cambridge University Press, 2023).

10. Atossa Araxia Abrahamian, "Who Loses When a Country Puts Citizenship Up for Sale?" *New York Times,* January 5, 2018.

11. Abrahamian, "Who Loses?" La Redaction, "Citoyenneté économique: aucun nouveau passeport émis par le présent régime," *Comores-Infos,* January 19, 2018.

12. Citizenship in the United Arab Emirates is segmented by differential rights and privileges determined by one's documents. People with a "family book"— effectively, a family registry—from the central government, and who also have a passport from it, are able to claim the highest grade of membership. Under them lies a gray zone of individuals who may have citizenship documents of some sort or a passport from, for example, an individual emirate, but not a passport-plus-family-book combination from the central government. Others may have a letter from the royal family granting them unlimited residence in the country, which could come with an Emirati passport, though not a family book. The documentary disorder is a byproduct of the slow centralization process and delay in constitution-building in post-independence UAE, which is layered on a history of hierarchical membership dating back to its time as a British protectorate. See Manal A. Jamal, "The Tiering of Citizenship and Residency and the Hierarchization of Migrant Communities: The United Arab Emirates in Historical Context," *International Migration Review* 49, no. 3 (2015): 601–632. In 1996, a new constitution finally centralized political control, and since then the government in Abu Dhabi has attempted to clear up the gray area, but with varying success. Some people have been able to convert their emirate-level documents into ones issued by the central government, but others have not, leaving them exposed to moves like the government's Comoros scheme.

13. David Lewis and Ali Amir Ahmed, "Comoros Passport Scheme Was Unlawful, Abused by 'Mafia' Networks—Report," Reuters, March 24, 2018, https://www .reuters.com/article/us-comoros-passports-exclusive-idUSKBN1GZ37H.

14. The CIIP was suspended in 2015. The government attests that it is no longer accepting applications through this route, though the Vanuatu Registry Service's contract runs through 2024.

15. In 2014, Vanuatu passed a further law establishing the Real Estate Option (REO) Program. Similar in form to Bulgaria's residence-into-citizenship option but aimed at the Chinese market, it allowed investors to gain residence in the country for $260,000, and they could later decide to become a citizen by paying an additional fee.

16. Dan McGarry, "Passport Sales Skyrocket," *Vanuatu Daily Post,* April 29, 2019.

17. Ana Maria Touma, "Moldova Offers Passports to Cash-Rich Foreigners," *Balkan Insight,* September 28, 2017. Republic of Moldova Government, Regulations for Citizenship by Investment, https://gov.md/sites/default/files/document/attach ments/intr20_89.pdf.

18. "Igor Grosu: Astăzi, R.Moldova a mai îndeplinit o condiționalitate pentru a putea beneficia de a doua tranșă din partea UE," Radio Chisinau, June 18, 2020, https://radiochisinau.md/igor-grosu-astazi-rmoldova-a-mai-indeplinit-o -conditionalitate-pentru-a-putea-beneficia-de-a-doua-transa-din-partea-ue— 111349.html.

19. Mike Eckel and Liliana Barbarosie, "Powerful Oligarch Who Fled Moldova Last Year Sought Political Asylum in U.S.," Radio Free Europe Radio Liberty, June 11, 2020.

20. Redactia Unimedia, "Guvernul a instituit moratoriu asupra acordării cetățeniei Republicii Moldova prin investitii," Unimedia, July 26, 2019. "Moratorium on Citizenship through Investments Programme to Be Extended by Another Two Months in Moldova," Moldpres, Chisinau, December 17, 2019.

21. Christian Henrik Nesheim, "Canceling Moldova CIP Now Would Mean €3–4 Million Fine: Parliament Approves 4-Month Freeze in Dual Reading," *Investment Migration Insider,* August 3, 2019. "Prime Minister Ion Chicu: Canceling Citizenship-by-Investment Could Cost the State 3.5 Million Euros," *Publika* (Moldova), February 17, 2020.

22. "Moldova Required to Pass Necessary Laws by May 31, to Obtain EU Aid's Second Tranche," *Publika* (Moldova), May 26, 2020. "Parliament Speaker, PM Having Meeting with Head of EU Delegation to Moldova," Moldpres, Chisinau, April 16, 2020.

23. Alice Elizabeth Taylor, "EU Commissioner for Justice: Albania Should Refrain from Selling Passports If It Wants to Join EU," *Exit News,* December 6, 2019.

24. For a general overview of the program and its trajectory, see also Eleanor Knott, "Recent Updates to Moldovan Citizenship Legislation," Country Report 2021/02, Robert Schuman Centre for Advanced Studies, European University Institute, February 2021, https://cadmus.eui.eu/handle/1814/69868.

25. "Prime Minister Ion Chicu." "No Applications for Getting Moldovan Citizenship through Investments to Be Received Till 1 September 2020," Moldpres, Chisinau, February 28, 2020.

26. Taylor, "EU Commissioner for Justice."

27. Albania, Law No. 113/2020, Article 9.

28. Marine Madatyan, "Global Firm Has Advice for Armenia: Bargain-Priced Golden Visas," *Organized Crime and Corruption Reporting Project*, March 5, 2018, https://www.occrp.org/en/goldforvisas/global-firm-has-advice-for -yerevan-bargain-priced-golden-visas.

29. On Armenian politics, see also Georgi Derluguian, "A Small World War," *New Left Review* 128, March-April 2021.

30. "Over 2,600 Foreign Investors Naturalized in Turkey," *Hürriyet Daily News,* September 27, 2019.

31. On serial investor migrants, see Kristin Surak, "Who Wants to Buy a Visa: Comparing the Uptake of Residence by Investment Programs in the European Union," *Journal of Contemporary European Studies* 30, no. 1 (2020): 151–169.

32. "Over 5000 Foreign Investors Granted Citizenship," *Daily Sabah,* February 28, 2020.

33. "Solomon Islands to Consider Selling Citizenship for Investment," *ABC Radio Australia,* March 20, 2020, https://www.abc.net.au/radio-australia/programs /pacificbeat/sols-passport/12073908.

5. Geopolitical Maneuvering

1. "US Cautions Caribbean Countries Offering Economic Citizenship," *Caribbean 360 News,* April 20, 2016, Dutch Caribbean Legal Portal, http://www .dutchcaribbeanlegalportal.com/news/crime/6848-us-cautions-caribbean -countries-offering-economic-citizenship.

2. "2018 International Narcotics Control Strategy Report," US Department of State, March 17, 2018, https://www.state.gov/2018-international-narcotics-control -strategy-report/.

3. The prime minister made clear the impetus behind the change. "The US continues to say what it's always been saying: that they have concerns with regard to the CIP [citizenship investment program], that they want to ensure that the CIP is away from the politicians," and in response, "we continue to do things to distance my office from the CIP," he announced. The most recent move, he noted, was to move the rejection appeals procedure from the "Minister Responsible for the CIP"—typically the prime minister—to an independent panel of due diligence professionals not associated with the program. "PM Addresses CIP Concerns in US Money Laundering Report," *HTS News 4orce,* April 12, 2018.

4. "Abuse of the Citizenship-by-Investment Program Sponsored by the Federation of St. Kitts and Nevis," Advisory FIN-2014-A004, Financial Crimes Enforce- ment Network, U.S. Department of the Treasury, May 20, 2014, https://www .fincen.gov/resources/advisories/fincen-advisory-fin-2014-a004.

5. "St. Kitts and Nevis: Staff Concluding Statement of the 2017 Article IV Mis- sion," January 31, 2023, https://www.imf.org/en/News/Articles/2023/01/31 /cs13123-st-kitts-and-nevis-staff-concluding-statement-of-the-2023-article-iv -mission.

6. The European Council and the European Court of Justice have yet to voice an opinion on the programs.

7. "A Comprehensive Union Policy on Preventing Money Laundering and Terrorist Financing—The Commission's Action Plan and Other Recent Developments," European Parliament, April 2020, and similar from July 2020, https://www .europarl.europa.eu/doceo/document/TA-9-2020-0204_EN.html.

8. Annette Chrysosotomou, "EU Commissioner on Citizenship Sale Fact-Finding Visit," *Cyprus Mail,* September 21, 2018.

9. Christoph B. Schiltz, "Brüssel geht gegen EU-Länder vor, die mit Pässen handeln," *Die Welt,* July 8, 2018.

10. European Parliament, Civil Liberties, Justice, and Home Affairs (LIBE) Committee Meeting LIBE/9/05606 2021 / 2026(INL), https://emeeting.europarl .europa.eu/emeeting/committee/en/agenda/202111/LIBE?meeting=LIBE-2021 -1129_1&session=11-29-14-45.

11. Edinburgh Decision: "The question whether an individual possesses the nationality of a member state will be settled solely by reference to the national law of the member state concerned." The decision was subsequently incorporated into the Lisbon Treaty and became a part of EU primary law. See Thomas Horsley, *The Court of Justice of the European Union as an Institutional Actor: Judicial Lawmaking and Its Limits* (Cambridge: Cambridge University Press, 2018), 43.

12. Perry Anderson, "The European Coup," *London Review of Books,* December 17, 2020. Perry Anderson, "Ever Closer Union?" *London Review of Books,* January 7, 2021. Paul Craig and Gráinne de Búrca, *EU Law: Text, Cases, and Materials,* 7th ed. (Oxford: Oxford University Press, 2020).

13. Anderson, "Ever Closer Union?" Dieter Grimm, *The Constitution of European Democracy* (Oxford: Oxford University Press, 2017). Horsley, *The Court of Justice.*

14. Beppe Galea, "Malta Must Do More against Money Laundering—Jourova," *Newsbook,* September 10, 2018.

15. Lorenzo Tondo, "Revealed: 2000 Refugee Deaths Linked to Illegal EU Push-backs," *Guardian,* May 5, 2021. On the similarly dire condition of those who end up in EU-funded detention camps in Libya, see Ian Urbina, "The Secretive Prisons That Keep Migrants Out of Europe," *New Yorker,* November 22, 2021.

16. Civitas Post, "The Cyprus Papers," https://civitaspost.com/wp-content/uploads /2020/09/CIVITAS-POST-Cyprus-Papers-Analysis-FINAL-2.pdf.

17. Kristin Surak, "Citizenship and Residence by Investment Schemes: State of Play and Avenues for EU Action," European Added Value Assessment, European Parliamentary Research Service, European Union, Brussels, 2021.

18. "Investor Citizenship Schemes: European Commission Opens Infringements against Cyprus and Malta for 'Selling' EU Citizenship," press release, European Commission, October 20, 2020. See also, for example, Galea, "Malta Must Do More."

19. The ruling stated that as a matter of consular protection, genuine links can be expected for a state to sue another state concerning the rights of a citizen.

20. Peter J. Spiro, "*Nottebohm* and 'Genuine Link': Anatomy of a Jurisprudential Illusion," IMC 2019 / 1, Investment Migration Working Paper, Investment Migration Council, 2019.

21. The reasoning is that because investor citizens do not usually reside—or spend much time at all—in their new country, they develop no genuine link to it.

Interestingly, the argument is not extended to other migration streams that facilitate naturalization in the absence of physical presence, which commonly see much larger uptake. Most notable are ancestry options that allow the descendants of former citizens to naturalize, often quite easily, through mere "declaration," or simply by producing documentation. Indeed, more than 2 million people have naturalized as Italian citizens at its embassies abroad, showing no evidence that they have ever been to Italy at all. Guido Tintori, "More than One Million Individuals Got Italian Citizenship Abroad in Twelve Years (1998–2010)," EUI Global Citizenship Observatory, November 21, 2012, https://globalcit.eu/more-than-one-million-individuals-got-italian-citizenship-abroad-in-the-twelve-years-1998-2010/.

22. In response to my query into the motives for launching infringement proceedings against Malta and Cyprus, I was told, "The Commission considers that the granting by these Member States of their nationality—and thereby EU citizenship—in exchange for a pre-determined payment or investment and without a genuine link with the Member States concerned, is not compatible with the principle of sincere cooperation enshrined in Article 4(3) of the Treaty on European Union. This also undermines the integrity of the status of EU citizenship provided for in Article 20 of the Treaty on the Functioning of the European Union." Email from the European Commission Directorate-General of Justice and Consumers registered under JUST.D.3 / JS / FW(2020)7202513S, November 10, 2021.

23. Alice Elizabeth Taylor, "EU Commissioner for Justice: Albania Should Refrain from Selling Passports If It Wants to Join the EU," *Exit News,* December 6, 2019.

24. The EU also gives better access to elites. Turkish citizens who receive a green passport—usually those with the closest ties to Erdoğan—have visa-free access to the EU, while the majority, who receive red passports, must apply for a visa.

25. "MEPs Demand a Ban on Golden Passports and Specific Rules for Golden Visas," *European Parliament News,* March 9, 2022.

26. "Cyprus: 2017 Article IV Consultation—Press Release; Staff Report; and Statement by the Executive Director," IMF Report No. 17/375.

27. "IMF Staff Completes 2016 Article IV Mission to St. Kitts and Nevis," press release, International Monetary Fund, May 13, 2016.

28. "St. Kitts and Nevis: Staff Report for the 2016 Article IV Consultation," International Monetary Fund, July 26, 2016.

29. Alex Muscat, "Defending What Is Ours by Right," *Times of Malta,* December 4, 2020.

30. Before Antigua's sale, Dominica announced that its donation option would increase from $100,000 to $175,000 for a single applicant to more closely match the regional standard that ranged from $200,000 to $250,000. As a result, Dominica enjoyed a bump in applications as investors sought to get in before the price hike. Afterward, however, it did not follow through with the promised cost increase and remained the cheapest option. Officials in Antigua explained that their own price drop was in reaction to Dominica's strategic fake to gain market share.

31. For a sample of these, see "Third Annual Report ORiip," Office of the Regulator, Government of Malta, October 2016, 31–34.

32. Russians account for around half of all CBI approvals in the EU and 20 percent of the far more numerous RBI approvals. Surak, "Citizenship and Residence."

33. The law was revised after the Russian invasion of Ukraine to require that naturalizers through the route prove also a connection to Portugal. This, however, did not affect Abramovich's status as a citizen. Camille Gijs, "Portugal Changes Law That Allowed Russian Oligarch Abramovich to Obtain Citizenship," *Politico,* March 16, 2022. On how Abramovich naturalized via Sephardic connections, see also Cnaan Liphshiz, "Documents Linked to Abramovich's Controversial Portuguese Citizenship Leak Online," *Times of Israel,* April 2, 2022.

34. "HS Learned the Language Skills of the Oligarchs Who Acquired Finnish Citizenship," *News Founded,* n.d., https://newsfounded.com/finlandeng/hs -learned-the-language-skills-of-the-oligarchs-who-acquired-finnish-citizenship/.

35. On this, see David FitzGerald, *Refuge beyond Reach: How Rich Democracies Repel Asylum Seekers* (Oxford: Oxford University Press, 2019).

6. The Citizenship Industry

1. This figure is calculated from the InvestMig dataset and obtained by multiplying the minimum investment amount with the number of approved applications. The limits of this mode of calculation are discussed in Chapter 7.

2. Many businesses profit from naturalization procedures outside the world of citizenship by investment. Examples include law firms that help with the paperwork for spousal applications or companies that assist with finding the documentation for naturalization through ancestry channels.

3. On the migration industry, see also Thomas Gammeltoft-Hansen and Ninna Nyberg Sørensen, eds., *The Migration Industry and the Commercialization of International Migration*(London: Routledge, 2013). Kristin Surak, "Migration Industries and the State: Guestwork Programs in East Asia," *International Migration Review* 52, no. 2 (2018): 487–523. Kristin Surak, "Global Citizenship 2.0: The Growth of Citizenship by Investment," IMC Working Paper IMC-RP 2016 / 3, Investment Migration Council, Geneva, November 15, 2016.

4. Many studied at Canadian universities in the 1990s, when exit was strictly controlled, and found upon returning to China that the knowledge they gained earning PhDs in the sciences was not nearly as lucrative as their practical knowledge of migration possibilities.

5. Kristin Surak and Yusuke Tsuzuki, "Are Golden Visas a Golden Opportunity? Assessing the Economic Origins and Outcomes of Residence by Investment Programmes in the EU," *Journal of Ethnic and Migration Studies* 47, no. 15 (2021): 3367–3389.

6. Note too that many service providers are themselves "multizens" who have picked up an extra citizenship—or six or seven—along the way. Some do it for marketing, displaying their own collection to potential clients. Others seek them out for business reasons: in some countries, only citizens can register as licensed agents. Travel convenience can be an allure as well: bigger players in

the citizenship industry jet frequently between clients and countries, filling passports quickly.

7. The QIIP remained open after the FIIP closed, but it imposed an annual cap that fluctuated around 1,800 approved applications per year. The limit left service providers still looking for other options.

8. In evaluating vetting procedures, actual rejection rates can be a poor indicator of the strength of background checks. If service providers are kept in line via a licensing system and required to carry out their own due diligence investigations, dodgy applications may be rejected even before they approach the country, and thus not impact the official figures. If the supply chain is solid, rejections by the government could conceivably be near zero. It's possible too that countries will reject a symbolic number of individuals to show that they're doing something, but the upshot is not effective. Rejections may be politically motivated, with numbers disproportionately high for people from some countries, such as Iran or Russia. In these cases, the rejections may have more to do with the status of geopolitical conflicts than with the quality of the application. Service providers with good connections to a government may also negotiate exceptions for clients who would not otherwise pass background checks.

9. Ann Marlowe, "How Cambridge Analytica Fueled a Shady Global Passport Bonanza," *Fast Company,* January 2018, https://www.fastcompany.com /40571052/how-cambridge-analytica-fueled-a-shady-global-passport -bonanza.

10. See the study by Liao Xiao Hua, "Immigration," https://mp.weixin.qq.com/s /VYcAVBQ3Wtgv4VocSfjFAQ.

11. Of course, commissions paid by governments are also extracted from the investor in the end, but in this case, the more direct cost is borne by the government as it reallocates its fee revenue.

12. On how this works, see Surak, "Migration Industries and the State."

7. Do the Programs Pay Off?

1. Terri-Ann Williams, "Investors Buying $1.3m Dream Homes in Dubai Get Backdoor Access to Europe Thrown in for Free Thanks to New Scheme Slammed as 'Serious Security Risk,'" *Daily Mail,* June 12, 2019.

2. John Dennehy, "Dubai Developer's Visa-Free Travel in Europe Offer Generates Interest in UAE," *The National,* June 20, 2019.

3. This is how Bloomberg and Knight Frank reach their calculations, for example.

4. I also exclude the Comoros from the overall count due to the irregularities around the scheme, which render it more akin to a discretionary channel than a fully formalized program.

5. In 2017 it would have done so even without the CBI program, but in 2016 and 2018 the surplus was due entirely to it. "Malta—Concluding Statement of the 2019 Article IV Mission," International Monetary Fund, January 16, 2019. "Malta: 2020 Article IV Consultation—Press Release and Staff Report," Country Report, International Monetary Fund, April 10, 2020.

6. "Malta: 2020 Article IV Consultation." "Malta Budget 2020: Connecting the Dots," Deloitte, October 2019, https://www2.deloitte.com/content/dam/Deloitte /mt/Documents/tax/publications/dt_mt_pub_budget_2020_summary.pdf.

7. "KPMG Cyprus Real Estate Market Report—The Insights," 11th ed., KPMG, July 2020, https://home.kpmg/cy/en/home/insights/2020/07/kpmg-cyprus-real -estate-market-report-the-insights.html.

8. "St. Kitts and Nevis: 2016 Article IV Consultation," Staff Report, IMF Country Report no. 16/250, International Monetary Fund, June 23, 2016.

9. "St. Kitts and Nevis: Staff Concluding Statement of the 2021 Article IV Mission," International Monetary Fund, July 6, 2021.

10. Vanessa Ogle, "Archipelago Capitalism: Tax Havens, Offshore Money, and the State," *American Historical Review* 122, no. 5 (2017): 1431–1458. Ronen Palan, Richard Murphy, and Christian Chavagneux, *Tax Havens: How Globalization Really Works* (Ithaca, NY: Cornell University Press, 2013).

11. Palan, Murphy, and Chavagneux, *Tax Havens*, 8.

12. Oliver Bullough, *Moneyland: Why Thieves and Crooks Now Rule the World and How to Take It Back* (London: Profile Books, 2018).

13. Ronen Palan, *The Offshore World: Sovereign Markets, Virtual Places, and Nomad Millionaires* (Ithaca, NY: Cornell University Press, 2003). Palan, Murphy, and Chavagneux, *Tax Havens*.

14. Max Holleran, "Buying Up the Semi-Periphery: Spain's Economy of 'Golden Visas,'" *Ethnos: Journal of Anthropology* 86, no. 4 (2019): 730–749. Amandine Marie Anne Scherrer and Elodie Thirion, "Citizenship by Investment (CBI) and Residency by Investment (RBI) Schemes in the EU," European Parliamentary Research Service, PE 627.128), European Parliament, October 17, 2018.

15. On RBI cases, see also Kristin Surak and Yusuke Tsuzuki, "Are Golden Visas a Golden Opportunity? Assessing the Economic Origins and Outcomes of Residence by Investment Programmes in the EU," *Journal of Ethnic and Migration Studies* 47, no. 15 (2021): 3367–3389.

16. "Cyprus: 2019 Article IV Consultation—Press Release; Staff Report; and Statement by the Executive Director for Cyprus," IMF Country Report No. 19/362, International Monetary Fund, December 2019, https://www.imf.org /en/Publications/CR/Issues/2019/12/09/Cyprus-2019-Article-IV-Consultation -Press-Release-Staff-Report-and-Statement-by-the-48863. "KPMG Cyprus Real Estate Market Report—The Insights."

17. The figure is calculated for the 12,000 main applicants and excludes family members who would also become investor citizens but under the same investment as the main applicant. See "Contractors in Turkey Expect Recovery in Building Trade," *Hurriyet Daily News,* December 6, 2019. "Effects of the Covid 19 on Overseas Real Estate Sales in Turkey," Gigder, Istanbul, April 21, 2020, https:// gigder.org.tr/en/effects-of-the-covid-19-on-overseas-real-estate-sales-in-turkey/.

18. See also Surak and Tsuzuki, "Are Golden Visas a Golden Opportunity?"

19. Limassol Chamber of Commerce, "Limassol Marina: The Flagship Project has been Completed," 2021, https://www.limassolchamber.eu/En/articles/1361/2021 /07/04/Limassol-Marina--The-flagship-project-has-been-completed.

20. Cyprus Department of Land and Surveys data.

21. Alexander Michaelides, "Cyprus: From Boom to Bail-in," *Economic Policy* 29, no. 80 (2014): 639–689, 689.

22. "KPMG Cyprus Real Estate Market Report—The Insights." The IMF, too, has noted the program's importance to reviving real estate. "2019 Article IV Consultation," IMF Country Report.

23. Cyprus Department of Land and Surveys data.

24. Since its establishment, Cyprus's RBI program has been directed at Chinese nationals, who do not always want a second citizenship, and they have been the source of most demand, which before Covid-19 focused on real estate projects around the city of Paphos.

25. "Linton Wants Criminal Investigation in Failed Layou River Hotel Project," *Dominica News Online,* February 11, 2016.

26. Statement from the Office of the Prime Minister, Government of Antigua and Barbuda, December 5, 2014.

27. See *Hardip Singh aka Peter Virdee and Dieter Trutschler v. The National Crime Agency* (2018) EWHC 1119 (Admin), Case No: CO/4157/2017 & CO/5692/2017, https://vlex.co.uk/vid/hardip-singh-aka-peter-792007377. Theo Andrew, "Fraudster Ordered to Pay £172,000 over Illegal Fund," *City Wire,* December 20, 2019. Lauren Fruen, "Top Conservative Party Donor Arrested at Heathrow and Faces Extradition to Germany over Alleged £100m VAT Scam," *The Sun,* January 16, 2017.

28. "Exposing Foggy Caribbean Business of Henley Partners," *Weekly Blitz,* March 24, 2022.

29. Antigua and Barbuda Citizenship by Investment Unit Six-Monthly Report (January–June 2019); Antigua and Barbuda Citizenship by Investment Unit Six-Monthly Report (July–December 2019).

30. There is not yet enough of a track record from the current program, launched in 2021, to make a similar assessment.

31. "Malta—Concluding Statement of the 2019 Article IV Mission," IMF. "Malta—2020 Article IV Consultation," IMF.

32. "Former AG Delano Bart Named in Alleged SIDF Corruption," *Saint Kitts and Nevis Observer,* April 24, 2015.

33. *Virdee & Trutschler v. NCA.*

34. To ensure that developers complete the promised project, some countries have started to monitor completion by dividing up the allotted citizenship slots and releasing them in tranches only after defined stages of construction have been cleared. The upshot in some cases, however, is that companies that simply tick the right boxes to collect the first and second tranches and then disappear before finishing the building.

35. Yuen Yuen Ang, *China's Gilded Age: The Paradox of Economic Boom and Vast Corruption* (Cambridge: Cambridge University Press, 2020).

8. Local Perspectives

1. US Department of State, Nonimmigrant Visa Statistics, https://travel.state.gov/content/travel/en/legal/visa-law0/visa-statistics/nonimmigrant-visa-statistics.html.

2. James Debono, "*Malta Today* Survey: Malta Says Yes to Budget, No to Sale of Citizenship," *Malta Today,* November 11, 2013. Over time, the Labour Party numbers have dropped slightly. In 2019, a similar survey found that still only 10 percent of Nationalist Party voters supported the program, while the proportion of Labour voters backing the program fell to 56 percent, with 31 percent against it. Kurt Sansone, "Majority Disagree with Sale of Maltese Citizenship, Show Strong Support for Road Widening," *Malta Today,* October 8, 2019.

9. Who Wants to Buy a Passport?

1. "How Rich Russians Turned Cyprus into 'Moscow on the Med,'" *Al Jazeera,* August 25, 2020. Al Jazeera, "The Cyprus Papers," 2020, https://interactive .aljazeera.com/aje/2020/cyprus-papers/index.html.
2. On Ogyen Trinley Dorje's travel challenges, as well as those of other Tibetan refugees, see also Jyoti Malhotra, "Karmapa's Caribbean Citizenship Cost Him Indian Recognition," *The Print,* December 28, 2018, https://theprint.in/india /governance/karmapas-caribbean-citizenship-may-have-cost-him-indian -recognition/170022/. Koh Phangan, "New Delhi Successful in Alienating Karmapa," *Tibet Sun,* January 31, 2019.
3. Isabelle Khurshudyan, "How the Founder of Telegram Messaging App Stood Up to the Kremlin—and Won," *Washington Post,* June 28, 2020.
4. Leonid Bershidsky, "Why Russians Are Choosing Malta over Putin," *Bloomberg,* January 11, 2018.
5. Samson Martirosyan and Edik Baghdasaryan, "The Pyramid of Lies Collapsed: President Armen Sarkissian Had to Resign," *HETQ,* January 24, 2022, https:// hetq.am/en/article/140389.
6. "Cambodian Government Denies PM Has Cyprus Passport," *Cyprus Mail,* October 6, 2021.
7. Al Jazeera, "Cyprus Papers."
8. "Government Seeks Legal Advice as Investigation Reveals Opposition Leader Holds Dominica Diplomatic Passport," *St Kitts and Nevis Observer,* October 25, 2017.
9. Attorney General of Saint Christopher and Nevis v. Dr. Denzil Douglas (Court of Appeal Judgment), appeal allowed, 0007/2019 Caribbean Supreme Court (2020). Note, too, that diplomats are not always nationals of the countries they represent, which can be one of the conveniences of a diplomatic passport.
10. Michael Peel and Kerin Hope, "Cyprus Defends 'Golden Passport' Scheme after Jho Low Link," *Financial Times,* November 5, 2019.
11. "The Cyprus Papers Analyzed: Is Al Jazeera's Reporting Balanced?" editorial, *Civitas Post,* September 2, 2020. The figure of 4 percent included all "politically exposed persons" (PEPs), or people in any position of power within a country, such as high-level politicians, judges, ambassadors, and managers of state-owned enterprises, as well as their family members and close business associates. Because such individuals may carry a higher risk of money laundering, they are generally accorded stronger due diligence checks than others even if they have not committed any crimes.

12. "Global Wealth Report 2018," Credit Suisse, October 2018, 16.

13. Kristin Surak, "Millionaire Mobility and the Sale of Citizenship," *Journal of Ethnic and Migration Studies* 47, no. 1 (2020): 166–189.

14. David Leonhardt and Sanam Yar, "Lebanon's Crisis," *New York Times*, October 15, 2021.

15. Government of Malta, "Fourth Annual Report on the Individual Investor Programme of the Government of Malta," Office of the Regulator, Individual Investment Programme (Oriip), 1 July 2016–30 June 2017, https://cupdf.com/document/office-of-the-regulator-oriipgovmt-report-2017pdf-level-2-evans-building.html?page=1.

16. The upshot for the UK investor visa program was that Saint Kitts, with a middling per capita income, was the country with the highest proportion of its population gaining residence through this means—followed by a less surprising Monaco and a more surprising Dominica (unless one knows that Dominica has a CBI program too). Kristin Surak, "Who Wants to Buy a Visa? Comparing the Uptake of Residence by Investment Programs in the European Union," *Journal of Contemporary European Studies* 30, no. 1 (2020): 151–169.

17. Kimberly Kay Hoang, "Risky Investments: How Local and Foreign Investors Finesse Corruption-Rife Emerging Markets," *American Sociological Review* 83, no. 4 (2018): 657–685. Alexander A. Cooley and John Heathershaw, *Dictators without Borders: Power and Money in Central Asia* (New Haven: Yale University Press, 2017).

18. Eleanor Knott, "Strategy, Identity or Legitimacy? Analysing Engagement with Dual Citizenship from the Bottom-Up," *Journal of Ethnic and Migration Studies* 45, no. 6 (2019): 994–1014. David Cook-Martin, *The Scramble for Citizens: Dual Nationality and State Competition for Immigrants* (Stanford: Stanford University Press, 2013). Pablo Mateos, "The Mestizo Nation Unbound: Dual Citizenship of Euro-Mexicans and US-Mexicans," *Journal of Ethnic and Migration Studies* 45, no. 6 (2019): 917–938.

19. Generally only one dependent spouse is allowed on an application—additional spouses require a second investment—and newborn children can come in for free or, in the case of Grenada, require an additional fee.

20. See Kristin Surak, "Citizenship and Residence by Investment Schemes: State of Play and Avenues for EU Action," European Added Value Assessment, European Parliamentary Research Service, European Union, Brussels, 2021.

21. Compare with Jelena Dzankic, *The Global Market for Investor Citizenship* (London: Palgrave Macmillan, 2019).

22. These include a reduced tax rate on income arising in the country and a zero tax rate on income or capital gains arising outside the country that are not remitted to it.

23. Morris Pearl, "How the Wealthiest Americans Get Away with Paying No Tax," *Financial Times*, June 14, 2021.

24. Surak, "Who Wants to Buy a Visa?"

25. See Benedict Anderson, *Imagined Communities: Reflections on the Origin and Spread of Nationalism* (London: Verso, 2016).

26. Yossi Harpaz, *Global Citizenship 2.0: Dual Nationality as a Global Asset* (Princeton: Princeton University Press, 2019).

27. Kristin Surak, "What Money Can Buy: Citizenship by Investment on a Global Scale," in *Deepening Divides: How Physical Borders and Social Boundaries Delineate Our World,* ed. Didier Fassin (London: Pluto Press, 2019).

28. Dimitry Kochenov, *Citizenship* (Cambridge, MA: MIT Press, 2019).

29. "China's Outward Investment Tops $161 Billion in 2016: Minister," Reuters, December 26, 2016.

30. Filip Novokmet, Thomas Piketty, and Gabriel Zucman, "From Soviets to Oligarchs: Inequality and Property in Russia 1905–2016," *Journal of Economic Inequality* 16, no. 2 (2018): 189–223.

10. Citizenship in the Twenty-First Century

1. Jens Beckert and Frank Wehinger, "In the Shadow: Illegal Markets and Economic Sociology," *Socio-Economic Review* 11, no. 1 (2013): 5–30.

2. Compare with Yossi Harpaz who analyzes mobility in the citizenship hierarchy but focuses only on those moving upward. Harpaz, "Compensatory Citizenship: Dual Nationality as a Strategy of Global Upward Mobility," *Journal of Ethnic and Migration Studies* 45, no. 6 (2019): 897–916.

3. Lorie Konish, "More Americans Are Considering Cutting Their Ties with the US—Here's Why," *CNBC News,* June 30, 2018.

4. On citizenship as a liability, see Kochenov, *Citizenship.*

5. Kimberly Kay Hoang, "Risky Investments: How Local and Foreign Investors Finesse Corruption-rife Emerging Markets," *American Sociological Review* 83, no. 4 (2018): 657–685. Kristin Surak, "Millionaire Mobility and the Sale of Citizenship," *Journal of Ethnic and Migration Studies* 47, no. 1 (2020): 166–189.

6. Yossi Harpaz, *Citizenship 2.0: Dual Nationality as a Global Asset* (Princeton: Princeton University Press, 2019).

7. Thomas Humphrey Marshall, *Citizenship and Social Class: And Other Essays* (Cambridge: Cambridge University Press, 1950), 43.

8. Marshall, *Citizenship and Social Class,* 77.

9. Lant Pritchett, *Let Their People Come: Breaking the Gridlock on Global Labor Mobility* (Washington, DC: Center for Global Development, 2006), 72.

10. Bridget Anderson, Nandita Sharma, and Cynthia Wright, "Why No Borders?" *Refuge: Canada's Journal on Refugees* 26, no. 2 (2009): 5–18, 11.

11. Even the Chinese Exclusion Act of 1882, often taken as the first racist immigration law in the United States, was aimed only at laborers: Chinese nationals who could demonstrate sufficient resources could still enter.

12. David FitzGerald, *Negotiating Extra-Territorial Citizenship: Mexican Migration and the Transnational Politics of Community.* (La Jolla: Center for Comparative Immigration Studies, UC San Diego, 2000).

13. Cook-Martin, *The Scramble for Citizens.* Harpaz, *Citizenship 2.0.*

14. See also Surak, "Millionaire Mobility," Kristin Surak, "What Money Can Buy: Citizenship by Investment on a Global Scale," in *Deepening Divides: How Physical Borders and Social Boundaries Delineate Our World,* ed. Didier Fassin (London: Pluto Press, 2019).

15. "The Rise of Global Citizen?" (Barclays Wealth Insights vol. 18, 2014), 11.

16. Harpaz, *Citizenship 2.0.*

17. Compare with Harpaz *Citizenship 2.0.*

18. On these "intercitizenships," see Dimitry Kochenov, "Intercitizenships of the World," *Quality of Nationality Index,* 3rd ed., (Zurich: Ideos Publishers, 2018).

19. Dimitry Kochenov and Justin Lindeboom, "Empirical Assessment of the Quality of Nationalities," *European Journal of Comparative Law and Governance* 4, no. 4 (2017): 314–336.

20. On this common myth, see Kochenov and Lindeboom, "Empirical Assessment."

21. Andrew Ellis, Carlos Navarro, Isabel Morales, Maria Gratschew, and Nadja Braun, *Voting from Abroad: The International IDEA Handbook* (Stockholm: International IDEA, 2007), 12–13.

22. John G. A. Pocock, "The Ideal of Citizenship since Classical Times," in *Theorizing Citizenship,* ed. Ronald Beiner (Albany: State University of New York Press, 1995).

23. Peter Mair, *Ruling the Void: The Hollowing of Western Democracy* (London: Verso, 2013). Wolfgang Streeck, *Buying Time: The Delayed Crisis of Democratic Capitalism* (New York: Verso, 2014).

24. Kristin Surak, "Global Citizenship 2.0: The Growth of Citizenship by Investment Programs." Investment Migration Council Working Papers, IMC-RP 2016/3.

25. Compare with Noora Lori, *Offshore Citizens: Permanent Temporary Status in the Gulf* (Cambridge: Cambridge University Press, 2019).

26. Nicholas Shaxson, *Treasure Islands: Tax Havens and the Men Who Stole the World* (London: Vintage Books, 2011). Ronen Palan, *The Offshore World: Sovereign Markets, Virtual Places, and Nomad Millionaires* (Ithaca, NY: Cornell University Press, 2006).

27. Salahi Sonyel, "The Protégé System in the Ottoman Empire," *Journal of Islamic Studies* 2, no. 1 (1991): 56–66.

28. Sonyel, "The Protégé System." See also Will Hanley, *Identifying with Nationality: European, Ottomans, and Egyptians in Alexandria* (New York: Columbia University Press, 2017).

29. Christopher A. Casey, *Nationals Abroad: Globalization, Individual Rights, and the Making of Modern International Law* (Cambridge: Cambridge University Press, 2020).

30. Casey, *Nationals Abroad.* Hanley, *Identifying with Nationality.*

31. These possibilities were racially exclusive as well, with variation across time and space. See David FitzGerald and David Cook Martín, *Culling the Masses: The Democratic Origins of Racist Immigration Policy in the Americas* (Cambridge, MA: Harvard University Press, 2014).

32. Casey, *Nationals Abroad,* 69–73. See also Hanley, *Identifying with Nationality,* and Sonyel, "The Protégé System."

33. There are two known exceptions—the Sweet Homes and Heart of Europe developments—discussed in Chapter 7.

34. David Fitzgerald, "Rethinking Emigrant Citizenship, *New York University Law Review* 81, no. 1 (2006): 90–116, 105.

35. Rogers Brubaker, *Citizenship and Nationhood in France and Germany* (Cambridge, MA: Harvard University Press, 1992), 21.

36. On governments structuring the market, see also Robert Hockett and Saule Omarova, "'Private' Means to 'Public' Ends: Governments as Market Actors," *Theoretical Inquiries in Law* 15, no. 1 (2014): 53–76. On governments incorporating market forces into modes of governance, see also David Harvey, *A Brief History of Neoliberalism* (Oxford: Oxford University Press, 2005). Aihwa Ong, *Neoliberalism as Exception: Mutations in Citizenship and Sovereignty* (Durham, NC: Duke University Press, 2006). Margaret R. Somers, *Genealogies of Citizenship: Markets, Statelessness, and the Right to Have Rights* (Cambridge: Cambridge University Press, 2008). Gaston A. Brown, "Rebuilding a Stronger, Safer, and Prosperous Antigua and Barbuda," 2016 Budget Statement, Minister of Finance and Corporate Governance, Antigua and Barbuda, January 21, 2016, https://ab.gov.ag/pdf /budget_speech_2016.pdf.

37. Kristin Surak, "Marketizing Sovereign Prerogatives: How to Sell Citizenship," *European Journal of Sociology* 62, no. 2 (2021): 275–308.

38. Bruce G. Carruthers and Arthur L. Stinchcombe, "The Social Structure of Liquidity: Flexibility, Markets, and States," *Theory and Society* 28, no. 3 (1999): 353–382. Of course, most sovereign debt is never repaid; it's the credibility that matters.

39. Marc Flandreau and Juan H. Flores, "Bonds and Brands: Foundations of Sovereign Debt Markets 1820–1830," *Journal of Economic History* 69, no. 3 (2009): 646–684.

40. Christopher M. Bruner and Rawi Abdelal, "To Judge Leviathan: Sovereign Credit Ratings, National Law, and the World Economy," *Journal of Public Policy* 25, no. 2 (2005): 191–217. Marion Fourcade, "State Metrology: The Ratings of Sovereigns and the Judgment of Nations," in *The Many Hands of the State: Theorizing Political Authority and Social Control*, ed. Kimberly Morgan and Ann Shola Orloff (Cambridge: Cambridge University Press, 2017).

41. Christine Trampusch, "The Financialization of the State: Government Debt Management Reforms in New Zealand and Ireland, " *Competition and Change* 23, no. 1 (2019): 3–22.

42. Glen Biglaiser and Joseph Staats, "Finding the 'Democratic Advantage' in Sovereign Bond Ratings: The Importance of Strong Courts, Property Rights Protection, and the Rule of Law," *International Organization* 66, no.3 (2012): 515–535. Sebastian Saiegh, "Coalition Governments and Sovereign Debt Crises," *Economics and Politics* 21, no. 2 (2009): 232–254.

43. See also Kristin Surak, "Guestworkers: A Taxonomy," *New Left Review* 84 (2013): 84–102. Kristin Surak, "Migration Industries and the State: Guestwork Programs in East Asia," *International Migration Review* 52, no. 2 (2018): 487–523. George Menz, "The Neoliberalized State and the Growth of the Migration Industry," in *The Migration Industry and the Commercialization of International Migration*, ed. Thomas Gammeltoft-Hansen and Ninna Nyberg Sørensen (London: Routledge, 2013).

44. On privatization of core state functions, see also Paul R. Verkuil, *Outsourcing Sovereignty: Why Privatization of Government Functions Threatens Democracy and*

What We Can Do about It (Cambridge: Cambridge University Press, 2007). For the cases of military intervention, see Deborah D. Avant, *The Market for Force: The Consequences of Privatizing Security* (Cambridge: Cambridge University Press, 2005). Dexter Whitfield, *Public Services or Corporate Welfare: Rethinking the Nation State in the Global Economy* (London: Pluto Press, 2001). For migration management, see Surak, "Guestworkers." Menz, "The Neoliberalized State."

45. Corporate Europe Observatory, *Lobby Planet Brussels: The Corporate Europe Observatory Guide to the Murky World of EU Lobbying* (Brussels: Corporate Europe Observatory, 2017), https://corporateeurope.org/en/lobbyplanet. On the ambiguous role of "lawyer-lobbyists" in Brussels, see Emilia Korkea-aho, "Legal Lobbying: The Evolving (But Hidden) Role of Lawyers and Law Firms in the EU Public Affairs Market," *German Law Journal* 22, no. 1 (2021): 65–84.

46. John Torpey, *The Invention of the Passport: Surveillance, Citizenship, and the State* (Cambridge: Cambridge University Press, 1999).

47. Tanja Brøndsted Sejersen, "'I Vow to Thee My Countries': The Expansion of Dual Citizenship in the 21st Century," *International Migration Review* 42, no. 3 (2008): 523–549. "Global Dual Citizenship Database" (Maastricht Centre for Citizenship, Migration and Development, Maastricht University, 2020).

48. Thomas Faist and Jürgen Gerdes, "Dual Citizenship in the Age of Mobility," *Delivering Citizenship: The Transatlantic Council on Migration* (Gütersloh: Bertelsmann Stiftung, 2008), 531. Harpaz, *Citizenship 2.0.*

49. Fitzgerald, "Rethinking Emigrant Citizenship." Rainer Bauböck and Thomas Faist, *Diaspora and Transnationalism: Concepts, Theories and Methods* (Amsterdam: Amsterdam University Press, 2010).

50. Evren Balta and Özlem Altan-Olcay, "Strategic Citizens of America: Transnational Inequalities and Transformation of Citizenship," *Ethnic and Racial Studies* 39, no. 6 (2016): 939–957.

51. Cook-Martín, *Scramble for Citizens.*

52. Yossi Harpaz, "Ancestry into Opportunity," *Journal of Ethnic and Migration Studies* 41, no. 13 (2015): 2081–2104. Harpaz, *Global Citizenship 2.0.*

53. Guillermina Jasso and Mark R. Rosenzweig, "Family Reunification and the Immigration Multiplier: US Immigration Law, Origin-Country Conditions, and the Reproduction of Immigrants," *Demography* 23, no. 3 (1986): 291–311, 303. Jaap Dronkers and Maarten Peter Vink, "Explaining Access to Citizenship in Europe: How Citizenship Policies Affect Naturalization Rates," *European Union Politics* 13, no. 3 (2012): 390–412.

54. Harpaz, "Ancestry into Opportunity." Cook-Martin, *The Scramble for Citizens;* Balta and Altan-Olcay, "Strategic Citizens of America."

55. See Christian Joppke, "The Instrumental Turn of Citizenship," *Journal of Ethnic and Migration Studies* 45, no. 26 (2019): 858–878.

56. Fitzgerald, "Rethinking Emigrant Citizenship."

57. Christian Joppke, "The Inevitable Lightening of Citizenship," *European Journal of Sociology* 51, no. 1 (2010): 29.

58. Spiro, *Beyond Citizenship.*

59. See Chapter 4 on the workaround Turkey provides for its military service obligations.

60. Ong, *Flexible Citizenship*. Cook-Martín, *Scramble for Citizens*.

61. Harpaz, *Citizenship 2.0*.

62. Ayelet Shachar, "The Race for Talent: Highly Skilled Migrants and Competitive Immigration Regimes," *New York University Law Review* 81, no. 1 (2006): 148–206. Ayelet Shachar, "Picking Winners: Olympic Citizenship and the Global Race for Talent," *Yale Law Journal* 120, no. 8 (2011): 2088–2139.

63. Fiona Adamson and Gerasimos Tsourapas, "The Migration State in the Global South: Nationalizing, Developmental, and Neoliberal Models of Migration Management," *International Migration Review* 54, no. 3 (2020): 853–882.

Methodological Appendix

1. For related statistical work using the InvestMig database, see Kristin Surak, "Citizenship and Residence by Investment Schemes: State of Play and Avenues for EU Action," European Added Value Assessment, European Parliamentary Research Service, European Union, Brussels, 2021, and Kristin Surak and Yusuke Tsuzuki, "Are Golden Visas a Golden Opportunity? Assessing the Economic Outcomes of Residence by Investment Programs in the EU," *Journal of Ethnic and Migration Studies* 47, no. 15 (2021): 3367–89.

Index